VOICES FROM A WILDERNESS EXPEDITION

THE JOURNALS AND MEN OF BENEDICT ARNOLD'S EXPEDITION TO QUEBEC IN 1775

Stephen Darley

authorHOUSE®

AuthorHouse™
1663 Liberty Drive
Bloomington, IN 47403
www.authorhouse.com
Phone: 1-800-839-8640

First published by AuthorHouse 6/29/2011

ISBN: 978-1-4567-6106-6 (sc)
ISBN: 978-1-4567-6107-3 (ebk)
ISBN: 978-1-4567-6108-0 (hc)

Library of Congress Control Number: 2011908006

Printed in the United States of America

"While we their children gather as our own

The harvest that the dead have sown"

TABLE OF CONTENTS

LIST OF ILLUSTRATIONS

Portrait of Gen. Benedict Arnold. Drawn from Life at Philadelphia by Du Simitier. The European Magazine and London Review, March 1, 1783. Author's copy.

Map of Route of Arnold Expedition. From the Atlas of John Marshall's The Life of George Washington, 1805.

Portrait of Lieut. Col. Eleazer Oswald. Courtesy of New York Public Library Digital Gallery, Emmet Collection of Manuscripts, Print Collection, Division of Art, Prints and Photographs. Image 422790.

Portrait of Maj. Gen. Henry Dearborn (1872). Courtesy of New York Public Library Digital Collection Gallery, Emmet Collection of Manuscripts, Print Collection, Division of Art, Prints and Photographs. Image 422941.

Portrait of Return Jonathan Meigs, Sr. Courtesy of New York Public Library Digital Gallery, Emmet Collection of Manuscripts, Print Collection, Division of Art, Prints and Photographs. Image 1686870.

Portrait of John Joseph Henry. Courtesy of Historical Society of Pennsylvania, Portrait Collection.

Portrait of Lieutenant William Heth. From miniature in possession of family. Taken from Arnold's Expedition to Quebec by John Codman. Special edition published for William Abbatt, 1903.

Working Against the Flood on Dead River. Illustration by Sydney Adamson, 1903. Courtesy of Library of Congress, Prints & Photographs Online Catalog, Image USZ62-108233.

Portrait of Colonel Roger Enos. From only known portrait in possession of family. Taken from Arnold's Expedition to Quebec by John Codman. Special edition published for William Abbatt, 1903.

Portrait of Dr. Isaac Senter. c. 1793. Oil on canvass painting by Samuel King. Courtesy of the Rhode Island Historical Society, RHi X5 15.

The illustration on the front cover is Benedict Arnold's Attack on the British in Quebec in the Winter of 1775 by F. C. Yohn from The Story of the Revolution by Henry Cabot Lodge, 1898.

GENERAL ARNOLD.

Drawn from Life at Philadelphia by Du Similier.

Published Mar. 1st 1783, by J. Fielding Pater noster Row, J. Sewell Cornhill and J. Debrett, Piccadilly.

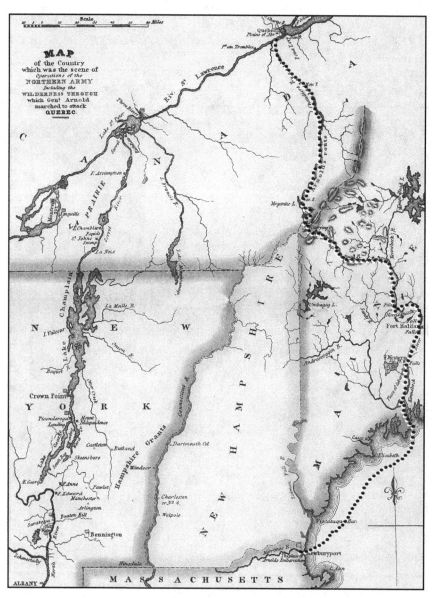

Map of Arnold Expedition Route to Quebec

PREFACE

The expedition to Quebec led by Colonel Benedict Arnold in the fall of 1775 was arguably the most difficult, noteworthy and subsequently neglected military expedition of the Revolutionary War. This is confirmed in the writings of Dr. Charles E. Banks, who spent a lifetime studying the Arnold expedition.

> There will be found in it more of the personal daring than at Stony Point; more of the terrible sufferings, disease and death from privation than at Valley Forge which sat amidst comparative plenty; greater losses in leadership than at Germantown; and the little army that invested Montreal and Quebec, though denied its quarry, came back unconquered... it has been left an heir to oblivion, almost unwept, unhonored and sung only in a minor key.

He concludes, as have others before and since, that "the march of Hannibal over the Alps has nothing in it of superior merit to the march of Arnold." The expedition deserves more study in order to understand and appreciate its historical significance and the sacrifices made by its participants.[1]

This book is not a history of the Arnold expedition. I will not attempt to chronicle the history of the expedition found in other sources. Many excellent books and magazine articles have been written detailing the rigors of the march and how hard the men struggled in their heroic effort to reach Quebec through the back woods of Maine. The first such book was written by Charles Henry Jones, who's *History of the Campaign for the Conquest of Canada* was published in 1882. Most biographies of Arnold have also described details about the expedition because of his significant role in that campaign. Readers are urged to read one or more of the expedition histories or Arnold biographies if they wish to understand the complete chronology of events.

This book is also not intended to replace or replicate *March to Quebec*, Kenneth Roberts' seminal book on the expedition journals which reproduced thirteen expedition journals. However, a highlight of the book is my discovery and transcription of three previously unknown manuscript journals, known collectively as the "Durben Journal." I located these journals in the Special Collections Division of the University of Glasgow Library while doing an internet search on Arnold expedition journals. These three journals add new primary source material to the historical record. I have transcribed a copy of the Durben manuscript and two other shorter journals that are reproduced and explained in detail in Chapter Two, where Durben's identification is revealed.

In addition to the three Glasgow Library journals, the following three journals have never been published and are presented here for the first time.

- The second Senter Journal which is in the Rhode Island Historical Society. Transcribed by Stephen Darley and reproduced in Chapter Four.
- Samuel Barney Journal. Transcribed by his grandson, Frances Bishop Barney. Edited by Stephen Darley and reproduced in Chapter Five.
- Moses Kimball Journal. Transcribed by Dr. L.C.
- Walker. Edited by Stephen Darley and reproduced in Chapter Five.

By presenting a bibliography of all of the expedition journals, one of the purposes of this book is to reawaken the voices of the men, both the known and the previously unknown, who recorded this unparalleled wilderness expedition. This book also provides details about the lives of some of the expedition officers and will reveal the identity of the men who marched with Arnold to Quebec by listing their names in a comprehensive roster of over eleven hundred men located in Appendix II. The roster includes pertinent information further identifying the officers and all but a handful of the privates. No such roster has been previously published.

The expedition voices are brought to life in this book through information about the journals that chronicle the experiences of the brave men who survived the hardships of the march. The book begins by presenting specific bibliographic information regarding all of the printings of the thirty journals that recorded the very personal accounts of their authors. These surviving expedition voices do not always speak in unison, often disagreeing on details. Some omit important events and focus on minor details. Some are descriptive while others are short and crisp to the point of obscuring key events. Many of the journal writers provide personal observations of their travels including the places and people they encountered. Others write objectively about factual occurrences with little supporting detail. These voices take us back two hundred thirty plus years and, together, provide a personal and more comprehensive understanding of one of the seminal events of the Revolutionary War.

It is fortunate that so many personal accounts survived the passage of time. The breadth of the journalistic record for this expedition will be evident from the number and variety of journals listed in the first chapter. Heretofore, too little attention has been paid to the personal accounts that recorded this historic event.

Although there are an unusually large number of expedition journals, there is also unanswered questions and controversy about these written accounts. Because there are still many questions that have not been satisfactorily answered, one chapter of the book investigates specific aspects of the five Ward Company journals that pose unresolved historical questions, including authenticity issues. One major conclusion from prior expedition historians regarding these journals, thought to be valid, is questioned and rejected.

The company commander about whom the least is known is Captain Scott, who led one of the companies in the Enos Division. Until now, Captain Scott has been a mystery because no one has successfully identified his first name or his hometown. The identity of Scott has been a glaring omission from the historical record of the Arnold expedition for too many years. In the early twentieth century, Charles Banks tried and failed to determine Scott's identity. I will reveal the identity of Captain Scott in this book.

The life and career of Lieutenant Colonel Roger Enos of Simsbury, Connecticut, one of the two initial division commanders, will be explored in detail. One of the more notable events that occurred during the expedition was the lingering controversy involving the decision by Enos' division to return to Cambridge before the expedition reached Quebec This decision, involving the unauthorized return of over two hundred men, was arguably the single most significant event of the march and too little attention has been paid to its impact on the expedition's mission.

Only six of the thirteen company commanders serving under Arnold have had their lives previously documented. The remaining seven have been relegated to obscurity ever since the news of the expedition's defeat reached the lower thirteen colonies. This book offers the most thorough study of the lives of these seven company commanders made to date.[2]

Four individuals deserve special mention for their previous contributions to the history of the expedition and their work to keep the voices of the participants alive. Their high standards for historical research and their work on the expedition inspired this book. First and foremost, anyone researching the expedition quickly realizes the important contribution of Professor Justin H. Smith, who, in 1903, published *Arnold's March from Cambridge to Quebec*, the most definitive and thoroughly researched book about the Arnold expedition published to that date. It not only included a history of the expedition, it also provided important details regarding many of the expedition journals. He also included an appendix containing Arnold's journal. This journal had been overlooked and neglected by historians until Smith brought it to the forefront in his book.[3]

Second, significant credit and recognition goes to Kenneth Roberts. His *March to Quebec* reprinted thirteen of the Arnold expedition journals, including the previously unpublished John Pierce journal. He introduced me, and many others, to Benedict Arnold and to the neglected history of the northern army from 1775 to 1777. Roberts' two well-known books of fiction presented a new and unique historical perspective on Arnold that caught many people's attention. I, and almost every person I know who has a special interest in Benedict Arnold, can trace their interest to Kenneth Roberts' books. Prior to *March to Quebec*, the expedition journals had not been compiled in one book. Roberts' book has been extensively used by a wide range of historians because of its importance as a single source for thirteen expedition journals.

Third, appropriate recognition should be given to the *Magazine of History with Notes and Queries*, published in the early twentieth century by William Abbatt of Tarrytown, New York. Abbatt reprinted eleven journals of the Arnold expedition in what he titled the "Extras" of his magazine, beginning with the Senter journal in Extra # 42 (1915) and ending with the Humphrey journal in Extra # 166 (1931). Prior to Kenneth Roberts, Abbatt's magazine served as primary source material for research regarding the expedition. Unfortunately, the individual Extras of his Magazine are very difficult to locate today because they have become almost as rare as the earlier and scarce printings of the journals. The Magazine of History Extras are housed in only a few libraries and are rarely available from book dealers.

Fourth, long overdue recognition needs to be given to Dr. Charles E. Banks, a little known physician and historian who devoted much of his spare time in the early twentieth century to the study of early American history. He spent many hours studying the journals of the Arnold expedition. He also attempted to identify the first name of Captain Scott. Most importantly, he did ground breaking research to produce a comprehensive list of the men who participated in the memorable march. Although others may have since researched the men who participated in the expedition, no additional listing of the names of the participants has been made public since Banks' death in 1931. I found Banks' roster and card file to be indispensable aids in compiling the list contained in Appendix II.

Charles E. Banks' has effectively articulated the importance of remembering Arnold's expedition.

> The unknown heroes of this remarkable campaign may be given the credit due for participation in one of the most trying tests of physical endurance in the annals of the Revolution. This military movement,

though a failure, was one of the most thrilling and picturesque of the war, and like all of the campaigns in which Arnold had a leading part, it was dramatic and spectacular from the start to the finish. Its participants earned a distinction not equaled in any of the subsequent campaigns of that war, and anyone whose ancestor took part in the march of three hundred miles through the wilderness of Maine and Canada has reason to be proud of the courage and fortitude of his Revolutionary grandsire.[4]

While researching this book, it became evident that misinformation about the men who served in the expedition is more pervasive than I anticipated. I found references in numerous publications to men who allegedly participated in the expedition. Subsequent research, however, revealed that some were not actually participants. In several instances, I examined many different sources before concluding whether a particular man was actually on the march. I also discovered that a number of men who were veterans of the expedition did not reveal their participation to family or friends. Therefore, their family history or town history does not make any reference to their presence on the expedition. This cover up was particularly true of men who served in the Enos division. The misinformation I encountered made the task of identifying the men who served with Arnold difficult and time consuming.

In addition to the problem of finding supporting evidence verifying the service of the men, evidence about their non-military lives is often contradictory. Many times publications containing information about the men disagreed on dates, the names of spouses, hometowns, and subsequent careers. This was more problematic for lesser known participants.

Providing details about the lives of the men is further complicated because often more than one person with the same name served in the military or lived in the same state. Sometimes the men with the same name were relatives and lived in the same town. As a result, there are still facts about the men that cannot be verified and inconsistent information that remains unresolved. This book, however, will provide a more historically accurate account of the lives of the leaders of the expedition than has been previously presented.

This book is unique because it contains three separate bibliographical source lists in three different locations. The first is the bibliographical sources for all of the printings of the thirty expedition journals that are included in Chapter One. The bibliographical details for the printings of each journal are included in the section of Chapter One for that journal. The second listing is the 147 numbered sources that are listed in the roster next to their names to document the men who were on the expedition. That listing is found starting on page 261, which is at the end of Appendix II, following the Roster. The final listing is the traditional bibliography which is located on page 278, just before the End Notes, under the heading "Works Consulted." Each list, including the Chapter One bibliography, has an introduction that explains what is included in that particular list.

ACKNOWLEDGEMENTS

This book could not have been completed without the assistance and cooperation of many individuals and institutions. With the emphasis on personal accounts and the need to identify the location of the more than thirty potential manuscript journals, I could only achieve that objective by examining the extant manuscripts either in person or by reviewing a photocopy. This could not have been done without the assistance of the librarians and staff at the institutions where the manuscripts are housed. Those institutions include the Massachusetts Historical Society, the Rhode Island Historical Society, the Historical Society of Pennsylvania, the Boston Public Library Rare Books and Manuscripts Department, Houghton Library of Harvard University, Rauner Special Collections Library at Dartmouth College, Judy Lacey of the New England Historical Genealogical Society and the Manuscript Division of the Library of Congress.

As will be apparent from the book, some of the officers and men whose story is included were difficult to research and information on their lives could not have been found without the help of local historical societies and genealogical libraries. Those most helpful were Orson Kingsley of the Henry Sheldon Museum in Middlebury, Vermont; Barbara Allen of the Local History Museum and Archives of the Stockbridge Library; the Dewey Research Center of the Sheffield Historical Society; the Berkshire Family History Center in Pittsfield, Massachusetts; Karen L. Aurand of the Mifflin County Historical Society; the Cumberland County Historical Society and Hamilton Library Association; Donna Heller Zinn of The Perry Historians; and Phyllis Hughes, genealogist of the Hull Family Association.

In addition, I examined family histories and genealogies in the Connecticut State Library, the Connecticut Historical Society, Yale University Library and the Godfrey Memorial Library of Middletown, CT. I examined Muster Rolls of two of the companies in Arnold's Detachment in the Massachusetts Archives and examined information on Connecticut officers on microfilm in the Connecticut Archives.

The following institutions provided photocopies of important documents that helped me in my research: Donald Mennerich of the New York Public Library; Pennsylvania State Archives; Joy Werlink of the Washington State History Research Center; the Wisconsin Historical Society; and Patrice N. Kane at the Archives and Special Collections of the Fordham University Library.

I would like to thank the Special Collection librarians of the University of Glasgow Library in Scotland for their assistance and cooperation in providing a copy of the Durben manuscript for inclusion in this book. They readily copied the entire file and sent it out in a very timely manner. They also included the four Appendices detailed in Chapter Two and the notations by Robertson and Hunter. Their generous assistance made this rare find available to the readers of the book.

Special appreciation is due to the New Haven Historical and Museum Society library that served as my home base as well as providing important information on Benedict Arnold, the manuscript journal of Samuel Barney, many books and journals on the expedition, various family and town histories and the Roster of Arnold's Detachment. I would like to thank James W. Campbell, the Librarian and Curator, and his staff.

The following online sites were particularly helpful by making the research more accessible without leaving my office: www.footnote.com, which has Revolutionary War muster rolls, pension applications, Pennsylvania Archives and Papers of the Continental Congress; www.ancestry.com, a genealogical web site that I used to find details many of the lives contained in this book; www.NewEnglandAncestors.org, which is the web site for the New England Historical and Genealogical Society; www.usgenweb.org, a genealogical website with information by state; www.mass.gov, which has the 17 volume Massachusetts Soldiers and Sailors in the Revolutionary War; www.memory.loc.gov, the web site for the Library of Congress which has the Washington Papers and the Journals of the Continental Congress; www.archive.org, which has a number of books printed prior to 1921; www.books.google.com, Google Books which also contains a large number of books; www.arnoldsmarch.com, the Arnold Expedition Historical Society; and the LDS Family History Center.

Special thanks to my proofreader, Eileen Albrizio, whose thorough approach to proofing not only identified all of the typical spelling, spacing and punctuation errors but also provided many helpful language changes that made this a more understandable and readable manuscript.

This book could not have been completed without the assistance and support of my wife, Peg Brennan. Not only did she encourage me, she also served as my preliminary proofreader and editor for the manuscript. Her suggestions and edits were significant and her work made this a much better book. My son, Eric, read an initial version of the manuscript and offered two extremely helpful suggestions regarding the approach to its writing. He also introduced me to *The Elements of Style* by Strunk and White. My step-son Dave was also instrumental in finalizing this book. He set up two of the illustrations and maps that are used in the book in a way that made the final result more interesting.

CHAPTER ONE

BIBLIOGRAPHY OF THIRTY EXPEDITION JOURNALS

A unique aspect of the Quebec expedition is the large number of journals written by its participants as compared to any other Revolutionary War campaign or battle. Expedition historian Charles E. Banks wrote, "Indeed it may be repeated that no campaign of the Revolution was more thoroughly journalized than by the men who marched under Arnold to Quebec".[5] Christopher Ward concluded: "Probably no other expedition of similar length made by so few men has produced so many contemporary records".[6] Encountering this number of journals written about one campaign in an eight-year war is such an extraordinary occurrence that it cries out for further study. The extent of the personal accounts of this march will allow the modern day reader to better understand the successes, as few as they were, as well as the hardships that were encountered in this Revolutionary War campaign of unsurpassed heroism.[7]

Thirty journals kept by members of the Arnold expedition are identified in this chapter and all of the printings for each are listed. The only journals not included are the three journals recently discovered in the University of Glasgow Library, described in Chapter Two. Officers wrote thirteen of the thirty journals presented in this chapter. Included in this category is Isaac Senter, who was the expedition's doctor, but did not make it to officer status. Also included is Matthias Ogden, who was a volunteer but was referred to in other journals as an officer. John Pierce, the expedition surveyor, and William McCoy of Hendricks' company, are also included although they were sergeants and not commissioned officers.

The seventeen remaining journals in this chapter were personal accounts kept by privates on the expedition. The journal attributed to Ebenezer Wild is included here, even though he was not on the expedition. The Anonymous Journal is also included in this category because it is clear from its entries that it was not written by an officer. There is no other Revolutionary War event that has so many surviving personal accounts written by privates.

Despite the fact that there are thirty journals containing accounts of the expedition, neither the journals nor the expedition has received the historical recognition that they deserve. The significance of the expedition's accomplishments is still unappreciated. One explanation for this was contained in William Abbatt's introduction to Topham's journal that appeared in the Magazine of History, Extra # 50.

The rank and file who returned to tell the tale were few in number, weak in influence and widely scattered. Many of them re-enlisted and perished during the war. Most of the surviving officers gained a wider reputation by brilliant exploits in more conspicuous fields, and continued to live the active lives which make history, but afford little time to write it. Moreover, this was one of the first military movements of importance in the war, and records at that time were not preserved with much care, so that a great deal of valuable information has only been recently accessible, while perhaps still more has been destroyed or lost forever. The young nation was not likely to dwell with pride on the failure of the invasion of Canada, and gladly allowed everything connected with it to fall into oblivion. Doubtless, also, a campaign which was so closely associated with the name of the traitor Arnold, the truthful account of which could not fail to reflect credit on that evil genius, was willingly slighted.[8]

Abbatt's point about the expedition being a failure is a major reason why it was forgotten so quickly. The negative impact of the news from Canada about the failure of the assault, the death of Montgomery, the wounding of Arnold, the capture of most of Arnold's detachment and the scourge of smallpox in Canada cannot be over emphasized. The northern army had just been devastated and it being so early in the war, no one wanted to focus very long on failure. Moreover, some of the blame for the failure was on the head of the Continental Congress and the leaders of the thirteen colonies that made up its member states. If it had been successful in accomplishing its mission and Canada had been brought to the American side, the Arnold expedition would be as well-known today as Valley Forge. However, its failure, followed five years later by its commander changing sides, made such a negative impression on the collective American consciousness that the only positive recognition it could be given was by those participants who wrote a personal account of the expedition. These personal accounts were few and far between so the singular accomplishments of the expedition were forgotten, and faded into an obscurity from which it has never managed to fully emerge. The fact that Americans were able to subsequently ignore the history of the invasion of Canada is evident by the fact that its first book length history did not appear in print until 1882.[9]

The difficulty of authenticating the authorship of some of the journals will be evident from the bibliographic information presented in this chapter. It may never be possible to determine whether some of these journals were actually written by the individuals whose names are associated with them, or whether they were copied from someone else's journal and claimed by the alleged author or a family member to be an authentic account. As each of the journals was examined, it became clear that questions about the authenticity and authorship of certain journals deserved further explanation. Chapters Three and Four provide a more detailed analysis of six journals that raise the most questions.

The publishing history of the Arnold expedition journals reflects the intellectual life of nineteenth century America in a way not found in the sources of any other Revolutionary War event. Researching the journals led to long forgotten intellectual periodicals that first published many of these expedition journals in the nineteenth century. Most of these periodicals have long since ceased publication and are largely unknown today, although in their time they were considered the cutting edge of intellectual thought. It was surprising to realize that so many journals with so many different perspectives were published between 1800 and 1900.

The individuals involved in finding, authenticating, transcribing and publishing the expedition journals represent an interesting array of scholars and amateur historians from nineteenth century America. They include lawyers, doctors and businessmen with sterling reputations who did this work in their spare time. All were members of the various historical or intellectual societies that dotted the landscape of nineteenth century America. Their contribution to our understanding of the history of the Revolutionary period and their service in finding the expedition journals are enormous. Without their work, important pieces of Revolutionary War history, including the Arnold expedition, would have been lost.

This chapter identifies all the known printings of each of the thirty known journals with sufficient detail on each printing to provide an authoritative bibliographical record. It contains a description of each journal as well as other relevant information about the journal, including the location of the original manuscript. A biography of each journalist is included so the reader can better understand the journal by knowing more about its author. There is a table in Appendix I summarizing information on the thirty expedition journalists from this chapter.

In addition to their historical significance, the number and variety of journals and the broad range of the authors' backgrounds reveal enlightening facts about the journals and authors that are not always expected. The following is a summary of factual information from the thirty expedition journals that is not clearly evident from the pages of this chapter or from any previous history.

- The life span of the thirty expedition journalists was 63.68 years, which is well above the average for that time. Two of the journalists died in their nineties and thirteen lived to be over the age of seventy-five.

- Only one of the journalists, Charles Porterfield, was killed in action during the war even though others served throughout the war.
- The most popular journal is the one written by Return J. Meigs, which has been reprinted eleven times in a variety of publications, some of them quite rare. The least known journal is the one by Samuel Barney of New Haven, which has never been printed or previously identified in any publication.
- Not including the newly discovered journals in this book, the dates of the first printings of the journals range from 1776 to 2000, a span of two hundred twenty-four years.
- The longest journal is the one written by John Joseph Henry, which was written on his sick bed and was not published during his lifetime. Its first printing in 1812 contained 224 pages.
- The shortest journal with the fewest words and entries is the one by John Flanders of Boscawen, New Hampshire, which was only preserved in a town history.
- The company that generated the most journals was the Ward Company with five, not counting the one ascribed to Wild. Dearborn's Company had three journalists as did Hendricks and Hubbard. Thayer, Morgan, Hanchett and Smith each had two. Scott and Topham had one journalist each. Goodrich's Company is the only one that went all the way to Quebec but produced no journals.
- The original manuscripts of fifteen journals have tragically been lost. On the other hand, there are still thirteen original manuscripts available and two existing manuscripts that are less clearly originals. Four of the most significant manuscript journals that have been preserved, Arnold, Pierce, Haskell and one of the Senter's, were not placed in public repositories until the first quarter of the twentieth century, over one hundred fifty years after the expedition occurred.
- There are no journalists from Maine, Vermont or New York. All other states that provided men for the expedition are represented including Virginia (2), New Jersey (1), Pennsylvania (4), Connecticut (6), Massachusetts (5), Rhode Island (5) and New Hampshire (5).
- In 1775, the youngest journalist at age eighteen was Private William Dorr and the oldest journalist was forty-year-old Major Return Jonathan Meigs, who also had the most unusual name.
- Five journalists, Dorr, Henry, McCoy, Kimball and Senter, did not serve in the military after the Quebec expedition. For one reason or

another, the expedition took its toll on these men so they declined to continue to serve and looked elsewhere for future employment.

- The journals of Heth, Nichols and Porterfield, all of whom were in the rifle companies, only have entries covering their time as prisoners of war in Quebec. It is likely that all three journals originally had entries covering the entire expedition, but those portions of their journals relating to the march have been lost or destroyed.
- Greenman and Dearborn are in a special category because they wrote journals that covered most of the period from their release from prison in Quebec until the end of the war. Greenman's journal is especially unique because it is one of only a handful of journals written by a private that provides an account of the entire war.[10] Despite the comprehensiveness of Greenman's account, his journal is not well known and the only book containing the transcription of his journal has only had four print runs.
- The rarest and most valuable printed journal is the Meigs journal, which was printed in the United States in 1776 in a limited edition of an unknown number of copies. The second rarest printed journal is the Abner Stocking journal first published in 1810. Although that first printing has appeared in rare book dealer catalogs during the twentieth century, it cannot be found in any public repository today.
- The journal with the most limited edition printings is the Melvin journal, which was published in the middle of the nineteenth century two different times by two different publishers in printings of only one hundred copies each. It was also published again in 1902 with a limited printing of 250 copies. Being a journal with no special content, it is a surprising choice to be the subject of multiple limited printings.
- With the reproduction in this book of the previously unpublished journals, all of the extant expedition journals have now been published at least once.

Both the terms diary and journal are used in many of the journal titles and have previously been used by others to describe the journals that appear in this chapter. The preferred use of one of these words in a particular title or as a designation by previous writers is based on individual preference as these designations in my view are interchangeable. I have preferred to designate the thirty personal accounts included in this book as journals rather than diaries, regardless of the wording in their title or the designation in previous publications.

BIBLIOGRAPHY OF THE JOURNALS

I. BENEDICT ARNOLD

A. <u>Description of Journal</u>.

The expedition leader, Colonel Benedict Arnold, kept the most relevant expedition journal, which unfortunately, only covered the first month of the trek. He left it behind when he fled from West Point after his treason was uncovered by the capture of British Major John Andre. It was found among his personal papers by Judge Pierpont Edwards, who was appointed as the administrator of Arnold's Connecticut estate as a result of the act of confiscation of loyalists estates passed by the Connecticut legislature. "The manuscript was in existence in 1835, though "in a rather dilapidated state" as stated by James Parton in his introduction to the Arnold journal published in the Appendix of the Life of Aaron Burr. Parton's introduction provides his authentication of the Arnold journal.

> There cannot be the slightest doubt of its being an original document, from the history of its preservation, from its antiquated appearance, from internal evidence, and a comparison of hand-writing, which we had an opportunity of making, from finding several letters from Arnold in the possession of those well acquainted with his chirography. It is the writing which was common in that day among well educated men, holding, like that of Washington, and also of Hancock, the middle style between copy and running hand.[11]

In 1886, Justin Windsor noted that the S.L.M. Barlow of New York then owned the Arnold journal. Barlow's collection was sold at auction in 1889. The auction catalogue includes an item described as *The Original Manuscript of Colonel Benedict Arnold's Journal of the Expedition to Quebec*, which was purchased at the auction for $405 by the famous bibliographer, Joseph Sabin, and then disappeared from view for a period of time. The Harvard Library manuscript was bound by Barlow as his bookplate is on the inside of the front cover of the cloth binding.

The manuscript subsequently showed up in Ogden Goelet's library, and was purchased by Gabriel Wells for $4500 at the auction of the Goelet library held on January 24 and 25, 1935. The journal then disappeared from view again until it showed up in the *Sale of the Estate of the late Gabriel Wells*, which was held in 1948 in New York. In the published Catalogue No. 1 containing Rare Books, first editions, manuscripts, autograph letters, Entry

8, is entitled *"ARNOLD, BENEDICT. Original Manuscript Journal of the Expedition to Quebec."* It was described as being 40 pages with entries from September 26 to October 30, 1775, "bound in full rose levant morocco gilt, gilt top, by Bedford."[12] The price on the journal was $5,500.00. There is no doubt that the journal listed in the Wells' catalogue is the same Arnold journal that he purchased from the estate of Goelet in 1935. It disappeared again for a period of time after the Wells auction and was finally donated to the Harvard University Library by Alfred C. Berol in 1970.[13]

A handwritten copy was used to reproduce the Arnold journal in the Appendix of Justin Smith's book. It turns out that a duplicate of the Arnold manuscript journal, then in the possession of Judge Pierpont Edwards, was given to Jared Sparks by Mr. R.R. Ward in February of 1833, and is now in the Spark's Collection of Documents Relating to the American Revolution in the Harvard University Library. It is not in Arnold's handwriting but it is a handwritten copy of the original journal. The Sparks copy is not the same as the original manuscript in the Harvard Library.[14]

The Harvard Library manuscript has a number of cross outs and word insertions by Arnold which indicates that the journal was written by him during the expedition. It is approx 5 X 7" and ends on page 40 with an entry for October 30th, which is not legible. Its condition has been preserved by the binding that was added by SLA Barlow prior to his estate being sold in 1889.

In his 1903 book on the Arnold expedition, Justin Smith states that "the first rank must certainly be given to the one extant journal that has never been printed in full until now. That is Arnold's."[15] Although other expedition journals were published prior to 1903, Arnold's was not, likely due to his reputation as a traitor. Smith made a significant contribution to the history of the Arnold expedition by reprinting Arnold's journal in its entirety.

B. <u>Notes on Journal</u>.
The Arnold journal is supplemented by another journal, prepared by Arnold aide, Eleazer Oswald, which starts twelve days earlier than Arnold's and continues on for some of the same time period. (See description of the next journal). The description of the Arnold journal in the Goelet catalog states that the "first few pages of the journal are missing (hence the starting date of September 25, 1775 rather than September 15th as contained in the Oswald journal), as are, apparently, a leaf or two at the end; a few corners have been torn off, affecting some words; and the last leaf is dim. Yet as a whole the manuscript is clear and legible considering the fearful

circumstances in which it was written." The journal as it now appears in the library starts on Wednesday, September 27, 1775 with an entry that is obviously a continuation. It states, "A number of our men employ'd in bring provisions."[16]

C. Period Covered.
The Arnold journal begins on Wednesday, September 26, 1775 and ends on Thursday, October 26, 1781, except for the one in the Life of Burr which ends on October 30, 1775. This leads to the conclusion that the journal in 1835 had a few more pages at the end than it did in 1903, and later when it was sold at the Goelet auction in 1935 and subsequently donated to Harvard.

D. Publishing History.
1st Printing. Samuel L. Knapp. *The Life of Aaron Burr*. New York: Wiley& Long, 1835. Appendix, pp. 205-223.

2nd Printing. *Arnold's Journal of His Expedition to Canada*. The journal was reproduced in its entirety as an Appendix in Justin H. Smith, Arnold's March from Cambridge to Quebec, A Critical Study Together with a Reprint of Arnold's Journal. New York and London: G.P. Putnam's Sons, 1903, pp. 467-486.

3rd Printing. *March to Quebec, Journals of the Members of Arnold's Expedition. Compiled and Annotated by Kenneth Roberts During the Writing of Arundel*. Garden City, New York: Doubleday & Company, Inc., 1948, pp. 45-66.

E. Location of Original.
Harvard University Library. Houghton MS Am 1859. Bound in full red morocco by Bedford. In a tray case. The Harvard manuscript journal is described as an "autograph manuscript, unsigned, dated at various places." It has the bookplate and signature of S.M.L. Barlow

The description of the manuscript in the Goelet catalog is as follows: "*Original Autograph Manuscript Journal of the Expedition to Quebec, 40 pp., over 4,000 words, small 4to. Sept. 26 to Oct. 30, 1775. Bound in full rose levant morocco, gilt tooled, gilt top, uncut, by Bedford. The day-by-day journal of the heroic struggle through an unknown wilderness by an American army during the American Revolution, Written by the indomitable leader of the expedition amidst almost constant storm or cold.*"

F. Biography of Author.
Benedict Arnold's involvement in the Quebec expedition is a story of heroism and superior leadership. However, except for George Washington, more books and articles have been written about Benedict Arnold than any other

American Revolutionary War officer. It is beyond the scope of this book to include another study of the life and services of Arnold, particularly when there is an excellent biography of his life written in 1997 by James Kirby Martin. Martin presents a fair and balanced study of this controversial "Revolutionary Hero".[17] Readers who want to understand more about the life and services of Benedict Arnold are encouraged to read Martin's superb biography.

II. ELEAZER OSWALD

A. Description of Journal.
Eleazer Oswald was a New Haven associate and aide to Benedict Arnold. While his journal is somewhat similar to the Arnold journal mentioned above, it does have different entries on some of the comparable days that are included in each journal.

B. Notes on Journal.
The Oswald journal is not the missing first pages of Arnold's journal as indicated by John H. Codman. Justin Smith suggests that it could be "the copy of my journal" that Arnold sent to Washington on October 13th.[18] Since it ends on October 13, this conclusion makes perfect sense. Charles E. Banks has a handwritten copy of Oswald's journal in the Banks Papers at the Massachusetts Historical Society.

C. Period Covered.
The Oswald journal starts on September 15 and runs through October 13, 1775.

D. Publishing History.
1st Printing. *A Journal of an Intended Tour from CAMBRIDGE to QUEBECK, Via KENNEBECK, with a detachment of two Regiments of Musketeers and three Companies of Riflers, consisting of about eleven hundred effective men, commanded by BENEDICT ARNOLD.* The journal is signed by ELEAZER OSWALD, Sec'y pro tem. Peter Force, American Archives, Ser. 4, Vol. III. Washington, D.C.: Peter Force, 1837-1853, page 1058.
2nd Printing. Kenneth Roberts. *March to Quebec.* Garden City, New York: Doubleday & Company, Inc., 1946. Extracts of Oswald's journal found on pages 44, 44a, and 44b.

E. Location of Original. The original of the Oswald journal is located in the Continental Army Papers, Ltrs. from General Officers, 1776-1789, Vol.

1, p. 28, NARA M247, National Archives and Record Administration, Washington, D.C. A copy is available on the web site of www.footnote. com.

F. Biography of Author.

Although Eleazer Oswald is listed as the author of this journal, he was acting as Arnold's personal secretary on the expedition and in the writing of the journal. He was born in Falmouth, England in1750. His parents were Eliazer Oswald, a ship's captain, and Rebekah Thomas. Eleazer came to America in 1770 after his father disappeared. He first landed in New York where he became an apprentice to the printer John Holt, who published a newspaper, *The New York Journal.* He subsequently married Holt's daughter, Elizabeth, on December 31, 1771 and they had at least seven children. One of his relatives in England was Richard Oswald, who was one of the signers of the Treaty of Peace between America and Great Britain to end the war.

He moved to New Haven after his marriage and continued his printing occupation. Although a recent emigrant, he was sympathetic to the patriot cause. On March 2, 1775, Oswald and Benedict Arnold were among fifty-eight men who formed a military company in New Haven, subsequently known as the Second Company Governor's Foot Guard. Arnold was soon appointed Captain, and Oswald served under him. After the Lexington Alarm, when Arnold marched with his company to Cambridge, Oswald was one of the men in the company who enlisted in the service. He was Arnold's aide at Fort Ticonderoga with the brevet rank of Captain and served as the Captain of Marines on the schooner *Liberty* in the raid on St. John's in May of 1775. Arnold appointed Oswald as a volunteer aide-de-camp and military secretary, with the same brevet rank, in the expedition to Quebec.

According to a letter written by Arnold after the assault, Oswald was the leader of the "Forlorn Hope," which was the designation of the troops at the head of the assault on the barricades during the December 31st assault on Quebec. It is obvious from the letter that Arnold had very high regard for Oswald and described Oswald as one whom "behaved extremely well." The forlorn hope carried the day at the first barrier using bayonets and captured the Captain of the Guard.

ELEAZER OSWALD,
Lieut. Colonel of the Revolutionary War
Nat. 1755 – Ob 1795

From a print in the collection of C.R. Hildeburn Esq.

Lieut. Col. Eleazer Oswald

Oswald was taken prisoner by the British in the assault and, along with other captured expedition officers, was exchanged in January of 1777. After being exchanged, he was appointed as a Lieutenant Colonel in the 2nd Continental Artillery Company commanded by Colonel John Lamb, who was also a veteran of the Quebec assault having reached Quebec with the Montgomery expedition. Oswald served with Lamb's company in opposing the British raid on Danbury and later distinguished himself at the Battle of Monmouth.

In May of 1778, Arnold wrote a letter on behalf of Oswald in which he says, "In the course of Lieut. Col. Oswald's service, he has ever acted with the highest honor & been universally estimed by the officers of the Army, & has been with me in several warm actions and has ever behaved with that calmness & Intrepity & good conduct which would have done honor to the oldest veteran. He has also to my knowledge made great sacrifices of his private interest by being in the Public Service." The Arnold letter was apparently written in support of Oswald, who was in a dispute with Congress over his seniority. Neither Arnold's letter nor any other action taken on Oswald's behalf resulted in a satisfactory resolution to his problem so he resigned from the Army on October 28th. His letter to Washington says that he could not possibly remain in camp "and subject myself to the Commands of a junior Officer." His letter goes on to tell Washington that he appreciates Washington's expressed concern for the "loss of a good Officer" but that he feels he must resign because "nothing but Injustice, by depriving me of my right, and transferring it to another, determines me to leave the Army." Oswald ends his letter by telling Washington: "I am sorry to observe, that there has not been more Attention paid to many brave and deserving Officers."

After his army service, Oswald returned to his previous occupation of printer, first in Baltimore with the Maryland Journal being published by William Goddard, and then with his own newspaper, the Independent Gazetteer in Philadelphia, which published its first issue on April 13, 1782. During the period after the war, his newspaper continually attacked Alexander Hamilton's policies regarding American finances and ultimately challenged Hamilton to a duel, but the matter was resolved and no duel was fought. He did, however, fight a duel in 1786 with another opponent, publisher Matthew Carey, who he wounded in the thigh. Carey had published a scathing poem dedicated to Oswald after a political attack on him by Oswald's paper.

Oswald was an avid anti-federalist and strongly opposed the adoption of the new Constitution, although he supported the Bill of Rights. His newspaper published twenty-four essays written by Pennsylvania Antifederalist leader Samuel Bryan under the name of "Centinel." Some writers consider this the leading argument against the constitution. In 1788, Oswald was charged with contempt of court by Pennsylvania Supreme Court Chief Justice Thomas McKean for his writings about the Constitution and his charges against a former business partner, who had charged him with libel. McKean called Oswald a "seditious turbulent man." In a highly publicized case, Oswald was convicted and then sentenced to a fine of ten pounds and a month in jail. His confrontation with McKean led to Oswald's unsuccessful attempt to get the Pennsylvania legislature to impeach Chief Justice McKean.

In 1793, after giving up his personal involvement in the printing business, Oswald went to England and then to France where he was commissioned as a colonel of artillery and regimental commander under General Dumourier in the French Republican army. His regiment fought in two or three battles. He was commissioned to take a trip to Ireland on behalf of the French government to assist the revolutionists in that country. He subsequently returned to France where he experienced problems with the Republican government over the purpose of his mission and back pay that he claimed he was owed. Being disgusted with the French Republicans, he returned to the U.S. in 1794. Prior to his death, Oswald sold his printing business, which had been operating under the leadership of his wife, to Joseph Gales. Eleazer Oswald died of yellow fever on December 2, 1795, after visiting a stricken friend, Major Charles Tillinghast. Oswald is one of the forgotten heroes of the Arnold expedition, and his efforts that greatly contributed to the passage of the Bill of Rights are also forgotten.[19]

III. HENRY DEARBORN

A. <u>Description of Journal</u>.
Captain Henry Dearborn was a company commander on the expedition to Quebec. His MHS journal, one of six journals regarding his experiences during the Revolutionary War, consists of forty pages of manuscript relating to Arnold's expedition. See Chapter Two for a newly discovered Dearborn journal.

In the introduction to The Journals of Henry Dearborn, published by the Caxton Club, the editor points out that the Quebec journal is the only one of the six journals "not in Dearborn's handwriting, although corrected in a score of places by the author." The manuscript of the Dearborn journal, which was originally published by the Massachusetts Historical Society, was purchased by the Boston Public Library at the sale of the John Wingate Thornton Manuscripts held on October 15, 1878. Thornton, an attorney, was the executor of the will of Henry A. S. Dearborn, the son of the author. Thornton's interests also included history and he was a well-known book collector of his time.[20]

MAJ. GEN HENRY DEARBORN.

Maj. Gen. Henry Dearborn

The MHS journal is not the original Dearborn journal as will be revealed in the next chapter, which presents information on a new manuscript that has come to light in Scotland. This section, however, contains the same information on the Dearborn journal published by MHS as is provided in all of the other expedition journals.

B. <u>Notes on Journal</u>. Judge Mellen Chamberlain, who introduced the Dearborn journal in its original publication in the Massachusetts Historical

Society Proceedings, states that the journal "relates the suffering of the men who marched from Boston through the wilderness to Quebec, and narrates the capture of the city which followed." Dearborn's MHS journal includes a list of officers in the initial organization of the detachment, which included two musket divisions and the three rifle companies.

Charles E. Banks concludes that this journal "is identical in its daily entries with the journal of Meigs, and is not in the [handwriting] of Dearborn, although it has some interlineations written by him. It is probable that he borrowed the journal kept by Meigs, had it copied and added it to his own personal recollections of events occurring in his experiences."[21] Although the title of Dearborn's journal is similar to the Meigs' journal title, the entries are quite different. One could argue that they are similar but the connection that seems most likely is that Dearborn used Meigs as a guide in the preparation of his journal. Additional details on the Dearborn journal are provided in the next chapter.

C. Period Covered.
The Dearborn journal covers the period between September 10, 1775 and July 16, 1776.

D. Publishing History.
1st Printing. *Journal Kept by Capt. Henry Dearborn of the Proceedings and Particular Occurrences, which happened within my Knowledge to the Troops, under the Command of Colonel Benedict Arnold in the year 1775 which troops were detached from the American Army lying before the Town of Boston, for the purpose of marching to, and taking possession of Quebec, Said detachment consisted of Eleven Hundred men, two battalions of musket men, and three companies of riflemen as Light-Infantry.* Proceedings of the Massachusetts Historical Society, Vol. II, Second Series, 1885-1886, pp. 275-305.
2nd Printing. Pamphlet with a gray cover. *Journal of Captain Henry Dearborn in the Quebec Expedition 1775.* Reprinted from the Proceedings of the Massachusetts Historical Society, 1886. Cambridge: John Wilson and Son. University Press. 1886. 33 pages.
3rd Printing. *Magazine of History with Notes and Queries,* Vol. XXXIV, Extra # 135, William Abbatt, Tarrytown, N.Y., 1928. 45 pages.
4th Printing. *March to Quebec Journals of the Members of Arnold's Expedition. Compiled and annotated by Kenneth Roberts during the Writing of Arundel.* Garden City, New York: Doubleday & Company, Inc., 1938, pp. 129-170.
5th Printing. *Revolutionary War Journals of Henry Dearborn 1775-1783.* Edited from the original manuscripts by Lloyd A. Brown and Howard E. Peckham. Chicago: The Caxon Club, 1939, pp. 35-96.

6th Printing. *Revolutionary War Journals of Henry Dearborn*. Westminster, MD: Heritage Books, 2004.

E. Location of Original.
The original manuscript of this Dearborn journal is located in the Boston Public Library Rare Book Room.

F. Biography of Author.
Henry Dearborn was born in North Hampton, New Hampshire, on February 23, 1751. He attended a local district school and then studied medicine under Dr. Hall Jackson in Portsmouth, New Hampshire. By 1772, he was practicing medicine in Nottingham Square, N.H. and prior to the beginning of the war, he was appointed as captain of a militia company of sixty men. When the Lexington Alarm broke out, Dearborn marched to Boston with his company, where they were incorporated into Col. John Stark's regiment and fought in the Battle of Bunker Hill.

In September of 1775, he volunteered for Arnold's expedition to Quebec and was designated as a company commander. Dearborn was late to report on the day of the assault and therefore was not in the main body of Arnold's troops, but he and his company were taken prisoner as they were marching to join the rest of the assault force. He was released on parole early, along with Return J. Meigs, in May of 1776, but was not formally exchanged until March 1777.

On March 19, 1777, he was appointed Major of the 3rd New Hampshire Regiment and in September of 1777, he was transferred to the 1st New Hampshire Regiment with the rank of lieutenant colonel. He was in the Battle of Saratoga and then spent the winter of 77-78 at Valley Forge with Washington's army. His unit was involved in the Battle of Monmouth in June of 1778, where his regiment won commendation from Washington for its actions on the field.

In the summer of 1779, his regiment formed part of the army in General John Sullivan's campaign against the Six Nations of Iroquois Indians in central New York. He then served on Washington's staff with the rank of colonel as Deputy Quartermaster in 1781, where he participated in the Battle of Yorktown.

Dearborn was discharged from the army in 1783 and settled in Gardiner, Maine with his family. After his discharge from the army, Dearborn was appointed fist as a Brigadier General and later a Major General of the Maine

State Militia. He was also appointed as United States Marshall for the District of Maine. He represented his district in Congress from 1793 to 1797. In 1801, President Thomas Jefferson appointed him Secretary of War and he served in that position until 1808. From 1809 until 1812, Dearborn was Collector of the Port of Boston.

At the beginning of the War of 1812, President James Madison appointed him as the Senior Major General in the United States Army and placed him in command of the northeast sector from the Niagara River to the New England coast. His ability to command was generally considered to be ineffective and by 1813, he was relieved of command and assigned to an administrative position in New York. He was honorably discharged from the army on June 15, 1815, but with a less than stellar reputation.

President Madison nominated him to again be Secretary of War but the nomination was rejected by the senate. From 1822 to 1824, he served as Minister Plenipotentiary to Portugal and then retired to his home in Roxbury, Massachusetts, where he died on June 6, 1829. Dearborn was married three times, to Mary Bartlet in 1771, to Dorcas Marble in 1780 and finally to Sarah, the widow of James Bowdoin. His son, Harry Scammell Dearborn, was a Brigadier General in the War of 1812, served in Congress for two years and was adjutant general of Massachusetts for nine years. Henry Dearborn was probably the best known Arnold expedition alumnus because of the various positions he held subsequent to the Revolutionary War.[22]

IV. RETURN JONATHAN MEIGS

A. Description of Journal.
Return J. Meigs was the highest ranking officer after Arnold to write a journal of the expedition. The Meigs' journal is significant for three reasons. First, it was the first journal of the Arnold expedition to be published. It was published in 1776 in the United States, which was less than a year after the expedition reached Quebec. The Almon printing, which was subsequent to the first printing but the same version, raised questions about its authorship by stating that the journal was "supposed" to be written by Meigs. The publishing date of the first printing of the Meigs journal proves that it is an authentic original journal written contemporaneously with the events he describes.

Second, the Meigs journal has been published more frequently than any other journal. Perhaps the 1776 date of the initial publication accounts for the preference that has been shown toward the Meigs journal in its publishing history. The breadth of publications in which it has appeared range from Almon to the Winchester Historical Society to the Quebec Literary and Historical Society. It was also reprinted by Charles Bushnell in the middle of the 19th century in a private publication as well as other printings spelled out below. This publishing history makes it one of the most unique Arnold expedition journals.

Third, there are two different versions of the journal that are so similar in style and content that there can be no doubt that Meigs penned both. The first journal was the one published in *Almon's Remembrancer*. The second version was the one published by the Massachusetts Historical Society, which was found among the papers of Yale College President Ezra Stiles. The MHS publication states that the journal was provided to Stiles by Meigs' brother, Josiah Meigs, who was a tutor at Yale College during the Revolutionary War. The MHS introduction states that the original was written by Meigs and "faithfully and intelligently edited" by someone else, presumably his brother.

Justin Smith makes a good point that the MHS journal was published while Meigs was still alive and that if that journal was not his, he could have said so. Even if Meigs did not edit the MHS proof, Smith concludes, "it seems reasonable to suppose that he was consulted."

B. Notes on Journal.

C. Period Covered.
The Almon journal covers the period of September 9, 1775 to November 20, 1775 and the MHS journal begins on September 9, 1775 and ends on January 1, 1776.

D. Publishing History.
1st Printing. Paper wraps. *A Journal of Occurrences which Happened Within the Circle of Observation in the Detachment Commanded by Colonel Benedictine Arnold, Consisting of Two Battalions, which were Detached from the Army at Cambridge, in the Year 1775.* By Major Ret. J. Meigs. Rich's Bibliotheca Americana Nova, published in 1835, Vol. 1, page 211, says, "This interesting tract contains an account of the attack on Quebec, in which General Montgomery was killed. It has no place, date or printer's name, but has the appearance of having been printed in America. A part of this journal is printed in the 'Remembrancer', iii; said to be taken from the American copy, 'supposed to be written by Major Meigs'." According to

a printed catalogue of the Library of the Massachusetts Historical Society, published by MHS in 1860, there is a copy of this first printing in that library. However, this author was unable to find any copy of this important publication in the MHS library.

Maj. Return Jonathan Meigs, Sr.

Fortunately, however, there is an extant copy of this first printing in the Harvard Library. That copy has been bound with a cloth binding. It was presented to the Harvard Library in 1865 by the Honorable William Prescott with a pencil notation "Rec'd May 6, 1865." The journal has a total of eleven pages unnumbered. At the top of the first paper page there is an ink notation that says: "1775 No 12." From this we can surmise that there were at least 12 copies printed. Other than this notation, there is no indication of how many copies of this pamphlet were printed. However, the 1775 version of the Meigs journal is undoubtedly the rarest publication of any of the expedition journal.

2nd Printing. *A Journal of Occurrences Which Happened Within the Circle of my Observation, in the Detachment Commanded by Col. Benedict Arnold, Consisting of Two Battalions which were detached from the army at Cambridge, in the year 1775.* The Almon journal states that it is printed from the "American Copy. (Supposed to be written by Major Meigs)." The Remembrancer, Impartial Repository of Public Events. Part II. For the Year 1776. London: Printed for J. Almon, 1776. pp. 295-302.

3rd Printing. *A Journal of Occurrences Which Happened Within the Circle of My Observation in the Detachment Commanded by Col. Benedict Arnold, Consisting of Two Battalions which were detached from the army at Cambridge, in the year 1775.* London Magazine, Vol. 45, 1776, p. 480, with a map titled "A View of the Rivers Kennebec and Chadiere, with Col. Arnold's Route to Quebec." The author has not viewed this publication but does have a copy of the original scarce map that is included in the London Magazine printing of the journal.

4th Printing. Robert Beatson. *Naval and Military Memoirs of Great Britain from 1727 to 1783.* London: Longman Hurst, Rees and Orme, 1804, Appendix, pp. 30-40.

5th Printing. A Journal of Occurrences... (Same title as above*). Collections of the Massachusetts Historical Society,* Vol. II, Second Series Boston, 1814. pp. 227-247. This publication is where the second version of the Meigs journal was first introduced.

6th Printing. *Journal of the Expedition against Quebec under Command of Benedict Arnold in the Year 1775, by Return J. Meigs,* With an Introduction and Notes by Charles I. Bushnell. New York: Privately Printed, 1864. This is Bushnell's first printing the Meigs journal as its own separate edition. It was then printed by Bushnell again that same year along with five other journals that were combined into one volume of a two volume series. (See the next entry).

7th Printing. (Same title as above). *Crumbs for Antiquarians, Charles I. Bushnell.* (2 vols.) Vol. 1. New York: Privately Printed, 1864. Dedicated to "My Antiquarian Friends, and to students of American history generally." pp. 1-57. Meigs' journal is one of six tracts bound together and included in Volume I. The tracts include an essay by Bushnell on early NYC tokens and five Revolutionary War memoirs including the one by Meigs. According to Sabin, Bushnell printed about 100 copies of the Meigs' journal so this book in both volumes is rare. However, the 100 copies include both the separate printing of the journal by Bushnell and the printing of Crumbs, which includes the Meigs journal. Per a note in OCLC and the Catalogue of the Collection of Books and Manuscripts Belonging to Mr. Branton Ives of New

York, only 50 copies of Crumbs were actually printed. Therefore, only 50 copies of the separate journal by Bushnell were printed. Crumbs is a rare item but is available from time to time from rare book dealers.

8th Printing. *Major Meig's: Journal of Operations against Quebec.* Literary and Historical Society of Quebec, Quebec, *Canada.* Transactions, Vol. NS (New Series), No. 12, 1876. pp. 31-36. The extract of the Meig's journal is included in an address by Lt.-Colonel Strange at the Centenary Celebration at the rooms of the Literary and Historical Society of Quebec, of the Centennial Anniversary of the siege of Quebec, 1775-1776, held on December 29, 1875.

9th Printing. *Journal of Major Return Jonathan Meigs, With Annotations by Mrs. Melvin Green.* Annual Papers of Winchester Virginia Historical Society, Vol. I, Winchester, Virginia, 1931, pp. 119-155.

10th Printing. Kenneth Roberts. *March to Quebec.* Garden City, New York: Doubleday, 1938, pp. 171-196.

11th Printing. Richard A. Mason. *The Quiet Patriot, Colonel Return Jonathan Meigs with Meig's 1775 Journal of the Quebec Expedition.* Westminster, MD: Heritage Books, 2010, pp. 309-337.

E. Location of Original.
The original version of the Meigs' journal has not been located. However, the Library of Congress has a copy of a letter from Sir George Beckwith to Josiah Meigs, written in 1818, regarding the loss of Col. Meigs' journal.

F. Biography of Author
Return Jonathan Meigs was born in Middletown, Connecticut, on December 16, 1740 and was the son of Return Meigs, who was a hatter. Apparently the Meigs family had a history of unusual names for children. Among the family names from the eighteenth century are: Concurrence, Mindwell, Recompense, Silence, Submit, Thankful, Mercy, Wait-still and Church.

In 1772, Meigs was commissioned as a lieutenant in the 6th Connecticut Regiment and two years later was promoted to Captain of the Light Infantry in that Regiment. Shortly after the Lexington Alarm, Meigs led his company to Boston. When the Connecticut regiments were reorganized, Meigs was promoted to Major in Colonel Joseph Spencer's 2nd Connecticut Regiment. Meigs later joined the Arnold expedition as one of its higher ranking field officers. He is the highest ranking officer after Arnold to write a journal of his experiences on the expedition.

In the assault on Quebec, Meigs was taken prisoner but was one of two officers first released on parole in May of 1776 by British commander Guy

Carleton. He was finally exchanged in January of 1777. On February 10, 1777, he was appointed as the Lieutenant Colonel of Sherburne's regiment. He later conducted a whaleboat raid on Sag Harbor, Long Island, in May of 1777 with 170 men. Meigs' troops charged the encampment, surprising the British troops stationed there, taking ninety prisoners and killing six without losing any of his men. His success was immediately recognized and on July 23, 1777, Congress passed a resolution praising his conduct and presenting him with a sword.

Meigs served with General Anthony Wayne in 1779 in the assault on Stony Point in New York and his regiment was a key factor in the capture of that fortified position. Following this activity, Meigs' regiment went into winter quarters with the rest of Washington's army at Morristown, New Jersey and in the spring of 1780 he played an important role in stopping a mutiny in the Connecticut line for which he received a personal note of thanks from Washington. Return J. Meigs retired from military service on January 1, 1781. Apparently he was offered an appointment as a Brigadier General in the Connecticut forces but declined it.

After the war, Meigs became a surveyor in the Ohio country and in 1787 became one of its first settlers. He was in Ohio for a number of years and held an office there as Judge of the Court of Quarter Sessions. He was involved in the Treaty of Grenville, where he worked to get a fair settlement for both the frontiersmen and the Native Americans. In 1801, Meigs was appointed by President Jefferson as Cherokee Indian Agent and Agent of the War Department in Tennessee. Meigs worked for what he considered to be the best interests of the Cherokees, which included removal of the Indians off their tribal lands, but he always maintained the respect of the Indians who named him "The White Path." He died of pneumonia on January 28, 1823 at the Cherokee Indian Agency in Tennessee.

Return J. Meigs was married twice and had a total of seven children He named his oldest son Return Jonathan Meigs II. That son had his own illustrious career which included appointment as the first Chief Justice of the Ohio Supreme Court, U.S. Senator from Ohio, Governor of Ohio and, in 1814, he was appointed by President Madison as Postmaster General.[23]

V. ISAAC SENTER.

A. Description of Journal.
Isaac Senter's account of the Arnold expedition is unique because he

apparently wrote two very distinct accounts at two different times. The manuscripts for each of these accounts are in different public repositories and are therefore available for examination. However, each of these manuscripts tells the history in a different way. Further information on the two Senter journals is presented in Chapter Four.

The only Senter journal that has been printed is the one first published by the Historical Society of Pennsylvania and is now housed in the Fordham University Library. William Matthews states that Senter's journal contains "long & well-written entries about camp life, his own work, and the progress of the campaign".[24] A review from 1846 says that this "little work is a plain but graphic narrative of the difficulties, dangers and sufferings, of that memorable expedition."[25] A more recent book dealer described the journal as a "vivid narrative of the sufferings of the American troops, as witnessed by the surgeon under Benedict Arnold".[26] Jared Sparks, President of Harvard University and nineteenth century historian, wrote in one of his letters that the Senter journal "is an interesting addition to our Revolutionary History, and gives a more exact picture of the celebrated March through the Wilderness, I think, than any other record".[27] The Sparks letter, however, was written before some of the other expedition journals were transcribed and published so he might have taken a different point of view if he had access to all of the journals that are included in this chapter.

B. <u>Notes on Journal</u>.
See Chapter Four.

C. <u>Period Covered</u>.
Journal begins on September 13, 1775 and ends on January 6, 1776.

D. <u>Publishing History</u>.
<u>1st Printing</u>. Paper wraps. *The Journal of Isaac Senter, physician and surgeon to the troops detached from the American army encamped at Cambridge, Mass., on a secret expedition against Quebec, under the command of Col. Benedict Arnold, in September, 1775.* Bulletin of the Historical Society of Pennsylvania, Vol. I, No. 5, March, 1846. Printed by Townsend, Ward, Philadelphia. The first edition of the Senter journal is printed as a Bulletin of the HSP with 40 uncut and untrimmed pages along with five introductory pages of minutes of the HSP meeting of December 22, 1845, which are page number 1 and then 66 through 69. This separate printing of Senter's journal by the HSP has a title page following the minutes, then a Notice, a Preface and then the journal with pages numbered 2 through 40.

According to Joseph Sabin, the Senter journal published by HSP was transcribed and edited by Edward D. Ingraham and the Preface to the journal was written by Henry Pennington. The HSP, realizing they had a rare journal of the Revolutionary War, wanted to get it published to a wider audience as quickly as possible.

Dr. Isaac Senter

<u>2nd Printing</u>. A series of thirteen Bulletins published by HSP in one volume that was entitled *Volume 1 of the Proceedings of the Historical Society of Pennsylvania,* but was also called *Volume 1 of The Bulletin of the Historical Society of Pennsylvania, 1845-1847.* This volume was printed in 1848 for the society by Merrihew & Thompson, Philadelphia. Each of the thirteen bulletins, including the Senter journal as Bulletin No. 5, was printed with its own date corresponding to a meeting date of the HSP beginning with February 2, 1845 and ending with November 1, 1847. The Senter Journal has the same title as in the first printing. *The Journal of Isaac Senter Physician and Surgeon to the Troops Detached from the American Army Encamped at*

Cambridge, Mass. on a Secret Expedition against Quebec under the Command of Col. Benedict Arnold in September, 1775. This printing has the same pagination as the first printing.

3rd Printing. A very short extract of the Senter journal appears in *The History of Norridgewock*, William Allen. Norridgewock, ME: William Allen, 1849. pp. 76-79.

4th Printing. *The Journal of Isaac Senter, physician and surgeon to the troops detached from the American army encamped at Cambridge, Mass., on a secret expedition against Quebec, under the command of Col. Benedict Arnold, in September, 1775.* The Magazine of History with Notes and Queries, Vol. XI, Extra Number 42, 1916. William Abbatt, Tarrytown, New York. pp. 85-144.

5th Printing. Kenneth Roberts. *March to Quebec.* pp. 197-246.

6th Printing. *The Journal of Isaac Senter...* Part of the series entitled Eyewitness Accounts of the American Revolution. New York: The New York Times & Arno Press, 1969, 40 pages. Cloth cover.

7th Printing. Excerpts from Senter's journal in *The American Revolution: Writings from the War of Independence.* New York: Library of America, 2001. pp. 218-235.

E. Location of Originals.

1st Original Manuscript Journal. Charles Allen Munn Collection, Archives & Special Collections, Fordham University Library. The journal consists of 86 leaves written on one side only. Enclosed in a pigskin case. This is the journal that has been published in all of the above printings using the HSP publication as the template.

2nd Original Manuscript Journal. Rhode Island Historical Society. Dr. Isaac Senter Papers. MSS 165. Box 2, folder 6. Journal of Isaac Senter. There is a notation that this "journal is very difficult to read" but that another version that is more readable has been published as per the above notes. See the transcription of the journal in Chapter Four.

F. Biography of Author.

Isaac Senter was born in Londonderry, New Hampshire, in 1753 and moved to Rhode Island with his family when he was a young boy. It seems likely that the Senter family came from Ireland because they lived in the "Irish settlement" of Londonderry. He studied to be a physician under Dr. Thomas Moffat, a physician in Newport. When the Revolutionary War broke out, he marched to Boston as a physician with the Rhode Island troops under the command of Colonel John Church.

Senter was appointed as the physician and surgeon to the Arnold expedition in September of 1775 while still in Cambridge, and marched with the troops to Quebec recording his experiences in two different journals. In his HSP journal, he records the initial treatment of Benedict Arnold's leg wound. "Daylight had scarce made its appearance ere Colonel Arnold was brought in, supported by two soldiers. He was wounded in one leg by a piece of a musket-ball. It had probably come into contact with a stone, or the like, which had cleft off nigh a third of it, ere it entered the leg. The other two-thirds entered the outer side of the leg about mid-way and in an oblique curve passed between the tibia and fibula, and lodged in the gastroeunemia muscle at the rise of the tendon Achilles, whereupon examination I easily discovered and extracted it." After the attack on Quebec, he treated the wounded troops, in addition to Arnold, at the General Hospital near Quebec. He returned home with the Arnold forces in the terrible retreat of 1776 and settled in Cranston to practice medicine. The Quebec expedition was his only Revolutionary War experience.

In 1776, Senter was appointed Surgeon-General of Rhode Island and served as the Cranston representative to the Rhode Island General Assembly from 1778 to 1780. He married Elizabeth (Betsy), the daughter of Capt. Rhodes Arnold of Pawtucket on November 8, 1778. Senter moved from Cranston to Newport in 1780, and lived there, practicing medicine, for the rest of his life. He had honorary membership in several U.S. and European medical societies. He was also a contributor to various medical journals. He obtained an honorary M.D. degree from Brown University in 1787 and was on their Board of Trustees until his death. He also received an honorary medical degree from both Harvard and Yale. The Massachusetts Historical Society elected him a corresponding member and he was also a member of the American Philosophical Society.

Because of his eminent status in Rhode Island, Senter was an early president of the Rhode Island Society of the Cincinnati and held that office for many years. He was also director of the Rhode Island military hospital from 1794 to his death in 1799. Senter was a tall man known to have a dignified appearance. In George Channing's "Recollections of Newport", he states, "Dr. Senter exerted a sort of enchantment when summoned to a sick-bed; if the case demanded only simples, his smile proved more potent than his prescription." One source says "He was the earliest writer of note among Rhode Island physicians and contributed four articles to the first volume of the Transactions of the Philadelphia College of Physicians, published in 1783."

Senter was a close friend of the Nathaniel Greene family and actively treated that family for a period of time until they moved their residence to South Carolina. Senter died in Newport on December 20, 1799, at the young age of 45, leaving his widow and six children. At his death, he left an extensive and valuable medical library which was donated to the Rhode Island Medical Society in 1881.

One of Isaac Senter's sons, Horatio, also became a doctor and after practicing in Newport for a few years, he moved to Savannah, presumably to be near his lover, the wife of John Rutledge, Jr. Rutledge came home one day and caught Senter leaving his wife's bedroom and challenged him to a duel. In the duel, Senter was wounded in the leg below the knee. The leg was amputated but gangrene set in and young Dr. Senter died. A newspaper account said of the fallout" "This cruel business has been the means of destroying Mr. R's peace of mind, and ruining his wife's character forever."[28]

VI. SIMEON THAYER

A. Description of Journal.
The Thayer journal has been described in one review as containing, "a careful and well-written account of the 'invasion of Canada'. The Journal of Captain Thayer is a simple and interesting narrative of one of the Rhode Island officers under Arnold. There are few passages in it of special historical importance, but it gives a vivid impression of the hardships of the expedition."[29]

Justin Smith makes the argument that Thayer's journal bears a strong resemblance to the journals of John Topham and William Humphrey, both of whom were Rhode Islanders and friends of Thayer.[30] Humphrey was a second lieutenant in Thayer's company. Smith believes that Thayer's journal has significant merit even though Thayer used Humphrey as a guide. Kenneth Roberts agrees with Smith when he labels the journals as "identical" but that Thayer "contains more detail than the other two."[31]

Smith reports that Edwin M. Stone, the transcriber and annotator of Thayer's journal, "permitted himself a great number of slight departures from the manuscript, with some considerable significance".[32] Although it has not been done yet, hopefully someone will update the transcription of this journal and correct those irregularities.

One of the significant contributions of Stone's book is the short personal sketches of some of the expedition personnel. This is the first publication containing comprehensive sketches of the key Arnold personnel and as such is a valuable resource. Stone has information not found anywhere else.

A different perspective of Stone's publication was contained in the 1868 North American Review.

> There are few passages in it of special historical importance, but it gives a vivid impression of the hardships of the expedition, and now and then there is a touch of character or feeling which is of value as an expression of human nature ... Mr. Stone has supplied, in a very elaborate Appendix, all the illustration required by the Journal. His work is thoroughly done; and the volume forms a very worthy contribution to the history of the Revolution.[33]

B. <u>Notes on the Journal</u>.
This author examined the Thayer journal and found it to be in a tattered condition with a rather elaborate design pattern located in three places in the manuscript. Based on the elaborate design, it was not written while Thayer was in prison and is most likely a handwritten version copied by Edwin M. Stone from an original. Smith states that the manuscript is not in Thayer's handwriting but goes on to say that it was written by a captain in Greene's division and Thayer is the only possible choice because of the other two captains Topham wrote his own journal and Hubbard was killed in the assault on Quebec.

C. <u>Period Covered</u>.
The journal starts on September 11, 1775 and ends on August 12, 1776.

D. <u>Publishing History</u>.
<u>1st Printing</u> Extracts. Benjamin Cowell. *The Spirit of 76 in Rhode Island*. 8 vols. Boston, 1850. Appendix, pp. 283-294 includes extracts of Thayer's journal entries from November 22, 1775 to January 1, 1776. This publication also includes a biography of Thayer.
<u>2nd Printing</u>. Edwin M. Stone. *The Invasion of Canada in 1775: Including the Journal of Captain Simeon Thayer, Describing the Perils and Sufferings of the Army under Colonel Benedict Arnold in its March Through the Wilderness to Quebec: With Notes and Appendix*. Providence, RI: Hammond, Angell & Co., Printers, 1867. Included in the Collections of the Rhode Island Historical Society, Vol. 6. Preface and Introduction plus pp. 1-104. Brown cloth binding. No maps and portraits. This is the first printing of the entire Thayer journal.
<u>3rd Printing</u>. Edwin Martin Stone. *The Invasion of Canada in 1775: Including*

the Journal of Captain Simeon Thayer Describing the Perils and Sufferings of the Army Under Colonel Benedict Arnold in its March Through the Wilderness to Quebec, with Notes and Appendix. Includes one map, two portraits and two errata slips. Providence, RI: Knowles, Anthony & Co., Printers, 1867, 104 pages. 100 copies printed. Although this is not the first printing of the entire Thayer journal, it is rare because it was a limited private printing by E.M. Stone. The Rhode Island Historical Society says that this printing of the Thayer journal is reprinted from the RIHS journal described in the 2nd printing.

There are two versions of the first printing. One version is on 8vo paper with two portraits and a map. This is the version printed on smaller paper and in the SLM Barlow catalogue it is listed as having "half morocco, gilt top, uncut pages" The second version is printed on large uncut paper, known as the large paper copy, and includes a map and two portraits. It is in half morocco binding with gilt lettering on the spine and the pages are trimmed but uncut. The Charles I. Bushnell catalogue says there were "only a few copies, privately printed" and the Barlow catalogue says there were "only a limited edition privately printed ... half morocco, gilt top, uncut, by Bradstreet." The sales catalog of the Anderson Galleries from 1920 offered a copy of the printing in wraps with no cloth cover.

4th Printing. Kenneth Roberts *March to Quebec*. pp. 247-298.

5th Printing. Edwin Martin Stone. *The Invasion of Canada in 1775: Including the Journal of Captain Simeon Thayer.* Bowie, Maryland: Heritage Books, Inc., 1997. Facsimile reprint of R.I. Collections.

6th Printing. Edwin Martin Stone. *The Invasion of Canada in 1775.* The Scholars Bookshelf, Cranbury, N.J., 2007. Soft cover.

Arnold Expedition Historical Society. Eyewitness Accounts. Simeon Thayer's Journal. www.arnoldsmarch.com/research.html.

E. Location of Original.

Rhode Island Historical Society. MSS 24. Simeon Thayer Papers. Diary. (1 box). The original manuscript in RIHS is written on large paper, almost the same as our legal size.

F. Biography of Author.

Simeon Thayer was born in Mendon, Massachusetts on April 30, 1737. As a young man he was apprenticed to a peruke (wig) maker in Rhode Island. In 1756, he joined a Rhode Island regiment to fight in the French and Indian War and was a member of the Massachusetts regiment at Fort William Henry when it surrendered to Montcalm in 1757. When he returned to Providence, he resumed his occupation and married his first wife in 1761.

In May of 1775, he was appointed as a Captain of a Rhode Island company, which he raised himself, and then marched his company to Roxbury to join the American army. In August of 1775, Thayer joined Arnold's expedition as a company commander and was captured in the failed attack on Quebec. He was released on parole in September of 1776 with other captured officers and was finally exchanged in July of 1777. He was appointed Major in the Rhode Island regiment commanded by Colonel Olney, which marched to Red Bank in 1777. Thayer's regiment of five hundred men was successful in defending the position at Red Bank in the face of an attack by 1200 Hessian soldiers. The next day Thayer went across the river to Fort Mifflin to take command of that Fort after its commander, Colonel Smith, was wounded. He successfully thwarted a couple of attacks on the Fort before he was finally forced to evacuate in the face of superior manpower.

In 1778, Thayer's regiment was in the Battle of Monmouth and he was injured in that battle by a cannon ball. He went to Morristown to recuperate and, while there, his regiment was ordered to Rhode Island to participate in the Battle for Rhode Island. The regiment arrived just days before the American army retreated. Major Thayer and his unit were with General Anthony Wayne in the successful storming of the Fort at Stony Point in New York. Thayer was in the front ranks in the assault and performed distinguished service.

In 1780, he was a Major in Colonel Angell's Rhode Island regiment located in New Jersey. In October of 1780, the two Rhode Island regiments were merged into one and Thayer retired from the service. After his Continental Army service, Thayer was appointed to be Brigadier General in the Rhode Island militia. He was also a member of the Rhode Island Society of Cincinnati until his death.

Thayer was married three times and had nine children. After retiring from the army, he opened a tavern and public house in Providence known as the Montgomery Hotel. After a few years, he sold the tavern and bought a farm in Cumberland where he lived until October 14, 1800. Thayer was thrown from a horse and killed while returning home from Providence.[34]

VII. JOHN TOPHAM

A. Description of Journal.
John Topham was another Rhode Islander who was a company commander on Arnold's expedition. Although he was put in charge of one of the

expedition companies, as was Thayer, he is not as well known. William Abbatt in his reprinting of the journal in the *Magazine of History* describes the Topham journal as "one of the rarest journals" of the Arnold expedition.[35] Abbatt's statement is a slight exaggeration because there are a number of journals that are rarer than Topham's.

Five entries from the Topham journal were included in *The Spirit of Rhode Island in 76,* published by Benjamin Cowell in 1850. The editor of The Rhode Island Sons of the Revolution printing of the Topham journal states that it ends "abruptly" at the end of a page and indicates that it is likely that there is a continuation of the journal "in another book."[36]

Both Smith and Roberts count the Topham journal as being similar to the Thayer and Humphrey journals and this author agrees. However, their entries are not identical so each wrote from his own perspective. Unfortunately, there is little evidence that Topham was the author of the journal attributed to him. The title to the manuscript journal using John Topham's name is in a different handwriting and was almost certainly inserted by someone other than its author. The only supporting evidence that Topham was the author is that the manuscript was in the possession of the Topham family at the time it appeared in the Newport Mercury in 1897, and that it was published by Cowell in 1850 as a Topham journal. There is nothing in the journal manuscript that confirms it to be a Topham journal.

B. Notes on the Journal.
Prior to the publication of his book, Justin Smith transcribed the Topham journal from the original, then owned by Topham's grandson, but it was never printed. There is no record of where Smith's transcription is located. It was Topham's grandson who allowed the Topham journal to be published in 1902 by the Rhode Island Sons of the Revolution. Either he or another family member donated the journal to the Rhode Island Historical Society where it now resides.

C. Period Covered.
The journal begins on October 6, 1775 and ends on November 30, 1776.

D. Publishing History.
1st Printing. Benjamin Cowell, *The Spirit of '76 in Rhode Island.* Boston, 1850. An appendix page 348-350, includes a brief biography of Topham. Contains five entries from Topham's journal.
2nd Printing. *Newport Mercury, Newport, RI.* Topham's journal was printed in eight issues beginning on May 15, 1897 in this Newport newspaper.

Smith says, "This version is substantially correct, but it does not begin until October 14th, whereas the MS is in part readable as early as October 6th, and it contains many slight and some astonishing departures from the original." A typed transcription of the Topham journal that was produced by the Newport Mercury is in the Rhode Island Historical Society. Its title is "A copy of a Journal Kept by Capt. Afterwards Col. John Topham of Newport, R.I. during Montgomery's Expedition." The word "Montgomery" has been crossed out and the word "Arnold" written in its place. RIHS has an original copy of the newspaper issues in which the Topham journal appeared. The journal as published in the Mercury ends on January 23rd, and the newspaper describes the reason. "Here the diary ends, practically, for the few remaining leaves are torn and disfigured so badly as to be unreadable." This author confirmed that statement by examining the original journal and finding the entries after January 23, 1776 almost impossible to read and a portion of the page remaining after the entries of January 23rd torn completely off.

3rd Printing. *Second Record Book of the Society of Sons of the Revolution in the State of Rhode Island.* Newport: The Mercury Publishing Company, 1902. Given the similarity of the name of the newspaper in the previous printing and the name of this printer, it is probable that the printer was the Newport Mercury. The only difference is that the journal in this printing ends on January 31st instead of January 23rd. Some unknown person, but not the transcriber for the Newport Mercury, took the time to examine the manuscript journal close enough to be able to reproduce portions of additional entries through January 31, 1776.

4th Printing. *The Journal of John Topham, 1775-6*. Magazine of History with Notes and Queries. Extra No. 50, William Abbatt, Tarrytown, NY, 1916, 46 pages. This printing, which is a reproduction of the third printing, also ends the journal on January 31, 1776, instead of January 23, 1776.

E. Location of original.
Rhode Island Historical Society. MSS 9001-T, John Topham journal.

F. Biography of Author.
John Topham was born in Newport, Rhode Island in 1742. Although there is no record of his early life, he must have either participated in the French and Indian War or else was active in the Rhode Island militia because when the Revolution broke out he was appointed as a captain in the company of Major Forrester of Colonel Church's regiment. In July of 1775, he is listed as commanding a company in the American army at Cambridge. When Colonel Benedict Arnold put together his officers for the Quebec expedition, Topham was designated as one of his company commanders. Other journalists in

their entries that covered the march through the wilderness indicate he was an active company commander.

During the attack on Quebec, Topham and most of his company were captured and taken prisoner. He was released along with the other expedition officers in the fall of 1776 and made his way home. In February of 1777, he was appointed a Captain in the 1st Rhode Island Continental Battalion and in June of 1777 was promoted to Lieutenant Colonel in the State Brigade under Colonel Crary, which was raised for fifteen months service within the state to respond to the British occupation of Newport. In December of 1777, he was transferred to Colonel Barton's regiment and in February of 1778 was made the commander of the Barton regiment, after Colonel Barton was transferred to the Continental line. Topham was in the siege of Newport and the subsequent Battle of Rhode Island in August of 1778. In 1779, he was a commander of one of two state battalions and subsequently became commander of both battalions still retaining the rank of Lieutenant Colonel.

In 1780, the British threat to Rhode Island was eliminated when the British left Newport and Topham and his regiment were discharged by the state. In May of 1780, the General Assembly of Rhode Island passed a resolution commending Topham and two other officers for their service to the state and gave them a vote of thanks for the "great fidelity and ability" with which they discharged their military duties during the war. Not surprising they authorized no money.

After his discharge from military service, Topham was elected as a Deputy in the Rhode Island General Assembly from Newport, and was consistently re-elected by his constituents until his death in 1793. He was an active businessman in Newport and became a prominent figure in the business community there. Unfortunately, Topham was one of many officers who did not get their full back pay for their Revolutionary War service even though a committee of the General Assembly concluded that both Topham and his men were owed a substantial amount of back pay. The General Assembly, however, claimed that the debt was the responsibility of Congress and not the State of Rhode Island. In 1790, Congress passed a law disallowing all claims against the new nation that had not been assumed by the states prior to 1788. Since the provisions of the law applied to the claims of Topham and his men, none were ever paid for their services.

John Codman offers this description of Topham's family. "Ten of his twelve sons went to sea; none of them ever returned, or were ever heard of (surely a most extraordinary record)." John Topham died in Newport on September 27, 1793 and was buried in the Island Cemetery. It was reported that his funeral was large and attended by many of the residents of Newport who were his constituents.[37]

VIII. WILLIAM HUMPHREY

A. <u>Description of Journal</u>.
Humphrey was a lieutenant in Thayer's company on the Arnold expedition. Smith finds more substantial evidence to support the authenticity of the Humphrey journal than he does for the Thayer and Topham accounts because Humphrey lived until 1832 and his wife lived until 1843. Smith believed the time proximity between the deaths of Humphrey and his wife to the first discovery of the Humphrey journal in 1883 provides a better authentication than is true for either Thayer or Topham. Humphrey's journal is significant because, in Smith's view, it is the basis for his own account as well as the accounts of Thayer and Topham.[38]

Based on this author's examination, the Humphrey journal appears to have been written during the expedition because of the variation in handwriting in its entries. There is also the name of William Humphrey written on the front cover of the book in which the manuscript is found as well as on the first page of the manuscript. There are also entries in the back of the book unrelated to the expedition, with the date of 1797, which have the name of William Humphrey written twice. The last three pages of the book have the heading, "List of Capt. Simeon Thayer's Company," with two pages of names and signed at the end "William Hum." All of this is good evidence that Humphrey wrote the journal attributed to him.

Although Smith concluded that Humphrey authored a journal that has a rougher style than Thayer and Topham, this conclusion is not supported by a comparison of the entries in the three journals. Humphrey's journal has entries that are just as detailed and well written as are the others. The others are not superior to his and Humphrey could have been the original from which the others copied.

The copy of the Humphrey journal now at the RIHS was in the possession of a Humphrey granddaughter, Elizabeth Kohr, as late as 1915. At some point after 1915, the journal was donated to the Rhode Island Historical Society. Its connection to Humphrey is relatively close in time and its provenance within the Humphrey family is convincing in establishing the authenticity of the journal.

B. <u>Notes on Journal</u>.
The editors of the most recent transcription state that the previous transcription from the Magazine of History was "incompletely edited and is rarely seen today."[39] Because this latest transcription, made in 1984, is an improvement in the quality of the transcription, it is a welcome addition and sets a higher standard of transcription for others to follow.

C. <u>Period Covered</u>.
The journal begins on September 9, 1775 and ends on August 11, 1776.

D. <u>Publishing History</u>.
1st Printing. *Diary of Lieut. William Humphrey of Arnold's Expedition (1775-1776)*. Magazine of History with Notes and Queries. *Extra No. 166*. William Abbatt, Tarrytown, NY, 1931, pp. 5-42.
2nd Printing. *Rhode Islanders Record the Revolution: The Journals of William Humphrey and Zuriel Waterman*. Introduced and Edited by Nathaniel Shipton and David Swain. Providence: Rhode Island Publication Society, 1984. This edition contains a new transcription of the journal that "corrects earlier misinterpretations and fills in previously illegible words. The editors also provided essential punctuation, corrected Humphrey's spelling and put superfluous capitals into lower case. Additional words and phrases in brackets are intended to clarify otherwise unintelligible passages." This is the later and the preferred transcription of the Humphrey journal.

E. <u>Location of Original</u>.
Rhode Island Historical Society. MSS 9001-H, William Humphrey Diary, 9/9/1775-8/1/1776.

F. <u>Biography of Author</u>.
William Humphrey was born in Rehoboth, Massachusetts in 1752. As is the case with most of the other journalists, Humphrey's early life is largely unknown. He entered the Revolutionary War by joining Varnum's Rhode Island regiment in June of 1775. When he volunteered for Arnold's expedition, he was assigned as first lieutenant in Captain Thayer's company. Humphrey was captured in the attack on Quebec and was paroled with the other expedition officers in September of 1776 and later exchanged.

After the Quebec expedition, Humphrey continued to serve in the military and was involved in many important conflicts throughout the war. On

January 1, 1777, he was appointed first lieutenant in the Second Rhode Island regiment and on October 22, 1778, he was promoted to Captain. He was transferred to the First Rhode Island regiment on January 1, 1781 under Colonel Israel Angell, where he served until the close of the war. He was with his regiment in the battles of Springfield, Red Bank, Monmouth and Yorktown and was discharged on June 15, 1783. Late in the war Humphrey was appointed a major but apparently the war ended before his commission was formally issued.

After the war, he returned to Rehoboth where he married Lydia Monroe on December 4, 1783. They had ten children. In 1787, he moved to Tiverton, Rhode Island where he received a large tract of land for his services in the Revolutionary war. Humphrey was Captain of the Tiverton militia for many years and was a senator in the Rhode Island General Assembly from 1802 to 1812. He was also a member of the Rhode Island Society of the Cincinnati for many years and a deacon in the Baptist Church. Humphrey received a pension for his service in 1828 and after he died, his widow was authorized a pension in 1838 when she was seventy-six years of age. Humphrey died in Tiverton on July 1, 1832 at the age of seventy-nine.[40]

IX. JOURNALS OF SIX PRIVATES IN SAMUEL WARD'S COMPANY

The Arnold expedition had thirteen companies, yet nearly one fourth of the journals were from the Ward Company. Ebenezer Tolman, Ebenezer Wild, Joseph Ware, Jeremiah Greenman, William Dorr and Caleb Haskell were six enlisted men in Captain Samuel Ward's Company who wrote extant journals. Some authors claim that these Ward Company journals are similar to each other. However, upon an examination of the journals, only four of the Ward Company journalists, Tolman, Wild, Ware and Dorr, are collaborators who wrote daily entries that are almost identical. Greenman and Haskell, wrote important journals in their own right, but did not collaborate with anyone else. Greenman and Haskell wrote independent accounts that are not copied from any other journal.

One other private in Ward's company, John Sleeper, writing in 1818 in support of Haskell's pension application, stated that he "kept a record of all our proceedings." This journal is listed here but no details are presented because it was never reproduced and no details are available. The four collaborative Ward Company journals are explored in more detail in Chapter Three because of questions about who wrote the primary journal. In this chapter, they will all be presented in the same format as the other expedition journals.

IX. 1. EBENEZER TOLMAN

A. <u>Description of Journal</u>.
The Tolman journal was not published until 1917 when it appeared in the publication prepared for the Town of Nelson, New Hampshire's 150th anniversary celebration. However, it achieved first class status and recognition as an important journal in the 1903 book by Justin H. Smith who asserted that the Tolman journal was the original journal and that all other similar journals from the Ward Company were copies. Smith based his conclusions on assertions made by a Tolman ancestor which will be explored in detail in Chapter Three.[41]

B. <u>Notes on the Journal</u>.
See Chapter Three for a more detailed analysis of the Tolman journal.

C. <u>Period Covered</u>.
Tolman's journal starts on September 13, 1775 and ends on September 6, 1778.

D. <u>Publishing History</u>.
<u>1st Printing</u>. Celebration of the One Hundred and Fiftieth Anniversary of the First Settlement of Nelson, New Hampshire, 1767-1917. Nelson, NH: Nelson Picnic Association, August 19, 1917, pp. 162-176. *A Journal of the Expedition Against Quebec, 1775,1776, written by Private Ebenezer Tolman of Captain Samuel Ward's Company in Colonel Benedict Arnold's Detachment.* (Includes a ten page personal history of Ebenezer Tolman).
<u>2nd Printing</u>. *Historical Society of Cheshire County.* Era 3: Revolution and the New Nation- 1763-1820, History Packet No. 3. A Journal of the Expedition against Quebec, 1775-1776, 8/14/2005. Web site: www.hsccnh.org/hps.cfm.

E. <u>Location of Original</u>.
There is a manuscript in the Harvard University, Houghton Library which was originally attributed to Wild and then to Tolman. The current catalog refers to the research of Justin H. Smith who the Library correctly says "attributes authorship to Tolman." On an inside page of the journal there is a notation written in ink that says: "MS copy of Wild's Journal of the Arnold Kennebec Expedition of 1775." It is probable that this notation was

written by Justin Winsor when he wrote the introduction to the so-called Wild journal that he published in the Massachusetts Historical Society (see the subsequent section of Ebenezer Wild). There is also pasted on one of the interior pages a notation written in ink that states, "Wild's Journal. This manuscript was given by Wm S. Stoddard, doorkeeper at the Statehouse in Boston. Oct. 8, 1850." The description in the catalog is: "1 v. (10 leaves); 16 x 25 cm. Bound in quarter green cloth with marbled paper boards. MS Am 831. A Journal of a March from Cambridge on an expedition against Quebeck in Col. Benedict Arnold's detachment, Sept. 13, 1775."

The manuscript contains twenty pages with the last entry on page 20 containing the date of June 6, 1776. There is a pencil notation on the last page of the journal that says: "Not the original but a copy." There is a serious question whether this is the journal examined by the three historians as described in Chapter Three.

F. Biography of Author.
Ebenezer Tolman was born in Attleboro, Massachusetts on May 31, 1748, the son of Henry Tolman. His father was dying when Tolman was a youth, so he lived with his grandfather, Benjamin Slack, until he was fourteen years old, when he was apprenticed to a local carpenter. Around 1769, he moved to Fitzwilliam, New Hampshire where he continued in the carpenter trade.

At the beginning of the war, Tolman enlisted in the company of Captain Jonathan Whitcomb in Colonel Reed's Regiment of New Hampshire troops. On June 17, 1775. Tolman fought in the Battle of Bunker Hill and then volunteered for the Arnold expedition in September of 1775. Tolman was captured in the attack on Quebec and remained a prisoner until August of 1776, suffering from a small pox attack during that time. He was released on parole and later exchanged.

In May of 1777, Tolman enlisted for three years in Captain Clayes Company in Colonel Nathan Hale's regiment. He was at Ticonderoga during the Burgoyne campaign as well as in the Battle of Hubbardston, and then was in the retreat to Stillwater. He became disabled due to sickness and hired a replacement to serve out the rest of his enlistment with the concurrence of his commander. Tolman left the service permanently prior to the Battle of Saratoga.

Tolman moved to Nelson, New Hampshire in 1780 and settled in the eastern part of town on a farm where he lived for the rest of his life. He received a pension for his Revolutionary War service at the age of eighty-six and died in

Nelson in 1838 at the age of ninety. At the time of his death, he was second to Ephraim Squier as the oldest journalist of the Quebec expedition.[42]

IX. 2. JOSEPH WARE

A. Description of Journal.
The Ware journal first surfaced in 1852 when it appeared in the New England Historical and Genealogical Register, courtesy of William B. Trask, and with explanatory notes prepared by Justin Winsor. That magazine states that it was "published for Joseph Ware, grandson of the journalist." Justin Winsor's notes indicate that the journal he examined contained the words "Joseph Ware, his book" written on the front page of the journal.[43]

A primary factor supporting the importance of the Ware journal is the inclusion of a detailed list of the officers and men, by company, who were killed, wounded or taken prisoner in the assault on Quebec. The importance of this list to identifying the casualties of the assault cannot be over emphasized.

B. Notes on the Journal.
The transcriber of the Ware journal was William B. Trask, of Dorchester. See Chapter Three for more information on the Ware journal.

C. Period Covered.
The same period as Tolman's journal, September 13 to September 6, 1776.

D. Publishing History.
1st Printing. *A Journal of a March from Cambridge on an Expedition against Quebec, in Col. Benedict Arnold's Detachment, Sept 13, 1775.* New England Historical and Genealogical Register. Vol. VI, Boston: April, 1852, pp. 129-150.
2nd Printing. *Journal of an Expedition against Quebec in 1775 under Col. Benedict Arnold by Joseph Ware, of Needham, Mass. To Which is Appended Notes and a Genealogy of the Ware Family.* Prepared for the New England Historical and Genealogical Register. Boston: Thomas Prince, Printer, 1852. 24 pages. Black cloth cover. 100 copies printed. "Annexed to the Journal are interesting explanatory Notes, by Mr. Justin Winsor, of Boston".
3rd Printing. Joseph Ware. *A Journal of the Expedition against Quebec (1775).* The Magazine of History with Notes and Queries. Vol. 34, No. 2, Extra No. 134, 1927. William Abbatt, Tarrytown, N.Y., pp. 5-35.

E. <u>Location of Original</u>.

The original Ware journal is located in the New England Historical and Genealogical Society, Mss C 2034. Unfortunately, the journal is not in good condition with only half of the first two pages still present and the entire journal being ripped in half. The Library of Congress has a handwritten copy of the Ware journal on microfilm, copied by Peter Force, located in the Peter Force Papers entitled: "Archival Manuscript Material (Collection). Papers and Collection of Peter Force. 0314B FORCE: Series 7E: entry 157. "

F. <u>Biography of Author</u>.

Joseph Ware was born in Needham, Massachusetts on October 15, 1753. His father, Josiah, was a farmer and was chosen as a selectman of Needham in 1773. Joseph was also a farmer until the start of the Revolutionary War. Ware enlisted for seven days in a company from Needham that marched to Cambridge on April 19th in response to the Lexington Alarm. He then apparently enlisted in Captain Whitney's Company of Heath's regiment on May 1, 1775, although there is an entry showing that Joseph Ware enlisted in Captain Worthly's Company of Phinney's Regiment on May 8, 1775. There is no explanation of this inconsistency unless there are two men with the same name, which is common in the ranks of Revolutionary War soldiers.

Ware joined Arnold's expedition and served in Captain Samuel Ward's company. He was captured during the attack on Quebec and was released at the same time as Tolman and the other privates in Arnold's command in August of 1776.

He then appears on the rolls in Captain Peter Pitts Company as of November 5, 1778. There is a Joseph Ware who was a sergeant in Captain James Tisdale's Company, 3rd Massachusetts Regiment on April 23, 1782. In the History of Wellesley, Mass., it states that the Joseph Ware who authored the journal was an orderly sergeant and recruiting officer during his service in the Revolution. Assuming the name on the muster rolls is the same Joseph Ware, he enlisted right after Lexington and served to 1782. Ware married Esther Smith on June 1, 1780 and they had seven children. There is no record as to Joseph Ware's occupation following the war. Joseph Ware died on November 12, 1805 at the age of fifty-two.[44]

IX. 3. EBENEZER WILD

A. <u>Description of Journal</u>.

Justin Winsor introduced the Wild journal in a volume of the Proceedings of the Massachusetts Historical Society in 1886 as Wild's authentic journal of his Arnold expedition experiences. However, it is clear that Wild was not in the Continental Army at that time so he was not in Ward's Company and was not a part of the expedition to Quebec. There is a journal of Wild's experiences during the Revolutionary War which contains many interesting details of various battles and skirmishes as well as the life of a continental soldier. That journal covers the period of 1776 through 1781.

B. Notes on Journal.
See Chapter Three for more information on the Wild journal and the reasons that Wild did not write the journal attributed to him.

C. Period Covered.
The same as Tolman's, September 13 to September 6, 1776

D. Publishing History.
1st Printing. Proceedings of the Massachusetts Historical Society, 2nd Series, Vol. II. Boston, 1886. *A Journal of a March from Cambridge, on an Expedition against Quebec in Colonel Benedict Arnold's Detachment, Sept 13, 1775.* pp. 265-275. This journal is attributed by Justin Winsor to Ebenezer Wild.
2nd Printing. Justin Winsor. *Arnold's Expedition against Quebec. 1775-1776. The Diary of Ebenezer Wild with a List of such Diaries.* Cambridge: John Wilson and Son, University Press, 1886. Privately Reprinted from the Proceedings of the Massachusetts Historical Society, April, 1886. 75 copies printed.
3rd Printing. *Journal of a March from Cambridge against Quebec, 1775.* The Magazine of History with Notes and Queries, Extra # 134, William Abbatt, Tarrytown, N.Y., 1927, pp. 37-47.

E. Location of Original.
There is no indication of what happened to the journal published by Winsor in 1885, but as stated in the section on the Tolman journal, there is an original of what is called the Wild/Tolman journal of the Quebec expedition in the Harvard Library. The original of the genuine Wild Revolutionary War journal, which covers the period after the Quebec expedition from 1776 to 1781, is also in the Harvard Library.

F. Biography of Author.
No biography is provided because Justin Smith has conclusively demonstrated that Wild was not on the Arnold expedition.

VI. 4. JEREMIAH GREENMAN

A. <u>Description of Journal</u>.
The journal of Private Jeremiah Greenman covers the entire period of the American Revolution from 1775 to 1784. Because it is one of the few personal accounts of the entire war, it has significant historical value. The Quebec expedition, which is only a small portion of the full journal, is just over twenty-one printed pages and covers the period from September 18, 1775, through November, 1776, including his time as a prisoner of war in Quebec.

The editors and transcribers of the Greenman journal state that they followed one basic principal, which was remaining "faithful to the original." They describe their very long and laborious transcription including the correction and clarification of punctuation and spelling to make it more understandable. The editors state that the main problem with the Greenman journal is that Greenman was writing only for himself so "what he wrote was a highly uncircumstantial account of his works and days, a kind of written remembrancer which years later would— through a brief and, to us, almost cryptic allusion—unlock his fuller memories of the Revolution."[45]

Due to its later discovery and transcription, there is only one publication of the journal, which is the book cited below. This book was issued in at least one hardback and three paperback printings and is still readily available.

B. <u>Notes on the Journal</u>.
The Greenman journal is more significant in understanding the history of the Arnold expedition than the Ware, Wild, Tolman and Dorr accounts. Greenman's entries are different from any of the other Ward company journals. They are much more detailed and descriptive than the others and show individuality that the others lack. That Greenman's journal covers the entire period of the war, beginning with the Quebec expedition, gives it an extra measure of historical significance as well as giving Greenman high credibility as a source. It is clear that Greenman wrote his own account and was not in collaboration with the other Ward Company journalists.

C. <u>Period Covered</u>.
The portion of Greenman's journal that covers the Quebec expedition starts on September 18, 1775 and ends on December 31, 1776.

D. <u>Publishing History</u>.
<u>1st Printing</u>. *Diary of a Common Soldier in the American Revolution, 1775-*

1783. An Annotated Edition of the Military Journal of Jeremiah Greenman. Edited by Robert Bray and Paul Bushnell. DeKalb, Illinois: Northern Illinois University Press, 1978.

E. <u>Location of Original</u>.
According to the editors, the original manuscript from which they transcribed the journal in 1978 was owned by Mrs. Edwin R. Lederer, of DeKalb, Illinois, a direct descendant of Jeremiah Greenman. It is likely that the journal is still in the possession of the Greenman/Lederer family.

F. <u>Biography of Author</u>.
Jeremiah Greenman was born in Newport, Rhode Island on May 7, 1758. He stated that he "received in his native town such education as the Common Schools afforded." He enlisted in a Rhode Island company after the Lexington Alarm and went to Cambridge. While there, he enlisted in Captain Samuel Ward's company for the expedition to Quebec. Greenman was captured in the attack and was held prisoner until August of 1776, when he was released on parole. He was exchanged in 1777.

Greenman enlisted in a Rhode Island regiment as a sergeant in the campaign of 1777 and later became first sergeant. In 1779, he was promoted to ensign and in 1781 was promoted again to first lieutenant. In 1782, Greenman was appointed as regimental adjutant for the Rhode Island troops, a position in which he served until the peace treaty was signed and his fellow officers had been mustered out.

In 1784, he moved from Providence to Swansea, Massachusetts to open a shop with his partner who was a fellow officer. In 1784, Greenman married Mary Eddy, whose family was involved in a successful shipyard business and by 1787 he joined the Eddy family business and became a seaman. By 1788, he had his master's certificate and was the captain of his own vessels. In the 1790's Greenman served as an officer in a revenue cutter on Long Island Sound. By the early 1800's he had part ownership of a schooner but that venture was not successful.

In 1806, Greenman's sailing business failed and he decided to migrate to homestead new lands in Ohio. His family settled in Marietta and he began life as a farmer. The life in Ohio was difficult and not financially rewarding. In 1818, Greenman applied for a pension as a surviving veteran of the war and was placed on the pension roles until 1821, when he was dropped. He was never able to get on the rolls again. Greenman died at his home in Ohio on November 15, 1828 of billious colic, at the age of seventy.[46]

IX. 5. WILLIAM DORR

A. <u>Description of Journal</u>.
The Dorr journal is located in the Massachusetts Historical Society but remained undiscovered until 2000 when Rebecca Goetz, a student at Bates College, transcribed and analyzed the journal for her senior thesis. According to the entry in the MHS listing, the Dorr journal has entries that "describe the journey to Maine up the Kennebec River and down the Chaudière to Quebec and the hardships incurred".[47] The journal contains the same list as the Ware journal of those men who were wounded, who died and who were taken prisoner in the assault, as well as a list of the carrying places on the Kennebec and Chaudière. It also includes a copy of the petition from the American prisoners to General Carleton of June 5, 1776.

The Dorr journal is identical to the Ware and Tolman journals in the wording of its entries. He was one of the Ward Company collaborators all of whom have the same daily entries.

B. <u>Notes on Journal</u>.
The Goetz transcription of Dorr's journal is titled "Journal Kept by William Dorr from 17 Sept. - 14 Dec. 1775 and 1-6 Aug. 1776 on Arnold's Expedition to Quebec while Serving with John Greaton's Regiment".

C. <u>Period Covered</u>.
The period covered by the journal is September 13, 1775 to September 6, 1776.

D. <u>Publishing History</u>.
1st Printing. Rebecca Anne Goetz. *Private William Dorr's March to Quebec: A Study in Historical Ambi*guity. Senior Thesis for Department of History, Bates College. Lewiston, Maine. March 17, 2000. [Typescript copy in Massachusetts Historical Society]. 146 pages.
2nd Printing. Charley Dorr. *Descendants of Edward Dorr*. www.gencircles. com/users/cdorr/1/data/959. The journal is reproduced in full on this web site.

E. <u>Location of Original</u>.
Massachusetts Historical Society. Manuscript Collections, Ms S-82a.

F. <u>Biography of Author</u>.
William Dorr was born in Roxbury, Massachusetts on July 13, 1757. Not much is known about his life prior to the start of the Revolutionary War,

except that he participated in the Boston Tea Party on December 16, 1773. Dorr joined the army and marched to Cambridge in 1775 in Whiting's Company of Minutemen.

According to a statement he filed on behalf of John Sleeper's pension application, Dorr was in Cambridge in August of 1775. At Cambridge, he enlisted into Captain Samuel Ward's company in the expedition to Quebec. He is listed on the return of Capt. Edward Payson William's Company of the 36th Regiment, dated at Fort No. 2, October 5, 1775, where he is reported as "Gone to Canada." Dorr says that he and Sleeper and "several hundred" others were taken prisoner the same day General Montgomery was killed and were confined in a Seminary.

Along with the others, Dorr was released and returned to New York by water in August of 1776. According to his pension application, he was in the army until October of 1776 when he was "discharged from the service at Kings Bridge in the State of New York" due to ill health, "having suffered by fatigue and exposure." There is no record of him enlisting in the military service again during the war.

The Dorr family tradition includes an interesting story involving the eighteen-year old William Dorr while on the Arnold expedition. As the expedition was proceeding up the Kennebec River, Dorr's company camped for the night in what is now Hallowell, Maine. The family says the camp was "by the spring of water on Main Street, near the Currier Tavern." Dorr was so impressed with the area that he told his friends in the company that he was going to come back there and settle down. "After the war he returned to Maine, stopping at Bath, where one or more of his children were born, and in Oct. 1788 came to the Hallowell area" and helped to found the town. The History of Hallowell states that his first house stood on what is now known as Sheppard's Point, which comprises the area where the Hallowell cemetery is located.

He married Jane Partridge of Roxbury on March 30, 1779 at Roxbury and they subsequently had seven children. He applied for a pension in 1830 at the age of seventy-three. Dorr died in Augusta, Maine, on August 13, 1840, making him one of the last survivors of the expedition.[48]

IX. 6. CALEB HASKELL

A. <u>Description of Journal</u>.

The Haskell journal covers the longest period of any of the Ward Company journals except for Greenman. It begins on May 5, 1775 and ends on May 30, 1776. Historian Israel N. Tarbox describes it as "a plain man's mention of events which he partook in and where the partakers have been raised to the rank of heroes." He described the journal entries as a "bare outline like entries in an almanac."[49] Haskell, like the rest of the Ward Company journal writers, does not provide detailed or elaborate descriptions of people or events. However, the journal has been reprinted many times and is a popular narrative of the events of the expedition.

Haskell's journal was given to the editor and publisher, Lothrop Withington, by Isaac Little around 1881. The journal that Withington published was a copy of an original in the possession of Caleb Haskell's son-in-law, Moses Pettingell. Mr. Little copied that journal from the Pettingell original.[50]

B. <u>Notes on Journal</u>.

Haskell's journal provides a personal account with unique observations in his daily entries. He differs from the other Ward company journalists because he was not taken prisoner during the attack. Perhaps this also accounts for his journal being different from the four collaborators. Haskell covered the same ground as the others so the places they went and where they spent the night are similar. However, Haskell's account contains more information and is historically more significant than the other collaborators. Both Haskell and Dorr were involved in Sleeper's pension application so it is apparent that the three men knew each other. There is no evidence, however, that the collaborators copied Haskell's account or that he used their accounts. Haskell's journal was written independently of any of the other Ward company journals. That both Withington and Little looked at a copy of the Haskell journal in the possession of his descendants confirms that it is an authentic original journal.

C. <u>Period Covered</u>.

This journal begins prior to Bunker Hill on May 5, 1775 and ends on May 30, 1776.

D. <u>Publishing History</u>.

<u>1st Printing</u>. Newburyport Herald newspaper. No dates are given.

<u>2nd Printing</u>. Extracts of Haskell Diary. *Life of Israel Putnam, Major General in the Continental Army*. Israel N. Tarbox. Boston: Lockwood, Brooks and

Company, 1876. pp. 214-215. When he wrote his book, Tarbox had access to the diary in the possession of A.W. Haskell of Boston, son of Caleb.

3rd Printing. Paper wraps. *Caleb Haskell's Diary.* Edited, with Notes, by Lothrop Withington. Newburyport: William H. Huse & Company, 1881, 23 pages.

4th Printing. *Ancestral History of the Pioneers of Deer Isle and Their Descendants. Benjamin Lake Noyes.* Privately Printed, 1899. *Also Deer Island Pioneers (including Stonington, Maine) plus an Appendix containing Caleb Haskell's war diary,* written by B. L. Noyes. Privately printed, 1901. pp. i-xxi.

5th Printing. Caleb Haskell's Diary. *The Magazine of History with Notes and Queries.* Extra Number 86. William Abbatt, Tarrytown, New York, 1922, 56 pages.

6th Printing. Kenneth Roberts. *March to Quebec.* 1946, pp. 459-504.

Web site: *www.hauleymusic.com/monthly.php* Extracts of Caleb Haskell's Diary.

E. Location of Original.

The manuscript of the Haskell Diary was one of the items in the William Randolph Hearst collection which was offered for sale at Parke-Bernet Galleries, New York, Nov. 16, 1938. The catalogue of the auction describes the journal as an "Autograph Manuscript Journal, 131 pp., 16mo, original limp boards. May 5, 1775 to May 30, 1776." The subheading states, "A FAMOUS JOURNAL CITED BY HISTORIANS AS THE SOURCE OF INFORMATION RELATING TO CAMP LIFE AT THE SIEGE OF BOSTON, THE BATTLE OF BUNKER HILL, THE HARDSHIPS OF A PRIVATE OVER THE WILDERNESS TRAIL TO QUEBEC, CAMP LIFE BEFORE QUEBEC, THE SIEGE OF THAT CITY, AND THE RETREAT OF THE ARMY ON THE St. LAWRENCE RIVER."[51]

The manuscript is now located in the Houghton Library, Harvard University, MS Am 1680. It is in a tray case and bound in paper wrappers. The manuscript is in a small book, approximately 3 X 6 inches and was given to the Harvard Library by a bequest of Gabriel Wells. It has a total of 129 pages and the pages are intact except for page 121 which has a section of approximately 1 X 2 inches missing.

The manuscript in the Harvard Library has nine pages with cross outs but no additional word insertions. In this author's opinion, the writing seems consistent throughout the book so Haskell likely recopied it after the expedition. There is no reason to doubt the historical accuracy of this manuscript.

F. Biography of Author.

Caleb Haskell was born on May 2, 1754 in Newburyport, Massachusetts, the son of Caleb and Elizabeth Haskell. He was one of the members of Captain Moses Newell's Company of men from Newburyport that responded on April 19th. In that company he is listed under "Drum & Fife" and some histories of Newburyport refer to him as a drummer and some as a fifer. He apparently returned home after the Lexington Alarm and then enlisted on May 5, 1775, in the company of Captain Ezra Lunt of Newburyport which went to Cambridge as one of eight companies in the Regiment of Colonel Moses Little. He fought in the Battle of Bunker Hill with Lunt's Regiment and his initial enlistment expired on August 1st. He stayed on with Lunt's Company after his enlistment and on September 10th, he volunteered for the Arnold expedition and was assigned to Captain Samuel Ward's Company. Fortunately, Haskell was not captured in the attack on Quebec and continued to serve in the army in Canada until May 30, 1776 when he was discharged by General Wooster in Canada. There is a receipt in his pension application for the return of his firelock into the store at St. Johns which was valued at three pounds lawful money.

There is no record of any military service after he was released from the army in Quebec. He did return to Newburyport where he lived for the rest of his life. He owned a lot adjoining his brother Nathan. In 1791, Caleb was chosen as a selectman for the Town of Newburyport. He was granted a pension for his war service in 1818 as a resident of Newburyport, which he continued to receive until he died in 1829. In the pension application, fellow expedition member John Sleeper provided a statement in support of Haskell where he stated that Haskell "was a good soldier and well attached to the service." His pension application only mentions his service in Cambridge and Quebec which covered a period of just over one year.

Even though his journal is a significant account of his Revolutionary War services and the expedition to Quebec, very little is known about his life prior to or subsequent to the Revolutionary War. One reason for this is that he did not continue to serve in the army and his pension application does not contain any personal information. He married Edna Hale of Newbury on April 10, 1781 and they had eleven children. Haskell died in Newburyport on January 12, 1829, at the age of seventy-five, and is buried in the Old Burying Hill. Rev. Mr. Molton conducted the funeral service and delivered a "discourse adapted to the solemnity of the occasion."[52] His gravestone describes him as a musician and a Revolutionary War soldier who was on the Quebec expedition.[53]

IX. 7. JOHN SLEEPER

A. <u>Description of Journal.</u>
There is no existing journal because according to Sleeper, in his 1818 affidavit of support for Caleb Haskell's pension application, his account of the experiences of his company had been "preserved several years but which is now destroyed".[54] There is no reason to doubt the truthfulness of his assertion as he was writing to support Haskell's claim, not his own. Sleeper knew Haskell because both were from Newburyport. As stated above, Haskell also supported Sleeper's pension application in 1832.

The interest here is that at least one other member of Captain Ward's company, who was not an officer, kept a journal. Sleeper's statement in support of Haskell indicates that he grew up with and was a friend of Haskell. Since Sleeper's journal has been lost, there is no way to tell whether he collaborated with Ware, Wild, Tolman, Haskell or Dorr or whether he wrote a separate and more personal account.

B. <u>Biography of Author.</u>
John Sleeper was born the son of Henry Sleeper in Newburyport, Massachusetts on August 11, 1754. There is no information about his family or his early life. Sleeper was part of the company of minutemen from Newburyport commanded by Captain Moses Nowell that marched to Cambridge at the Lexington Alarm on April 19, 1775. The company returned home a few days later and on May 1, 1775, Sleeper enlisted in Captain Ezra Lunt's company of Colonel Little's regiment and marched to Cambridge. Lunt's company participated in the Battle of Bunker Hill as Haskell's record confirms. There is no indication, however, in Sleeper's pension application that he was in that battle.

On September 10, Sleeper enlisted in Captain Samuel Ward's company for the Quebec expedition. He was taken prisoner by the British in the assault on Quebec and released from prison in August of 1776. After returning to Newburyport, he enlisted to serve on board the frigate *Boston* in late 1776 under Captain McNeil and was on the vessel when it captured a British sloop of war. He served on the frigate for more than one year as a ship's carpenter.

By 1818, Sleeper was residing in Chester, New Hampshire when he submitted a statement in support of a pension application for Caleb Haskell. Sleeper was awarded his own pension in 1832 and died in Chester on June 27, 1834, at the age of seventy-nine. His pension papers contain no information on a wife or family.[55]

X. JOHN JOSEPH HENRY

A. Description of Journal.
Although some of the expedition journals are questionable in terms of authorship or authenticity, Henry's journal is not one of these. Henry wrote his journal around 1808, some thirty-three years after the expedition, at the request of his children. At the time he wrote, he was confined to his room with a recurring illness from his campaign with Arnold resulting in seven years of, as he describes, "bodily suffering" and "deadly pains." According to Francis Jordan, the author of a biography of his father William, Henry wrote his account using "notes and memoranda" that he had in his possession.[56] In an 1808 letter to General Francis Nichols, who was with him on the expedition, Henry tells Nichols that he wrote from his own memory "assisted by the notes of General Meigs and Wm. McCoy, one of our sergeants." He tells Nichols that his memoirs are being transcribed by his eldest daughter and that it would consist of "250 pages octavo at least." [57]His widow finally published the manuscript in 1812, just one year after his death.

Henry's journal is different from almost every other expedition journal in that it is not written with the typical daily entries of a journal or diary, but is written as a narrative containing detailed descriptions of people, events and places. It is more a historical narrative by one of the participants than a daily journal. Although some dates are provided, the emphasis is on the narration and not the dates. Henry describes many activities in great detail and records experiences that are not present in any other accounts. It is considered by historians as the most readable and most interesting of the expedition journals.

B. Notes on Journal.
Henry's account is unique in that it was published in three different editions each with a different title and each with its own unique additional material. There is no question that the Henry journal, with all of its faults, is an authentic account. Henry produced the most extensive narration of the expedition. His journal contains more words than any other expedition journal, even though the one-year time period it covers is not as extensive as the time period of some of the other journals.

C. Period Covered.
Henry's narrative starts on September 11, 1775 and ends around September 26, 1776 at Long Island.

John Joseph Henry

D. Publishing History.
1st Printing. *An Accurate and Interesting Account of the Sufferings and Hardships of That Ban of Heroes, Who Traversed the Wilderness in the Campaign against Quebec in 1775.* Lancaster, PA: William Greer, 1812. 228 pages including notes. Very rare. Sabin calls this the "First and best edition of a narrative of rare interest."
2nd Printing. An abridged publication of Henry's journal appeared in the book *Adventures and Achievements of Americans; A Series of Narratives Illustrating Heroism, Self-reliance, Genius and Enterprise.* Henry Howe. Cincinnati: 1861. pp. 51-84.
3rd Printing. *Campaign against Quebec Being an Accurate and Interesting Account of the Hardships and Sufferings of That Band of Heroes Who Traversed*

the Wilderness, by the Route of the Kennebec and Chaudière River, to Quebec in the Year 1775. Revised Edition with Corrections and Alterations. Watertown, N.Y.: Knowlton & Rice, 1844. Also containing a Sketch of the Life of Arnold. 212 pages.

4th Printing. *Account of Arnold's Campaign Against Quebec, and of the hardships and Sufferings of that Band of Heroes who Traversed the Wilderness of Maine from Cambridge to the St. Lawrence in the Autumn of 1775.* Albany: Joel Munsell, 1877. Appendix containing letters of Arnold and Montgomery. 198 pages.

5th Printing. *Journal of the Campaign against Quebec by John Joseph Henry, 1775. Pennsylvania Archives, Series 2, Vol. XV, 1893, pp. 59-191.*

6th Printing. Kenneth Roberts. *March to Quebec.* 1946. pp. 299-432.

7th Printing. *Account of Arnold's Campaign against Quebec.* New York: Arno Press & N.Y. Times. Eyewitness Accounts of the American Revolution. 1968.

Also published by Ayer Company Publishers, North Stratford, N.H., 1968.

Also published by S.R. Publishers, East Ardley, Yorkshire, 1968.

E. Location of Original.
Historical Society of Pennsylvania. HSP Manuscripts Guide. #280, William Henry Papers.

F. Biography of Author.
John Joseph Henry was born in Lancaster, Pennsylvania on November 4, 1758. He was the son of William Henry who was a well-known gunsmith and a prominent leader in Lancaster County. At the age of fourteen, he was apprenticed to an uncle, who was also a gunsmith. The uncle subsequently moved to Detroit taking young John Joseph with him. Young John Joseph did not like Detroit so he returned home on foot with a guide who died in the wilderness along the way.

At the age of seventeen, he enlisted in Captain Matthew Smith's rifle company of Colonel Thompson's Battalion against his parent's wishes and without their permission. In early September, Smith's company was ordered to go to Quebec with Arnold, and Henry joined that company as a volunteer without his parent's consent. Henry was among those taken prisoner in the attack on Quebec and he was released on parole with the rest of Arnold's men in August of 1776 and arrived in Elizabethtown, New Jersey on October 1.

Henry spent two years recuperating from his injuries incurred during his time in Arnold's Army. Because they never completely healed, he never served in the army again. Henry then studied law first as a clerk for the court and then by entering the law office of Stephen Chambers, who was one of the prominent members of the Lancaster County Bar. Henry was admitted to the bar in 1785 and was appointed as a President of the Second Judicial District of Pennsylvania by Governor Mifflin in 1793.

Henry married the younger sister of his mentor Chambers and had eight children. His career as a lawyer and judge was cut short by the recurrence of the injuries he suffered during the expedition. He resigned from his judgeship in 1810, after serving seventeen years on the bench, mostly as a result of complaints about his inability to appear in court to handle his cases. He wrote his journal from his sick bed by dictating it to his daughter and it was finally completed in 1810. He died in Lancaster on April 15, 1811 at the age of fifty-three just a few months after he resigned from his judgeship. His widow published his journal in 1812, one year after his death.[58]

XI. JOHN PIERCE

A. Description of Journal.

Although the Pierce journal was listed as an Arnold expedition journal by various nineteenth century authors, it was not transcribed and published until Kenneth Roberts found the manuscript in the late 1930's while he was working on revising *March to Quebec*. Roberts calls this journal the "Lost Journal" because no previous historian had transcribed and published it. Gabriel Wells purchased the journal from the estate of Ogden Goelet, at a 1935 auction. Roberts purchased the manuscript journal from Gabriel Wells on January 19, 1939 for $525.00.

The Pierce journal is the only one that mentions the disputes between Arnold and the Hanchett, Hubbard and Goodrich companies after their arrival in Canada. Being a surveyor, his description of the route is more detailed than any other journal and is a primary source document for the route that was followed to get to Quebec. He also consistently includes a description of the weather, which was helpful to Roberts in writing his novel. Roberts argues that the Pierce journal is second in importance "only to Arnold's".[59] This is a questionable assertion and one could argue that Roberts had a vested interest in promoting its significance to help sell his book for there are other expedition journals of equal or more importance.

B. Notes on Journal.

The Goelet catalog describes the Pierce journal as follows.

This autograph manuscript journal supplies not only details but a contemporary record of matters of major importance absolutely unrecorded by historians. It is probably one of the most voluminous of the contemporary diaries of the terrible struggle over the wilderness trail... It is written by a well educated and careful observer who reveals facts and conditions unrecorded in the published journals of other participants, including many names of those who were killed, starved, or who fell by the way on the overland journey... and especially the unrecorded facts of the many discords that affected the morale of the army that undertook the most hazardous and fatal expedition of the American Revolution.[60]

The manuscript in the Dartmouth Library is written on two different sizes of paper. From the beginning of the journal through the entry for December 17th, the paper is approximately ½ inch smaller than the rest of the manuscript. The last readable entry is for January 16, 1776. The last page of the manuscript, which seems to cover entries for part of January 16th and part of January 17th, has pieces torn out so parts of it are illegible. There is also nothing in the wording of the title of the manuscript that has Pierce's name. It is entitled *Revolutionary War Diary on the Expedition from New England to Canada September 1775 to January 16, 1776.*

The manuscript has an interesting pencil notation on its first page which says "Topham." This may be why it was lost for so long because Goelet thought it was Topham's journal. Another observation by this author is that in the entry for November 17th, Pierce refers to General Arnold's Army. Arnold was not a general on November 17th. His appointment took place in January of 1776; therefore, it appears that the Pierce manuscript journal was not written while the expedition was underway.

C. <u>Period Covered</u>.
Journal begins on September 8, 1775 and ends on January 16, 1776.

D. <u>Publishing History.</u>
<u>1st Printing</u>. Kenneth Roberts. *March to Quebec*, 3rd edition published June 6, 1940. New York: Doubleday, Doran & Company, Inc, pp. 653-711.
<u>2nd Printing</u>. Paper Wraps. *John Pierce Journal of the Advance Surveyor with Col. Arnold on the March to Quebec, with an Introduction and Notes by Kenneth Roberts.* New York: Doubleday, Doran & Company, Inc., 1940. pp. 653-711, same pagination as the Roberts' book. Reprinted from third edition of *March to Quebec* by Kenneth Roberts. Only 60 copies were reportedly printed.

E. Location of Original.
Rauner Special Collections Library, Dartmouth College. Original manuscript bound in dark maroon leather with quarter brown leather slipcase by bindery of the Boston Public Library. 108 pages. The catalog says that the "last leaf torn and probably a leaf missing at the end."

F. Biography of Author.
John Pierce was born in Worcester, Massachusetts on October 12, 1744. He grew up in Worcester and married Lydia Jones on August 18, 1770. He was an experienced surveyor at the time the revolution broke out. He first served as a corporal in Capt. Timothy Bigelow's company of minutemen from Worcester who responded to the Lexington alarm. He then joined Captain Jonas Hubbard's company for the expedition to Quebec and was appointed a sergeant in that company.

Because of his surveying experience, he was assigned by Arnold to march ahead of the main body of the expedition, along with Lieutenants Steel and Church, to determine the route the expedition would take. Pierce was not captured during the siege of Quebec and his journal ends with him at Point-aux-Trembles waiting for instructions from his commanding officer.

Pierce subsequently enlisted in the 15th Massachusetts Regiment commanded by his old friend from Worcester, Colonel Timothy Bigelow. Effective January 1, 1777, he was appointed to be a lieutenant in Daniel Gates' company of that regiment. He was subsequently commissioned as a Captain on March 1, 1779 and confirmed by Congress on September 6, 1779. He then succeeded Gates as the company commander until he was discharged on December 31, 1780. Due to his rank, he was thereafter known around Worcester as Captain John Pierce.

After the war, Pierce stayed in Worcester for a period of time and continued his trade. In 1793, he assisted Charles Baker in extensively surveying Worcester County and he continued as a surveyor in Worcester at least until 1805. In 1793, a survey map of Worcester County, prepared by Captain John Pierce and Charles Baker, was utilized in a history of Worcester County written by Peter Whitney. After 1805, Pierce seems to have moved to Burlington, Vermont, where his eldest son was killed in a skating accident, but he later moved back to Worcester. He died in Worcester on March 2, 1808. No pension application exists for Pierce and there is no record of military service between the siege of Quebec and his appointment in the 15th Regiment one year later.[61]

XII. THREE JOURNALS OF PRIVATES IN CAPTAIN DEARBORN'S COMPANY

XII. I. JAMES MELVIN

A. Description of Journal.
James Melvin's journal was first published in 1857 by The Club in New York City, a predecessor to the Bradford Club founded by William J. Davis, J.B. and C.C. Moreau, Charles Cogden, William Menzies, Robert Macoy, and J. Carson Brevoort. Justin Smith concludes that the "printed version represents the original accurately" because the transcriber stated that the writing was "exceedingly neat", thus leading him to surmise that the transcriber could more easily discern the words in the journal.[62]

The first two printings of the Melvin journal are rare because both were issued in very limited printings. The copy of the journal published in Maine in 1902 is more readily available.

B. Notes on Journal.
In *March to Quebec,* Kenneth Roberts argued that Melvin's journal is not an original because it is very similar to the Kimball journal for which he provided extracts in his book. Roberts concluded that the Kimball journal is the original and that it was used and improved upon by Melvin, who wrote the superior journal. Roberts reproduced the entire Melvin journal because it "contains more detail, and is the one that should be reproduced."

One thing Melvin has over Kimball is 178 daily entries that are not in Kimball's journal. Melvin was a more consistent journalist and has daily entries from his Quebec prison in April, May and June of 1776 while Kimball does not.

This author compared both journals and found that 11% of the entries in the two journals are not alike at all and there are no entries that are identical. The comparison showed that only 15% of the total journal entries are similar. However, in their respective entries, Melvin and Kimball each have a number of entries that are superior in terms of description and wording than the other. What this author found, and what Roberts is really pointing out, is that Melvin wrote a longer journal with more daily entries, but it seems likely that neither journal is the original from which the other copied.

C. Period Covered.
Melvin's journal begins on September 13, 1775 and ends on August 5, 1776.

D. Publishing History.
1st Printing. *A Journal of the Expedition to Quebec, in the Year 1775, under the Command of Benedict Arnold, by James Melvin, a private in Captain Dearborn's Company.* Edited by W.J. Davis, a founding member. New York: The Club, 1857. 30 pages. 100 copies, privately printed. The first issue of The Club. Rare item. Note: The editor made up an unknown number of presentation copies that included a half morocco cover and 21 extra portraits and plates inserted into the publication. These presentation copies are even rarer than the original and none have been located.
2nd Printing. *A Journal of the Expedition to Quebec, in the Year 1775, under the Command of Benedict Arnold, by James Melvin, a private in Captain Dearborn's Company.* Philadelphia: Printed for the Franklin Club, 1864. Privately printed. 34 pages. Sabin says that this edition "consisted of one hundred copies in octavo, and twenty in quarto." The catalogue of SLM Barlow library says that the notes in this edition "are more extensive than the Bradford Club issue." The 20 large paper copies included a half morocco cover and 13 extra portraits and plates inserted. This is a rare item in either printing but the 20 large paper copies with the inserts are clearly the rarest.
3rd Printing. *The Life and Times of Aaron Burr, with Numerous Appendices, Containing New and Interesting Information.* James Parton. Boston and New York: Houghton Mifflin and Company, 1893. Appendix V. Arnold's Expedition to Quebec in 1775, pp. 375-390.
4th Printing. *The Journal of James Melvin Private Soldier in Arnold's Expedition against Quebec in the year 1775.* With Notes and Introduction by Andrew A. Melvin. Portland: Hubbard W. Bryant, Publisher, 1902. 90 pages. Limited to 250 copies.
5th Printing. Kenneth Roberts. *March to Quebec.* Pages 433-458.
6th Printing. Arnold Expedition Historical Society Research Room. Web site at www.arnoldsmarch.com/research.html.

E. Location of Original.
At one time in the nineteenth century the original manuscript was in the possession of the Melvin family but its location now is unknown.

F. Biography of Author.
James Melvin was born in Concord, Massachusetts. Vital records from Springfield show that his wife died in Springfield in 1825 and that he was eighty-one years old and still living at that time. If his age at the time of his

wife's death is correct, he was born prior to 1749. However, there are two sources that indicate he was born in 1752 or 1753. The first is the British Army's list of prisoners which lists Melvin as 22 years old which would mean he was born in 1753. In his application for reinstatement of his pension in 1821, he states that he is 69 years old, making his birth year 1752. It seems reasonable to conclude that he was born in 1752.

After the death of his mother when James was still very young, James' father moved to Chester, Massachusetts, where he married a second time. James did not get along with his stepmother so he was apprenticed to Jonathan Prescott, a friend of his father from Halifax, Nova Scotia. There is some evidence that James was a difficult boy and had trouble dealing with other children after his mother died. Sometime after that and prior to the start of the war, he left Nova Scotia and went back to Concord to live with his elder brother, Eleazer.

In April of 1775, as a result of the Lexington Alarm, Melvin enlisted from Hubbardston, Massachusetts in Colonel Doolittle's regiment and marched to Cambridge. There is no record of when or why he was in Hubbardston. In September, he enlisted in Captain Dearborn's company for the Arnold expedition and was captured in the attack on Quebec. He was confined in prison in Quebec until he was released on parole with the other officers and men and arrived in Elizabethtown, New Jersey in October of 1776. After returning from Canada, he served in Captain Bryant's company and then in Colonel John Cranes regiment of artillery from 1777 to 1779. During that period, he was stationed in Springfield, Massachusetts, and at one point his duties included making powder at the armory in Springfield. In 1780 he was again on the rolls of Captain Bryant's company from January 1, 1780 until December 31, 1780. In his letter to the Secretary of War, Melvin states that he served "faithfully until honorably discharged after the end of the war." Apparently he served in Springfield until he was discharged.

After the war, he stayed in Springfield because he had married a widow, Katherine Cooley in Springfield on December 29, 1778, and they subsequently had three children. Sometime later, Melvin purchased a farm in Chester, Massachusetts, where he lived for many years. He obtained a pension allowance in 1818 due to the fact that his wife was an invalid but was dropped from the rolls in 1820. In 1821, he applied to reinstate his pension for his services in the Revolutionary War with a very articulate letter explaining his living situation, the need for the pension and requesting reinstatement of his pension. He was turned down at that time and applied again in 1828. The exact date of his death is not known but it was after his reapplication in1828. According to his grandson, Melvin moved back to Springfield some years before he died.[63]

XII. II. MOSES KIMBALL

A. <u>Description of Journal</u>.
This journal is a sixteen-page account written by Private Moses Kimball of Dearborn's Company. In 1928, the original manuscript journal was in the possession of Dr. L. C. Walker of Jamestown, Ohio, who made a longhand copy of the journal. Walker describes the journal as being written "in an improvised book made of unruled paper 5" long by 4" wide, sewed by hand, without a back or cover." Walker says the journal came into his possession in 1914. Walker gave his handwritten copy of the journal to George E. Simmons, Professor of Agronomy at the University of Maine in December of 1928. Simmons turned the longhand copy into a typescript. Kenneth Roberts obtained a typescript copy of this journal from Simmons, which is in his papers at the Dartmouth Library. Roberts' copy of the journal includes his notations.[64]

B. <u>Notes on Journal</u>.
The complete Kimball journal is printed in Chapter Five. Its provenance is established by Mary A. Hovey, Kimball's great granddaughter. Hovey says, "This diary was written by my great grandfather Kimball, while he was a soldier in the years of 1775-76."

C. <u>Period Covered</u>.
Begins on September 2, 1775 and ends on September 20, 1776.

D. <u>Publishing History</u>.
<u>1st Printing</u>. Extracts of the Kimball journal are in the footnotes of James Melvin's Journal as found in *March to Quebec*. Since the Kimball journal in that book only consists of footnotes, it is technically not a printing. However, it is the only printing of entries from the journal that has been offered to date.

E. <u>Location of Original</u>.
Dr. L.C. Walker of Jamestown, Ohio owned the original in 1928. There is no indication of its current location. There is a longhand copy of the original at the University of Maine at Orono, which was provided to the library by Professor George E. Simmons in 1934. There is a typescript copy of the journal in the Kenneth Roberts' Collection at the Dartmouth Library.

F. Biography of Author.

Little is actually known about the Moses Kimball who was on the Arnold expedition. One reason for this is that there were a surprising number of Moses Kimballs who served in the Revolutionary War. This situation makes it difficult to make an accurate identification as to whether a certain Moses Kimball is the Moses Kimball who was on the Arnold expedition. Moreover, family genealogies or local histories have also been confused about which Moses Kimball served where. A Sergeant Moses Kimball from Hopkinton, New Hampshire is most often confused with the Moses Kimball who was on the expedition.

According to his great granddaughter and the Kimball family history, Moses Kimball was one of fifteen children and was born in Hampstead, New Hampshire on March 3, 1756 to Benjamin and Mary Kimball. The only thing known about his life before the war was that he was a blacksmith. He is shown on a muster roll of Captain Hezekiah Hutchins Company which was part of Colonel Reed's Regiment. Moses Kimball was enrolled in the company as of June 9, 1775. He is listed as a 19-year-old private with occupation as a blacksmith and being from Hampstead, New Hampshire. Since Reed's Regiment was in the Battle of Bunker Hill, it is reasonable to assume that Hutchins' company participated in that battle.

His name next appears on the muster rolls as a participant in the Quebec expedition with Captain Dearborn's company. In one of the rolls, Moses Kimball is listed as a 19-year-old private from Hampstead, New Hampshire. His civilian occupation is listed as a blacksmith. He was taken prisoner in the assault and is on the British army's list of prisoners taken in the attack on Quebec. There is no record of Kimball serving in the army after the Quebec expedition. According to the family history, he married a woman named Hannah and had three children. The family moved to Vassalboro, Maine after his military service was over. He died in Vassalboro in 1789 at the young age of thirty-three. The title of the journal in the Roberts' papers stating that he was the son of Joseph Kimball of Ipswich is not true. His father was Benjamin Kimball of Hampstead.[65]

XII. III. JOHN FLANDERS

A. Description of Journal.

The only known reference to this journal, which includes a limited number of journal entries, is found in *The History of Boscawen and Webster from 1733 to 1878*. The chapter on Military History states that while he was a prisoner in Quebec, John Flanders "kept a diary, which has been in part preserved. It contains a record of the weather from the first week in January, 1776, to April 25, together with a few items of interest, mostly written in cipher, the key to which has been discovered."[66]

The history includes excerpts from the Flanders' diary for January 3 through 21 and includes two entries written in cipher with the translation. It goes on to give the ultimate disposition of the Boscawen prisoners, including Flanders, who were released on parole on August 1, 1776, and were taken by ship to the port of New York and then released. They finally arrived back in Boscawen on September 25.

The entries provided in the book are minimal in nature being primarily about the weather. The journal as presented has no significance other than the fact that it was written in cipher and that it is yet another missing expedition journal. Given the brevity of the diary entries, there is no possibility that Flanders was relying on Melvin's account, or vice versa. It is also unlikely that Flanders was collaborating with Moses Kimball. Thus, we do have an interesting original diary that seems to be, at least partially, written in cipher. The original of this journal, if it still exists, is likely in the possession of the descendants of Flanders.

B. Biography of Author.

John Flanders was born in Boscawen, New Hampshire on October 13, 1752 to John Flanders, Sr. His grandfather, Jacob, was one of the first settlers of Boscawen, then called Contoocook. Not much is known about his early life before the Revolutionary War. He married Elizabeth Stevens, the widow of John Stevens about 1780 and they had ten children.

Flanders was one of sixteen men from Boscawen that responded to the Lexington Alarm in Captain Henry Gerrish's company which marched on April 21st. He was in the Battle of Bunker Hill and enlisted in Dearborn's company for the Quebec expedition. Flanders was taken prisoner in the assault on Quebec and was released with the other men in August of 1776. After returning home, he was one of twenty-three men from Boscawen who enlisted for the defense of Fort Ticonderoga in late 1776. On August 24, 1777, he enlisted in Captain Kimball's company in Colonel Stickney's regiment which took part in the Battle of Bennington. In 1778, he was in Captain Webster's company of Colonel Nichols regiment that participated in the defense of Rhode Island. In 1778, he was part of a committee established by the Town of Boscawen to develop a plan to enlist more soldiers for the war. Flanders enlisted for three years in the company of Captain Nathaniel

Hutchins, a Quebec expedition alumnus, in 1778. There is no further record of his service.

John Flanders purchased a lot in Boscawen in 1783 on which he operated a farm for many years. Flanders sold his farm in 1817. In 1783, Flanders was involved as the defendant in a lawsuit brought against him by Samuel Corser of Boscawen for hitting his wife and causing the death of his unborn child. Witnesses for both sides offered very different views of the incident with Flanders' witnesses asserting that he did not hit Mrs. Corser. The case was finally referred to a referee by agreement of both parties so no indication is provided in the records of its ultimate disposition. The date of John Flanders death is unknown but he is buried in the Water Street Cemetery in Boscawen.[67]

XIII. ABNER STOCKING

A. <u>Description of Journal</u>.
William Matthews describes the Stocking journal as "fairly interesting, but written up,"[68] and Howes describes it as a "day by day narrative of the Arnold expedition."[69] Kenneth Roberts says, "one of the most interesting features of Stocking's Journal is his own high opinion of himself that shines out from every page."[70]

In the introduction to the Stocking journal reproduced in *The Maine Reader*, Stocking is described as "an educated villager" who honed his writing skills from reading "both moral tracts and romantic novels."[71] There is no way to know whether this is true because there is no information on Stocking's early life and no source is cited to verify the conclusion that he was an educated villager. The only available evidence is the entries in the journal which are among the most extensive in terms of detail and the ability of articulate expression. The quality of the writing leaves the reader with the impression that Stocking was above average in the ability to express himself. Justin Smith observed that although he has questions about Stocking's journal, Stocking "was so evidently a careful, sensible man, observant and also reflective, that we cannot help regarding his narrative as in substance reliable."[72]

B. <u>Notes on Journal</u>.
Midland Rare Books listed a copy of this rare journal in a 1948 catalogue (41-196) and a copy of it also appeared in the Streeter sale so we know that copies of it have been available from rare book dealers in the past. The Midland catalogue describes the Stocking journal as a "splendid day by day

journal, and perhaps the rarest narrative of Arnold's Expedition."[73] This author agrees with the observation about it being a splendid journal but not with it being the rarest. The Meigs' journal published in 1776 is the rarest. Moreover, there are copies of the McCoy journal in two libraries in the U.K. and of the Morison journal in three public repositories in the U.S. There is no record of the first printing of this journal being in any repository in the U.S. and no record of the whereabouts of the original manuscript. The only source that was found on the Internet to have a copy of the 1810 printing was the Royal Society of Canada, which listed its copy in a 1906 catalogue of the books in its library. At this time, the library no longer exists and there is no indication of what happened to its copy of Stocking's journal.

C. Period Covered.
Starts on September 14, 1775 and ends on January 1, 1776.

D. Publishing History.
1st Printing. *An Interesting Journal of Abner Stocking of Chatham, Connecticut Detailing the Distressing Events of the Expedition Against Quebec, under the Command of Col. Arnold in the Year 1775.* Published by the relatives of Abner Stocking. Catskill, NY: Eagle Office, 1810, 36 pages. This is an extremely rare publication.
2nd Printing. *Magazine of History with Notes and Queries,* Extra Number 75, William Abbatt, Tarrytown, N.Y., 1921. 36 pages.
3rd Printing. Kenneth Roberts. *March to Quebec,* 1938, pp. 545-574.
4th Printing. *The Maine Reader,* Edited by Charles & Samuella Shain. Boston and New York: Houghton Mifflin and Company, 1991, pp. 38-49.

E. Location of Original.
No original Stocking manuscript journal has been found.

F. Biography of Author.
Abner Stocking, Jr. was born the son of sea captain Abner Stocking in Middle Haddam, Connecticut, on January 2, 1753. Middle Haddam at that time was part of the Town of Chatham, Connecticut, which is today called East Hampton. Captain Abner Stocking commanded a privateer that operated out of New York during the Revolution and participated in the Point Judith expedition. In addition to Abner Jr., Captain Abner had three sons who served in the Revolutionary War. Captain Abner's father was Captain George Stocking, who owned a grist mill prior to 1740 and was a captain of the militia in 1752. Abner Jr. was married to Lidea Bowers on February 20, 1777. The younger Abner Stocking is often confused with his

father of the same name so it is sometimes difficult to sort out who was who during the Revolutionary War.

On May 6, 1775, at the age of twenty-two, Abner Stocking Jr. enlisted in Captain Ezekiel Scott's Company and marched to Roxbury where he fought in the Battle of Bunker Hill. He then served in Captain Oliver Hanchett's Company on the expedition to Quebec and wrote a journal. In the attack on Quebec, Stocking was taken prisoner and during his captivity he states that he was "affected with scurvy and the flux" while in prison. He described his situation in the British prison as being "without comfortable clothing and many of us were entirely naked".

Stocking was released along with the rest of Arnold's men in August of 1776. They arrived in Elizabethtown, New Jersey on the 22nd of September and he met up with his father and two brothers at Kings Bridge, New York, while on his way home shortly afterward. His journal says he arrived at his father's house on October 6th at 11 o'clock in the morning. The journal says that the house was located in Chatham which encompasses what was in the eighteenth century called the Middle Haddam parish.

In April of 1780, he was on the roll as a Captain in the 23rd Regiment of the Connecticut Militia. If this is Abner, Jr., he would be the third Stocking who gained the title of Captain following in the footsteps of his father and grandfather.

Some previous authors in relaying biographical information about the journalist Abner Stocking have suggested that he captained a privateer and was in the Point Judith expedition, but that was most likely his father. There is no record that the Abner Stocking who was on the Quebec expedition was a sea captain or that he served on a privateer.

There are no records of Abner Stocking's life after the Revolutionary War including the number of children that he fathered. The exact date of his death is not known but one source suggests that it occurred about 1806 in Middle Haddam, Connecticut. Based on a reference in the first printing of the Stocking journal, he died before the journal was published in 1810, so therefore the 1806 date cannot be eliminated as his date of death. This author has been unable to find any definitive record of Stocking's death or his burial place.[74]

XIV. WILLIAM MCCOY ALSO KNOWN AS PROVINCIAL

A. <u>Description of Journal</u>.
In 1776, less than a year after the assault on Quebec by the Arnold and Montgomery forces, a printer in Glasgow, Scotland published an Arnold expedition journal. The logistics of getting this journal published in Scotland so soon after the event happened must have been astounding.

The title of the journal was "A Journal of the March of a Party of Provincials from Carlisle to Boston and from Thence to Quebec, Begin the 13th of July and Ended the 31st of December 1775, to which is Added An Account of the Attack and Engagement at Quebec, the 31st of December, 1775." It contains the record of the march made by the William Hendricks' rifle company from Pennsylvania to Cambridge and then on to Quebec. Its authenticity as an original source journal is established without question by its date of publication.

Kenneth Roberts places this journal in the same category as Stocking, Ware, Wild and Tolman. Roughly half of the entries do have similarities in word usage for some phrases or sentences, but there is no entry in the McCoy journal that contains identical or even closely similar language to those found in the Ward Company collaborative journals. Roberts' conclusion is not supported by the facts."

The McCoy journal also contains an addendum of a completely unrelated account "of the Engagement at Quebec, from a Gentleman to his Friend" because "the Writer of the above Journal leaves it rather unfinished." Joseph Sabin, the well-known bibliographer, states that the "account of the engagement at Quebec, is not by the American who wrote the journal, but by the gentleman who sent it to Glasgow."[75] Based on the information provided by John Joseph Henry that "Gentleman" was Major Murray, the Barracks Master of the British Army in Quebec.[76]

B. <u>Notes on Journal</u>.
In March of 1975, Dr. Henry J. Young, Dana Professor Emeritus of History at Dickinson College, in an article written for John and Mary's Journal, stated that the Hendricks journal "was started by Captain Hendricks himself, apparently taken up in early September by one of his sergeants, William McCoy, added to after 31 December by a British officer, Major Murray, barrack-master of Quebec, and then published in 1776 in Glasgow".[77] The support for this claim is found in Henry's journal where he says that Sergeant McCoy of the Hendricks Company, who he describes as "an excellent

clerk", gave a "genuine copy of his journal" to Major Murray of the Quebec garrison.[78] Henry's reference contains no indication of Hendricks being involved or that McCoy did more than give his journal to Major Murray. There is no indication that Murray added entries to the journal. Murray is a credible connection to the subsequent Glasgow publication in 1776. As a Scotsman, he would have had the family connections to get the journal back to Scotland and then to the publisher. The Murray connection supports McCoy as the author.

Henry's narrative account, which refers to McCoy writing a journal that he used as a guide, is even further substantiated by an 1808 letter written by Henry to Francis Nichols, second in command to Hendricks, where Henry describes the writing of his own journal. He states that he has been assisted in his own writing "by the notes of Gen. Meigs and Wm McCoy, one of our sergeants."[79] The Gen. Meigs referred to by Henry is Return J. Meigs whose account was first published in 1776. The McCoy "notes" that Henry refers to was this journal.

In their reprinting of the McCoy journal, Raymond M. Bell and Chauncey E. McCoy[80] argue persuasively for McCoy being the author for three reasons:

First, the Journal was written in the first person but Hendricks is referred to four times in the third person. This is very compelling argument that has not been made before.

Second, the concluding entries tell of the defeat at Quebec. Hendricks fell early in the assault and could not have known of the events recorded about the assault.

Third, Chambers, who is mentioned at the beginning of the Journal along with Hendricks, is designated as Capt. John Chambers. However, John Chambers is actually a private, not a Captain in William Hendricks' company. In his article, Dr. Young goes further and says that "in the entire Continental Army, or even in the Quebec Militia or the British army, there is no identifiable Captain John Chambers." It is unclear who inserted the name of Chambers in the Journal but certainly not McCoy, who would have known his rank.

C. Publishing History.
1st Printing. *A Journal of the March of a Party of Provincials from Carlisle to Boston and from Thence to Quebec, Begun the 13th of July, and ended the 31st of December, 1775, to which is added An Account of the Attack and Engagement*

at Quebec, the 31st of December, 1775. Glasgow, Scotland: R. Chapman and A. Duncan, MDCCLXXV (1776), 36 pages. The printers, Chapman and Duncan, were the printers of the Glasgow Mercury. The size of this printing is 4 7/8" X 7 5/8" and it is printed on bound paper wrappers

Sabin describes this as "a very rare piece." Only three original publications of this journal have been located. One is in the U.S. at the Williams College Library, although the catalogue lists it as unavailable. The second is in the U.S. at the John Carter Brown Library of Brown University in Providence, Rhode Island. The third is in Scotland at the University of Glasgow Library, Special Collections.

2nd Printing. *Journal of Captain William Hendricks*. Pennsylvania Archives, Series 2, Vol. 15, Harrisburg, Pennsylvania, 1893, pp. 21-58. This printing states that it is copied from "a rare pamphlet printed in Glasgow, Scotland, in connection with an account of the Siege of Quebec, from the hands of a British officer, and it has been given page for page as in the original."

3rd Printing. *Thompson's Battalion and/or the First Continental Regiment*. Oscar H. Stroh. Harrisburg, Pa: Graphic Services, 1975. Appendix: *The Journal of Captain William Hendricks*, pp. 47-51.

4th Printing. *Journal of Sergeant William McCoy of the March from Pennsylvania to Quebec July 13-1775 to December 31-1775, First published in 1776 in Glasgow, Scotland, reprinted in Pennsylvania Archives. Series 2, Volume 15, pp. 22-51*. Edited by Raymond M. Bell, Washington, Pennsylvania, and Chauncey E. McCoy, Romney, Indiana. Bell and McCoy, 1991, 16 typewritten pages.

5th Printing. http://files.usgwarchives.net/pa/1pa/military/revwar/hendricks01. txt.

Also see: Provincial Journal. Arnold Expedition Historical, The Research Room. www.arnoldsmarch.com/research.html.

D. Period Covered.
The journal starts on July13, 1775 and ends December 31, 1775.

E. Location of original.
There is no indication as to the location of the original journal. Presumably, if it still exists, it is somewhere in Scotland.

F. Biography of Author.
There is very little in the public record about the William McCoy who was on the Arnold expedition and authored the Provincial journal. William McCoy was born about 1747 in an unknown town in eastern Pennsylvania, probably in Lancaster County. John McCoy, his father, brought the family

to Rye Township (now Wheatfield Township) in Perry County, Pennsylvania in 1766 where he purchased 300 acres of land on Little Juniata Creek. This land was approximately two miles upstream from the present day town of Duncannon. At that time, it was still a part of Cumberland County. John McCoy, the father, died without a will in 1781/ 2. At his death, John Sr. had a total of six sons and three daughters. One source states that prior to the war, William became a schoolteacher and taught school in Mifflintown in present Juniata County. There is no record of where he got his education and training to be a schoolteacher.

In July of 1775, William was the first of the six McCoy sons to enter into the military service. A total of four of John Sr.'s sons served during the Revolutionary War. At that time, William enlisted in the Cumberland County Rifle Company of Captain William Hendricks. McCoy was a sergeant in the company, probably based on his friendship with Lieutenant John McClelland, who was his neighbor. The company marched to Boston, a distance of 432 miles, in just 27 days. Upon reaching Cambridge, the Hendricks Company was assigned by General Washington to the Quebec expedition.

McCoy's friend, Lieutenant McClelland, died on the way to Cambridge and his company commander, William Hendricks, was killed in the attack on Quebec. McCoy and most of his company were captured and taken prisoner. Henry described some activities involving McCoy while the Americans were confined in Quebec. One issue that the Americans had in confinement was the quality of food they were served. Henry says two sergeants from Pennsylvania were helpful in getting better quality food. "Our other resource was William McCoy, a sergeant of Hendrick's, an excellent clerk, who came into favor with the Governor, by giving to Major Murray of the garrison, a genuine copy of his journal of the route through the wilderness to Canada. He was a sedate and sensible man. He was installed 'clerk of the kitchen' and put me in mind of Gil Blas' clerk." Henry concludes his narrative of the food by stating that "friend McCoy gave us every advantage our melancholy situation afforded him."

At a later point in his narrative, Henry describes an escape attempt from the Dauphin Jail which he described as being "300 yards from St. John's gate." No month is given to designate how long into their confinement the plan was developed. In the organization of the escape, one of the men was designated as the general and McCoy was made a colonel along with some others. The men who were assigned to be with Henry were under the "command of McCoy", and were to act as a reserve to the main body that would be leading the escape. The escape never got beyond the planning stage because the plans for the escape were revealed to the British by one of the Americans. It is clear that McCoy was well thought of by the men, which explains the important position in the planning of the escape that he was given.

McCoy was one of the NCO's in Hendricks' company who wrote a letter of support on behalf of Lieutenant Francis Nichols who had been accused of cowardice in the attack on Quebec. McCoy's letter states that during the assault "Lieut. Nichols came up from the rear of the company and spiritedly and bravely encouraged the men 'push on my brave, brave fellows, we will all be well enough, the town will be our own', or words to that purpose and with that he push'd through the barrier, and we follow'd him and it appear'd to me that he behaved with ardour, bravery & Resolution."

On August 6, 1776, McCoy, along with the other prisoners, was sent by ship to Elizabethtown, New Jersey, which he reached on September 24th. One week later he was home. Despite his abilities as a soldier and leader, there is no indication of any other Revolutionary War service by Sergeant McCoy. A listing of the inhabitants of Cumberland County for 1778 has a William McCoy living in Rye Township. William married a wife named Rachael in the autumn of 1777 after his return from Quebec. The family genealogists claim that her last name was Means, although there is no Means family history that supports this assertion. This identification of Means is based on the children some of whom have Means for a second name.

After the war, one source claims that McCoy returned to his home in Mifflintown and lived near the school where he had taught before the war. If this is the case, it did not happen until after 1778. In 1789, William McCoy was appointed by the Provincial Council to be a Justice of the Peace for the Township of Fermanagh in what was then Mifflin County, Pennsylvania. It is also claimed that he was a land speculator. Two different genealogical books on the McCoy family have concluded that William McCoy maintained two different homes after his marriage. One was in Rye Township in Cumberland County, today known as Perry County. The other was in Fermanagh Township in what was then Mifflin County. Both of these locations would have been part of Cumberland County until 1789. In 1795, William McCoy is listed as one of the signers of a subscription to provide funds with which to complete a Presbyterian Church in Mifflintown, known today as the county seat of Juniata County, but then in Mifflin County. He is also listed as living in Mifflin County in the 1790 federal census with five members in his household. It seems more likely to me that he moved his family permanently to Mifflin County after 1778.

William McCoy died in 1797, probably at the home of his eldest son John in Mifflin County, leaving his wife and nine children. No burial place has been identified for William McCoy. He left a soldier's legacy with a grandson, Thomas Franklin McCoy, who was Civil War general, and his great grandson, General Frank Ross McCoy, a well-known soldier-diplomat in the first half of the twentieth century. The 1841 McCoy House, which is located in Lewistown and was built by General Thomas Franklin McCoy, is the premier historical landmark in Mifflin County. It was the birthplace and boyhood home of General Frank Ross McCoy and now serves as the Mifflin County Historical Society Museum.[81]

XV. SIMON FOBES

A. Description of Journal.
The first published account of the Fobes journal states that it was "given by himself, and recorded by his son, Joshua Fobes, Esq., in 1835," when Fobes was seventy-nine years old. Smith describes his account as "not a journal, but recollections out in writing sixty years after the events took place." Although Smith acknowledges that there are a number of errors in the Fobes journal, he finds that it does have value as an historical account.

Kenneth Roberts includes the Fobes' journal in his book primarily because it contains the only record of the return route followed by a group of soldiers who were in prison in Quebec but managed to escape. However, Roberts is troubled by a reference in the Fobes' journal of his meeting up with his expedition company commander, Captain Jonas Hubbard, on his way home. Hubbard was killed during the attack on Quebec so he could not have been alive in the fall of 1776, and therefore could not have met up with Fobes. For Roberts, this incident seriously negates the value of Fobes' narrative.[82] The 1835 date lends significant credibility to the argument that Fobes was writing his journal so long after the event itself that his memory was faulty on the Hubbard meeting. This mistaken identification tends to lessen the value of the Fobes journal as an accurate history of the expedition.

Matthews' book on American Diaries describes Fobes journal as "interesting."[83] Codman, Stone, Winsor and Banks did not think the Fobes journal was historically significant enough to be included in their list of Arnold expedition journals.

B. Notes on Journal.
The National Archives and Records Administration has prepared an

Elementary and Secondary School Teaching Guide entitled "Simon Fobes Goes to War. The Life of a Revolutionary War Soldier." The publication is intended for use by teachers bringing school children to visit the National Archives. The Fobes journal is not used in this teaching guide.[84]

C. Publishing History.
1st Printing. Simon Fobes' Journal. *Historical Collections of the Mahoning Valley.* Vol. I, Mahoning Valley Historical Society, Youngstown, 1876. pp. 345-394.
2nd Printing. *Magazine of History with Notes and Queries.* Extra No. 130. William Abbatt, Tarrytown, 1927, 53 pages.
3rd Printing. Kenneth Roberts. *March to Quebec*, 1938, pp. 575-613.
4th Printing. *Simon Fobes' Journal.* Arnold Expedition Historical Society, The Research Room. www.arnoldsmarch.com/research.html.

D. Period Covered.
The portion of the Fobes journal relating to the Quebec expedition covers the period from what he calls "about the middle of September" 1775 to September 30, 1776.

E. Location of Original.
The location of the Fobes original manuscript is unknown but it may be in the possession of the Fobes family.

F. Biography of Author.
Simon Fobes was born in Canterbury, Connecticut, on April 5, 1756, the son of Simon Fobes Sr., and he grew up on the family farm. His family moved to Amherst, Massachusetts, in 1770. After the Lexington alarm, he was in Cambridge with Captain Smith's Company of Ward's Regiment. He was in the Battle of Bunker Hill and then enlisted in Captain Hubbard's Company for the expedition to Quebec under Arnold.

He was captured in the assault on Quebec and was held until August of 1776, when he escaped from custody, eluded pursuit and after great hardships finally returned to his father's house on September 20, 1776. From December of 1776 until the spring of 1777, Fobes served in the place of someone else from Amherst as a corporal in the company of Captain Smith. His family moved to a farm in Somers, Connecticut, and in the spring of 1778, he enlisted as a sergeant for one year in Captain Robinson's company of the Connecticut militia under Colonel Roger Enos. In May of 1779, he enlisted as an Ensign in the Connecticut militia serving in New London, Connecticut and then in East Haven, CT until his nine-month commission expired. On

March 27, 1780, he obtained a lieutenant's commission and served for one year and two months, including duty as the commander of a whaleboat in Long Island Sound to monitor the British sailing activity.

Fobes was discharged with an honorable release in May of 1781. After the war, he married Elizabeth Jones of Somers and they had five sons and two daughters. In 1803, his family purchased land in Wayne Township in Ohio and in 1807 the entire family, including his parents, moved to Wayne. His mother died in 1808 and was the first recorded death in Wayne Township. Three days later his father died.

Simon moved to Kinsman, Ohio prior to 1829 and was living there when he obtained a pension for his Revolutionary War services. Simon Fobes died on January 30, 1840 at the age of 84, and is buried in the Wayne Center Cemetery.[85]

XVI. EPHRAIM SQUIER

A. Description of Journal.
The Squier journal was discovered in the U.S. Government Pension Office in the late nineteenth century. Squier provided it to the Pension Office in 1832 along with his application for a pension. Squier is the only journalist who was in the Enos Division and his journal contains the only contemporary account of the early return to Cambridge of that division. For that reason alone it is an important account.

Smith describes the Squier account as being the story "of a common soldier, very plain, simple and meagre, and not always accurate." He goes on to say that it is authentic and that his examination of the original manuscript journal convinces him that this is "a contemporary, unaltered record." He concludes that the journal "is of considerable importance" because of Squier's presence in the Enos Division.[86] Roberts included the Squier journal in his book but he finds it has significance only because it relates the history of the return of the Enos division.

B. Notes on Journal.
The Squier journal was transferred from the Pension Office to the Library of Congress on February 9, 1909.[87] The Squier family had previously requested the Pension Office to return the journal to their family but the request was refused. There is no question that this is an authentic original manuscript

written in Squier's own hand as the handwriting matches other documents by Squier that are in his pension application.

C. Publishing History.
1st Printing. *Diary of Ephraim Squier*. Magazine of American History, Vol. II, Part II, November, 1878, pp. 685-694.
2nd Printing. *Diary of Ephraim Squier*. Magazine of History with Notes and Queries, Extra No.160. William Abbatt, Tarrytown, 1930, pp. 39-48.
3rd Printing. Kenneth Roberts. *March to Quebec*, 1938. pp. 619-628.

D. Period Covered.
The journal covers the period from September 7, 1775 to November 25, 1775.

E. Location of Original.
The original manuscript is located in the Library of Congress, Journal of Ephraim Squier, 1775-1777, mm 81095687.

F. Biography of Author.
Ephraim Squier was born in Ashford, Connecticut, on February 9, 1747. He was the son of Phillip Squier, who was at the capture of Louisburg. Little is known of his early years, but on the 21st of April, 1775, he was one of eighty men who volunteered in the company of his next door neighbor, Captain Thomas Knowlton. The company marched to Charlestown and Squier remained in Knowlton's Company until sometime in June. At that point, he enlisted in the artillery company commanded by Captain Collander and fought with that company in the Battle of Bunker Hill. He then enlisted in Captain Pomeroy's Company of Colonel Fellows Regiment. Then, on September 7, 1775, Lieutenant James Sprague of Union, Connecticut enlisted him in Captain William Scott's Company for the expedition to Quebec.

Because Scott's company was in the Enos Division, Squier was one of the men who returned in October to the main army in Cambridge and arrived there on November 25th. He was the only person to write a journal of the Enos Division's return. After returning, he re-enlisted in Captain Pomeroy's company where he served until March 25, 1776. In April of 1776, he enlisted in Captain Hindee's Company in the Connecticut militia and served in White Plains and then in Providence, Rhode Island. In September of 1777, he was in Captain Isaac Stone's company of Colonel Latimer's Regiment and marched to Stillwater, New York, where he participated in the Battle of Saratoga. He was at the capture of Burgoyne's army. Squier's company was one of the Connecticut units that followed Arnold in the final attack on Breyman's redoubt that turned the course of the battle.

Squier married Priscilla Sibley on December 31, 1776 in Ashford and they had four children. Squier was one of the living survivors of the Bunker Hill battle who attended the laying of the corner stone of the Bunker Hill monument in 1825. At that time his age was listed as 72, but it should have been 78. He died in Ashford in 1841 at the age of 94, making him the oldest journalist and likely the longest living soldier from the Arnold expedition.[88]

XVII. GEORGE MORISON

A. Description of Journal.
Justin Smith says that the Morison journal is written with "an extensive imagination." Smith describes his journal as "both interesting and valuable as the picture of a brave, hopeful, patriotic soldier", but that it was "too often incomplete or incorrect in detail." Smith places the Morison journal in the same general category as the Provincial, Tolman, Ware and Wild journals, because he believes it shares a "certain family likeness" to those journals. Smith concludes that although Morison seems to have made use of one or more journals from the 1st Division as a guide to establish the "thread of his story", his account is more valuable than Tolman's because it is "fuller and more individual, but it must be followed with caution." Smith does not believe that Morison wrote a daily record on his own, but rather that he produced "a free reworking of something else, filled out with many additions."[89]

Roberts says, "Morison's Journal must be taken with an extra-large grain of salt", although he included it in his book because of its descriptive rhetoric, which he says rivals James Fennimore Cooper for flowery language.[90]

Morison's journal was the third Arnold expedition journal to find its way into print when it was published in 1803. Nothing has surfaced to explain how the journal came into the hands of the printer from Morison or his family. Since the original manuscript has not been found, there is no way to compare the transcription published in 1803 with the original. However, Morison's journal has credibility because of its early publishing date.

B. Notes on Journal.
This is a rare piece of Americana because only three existing copies of the

1803 first printing have been found. The three copies are in the William L. Clements Library, the Historical Society of Pennsylvania, and the Historical Society of Wisconsin Rare Book Collection. However, there is a copy of the 1st printing of the journal listed in Catalogue #321 published in 1940 by Goodspeed's Book Shop, Inc. in Boston. The book is described as being "12mo, removed from a bound volume (title and preliminary blank leaves slightly stained, lower margins cropped with injury to text, including bottom line of imprint...)." The catalogue also has a black and white illustration of the title page of Morison's journal. It is not known where that copy is currently located.

The copy in the Historical Society of Pennsylvania is 5" X 81/4 inches in size and at the top of the title page is written "No 4" which indicates that at least four copies were printed. Although the location of only four known copies can be identified, at least twenty or more copies must have been originally printed.

There is also a Goodspeed catalogue in 1946 that lists a copy of this rare 1803 journal and describes it as "12mo, removed from a bound volume (title and preliminary blank leaves slightly stained, lower margins cropped with injury to text, including bottom line of imprint." The description seems to be identical to the one listed in the 1940 catalogue. Both catalogues also describes the Morison journal as probably "the rarest of all narratives of Arnold's expedition," but then goes on to recognize the Stocking journal as a "rival." The Morison journal is actually the fourth rarest Arnold expedition journal after Meigs, McCoy and Stocking.

C. <u>Publishing History</u>.
<u>1st Printing</u>. *An Interesting Journal of Occurrences During the Expedition to Quebec Conducted by the Celebrated Arnold at the Commencement of the American Revolution: Giving a Particular Account of the Unparalleled Sufferings Sustained by that Detachment in Passing through the Wilderness: Together with a Description of the Battle of Quebec, Kept by George Morison, a Volunteer in the Company of Riflemen Commanded by Capt. Hendricks, Who Was Slain at the Attack on Quebec: Now Published from the Manuscript.* James Magee, Hagerstown, Maryland, 1803. This is now a very rare item (see above for explanation).
<u>2nd Printing</u>. Extracts of George Morison's journal. *An Assault on Quebec.* Pennsylvania Magazine of History and Biography, Vol. 14, January 1891, pp. 434-439.
<u>3rd Printing</u>. *The Magazine of History with Notes and Queries,* Extra Number 52, Part II. William Abbatt, Tarrytown, New York, 1916.

4th Printing. Kenneth Roberts. *March to Quebec*, 1938, pp. 505-544.
5th Printing. *An Interesting Journal of Occurrences...* Library Reprints, Inc.
44 pages.

D. Period Covered.
The journal begins on July 17th and ends on September 24, 1776.

E. Location of Original.
The original manuscript of the Morison journal is not in the Historical
Society of Pennsylvania and has not been located elsewhere. However, the
Houghton Library at Harvard University has a handwritten copy of the
journal published in 1803, which was given to the Library by the widow of
John Codman. Codman's book says he made his copy from a copy of the
original journal published by James Magee in 1803, which was located in
the Historical Society of Pennsylvania. The Massachusetts Historical Society
also has a handwritten copy of the journal in the Charles E. Banks Papers.
A note from Banks on this copy says that it was "made from the exceedingly
rare original in the Library of the Historical Society of Pennsylvania, and it
is a literal transcription with all typographical errors retained".

F. Biography of Author.
Although the Morison journal was among the earliest published, not much
is known about Morison's life. According to the DAR Patriot Index, George
Morison was born in Pennsylvania about 1739 and married Margaret
Morison. Both of these facts are incorrect. George Morison was born in
1754 or 1755, according to the British list of Prisoners in Quebec from 1776
which lists his age as 21. This age, given the other things we know about him,
makes sense. He did not marry Margaret Morrison. The George Morrison
who did marry Margaret Morison was born in Bucks County, Pennsylvania
and married Margaret in 1760. The expedition's George Morison was 5 or
6 years old in 1760. There is no record of a Cumberland County marriage
between George Morison and Margaret. The only marriage of a Margaret
Morrison in Cumberland County during the last half of the eighteenth
century was to a Revolutionary War soldier named George Black. This
author does not believe that Morison was married at all based on his early
death. Additionally, probable lingering effects of the Quebec expedition
and his subsequent military service could easily account for his unmarried
status.

A record of Early Perry County People lists two men named Morrison, James
and Anthony, who each purchased significant acreages of land in 1768 in
Toboyne Township, being some of the earliest settlers. It seems likely the

George is a son of one of these men, who may have been brothers, even though his last name is spelled differently than theirs. The early records of Toboyne show only one other Morison who spelled the name with one "R".

When he volunteered to serve in the Captain William Hendricks Company in 1775, Morison was living in Sherman's Valley, Cumberland County, Pennsylvania. He was with the Hendricks' Company in Arnold's army and was captured during the attack on Quebec. Sherman's Valley at an early time included all of the current day boundaries of Perry County, except for Pfoutz's Valley. It received its name from the creek running through the area, which was called Sherman's after an Indian trader who was drowned in the creek while attempting to cross with his horse and furs. Toboyne Township, where Morison lived after the war, is in Sherman's Valley. In 1775, it was the furthest town west in Perry County and dates its formation from before the Revolutionary War.

Morison served time in confinement in Quebec and was released in the fall of 1776. Sometime after he returned home, he enlisted in the army again. In 1780, Morison was listed as one of the men in the 8th company, 5th Battalion of the Cumberland County Militia. According to John Morison, who gave the journal to its original publisher, Morison was acting as a Quarter Master of his unit in winter quarters near Norristown, PA when he had a run in with a Colonel of the Maryland line. Morison ended up breaking the Colonel's arm with a shovel and was sentenced to one thousand lashes. Before the sentence was carried out, the Colonel intervened and his punishment was overturned. Morison was so upset by this experience that he obtained permission to quit the army. John Morison stated that "his feelings were so corroded by this circumstance that he destroyed the subsequent part of his journal, quitted the army and died some time after." Morison is not on the rolls of the Cumberland County militia in 1777, which included a large number of Toboyne men, but he is on a list of Cumberland County soldiers of the Revolutionary War who received pay for their service as a ranger on the frontier. The 1780 service is consistent with the above details.

Morison is shown on the taxable rolls in 1781 and 1782 of Toboyne Township then a part of Cumberland County, Pennsylvania. Morison's only property listed on the tax rolls was one cow and no land. Toboyne is now located in Perry County which was formed in 1820 so that the residents of the area would not have to cross the Conococheague Mountain to get to the county seat of Carlisle. The taxable list indicates he did not have substantial assets which supports the notion that he was living with his parents as an unmarried man. George Morison is not on the taxable list for Cumberland County in 1785. His name is not on the 1790 or 1800 federal census in Cumberland County. There is also no pension application for Morison and no mention of George Morison in any county record after 1782. If he was not married and owned no land, he would not have left a will.

The D.A.R. records indicating that he died in 1785 might be correct but no source for this date is given. The preface to his journal published in 1803 states that it was given to the publisher by a John Morison of Cumberland County, presumably a relative. John told the publisher that the journal had "lain in his [John's] hands for many years." He goes on to say that it had been George's intention to publish the journal but that "his death prevented it." This seems consistent with a death in 1785, which would have been 18 or 19 years prior to the publication. John Morison's statement that George Morison died after the end of his service is also consistent with the 1785 date. There is no record of a gravesite for George Morison in any of the cemeteries in the boundaries of the old Cumberland County so he was most likely buried in a family cemetery.[91]

XVIII. WILLIAM HETH

A. <u>Description of Journal</u>.
William Heth was a lieutenant in Morgan's rifle company in the expedition to Quebec. Even though Heth's journal was one of the later journals to be published, there are references to it in at least three earlier writings. The first was in Daniel Morgan's biographical sketch of his own life. On page 464, Morgan refers to a journal kept by Lieutenant Heth of his company.[92] Second, John Marshall, in a footnote on page 62 of his biography of Washington says that to write his account of the Arnold expedition to Quebec and the assault on the city on the night of December 31, 1775 "much use has been made of a journal kept by Colonel Heth."[93] Finally, there is a reference to the Heth journal in the *Proceedings of the Virginia Historical Society*, which identifies the descendant of Heth who owned the journal as Mr. Richard Heth Munford Harrison, Heth's great grandson of Richmond, Virginia.[94]

In 1896, the Heth journal was examined and copied by Charles E. Banks, who looked at the original then in the possession of Mrs. Richard Heth Munford Harrison. At the time Banks saw the journal, he described it as consisting of "about 150 leaves originally, but about forty of the first portion had been roughly cut out." Banks goes on to speculate that the portion that was removed covered the period "beginning about the first week of

December to, and including, the 31st of that month, when he was taken prisoner." He described the existing journal, which he believes was in the second of a total of three separate books, as "a book 4 x 6 1/2 inches, now in a shaky binding, of which but one cover remains." Banks points out that at the close of this second book Heth refers to "its continuation in the 'Blue Book', Vol. 3 now missing."[95]

LIEUTENANT WILLIAM HETH.
(AFTERWARD COLONEL THIRD VIRGINIA REGIMENT.)
*From miniature in possession of Mr. R. H. M.
Harrison, Richmond, Va.*

The editor of the Heth journal, B. Floyd Flickinger, states that the Winchester Virginia Historical Society obtained a photostat copy of the journal from its then owner, the Library of Congress, some years prior to his work transcribing the journal. In 1930, Mr. Flickinger examined the original in the Library of Congress and concluded that "at least twenty-five sheets had been clipped from the note book." Flickinger describes the existing journal as being in "two note books, each 4 by 6 3/4 inches, and totaling 202 pages." Flickinger indicates that the portion of the diary that has been preserved "does not add much to our factual knowledge of the period and events covered."[96]

The references to Heth's journal from two contemporary sources, Marshall and Morgan, demonstrates that it is an authentic account of the expedition for the period covered. If the missing portion of Heth's journal is of the same quality and detail as the surviving portion, then it is a significant loss of expedition history. Those surviving journal entries are superior to almost all of the other expedition journals. Heth wrote an important expedition journal even though the time period it covered is limited. Unfortunately, it covered only the time he spent in prison in Quebec and not an account of the expedition through the wilderness to get there.

B. <u>Notes on Journal</u>.
C. <u>Publishing History</u>.
<u>1st Printing</u>. *The Diary of Lieut. William Heth while a Prisoner in Quebec, 1776. Edited with Introduction and Notes by B. Floyd Flickinger, Department of History, College of William and Mary*. Annual Papers of Winchester Virginia Historical Society, Volume 1, Winchester, Virginia, 1931, pp. 37-118.
<u>2nd Printing</u>. Paper wraps. *The Diary of Lieut. William Heth while a Prisoner in Quebec, 1776*, Edited with Introduction and Notes by B. Floyd Flickinger. Reprinted from *Annual Papers of Winchester Virginia Historical Society*, 1931, Winchester, VA: Floyd Flickinger, 118 pages.

D. <u>Period Covered</u>.
The Heth journal starts on February 1, 1776 and ends on July 3, 1776.

E. <u>Location of Original</u>.
The original manuscript is located in the William Heth Papers, Manuscript Division, Library of Congress.

F. <u>Biography of Author</u>.
William Heth was born in Pennsylvania on July 19, 1750. His father moved to Virginia after he was born and he grew up in Winchester where one of his relatives kept a tavern. Heth joined Captain Daniel Morgan's company of the Frederick County militia in 1774 serving as a lieutenant. The company participated in Lord Dunmore's War in 1774. Prior to the Revolutionary War, Heth was clerk of the Frederick County Committee of Correspondence so he was active in the patriot movement.

Daniel Morgan raised a company of riflemen in June of 1775 and Heth was appointed his Second Lieutenant. On July 14, 1775, the company left Winchester to march to Cambridge. Morgan's company reached Cambridge on August 6th and then joined the Arnold expedition.

During the attack on Quebec, Heth was wounded and taken prisoner. He was released on parole with the rest of the captured officers and was later exchanged. On April 1, 1777, he was promoted to Lieutenant Colonel and was subsequently promoted to Colonel. His regiment was with General

Lincoln in the siege of Charleston and he served in the army until 1781, when his name appears on a list of supernumerary officers from Virginia.

In 1786, he was appointed by the Virginia Governor as one of the commissioners to settle the claims of the State of Virginia in the acquisition and defense of the Northwest Territory. He served for two years and three months and was commended by the Governor and the legislature for his services. He attended meetings of the State Council and was a member of the Virginia Convention that ratified the Constitution on June 25, 1788. Heth was appointed by President Washington as Collector of the Ports of Richmond, Petersburg and Bermuda Hundred. Because he was a Federalist, President Jefferson forced his removal from that post in 1802.

Heth was active in the Virginia Society of the Cincinnati and served as its Treasurer from 1786 until his death in April of 1807 at the age of fifty-seven. Heth has been described as stout and of medium height. He had two wives and five children and when he died he had an estate that included three farms, a number of slaves and some stocks.[97]

XIX. CHARLES PORTERFIELD

A. <u>Description of Journal</u>.
In the late 19th century, an old journal was discovered in with a group of books that were purchased from the estate of Judge John N. Hendren of Staunton, Virginia. After some research on the journal, it was determined that the author was Charles Porterfield, who served in the Revolutionary War and was on the expedition to Quebec.

The journal being located in the estate of Judge Hendren is logical because Charles Porterfield was the brother of General Robert Porterfield, who also served in the Revolution. Robert Porterfield was the heir to his brother's estate when Charles was killed at the Battle of Camden in 1780. The son-in-law of General Robert Porterfield was William Kinney of Staunton, Virginia, who was also the executor of General Porterfield's estate. Kinney likely obtained the journal as part of the inheritance. Judge Hendren was in turn the administrator of Kinney's estate, which is how the journal came to be in his possession. There is no indication why the journal was not passed down to a surviving member of the Porterfield family.

The journal is described in the Virginia Magazine of History & Biography as a diary "contained in a small book, of many pages, and in some parts the writing is difficult to decipher." It appears that no one examined the journal very closely so no one knew what it contained until Mr. Olivier found it in the Hendren estate. The almost unreadable name of "Charles Por___" was written on the front page of the book.

B. Notes on Journal.
The Porterfield journal is one of only two extant journals that recount the history of the Morgan Company on the expedition. The journal entries as published by the Southern History Association only covers the period that Porterfield was in prison in Quebec. It does not have any information from 1775 regarding the expedition from Cambridge to Quebec.

C. Publishing History.
1st Printing. *Memorable Attack on Quebec, December 21, 1775, Diary of Colonel Charles Porterfield. Magazine of American History with Notes and Queries,* Vol. XXI, January-June, New York, 1889, pp. 318-319. Extract.
2nd Printing. *Diary of a Prisoner of War at Quebec, 1776, communicated by J.A. Waddell, Esq. Virginia Magazine of History and Biography,* Vol. IX, No. 2, Richmond, 1901, pp. 144-145.
3rd Printing. Journal of Charles Porterfield from March 3, 1776 to July 23, 1776, while a prisoner of war in Quebec. *Publications of the Southern History Association,* Vol. VI, No.'s 2-5, Washington, D.C., 1902.

D. Period Covered.
Begins on March 3, 1776 and ends on July 23, 1776.

E. Location of Original.
At least one source has identified the Southern History Association as the location of the Porterfield manuscript journal. The SHA was disbanded by the 1920's so it has no library or collections and there is no evidence that any of its former collections are now in a specific repository. It is more likely that the manuscript is in the possession of a family member who inherited it from Colonel George A. Porterfield or that it was sold by SHA at the time it dissolved.

F. Biography of Author.
Charles Porterfield was born in Frederick, Virginia in 1750 and was living on his family's estate when the war broke out. He volunteered in the company of riflemen from Frederick County under the command of Captain Daniel Morgan, where he was listed as a sergeant. Soon after reaching Cambridge, the company was assigned to the Arnold expedition.

He was captured in the attack and was exchanged in 1776 with the rest of Morgan's men. He enlisted in Colonel Morgan's rifle regiment in the spring of 1777 and was promoted to Captain and served with Morgan's regiment during the Saratoga campaign of 1777 and for most of 1778. In 1778, he was appointed by the State of Virginia as brigade major to General William Woodford and served in that capacity until 1779. The State of Virginia appointed Porterfield as a lieutenant colonel of a state regiment being formed for the defense of the state, and in 1780 the regiment marched to the relief of Charlestown, South Carolina.

Porterfield's regiment subsequently joined with General Gates' army and was with Gates in the Battle of Camden. Porterfield was part of the advance force of Gates' army as it went into the battle. As he was defending his position on the night of August 16th, he received a wound in his left leg. He was captured by the British and taken from the field but did not receive any surgical attention for ten days. At that point his leg was amputated in an effort to save his life but the amputation was too late. He died of his wounds on the Santee River enroute to Charlestown to seek medical attention in October of 1780.[98]

XX. MATTHIAS OGDEN

A. <u>Description of Journal.</u>
Matthias Ogden was a volunteer from New Jersey who went on the expedition accompanied by his friend, Aaron Burr. Ogden's journal has rarely been cited in any other historical work. Although Ogden did go on to become a recognized Revolutionary War hero, his journal of the Quebec expedition has received little attention.

The authenticity of the Ogden journal was established by Marie Blades in the pamphlet published by the Morris County Historical Society in 1980. When she wrote her pamphlet, Ms. Blades was not aware that the journal had already been published in 1928 in the New Jersey Historical Society Proceedings and that it had been identified as Ogden's journal in the introduction.

The NJHS publication introduces the journal by stating that the "preserved manuscript starts with the date "27th" (October 27, 1775), but probably there was an earlier beginning. It is evident that what was written was done often under circumstances of haste, and we have occasionally supplied words where necessary and corrected misspellings."[99]

B. <u>Notes on Journal</u>.

Despite the minimal attention it has attracted since its first publication, the Ogden journal is a significant addition to the journals of the expedition. Perhaps some have discounted Ogden's account because he was a friend of Burr and was a volunteer on the expedition. However, Ogden was highly respected by Arnold and was given a bigger role during the expedition and the assault than his volunteer status would indicate.

C. <u>Publishing History</u>.

<u>1st Printing</u>. *Journal of Major Matthias Ogden: in Arnold's Campaign Against Quebec*. Morristown, N.J.: Washington Association of New Jersey, 1928, 16 pages. This is a very rare printing and only one copy has been located in the Library of Rutgers University, Special Collections.

<u>2nd Printing</u>. *Journal of Major Matthias Ogden in Arnold's Campaign against Quebec 1775*. *Proceedings of the New Jersey Historical Society*. Vol. XIII, No. 1, January 1928, pp. 17-30.

<u>3rd Printing</u>. *The March to Quebec: A Mystery Solved*. Marie E. Blades. Morristown, New Jersey: Morris County Historical Society, 1980, 24 pages.

<u>4th Printing</u>. *Journal of Major Matthias Ogden*. Morristown, NJ. www.digitalantiquaria.com, no date.

D. <u>Period Covered</u>.

Journal starts on October 27, 1775 and ends on December 15, 1775.

E. <u>Location of Original</u>.

The original of the Ogden journal was initially housed in the collections of the Washington Association of New Jersey, which was formed in 1874 in Morristown, New Jersey in order to preserve valuable relics of the American Revolution. However, in 1933, the Morristown National Historic Park acquired the entire library and collection of the Washington Association. The Ogden journal is now located in the Morristown National Historic Park Library & Archives.

F. <u>Biography of Author</u>.

Matthias Ogden was born in Elizabeth, New Jersey on October 12, 1754. His father was a prominent man in New Jersey prior to the Revolution serving as a lawyer and elected official. Matthias attended the College of New Jersey in Princeton where one of his classmates was Aaron Burr.

At the outbreak of war, Ogden and Burr joined the Arnold expedition together as volunteers. Ogden was wounded in the shoulder in the attack on Quebec and joined Arnold in the hospital. Arnold wrote a letter to Washington after the battle offering high praise for Ogden, Burr and Eleazer Oswald. "The loss of my detachment before I left it, was about twenty men killed and wounded; among the latter is Major Ogden, who with Capt. Oswald, Capt. Burr and the other volunteers behaved extremely well." Even though Ogden was a volunteer, Arnold gave him an important position in the plan of attack.

In March of 1776, when his injury healed sufficiently for him to travel, Ogden returned home. He was then commissioned as a lieutenant colonel in the First Regiment of the New Jersey line and he was subsequently promoted to full colonel on January 1, 1777. He served at Fort Ticonderoga in 1777 and was at the Battle of Monmouth.

In 1779, Ogden was accused by a fellow officer in the New Jersey Line of four different charges of misconduct for which he was court-martialed in March of 1779. The four counts were that he was neglectful of the affairs of his regiment, that he was dishonest, that he was a cowardly officer and that he engaged in gaming. The court-martial board found him not guilty on all of the charges except the charge of gaming. For that charge the board sentenced him to be "severely reprimanded in general orders." Washington's reprimand included the following words:

> The General approves the sentence of the Court and it gives him pleasure to find that Colonel Ogden of whom he always entertained a high opinion, has been acquitted of the first three charges exhibited against him… All General Orders are in force 'till they are set aside or altered by subsequent ones issuing from proper authority or 'till the occasion ceases which produced them. Colo. Ogden knows this and he must have known also that the particular order which was the subject of the Court-Martial's consideration of the 4th charge against him, remained unalter'd and the infraction of it is more censurable, if possible, than that of any other, inasmuch as the order was intended to prevent the most Pernicious Vice that can obtain in an Army, the vice of gaming.

There is no evidence that the charges against Ogden and the decision that he was guilty of gaming had any negative impact on Washington's feelings about Ogden.

Mathias Ogden was captured by the British in a skirmish at Elizabethtown, New Jersey, in November of 1780 but was exchanged after being held in New York for a few months. In September of 1781, Ogden conceived of and proposed a plan to Washington that involved the capture of Prince William Henry, who later became King William IV, to use as a hostage in negotiations with the British to end the war. The Prince at that time was with Admiral Digby in New York. Due to the circumstances that existed after the surrender at Yorktown, the plan was never implemented and was finally abandoned in 1782.

In an effort to try to secure a business relationship with the French on behalf of the colonies, Congress, upon the recommendation of the Commander-in-Chief, granted Ogden a leave of absence from his duties in April of 1783. His friend, General Lafayette, offered to introduce him to the King. While in France working to negotiate an arrangement with the French government, he was awarded the honor le droit du tabouret by the French King, Louis XVI. While he was in Europe, Congress commissioned him as a Brigadier General by brevet in September of 1783. He returned from France to personally deliver to Congress, on October 31, 1783, the news of the signing of the Treaty of Paris ending the Revolutionary War.

Following the war, Ogden served in the State of New Jersey Legislative Council and made his living operating one of the mints making a new state coin for New Jersey. It seems likely that Ogden's political connections helped him to get the contract to operate his mint in his hometown of Elizabethtown. He also engaged in land speculation on the western frontier, particularly in the Ohio Tract. In the 1789 presidential election, he served as an elector for the State of New Jersey. He died of yellow fever in Elizabethtown on March 31, 1791 at the age of thirty-six.

In April of 1776, Matthias Ogden married Hannah Drayton, the daughter of well- known patriot Elias Drayton, and they had four children. He is buried in the First Presbyterian Church cemetery in Elizabethtown next to his wife. The inscription on his tombstone includes these words: "In him were united those various virtues of the Soldier the Patriot and the Friend which endear men to society. Distress failed not to find relief in his bounty. Unfortunate merit a refuge in his generosity." [100]

XXI. SAMUEL BARNEY

A. Description of Journal.
Samuel Barney was a private in Oliver Hanchett's company on the expedition. His journal is written in a small paper book (3 ¾ X 6 ½ inches) bound together but with no cloth binding and with edges that are rough and

tattered. The journal is now in the possession of the New Haven Museum and Historical Society. It has been transcribed by his great grandson, Francis Bishop Barney, who states in the introduction of his transcription that "all the dates have been verified (and all are correct) also names of towns, rivers, etc. A few brief entries have been omitted, as adding nothing to the interest. But, as may be seen, not even illness deterred the writer from making an entry in his much-valued Diary each day."

The title of Barney's manuscript, which was designated by his great grandson, is "Diary of Samuel Barney of New Haven Kept during Arnold's Trip to Quebec in 1775." Presumably this manuscript was kept in the family until it was donated to the New Haven Museum and Historical Society. Although Barney's name does not appear in the original manuscript, it is clearly an original journal and relates an account of the Hanchett Company as it traveled on the expedition. Based on the wording of the entries, it is an original manuscript journal written as he went along rather than after the expedition was over. An interesting aspect of Barney's account is that he provides the names of a number of his fellow soldiers, which is different from any other journal, except for Pierce.

The Barney journal also has entries starting on July 8, 1775 and running until July 16th. These entries are not included in the Barney journal that is reproduced in Chapter Six because the entries omitted do not relate to the Quebec expedition. Since Barney purchased the book in which the journal was written in Newburyport when the expedition was there in September, he obviously made the July entries after that time. Those entries are inserted later in the book and not in their natural chronological order, which would be at the front of the book.

B. Notes on Journal
The Barney journal has never been published. It is one more example of the various expedition accounts kept by enlisted men. Barney has written a unique personal account told from the point of view of a private in one of the musket companies. His journal relates a personal experience and not a record of either his company or the expedition itself as is the case with some other journals. The details offered by Private Barney do add a different perspective to the march but they are almost all about him and his friends. Most importantly, Barney's journal is a previously unknown journal and, as such, it deserves to be recognized and he deserves to be remembered.

C. <u>Publishing History</u>.
The diary has never been published but see Chapter Seven where it is printed in its entirety.

D. <u>Period Covered</u>.
The journal begins on September 6, 1775 and ends on January 11, 1776.

E. <u>Location of Original</u>.
New Haven Museum and Historical Society. Benedict Arnold Papers. MSS 106, Box 1, Folder O.

F. <u>Biography of Author</u>.
Very little is known about Samuel Barney's life. He was born in New Haven, Connecticut in 1753 and enlisted in Captain Caleb Trowbridge's company in May of 1775. On September 6, 1775, he enlisted in Captain Oliver Hanchett's company for the expedition to Quebec. He was in the attack on Quebec but was not taken prisoner because, according to his daughter's statement in her mother's pension application, he helped to carry the wounded Arnold from the field. Barney continued to serve in Hanchett's company until May 27, 1776, when he was discharged by Arnold at Montreal and returned home.

In the pension application submitted by Barney's widow in 1837, their daughter described his service in the march to Quebec. "He bore his part of the dreadful sufferings of that well remembered march through the woods and wilds of America with an undaunted heart, although being among those who were destitute of shoes. The snow for many a weary mile was stain'd with his blood..." In 1777, Barney attempted to get back wages and travel money that he argued he was owed. There is no evidence that he was successful in this effort.

Barney enlisted again in March of 1779 under Captain Thomas Trowbridge, who was planning to sail to the West Indies. On the fourth day out to sea, his ship was captured by the British and Barney, along with his fellow shipmates, was imprisoned on the infamous Jersey prison ship. While there, he contracted a serious fever and suffered for many weeks. He was exchanged in August of 1779 and he returned home "in a very debilitated state." According to his daughter's statement, his war experiences resulted in "almost unparalleled sufferings" that impaired a "constitution naturally strong".

Barney married Sarah Bassett on August 20, 1778 and they had two children. Their daughter described the suffering of her mother when the British army invaded New Haven in July of 1779 while her father was sick in New Jersey.

> She was in the eighth month of pregnancy with her first child, and fled on foot four miles to attain a place of safety. The British soon left the Town, and she return'd home, but was persuaded and assisted by her neighbors to go to Woodbridge as a place for greater security in her unprotected state. Her child was born four weeks from the date the British troops enter'd New Haven and Mr. Barney being exchanged returned in a very debilitated state in the latter part of August, and found his wife with a son three weeks old.

After the war, he built a house on Church Street in New Haven where he lived the rest of his life. Barney died on July 17, 1805 and is buried in the Grove Street Cemetery in New Haven. Barney's wife and son, Samuel, Jr., are also buried in the Grove Street Cemetery. His tombstone is now so weathered and deteriorated by the passage of time that it is almost impossible to read the dates on the stone. His wife, Sarah, collected a pension for his services in 1838 at the age of eighty based on a bill approved by the U.S. House of Representatives which also approved payments to go back to a starting date of March 4, 1831. Barney was one of those forgotten heroes of the Quebec expedition who never received appropriate recognition for their service.[101]

XXII. FRANCIS NICHOLS

A. <u>Description of Journal.</u>
Francis Nichols was a lieutenant and second in command of the William Hendricks company of riflemen. His journal covers the period when he was a prisoner in Quebec. Upon the death of Hendricks during the siege, Nichols became the company commander, although his position was short-lived because the British captured him and his company.

The Nichols journal is a ten-page document containing entries from December 31, 1775 through September 27, 1776. It is primarily an account of the captivity of Nichols and the other officers who were held in the Quebec Seminary. Nichols provides a good account of the period when the men were held hostage by the British and of the difficulties that the officers and men suffered while in confinement.

B. <u>Notes on Journal</u>.
Although it has appeared in two publications, Nichols' journal is probably the

least well-known expedition journal written by an officer. The confinement of Nichols was preceded by "his account of the unsuccessful assault on Quebec ... in which he was captured. This account was written on February 9, 1776, in the Seminary at Quebec" and is entered under the date of December 31, 1775. The journal then skips to March 10, 1776, when the first entry begins to record the period that Nichols was a prisoner in Quebec.

C. Publishing History.

1st Printing. *Diary of Lieutenant Francis Nichols, of Colonel William Thompson's Battalion of Pennsylvania Riflemen, January to September, 1776. The Pennsylvania Magazine of History and Biography,* Vol. XX, Philadelphia, Historical Society of Pennsylvania, 1896, pp. 504-514.

2nd Printing. *A Prisoner of War-Extracts from the Diary of Gen. Francis Nichols- Captured during Arnold's Expedition against Quebec. Proceedings of the Delaware County Historical Society,* Volume One, Chester, PA, 1902, pp. 26-29.

D. Period Covered.
December 31, 1775 through September 27, 1776.

E. Location of Original.
The original manuscript is in the Historical Society of Pennsylvania. The Nichols manuscript is in the same binding as the John Joseph Henry journal. It follows the Henry journal and includes a letter from Henry to Nichols containing thirteen queries about the expedition to help Henry in the preparation of his own journal.

F. Biography of Author.
Francis Nichols was born in Crieve Hill, Inniskillen, Ireland in 1737 and came to America in 1769. He became a successful businessman and by 1774 he owned considerable lands in Northumberland County, PA, although he probably did not reside there. In June of 1775, he became a second lieutenant in Captain William Hendricks' rifle company, which was formed with officers from Cumberland County, and he was with the Hendricks' company when it marched to Cambridge and participated in the expedition to Quebec.

He was an active participant in the assault on Quebec on the night of December 31, 1775. When his company commander was killed in the assault, according to some of the men in his company, Nichols took charge of the company and led them with "Ardour, Bravery & Resolution." Nichols was listed as captured but not wounded on a list of prisoners from the

Quebec attack. There is a story that when Nichols was captured he refused to give up his sword to several private soldiers. He finally gave it to a British officer with the promise that he would get it back when he was released. As his journal details, he ultimately did get the sword back upon his release.

Nichols was exchanged by the British on October 10, 1776, and when he returned, he was appointed as a Captain in the 9th Pennsylvania Regiment. At about that time, rumors and accusations began to appear regarding Nichol's behavior during the assault on Quebec. Nichols responded to these allegations by compiling a package of material that supported and confirmed his actions as being above reproach. The package included affidavits by Nichols and letters from some of the lieutenants and sergeants who served under him in the Hendricks Company.

Nichols was subsequently promoted to major of the 9th Regiment on February 7, 1777 and continued to serve in the 9th Regiment in the battles of Brandywine, Germantown and Monmouth. He resigned from the army on May 12, 1779 and returned to private life.

Nichols was among a group of officers and important civilians who were at the house of James Wilson on the night of October 4, 1779. At that time, Wilson's house was attacked by a mob of unhappy citizens who were encouraged by the radical patriots in charge of the Pennsylvania government. The mob blamed Wilson, among others, for betraying the revolutionary cause and threatened to kill him and burn down his house. Nichols helped to hold the mob at bay until help arrived.

In 1782, Nichols worked for his friend Robert Morris, who was then helping to finance the war effort by supplying the Continental troops, who were encamped in Morristown, New Jersey, with provisions. At some point after the war, perhaps with the assistance of Morris or Wilson, he was appointed as a Brigadier General in the Pennsylvania militia. This is confirmed in an 1809 letter to Nichols from John Joseph Henry, in which he is addressed as "Gen. Francis Nichols." Nichols was a dedicated Federalist and strong supporter of Washington. For his support, Nichols was appointed by the Washington administration as the first U.S. Marshall in the eastern district of Pennsylvania. He died in Pottstown, Pennsylvania on February 13, 1812.[102]

XXIII. ANONYMOUS JOURNAL

A. <u>Description of Journal</u>.
Prior to 1900, this journal was located in the Washington State Historical Society. The journal was "a little old, brown covered book" that was presented to the Historical Society by Chaplain Robert S. Stubbs, who was both Chaplain and Superintendent of the Seaman's Bethel, first in Portland, Oregon and later in Tacoma, Washington.[103] The Seaman's Bethel was a non-denominational Christian seafarers association located in various ports around the country. The Chaplain apparently obtained the journal from a Mrs. Collins of Collins Landing. Perhaps her husband or some other family member was a sailor and had been helped by Chaplain Stubbs, who died in Tacoma in 1925.

The journal was ultimately given to Rev. Stephen D. Peet, Ph.D., who was the founder, editor and manager of a journal called The American Antiquarian and Oriental Journal. Peet started this journal in 1878 and was its primary manager until he retired in 1910. The journal was "devoted to Early American History, Ethnology and Archaeology." The journal stated that its scope included "the Early History, Exploration, Discoveries and Settlement of the different portions of the Continent...The Native Races ...The Antiquities of America...Pre-historic Man." The magazine was published monthly, bi-monthly and quarterly over its history and each issue contained numerous scholarly articles on a wide variety of subjects, but with an emphasis on archaeology.

Peet was born in Ohio in 1831. He graduated from Beloit College in Wisconsin in 1851 and went on to get his Ph.D. from that same institution. He also attended Yale Divinity School and graduated from Andover Theological Seminary in 1854. Peet was a prolific writer, not only for his own magazine but also for many other scholarly journals. He was an important scholar of the late nineteenth century.

The journal was given to Rev. Peet by one of his associates, James Wickersham. Wickersham was born in Illinois in 1857, and at the age of twenty he studied law under Senator John M. Palmer of Springfield. In 1883, he and his wife moved to Tacoma in Washington Territory and he began the practice of law. He was elected as Probate Judge in Tacoma and began to take an interest in the mound builders in Illinois. He soon expanded his interests to other anthropological issues, as well as the history of the northwest. At some point, his interest in the field of the early American Indians led him to Rev. Peet and he began writing articles for Peet's journal. He later moved to Alaska and played a major role in the settlement of that country. His achievements in Alaska have been summed up as follows: "James Wickersham was a statesman, author, historian and scholar ... No other man has made as deep and varied imprints on Alaska's heritage, whether it be in politics, government, commerce, literature, history or philosophy."[104]

Wickersham had an affiliation with the Washington Historical Society as well as with Peet. On July 2, 1891, he was one of a group of people who met in Tacoma to form a state historical society. In October of that year, Wickersham was one of the twenty-two charter members of the Washington State Historical Society. He likely had access to the records and collections of the society after that and was probably the one who found the Arnold expedition journal in the historical society's collections and sent it to Peet to be published. It is unclear whether Wickersham or Peet transcribed the diary, but in either case the transcriber had significant credibility. Based on the description of the journal by Peet, it seems likely that he was the one who transcribed it.

Peet, in his role as editor of The American Antiquarian, describes the diary as follows:

> Eleven pages of this diary are in very small script with the details of the memorable journey from Boston to Quebec of 1,200 men of a Boston army contingent, and of the terrible march through the wilderness of the Kennebec River, Maine. The narrative shows that the author was a man of more than ordinary intelligence, who fully appreciated the importance and magnitude of the contest in which the American colonies were engaged, and he graphically describes the perils and privations endured by the small force sent by General Washington under Colonel Benedict Arnold to assist General Schuyler and Montgomery's forces ... in the attack upon Quebec.

B. Notes on Journal.
Regardless of its overall significance to the history of the Arnold expedition, the journal is clearly a credible source and its authenticity seems beyond reproach due to the personal qualities and background of the two men who were involved in the publication of this journal.

From the text of the journal, it is clear that the author was in Captain Jonas Hubbard's company. He was from Massachusetts because he says he was one of the men who harassed the British troops on their way back to Boston on April 19th. He says he was in the Battle of Bunker Hill and that for a time he was a member of Captain William Smith's company while in the encampment around Boston. He was also in the Battle of Saratoga. However, he does not provide either his name or his hometown.

C. Publishing History.
1st and only known Printing. *Diary of Arnold's March to Quebec by a Soldier of the American Revolution. The American Antiquarian and Oriental Journal.* Rev. Stephen D. Peet, Editor. Volume XXII, January-December, 1900, Chicago, 1900, pp. 224-228.

D. Period Covered.
Journal begins on September 13, 1775 and ends on January 9, 1776.

E. Location of Original.
When the journal was published in Peet's magazine in 1900, it had been in the Washington Historical Society through the involvement of Chaplain Stubbs. In January of 2009, this author asked the Washington Historical Society if they still had the journal or if they have any record of it being there. On January 13, 2009, a response was received saying that they "have been unable to verify that the diary in question was ever part of our collection. However, our early donation records are incomplete..."[105] It appears that the anonymous diary has disappeared and is no longer available in the files of the WHS.

F. Biography of Author.
No author has been identified.

CHAPTER TWO

CAPTAIN DURBEN'S JOURNAL

The Captain Durben journal first became known to this author through an online Americana exhibit by the Special Collections section of the University of Glasgow Library. The exhibit contained photos and information on books and manuscripts relating to America from the Library's collections. A photo of the first page of the journal and a description of the manuscript as a journal written by a Captain Durben was presented on page four of the Americana Exhibit. Since there was no person named Captain Durben on the expedition, it was either a mistaken identification and did not have any relationship to the expedition or it was an authentic, but previously unknown, manuscript journal of the Arnold expedition. In order to make that determination, a copy was obtained from the University of Glasgow Library for a closer examination. What was discovered when the manuscripts were examined is explained below.

DESCRIPTION OF DURBEN MANUSCRIPT JOURNAL

The Captain Durben manuscript journal was among a number of different manuscripts from the personal library of William Hunter that were bequeathed to the Library of the University of Glasgow upon Hunter's death in 1783. Some of the manuscripts were retained in London until 1807 for the use of his nephew, Dr. Matthew Baillie. The University Library's note for the Durben journal says: "The MS. does not seem to have been published. At the end are four appendixes, containing copies of relative documents. The Author seems to have been an obscure individual. No account of him has been obtained." The Durben manuscript is described as being in a bound volume. It is referenced as MS Hunter 608 which is part of MS Hunter 1-658, entitled "Manuscripts from the Library of William Hunter."

William Hunter, a Scottish anatomist, physician, coin collector and book collector, was born in South Lanarkshire in 1718. He pursued the occupation of physician and trained in London at St. George's Hospital and as a resident pupil under William Smellie. He subsequently became physician to Queen Charlotte and was elected as a Fellow of the Royal Society and as Professor of Anatomy to the Royal Academy. In 1770, he built a nice house in Glasgow which later became the home of the University of Glasgow's Hunterian Museum and Art Gallery. He died in 1783 at the age of 64 and was buried in London. An avid book collector, Hunter purchased many important collections, including those of Horace Walpole, Thomas Crofts and Anthony Askew. He was such an important player in the collecting world that his major competitor for book and manuscript purchases was the British Museum. Hunter is an extremely credible source for the provenance of this journal.

How the journal got from Durben to Hunter is explained in the notations to the journal that were written by Dr. Hunter and Dr. Robert Robertson. Hunter clarifies in one of the notations that the journal was given to him by a colleague, Mr. Robertson, who was a surgeon on H.M.S. Juno. Hunter's comments in his notations make it clear that Robertson trusted him.

It makes sense that Robertson, who was also a surgeon, would give this manuscript to a colleague, Dr. Hunter, who was well known for his book and manuscript collections. The document does not indicate when the transcription of the Durben journal was completed or by whom. However, based on the various notes written on the journal, it is likely that Robertson made the transcription himself. It is also apparent that Hunter's stamp of approval was based on his assumption that Robertson transcribed the document that he gave to Hunter.

The Durben manuscript contains not only the Durben journal but also four additional appendices. The appendices reveal that Robertson obtained not just one, but a total of three previously unknown journals of the Arnold expedition while he was in Quebec. The entire package is a treasure trove of documents relating to the Arnold expedition containing the following documents.

1. Appendix I contains a second journal of the Arnold expedition that in the transcription and editing by Robertson is shorter with fewer daily entries and less detail than the Durben journal. Robertson, however, explains this in a note to the second journal which is set forth below as an introduction to the first Appendix. This journal, because of its brevity and its scrubbing by Robertson, does not contain sufficient information to identify the author, his rank or his unit. This journal is printed below as it appears in the manuscript.

2. Appendix II contains a third journal of the Arnold expedition which is even shorter and less detailed than the second journal. Robertson indicates this was another journal in his possession that covered the same march from Cambridge to Quebec as did the two previous journals. Robertson's remarks about the journals apply to both the second and third journals. This journal is also printed below as it appears in the manuscript.

3. Appendix III contains two items. The first item is an order from General

Carleton, described as follows: "Deliver'd out in Public Orders, by Order of General Carleton at Quebec, August 4th 1776." The order relates to any letter or message from the "Rebels, Traitors in Arms against the King, Rioters, Disturbers of the Public Peace, Plunderers, Robers, Assassins, or Murderers," and forbids anyone to accept such letters or messages. The order further goes on to say, "All Prisoners from the rebellious Provinces who chose to return home are to hold themselves in readiness to embark at a short notice ... General Howe will regulate their place of landing." The letter is signed by E. Foy, Dep. Adj. Gen.

The second item is a copy of the parole that prisoners in Quebec were required to sign before being released. Robertson says that both the officers and the men signed two copies, but that he never saw a copy of any of the parole's signed by the men. The language of this parole, which was signed by an officer, is undoubtedly the same as the paroles signed by other prisoners who were released from Quebec in 1776.

4. Appendix IV (although not labeled as such) is a copy of an epitaph that was found on a piece of wood placed over a group burial of dead American soldiers on Isle aux Noix. A parody to the epitaph was added on August 10, 1776 at Quebec. The epitaph and the parody, while interesting, do not have any bearing on the expedition, and are not reproduced here.

Since the most important document in this package is the Durben journal, it will be the first document analyzed in detail. This journal is the most relevant discovery of an Arnold expedition journal since the 1940 publication by Kenneth Roberts of the so-called lost journal written by John Pierce, the expedition surveyor.

EXPLANATION OF IDENTITY OF AUTHOR AND AUTHENTICATION OF THE JOURNAL

A close examination of the Durben manuscript journal reveals, for the reasons explained below, that it is a copy of a journal written by Captain Henry Dearborn contemporaneously to the time the events occurred. He either wrote it as he went along on the expedition or during the four and a half months he was in prison in Quebec. In any event, it was written over a hundred years before the Massachusetts Historical Society published its version of Captain Dearborn's journal in 1886.

The name Durben at first caused some difficulty because there is no officer in the Arnold expedition by that name. However, if one looks at names that sound like Durben, it becomes clear that the author must be Henry Dearborn because Durben sounds a lot like Dearborn. It would be easy to see how the initial transcriber, Dr. Robert Robertson, would have identified it as a Durben journal because of the way the name Dearborn was pronounced by people in Quebec. He spelled it the way it sounded to him. It is apparent that neither Robertson nor Hunter attempted to determine the identity of the original author.

There is no other officer in the Arnold expedition with a name that sounds anything like Durben except for Dearborn. No other name begins with the letter D except for Dearborn. The name Durben does not fit any other officer.

In the journal entries, two officers are mentioned by name and both of them were officers in Captain Dearborn's company. The first is Joseph Thomas. In his daily entry for the 18th of September, the journal author says that Thomas was appointed as his Ensign. The author also refers in another daily entry to a Lieutenant Hutchins being in his company. Both were officers in Dearborn's company and both are listed in New Hampshire Troops in the Quebec Expedition, The State of New Hampshire. Rolls of Soldiers in the Revolutionary War, 1775, to May, 1777, Concord, N.H., 1885, page 215, entitled *Roll of Capt Henry Dearborns Company in Col Arnolds detachment for Canada ... Sept 1st 1775.*

The author of the journal states that he left Quebec with Major Meigs before the rest of the officers were released. The journal has entries for the days of May 17 and 18 that describe the journal's author leaving on a boat with Meigs. Therefore, the author had to be someone who went home early with Meigs.

Dr. Robertson attached the following note at the end of the journal describing why he ended the journal at that point and how the journal got into his hands. The last sentence in this note also asserts that the author and Meigs left Quebec together.

> The original was continued for a few days longer; but as it contained nothing material or entertaining I thought it needless to copy it further. By some accident or another, the Schooner that they sailed in was obliged to return to Quebec; and a person on board of her stole the originals from the author, & gave it to one of his own friends a shore, who was so obliging as to lend it to me to take a copy of it- at least this is the history which I got from that gentleman, of it. The two Major Meigs and Captain Durben sail'd afterwards on board of His Majesty's ship Niger to Halifax.

Based on the last sentence in Robertson's note, he was told that both Dearborn and Meigs went home together. If this fact is documented in any of the other expedition journals or from some other contemporary source, it would be enough evidence to be certain that Dearborn is the author of the Durben journal.

In Private James Melvin's journal, the entry on May 18, 1776 reads: "Pleasant weather; hear that Major Meigs and Captain Dearborn are gone home."[106] This is the first additional supporting confirmation that the two did go home together. The second expedition journal confirmation is an entry in Thayer's journal for May 17 which says: "A small Sloop came up. Major Meigs had liberty to walk the town until 4 o'clock. Mr. Laveris [Levius] came and informed Capt. Dearborn that he had obtained liberty for him to go home on his parole, & that he must get ready to go on board immediately. In the Evening they took their leave of us, & went on board the Magdalen." May 18. "About ten o'clock they set sail for Halifax."[107] Dearborn's MHS journal also references his going home with Meigs.

The Melvin and Thayer journal entries demonstrate that it was well known by the officers and men in prison that Meigs and Dearborn went home together before any of the other officers. As a result, this presents compelling supportive evidence that the author of this journal is Henry Dearborn. Dearborn's MHS journal also states that he went home with Meigs. Based on the above four points, there is little doubt that this is the original journal of Captain Henry Dearborn.

TIME OF WRITING OF DURBEN JOURNAL AND AUTHENTICITY

Dr. Robert Robertson transcribed the Durben journal between June 4, 1776 and the death of William Hunter in 1783. Robertson was the Surgeon on H.M.S. Juno, which was given formal orders to go to Quebec on March 26, 1776. The Juno did not reach Quebec until the 4th of June, which was after the attack and the subsequent imprisonment of the captured officers and men of Arnold's army. The Juno also arrived after the ship carrying Meigs and Dearborn had left Quebec. The journal had to have been completed before May 18th because that was the date Dearborn and Meigs left Quebec, and the journal was taken from Dearborn while he was still in Quebec. It could not have been transcribed prior to June 4th because the Juno and Robertson did not arrive in Quebec until that day.

The note from Robertson explaining how he came into possession of the journal describes how it got from Dearborn to him. Robertson acknowledges that it was stolen from Dearborn and subsequently given to him by a third party. Robertson's notes are crucial in terms of authenticating the journal. He had no reason to fabricate the story contained in his note. The third party who stole the journal probably did not give the journal to Robertson right after the Juno arrived. It is more likely that he kept it in his possession for a few weeks. The Juno remained in Quebec until September 1776, so the journal could have been given to Robertson at any point in time prior to the day it left.

The Naval Documents of the American Revolution contain various entries for the Juno from the time it left England until it was burned in Providence Harbor on August 7, 1778, in order to prevent its capture by American forces. The information in the Naval Documents provides a record of a ship that was in a number of different ports after it left Quebec in September of 1776. First it sailed to Nova Scotia and remained in the Nova Scotia area until December of 1776. It then went to New York for about a month and then to Newport, Rhode Island, until April of 1777. For two months it was in the West Indies and from June to September of 1777, it was in the Cape Cod area. As of September 4, 1777, it was back in the Rhode Island area, where it stayed until the following August. According to an entry in NDAR, Dr. Robertson was on board the Juno on August 13, 1777.

William Hunter, the subsequent recipient of the manuscript from Robertson, died on March 30, 1783, and from his signed notation, the journal was in his possession before he died. Sometime between 1778 and 1783, Robertson gave this journal, transcribed in his hand, to Hunter. It has never been published, nor has the author of the journal been identified until now. The provenance of the journal can be established sufficiently to say with certainty that it followed Dr. Robertson on his voyages with the Juno, and when he returned to Scotland, the journal went with him. It was subsequently given to Hunter and has remained in his manuscript collection since then.

In summary, the Durben journal dates back to 1775 and 1776 and was originally in Dearborn's handwriting. A copy of the journal was given to Robertson who subsequently transcribed and edited it and gave it to Hunter. The original manuscript journal in Dearborn's handwriting was not given to Hunter and as a result it has long since disappeared. At this point, we are left only with Robertson's transcription and not the original manuscript.

Since the original manuscript in Dearborn's writing is not available, there is no way to determine how much of the original handwritten manuscript that Dr. Robertson transcribed is Robertson and how much is Dearborn. Robertson indicates in his notes that he had to make substantial changes to a number of the entries. Transcribers have been known to take great liberties with the text that they transcribe. Based on Robertson's statements, it is fair to conclude that the Durben journal presented here is almost as much Robertson as it is Dearborn.

THE MHS DEARBORN JOURNAL

When comparing this original journal from the University of Glasgow Library with the Dearborn journal published by the MHS, it is apparent that many of the entries and the events that are covered are similar. However, the Glasgow journal is shorter with more succinct entries. The brevity and language of its entries indicates that it was written during a significant army field maneuver, while the longer MHS journal was written in a more descriptive style by someone who was not so pressed for time.

Robertson's comments about the writing style of the text of the journal are important in determining the time frame of the writing of that journal by Dearborn. Robertson is critical of the content of the written manuscript that he had been given and the sometimes incoherent language that was used. He admits he made some significant changes in order to make it more understandable to the reader. Those comments infer that this was a hastily written journal by someone who made basic entries about events as he went along his way on the expedition. The MHS journal on the other hand is a more comprehensive account clearly written with more thought and with no time constraints. The MHS journal presents a narrative that has more internal consistency and is much better written than the Durben journal. It was, however, written approximately thirty years after the events took place, while the Durben journal was written at the time the events occurred.

The manuscript journal, which is now in the Boston Public Library and was first published in the MHS Proceedings in 1886, is not in Henry Dearborn's handwriting. That fact is indicated in the MHS introduction to the Dearborn journal as well as in the introduction to the Dearborn journals published by the Caxton Club in 1939. Even though Dearborn himself did not write it, subsequent writers have concluded that MHS journal's authenticity is established because Dearborn made handwritten notations in that journal.

This conclusion that Dearborn himself wrote the notations is based on a footnote in the MHS publication. Judge Mellen Chamberlain, a member of the MHS and a well recognized rare book collector and authority on Revolutionary War signatures, wrote the footnote. Chamberlain states that the additions and corrections are "from his own hand." He also acknowledges that unlike the other Dearborn journals, this one is not in Dearborn's handwriting. He says the journal came to the Boston Public Library from the estate of John Wingate Thornton, who was the executor of the younger Dearborn's will. Thornton was a book collector and author as well as a lawyer, and his estate contained an extensive collection of early Americana.

The argument by Charles E. Banks, that the Meigs journal was used as the guide for the writing of the MHS Dearborn journal, is a credible point. Given the discovery of the Durben journal, it offers a convincing explanation as to how Dearborn was able to recreate his lost journal. Banks provides a reasonable rationale for Meigs as the source used by Dearborn to provide details that he could use in writing that journal. The Meigs journal was in print early and was used by Henry as a guide in the writing of his account. It would be an obvious choice for the author of the Dearborn journal to use as well. Banks is wrong, however, in his conclusion that the Meigs and Dearborn journals are identical. They have some similarities but are not identical.

At the time the MHS journal was written, other expedition journals were in existence and could have been used as a guide. Henry's journal was published in 1812 so it could have been used, as he used the Meigs journal. The Morison, Hendricks and Stocking journals had also been published by 1812. Although they had limited printings, one or more of them could have been used as well.

It is well accepted that the senior Dearborn wrote other journals of his Revolutionary War experiences, including an account of the Battle of Bunker Hill written in 1818. With so many Dearborn Revolutionary War journals in his handwriting, the missing Quebec journal is a glaring omission of his Revolutionary War experiences. Until now, it was thought that an original manuscript journal did not exist. Now, however, thanks to Robertson, we have that journal, or at least his sanitized transcription of it.

CAPTAIN HENRY DEARBORN'S ORIGINAL MANUSCRIPT JOURNAL OF THE EXPEDITION TO QUEBEC UNDER COLONEL BENEDICT ARNOLD IN 1775

JOURNAL OF THE REBEL EXPEDITION

Introductory Note from the Transcriber Found in Journal

An exact copy of A Journal of the Route, and Proceedings of 1100 Rebels, who marched from Cambridge, in Massachusetts Bay, under the Command of

Colonel Arnold, in the fall of the year 1775; to attack Quebec: But providentially failed in their Rebellious Attempt to subdue it, Although there were not 100 Regular Troops in the Garrison, So bravely was it defended by the Seaman, the Militia & those few Regulars. I mean particularly that Body of the Militia called the British.

The Sense and Meaning of the Original, which was kept by a Captain Durben, are strictly adhered to in this copy; but the Orthography, Syntax, & diction of it were so extremely deficient, and even barbarous, if I may be allowed the Exception, that it would have been highly ridiculous to have transcribed it verbatim.

Yet notwithstanding all the Pains I have taken to render it clear and intelligible, some Pages are still obscure, and perhaps indistinct. But I know of no method by which I could amend them, unless by Fiction; and that I would not adopt. However, in Order to elucidate those in some measure I have subjoined a few notes, that I flatter myself will not, at least be entirely useless.

As to the proper Names, or even the Names of Places, should I unfortunately have mis-spelled them at times, I am hopeful the Error is venial.

(Note in Different Handwriting by William Hunter)

This was given to me by Mr. Robertson Surgeon of his Majesty's Ship Juno-- who procured a genuine copy of the Journal at Quebec. He assured me that I might depend on its being faithfully transcribed; and I know that I can depend on anything he asserts.

William Hunter

THIS AUTHOR'S INTRODUCTORY COMMENTS ON THE JOURNAL

Because the transcriber was a Scottish surgeon, he spelled certain words with a distinctly British spelling, typically involving our instead of or, as for example colour. It is not likely that Dearborn himself used this spelling, but there is no way to confirm this because the original Dearborn manuscript was lost. Robertson also used the abbreviation of 'd instead of ed quite often and I have kept that in the journal.

When Robertson refers to the distance measure in rods, it is spelled roods. I have changed the punctuation in a number of places so that it is easier to read.

There are also a few words that are difficult to make out, although Robertson's transcription is very readable.

DEARBORN'S JOURNAL

On the 13th of September 1775, we marched from Cambridge to Mystick; on the 14th to Salem; on the 15th to Ipswich; and on the 16th to Newborough Port.

The 17th being Sabath we attended meeting.

On the 18th we embarked on board of ten vessels, and waited for a wind.

The 19th we sailed for the mouth of the Kennebek River.

Before noon of the 20th we got into that River.

21st. We sailed up as high as Gardiner's Town and met with good entertainment at Doctor Gardiner of Boston's seat.

22nd. We got up to where the Bateaux were built; from thence we carried thirty three men of each Company in the Bateaux up to Fort Western; That is about forty miles up from the mouth of the River; and at night all our men had mostly got up to the Fort.

23d. One of the men shot another.

24th. The criminal was taken up.

On the 25th he was tried by a Court Martial, was found guilty & received Sentence of death.

26th. The convict was carried to the place of Execution, and there reprieved by Colonel Arnold. General Washington's pleasure could not be known.

27th. At three after noon we embarked on board the Bateaux with forty five days provisions; got four miles up the river; and encamped ashore.

28th. We encamped after getting two miles up.

The 29th before noon we got up four miles- to Fort Halifax; and after staying there about half an hour we crossed the River to the Portage, ninety seven roods in length. When we had haled our Bateaux, and carried everything else over the Portage, we encamped on the Rivers side.

On the 30th we went six miles up the River; it was extremely rapid with many little falls in it.

31st. We got up three miles; there, Major Meigs had got a Bullock killed for us; of which we eat heartily; and carried whatever left along with us, three miles further up, & there encamped.

October 1st. We reached ten miles up the River- the land that we passed was in general good, with a number of Inhabitants upon it.

2d. Before noon we got up to Sowegan Falls, there we hauled our Bateaux up, calked them, [and] carried them over the Portage, that was forty roods long; then we reloaded the Bateaux, crossed the River, encamped on the other side of it. Our course so far up the River was generally from N. to NE.

3d. We got twelve miles up the River to Norrywok. There was few Inhabitants on the shore we passed by. Our first Division of Musket Men had marched from thence the preceeding day only. There, too, we found our three Companies of Riflemen; the former left Fort Western two days (earlier); and the latter on a Day before us. At Norrywok are the Ruins of an Indian Fort; an appearance of some old Intrenchments; a Friars Grave with a cross at one end of it; and a good deal of cleared ground.

4th. We haled up our Bateaux at the Portage, and dried them. On the 5th we calked them & paid them; & repaked our Pork and Bread.

6th We haled & carried everything over the Portage that was a mile across, launched & loaded the Bateaux. Then we went two miles up the River, and encamped a shore.

The 7th we proceeded eight miles up the River, and then encamped.

On the 8th we reached up to Caratunkas. The River runs down there between two very high rocks, that are not above forty feet or under. After getting everything across the Portage, of eighty seven roods, we went up the River four miles, and encamped.

9th. We advanced nine miles up the River; then we put ashore and encamped.

The 10th we proceeded six miles up and arrived at one afternoon at the great Portage whereupon there is water. The course of the River upwards from that was about NW between two mountains.

11th. We began to carry our things across to the first pond that was about four miles distant from the River.

12th. A party of my men were set about building of a Block House; the rest of them assisted to carry everything to the Pond, to which we encamped at night.

13th. It blowed so hard that we could not cross the Pond. There was plenty of fine trout in it.

The 14th we crossed the pond. It was about three quarters of a mile over. Then we carried our things about half a mile to a second Pond, & crossed it about a mile and a half over. Afterwards we carried our things about a mile & a half and encamped.

On the 15th we carried our things a mile & a quarter further before we reached a third Pond that was a very fine two miles wide. After crossing it we carried our things nine miles, and encamped.

16th. We had our things to drag & carry three miles further over a Spruce Heath that was knee deep of mire; after that we launched our Bateaux in the Dead River; got up about half a mile and then put ashore, and encamped. The Dead River is only a continuation of the Kennebek and there makes the large flexure that employed us six days in crossing in that great winding the River is almost on continued fall, and no where passable the Indians said. Where we encamped it was very deep & still; and most probably that occasioned its being called the Dead River. The land on the other side of it was, apparently, fine.

17th. We reached ten miles up the River. The land seemed to be very good & pleasant. Then we crossed a Portage about eight roods over, and encamped by the River.

On the 18th we got fifteen miles up. There was found our first Division of Musket Men employed in making cartridges. My company filled some powder; and Joseph Thomas was appointed my Ensign. Each company had half a quarter of fresh Beef given to them.

19th. Our Division put off in their Bateaux and went about five miles up the

River. There were three little falls in it; and in every other place the current was gentle. It rained all day.

[20th] We got thirteen miles as we supposed. Up the River there were several little falls in it & we had one short Portage of about thirteen roods to cross. At night we encamped. It rained all day.

21st. We proceeded up the River about three miles, when we came to a Portage thirty five roods long, and carried our things across it. After getting up the River about two miles, we came to another Portage of thirty roods that we crossed, and then encamped. It rained hard all day.

22nd. The River rose about eight feet in the night, overflowed its banks hurt our Baggage considerably; and retarded us much. We only got three miles up and crossed a Portage of seventy four roods in length.

23d. We proceeded about nine miles up the River. Most of our advanced Foot, through a mistake, went up a River that runs into the Dead River. As we supposed that they had made the mistake my Bateau was sent up the River after them; but before it had reached them, about four miles, they had found out their error, and were carrying their things over the land into the Dead River. When the Bateaux returned, we went on up the River until we joined those Foot at a Portage where we all encamped, and held a Council of War.

The 24th. In consequence of the Council, I was ordered to proceed forward with fifty men up the River, to the Chaudière: and the sick were sent back under the care of an Officer and a Surgeon. At night I and my men put ashore and encamped.

25th. We got six miles up only but we have three Portages in the way to cross; two of them were about four roods each in length, and the other was ninety. It was squally with snow.

26th. We crossed a Pond two miles wide, and soon after a Gutter about four roods. Then we came to and passed over a second Pond about a mile in width; and went over a Portage of about a mile & a half in length. After that we had a third Pond about three miles wide to cross, & we got over a small Portage. We had a fourth Pond to cross 3 mile wide, before we got into a narrow River that we went up about four miles when we came to a small Portage of fifteen roods long, & crossed it. We came then to another pond half a mile in width; and after crossing over that we encamped very much fatigued.

27ᵗʰ. We crossed over the Portage of one mile; we crossed a Pond about fifty roods in width. We got over another Portage of about forty four roods long. Then we came to a Pond two miles wide and crossed it. We were now on the Portage of the Chaudière, where we left our Bateaux and went on, each man carrying his own share of the Provision. When we had walked about a mile we encamped. I found a Bark canoe left there by the Indians, I imagined, which I took to be carried in, as I had been taken ill the preceeding night.

28ᵗʰ. We got over the Portage; in all it was about four miles & a quarter long; and reached the Pond of Chaudière. On the east side of the Pond a River runs into it that my People could not ford; they therefore waded the Pond to an Island, that before they thought had been the Continent. I joined them in my canoe, and took into it Capt Goodrich, who had near perished on that Island, after wading breast high to it, and breaking the ice before him as he waded. Before he did that he attempted in vain to wade the River already mentioned. When we had gone up along the Island a little way; in the canoe we came to a good Indian House with a fire in it. One of our advanced Party was there, who had been obliged to stay behind for want of Provisions to carry him on. I sent my canoe to find out Captain Goodrich's Bateau that was gone, he knew not where, with a Sergeant & a man that were sick, but it being dark night the Bateau could not be found. The Island was low & swampy. We were both very uneasy about our men.

On the 29ᵗʰ early in the morning we returned to our men & found them in better spirits than we expected. We had begun to carry them over in my canoe when Captain Smith's Bateau arrived; the rest of them were carried over in that. After we had walked about sixty roods, we unexpectedly came to another River that we got over with great difficulty. Then we went as far as the Indian House that I had lodged at the night before, and encamped. Although my men were extremely fatigued they had got in all about thirteen miles. I was yet very ill.

The 30ᵗʰ my men marched early in the morning. I went down the Pond in my canoe, and met them at the lower end of it. When we found out the mouth of the Chaudière that looked less wild than it really proved to be. We got down that River about eighteen miles, but in going down many of the Bateaux run aground; some of them overset; and others filled. None except Colonel Arnold's Bateau, and my own canoe, lived. One man was drowned and many of our things was lost.

31ˢᵗ. My Party marched down along the River about twenty miles; and I went down the River in my canoe. The River was shallow, rocky, and very rapid; and besides I had two short Portages to cross over. At night we encamped.

November 1st. My men marched down about thirty miles; and I went down the River in my canoe; as the bottom of it was all worn and cut through from the rapidity and rockiness of the River, I resolved on using it no more. At night we encamped.

2nd. As we were journeying down we met five oxen, and two horses that Colonel Arnold had sent to meet us by some Canadians. The cattle were a very agreeable sight to us; for we had very near been starved through want of Provisions for some time. After advancing about four miles further we came to a Portage of a mile long-- when I found a good canoe. The River has a great fall there. At the foot of the fall there were two Indians in a canoe with Provisions for us. I went with them down the River, and my own canoe followed us. About six miles below the fall we reached the first houses of the Inhabitants at three [in the] afternoon. It was very difficult to get down the River. At four o'clock Lieutenant Hutching, and Ensign Thomas with my men arrived where I was. Provisions had been got ready for us there by the Colonel- and we stayed all night.

3rd. My men went on & I hired an Indian to carry me down the River in his canoe, about four miles where Colonel Arnold was. A number of Indians gathered about us to be hired, and we engaged with twenty two of them for forty eight shillings a month. I stayed there all night by the Colonel's advice, as I was still very bad. The People were kind to me.

4th. It rained hard all night, and snowed all day. I did not move.

5th. It was clear and moderate weather. I hired a horse & rode four miles, and put up at a tavern. Two of our Men were sent back with Horses to meet me. One of these men was Canadian born in Quebec, who spoke good French & tolerable English; he enlisted with us at Fort Western on the Kennebek River.

I hired an Indian on the 6th to carry me down the River eight miles in his canoe to one Pere St. Joses where I took lodgings as I yet continued ill. But my men marched on with the rest to Point Levi.

On the 7th, they arrived at St. Mary's; and on the 8th they got to Point Levi.

9th. Nothing happened. The Canadians were very kind to our people.

On the 10th they took a Midshipman Prisoner; he belonged to the Hunter Sloop of War & was a brother of the Captains- his name's Mackenzie.

11th & 12th. Nothing particular happened.

13th. At nine o'clock of the preceeding night our men began to embark on board of thirty-five canoes; and at four of the morning they landed safely on the other side of the River St. Laurence-- at the place where General Wolfe landed his army in the year 1759, now called Wolfe's Cove from thence they Marched across the Heights of Abraham, & took possession of some Houses for their Quarters. The Colonel took up his quarters in Major Caldwell's house.

14th. At noon the enemy surprised and took prisoner one of our sentinels. The Colonel drew up the men; marched them close to the Garrison; and gave the enemy three Hazzas; Then he marched our People in a circular form, full in their view, whilst they fired a number of cannon shot at them from the Garrison-- without hurting one of them, after that he carried them back to their Quarters. A number of the Houses in the suburbs were burnt by the enemy. The Inhabitants with what effects they could preserve were forced to go into the Country for shelter.

Captain Ogden was sent with a flag of truce to demand the Town and Citadel in the name and behalf of the United Colonies; but they fired upon him and would not suffer him to approach the Citadel. In the evening our Men were informed by a Gentleman from Quebec that they might expect an attack that night, or the next day from the Garrison. It was reported too that about two hundred Canadians belonging to the suburbs declared if the troops that were in the Garrison continued to burn their Houses, that they would apply to Colonel Arnold either for assistance or directions what to do. Our men were ordered to ly (lie) under arms to prevent their being surprised. The weather was fine for the season.

15th. An express was sent to General Montgomery. Captain Ogden was again sent with a flag of truce to demand the Town & Garrison to be delivered up; but he only met with the same reception that he did the day before. At noon our Men were alarmed with a report that the enemy were coming to attack them; and they turned out to receive them; but the report proved to be false. The Canadians came in daily to pay their respects to Colonel Arnold, and to beg his protection.

16th. The Colonel received an address from the Inhabitants of Point au Tremble, and he had certain advice that Montreal had surrendered to General Montgomery; who it was said had likewise taken twelve vessels with a large quantity of provisions, clothing, and a number of Prisoners. A company of our men (were) sent to take possession of the nunnery.

17th. The Canadians were continually coming in to express their satisfaction to the Colonel for having come into Canada. After-noon a deserter from the Garrison surrendered himself a Prisoner to one of our advanced sentinels; but he (gave?) us no particular intelligence. A party of men were sent by the Colonel to Point Levi to bring over some of our people, and provisions that had arrived there.

On the 18th nothing material happened. The weather was fine for the season.

19th. Our men left their Quarters; and were marched to Point au Tremble, about seven or eight leagues from Quebec. The part of the Country that they had passed through was well peopled, and cultivated; and most of the Inhabitants were very kind to them. The weather continued good.

20th. Before noon our express arrived from General Montgomery, mentioning that General Carleton had abandoned Montreal; that our People were in possession of it; that they intended to attack the ships lying there with boats, and Row Galleys that carried guns; and that as soon as they were taken he would proceed to join our party with men, artillery etc.

21st. Our People took a soldier of Colonel Maclean's Regiment in Quebec, whom they thought was a spy, a prisoner.

The 22d, an express arrived from Montreal telling the Colonel that the enemies ships were taken on the preceeding Sabbath; and that General Montgomery was obliged to march to Quebec.

On the 23d, they were informed by another express that the General was on his way to join them; and that clothing was coming down for our Detachment.

24th. Four sail of vessels were seen coming up the River before-noon. Colonel Arnold sent an express to acquaint our Troops that were coming down from Montreal by water there-with.

25th. The Hunter Sloop, a large scow commanded by Capt. Napier; and an armed schooner came up the River, and anchored opposite to our quarters. A canowe [canoe] was sent up the River to apprise the Troops, coming down in vessels thereof; and an express was sent up by land to inform those of it, who were coming that way.

26th. Nothing singular occurr'd.

27th. The Colonel was inform'd that the Kings Troops had burned Major Caldwell's House, where he held his quarters whilst he was before Quebec. It was very cold.

111

28th. The Colonel went up to Jacquartiere to meet the ammunition that was on the way from Montreal.

The 29th Captain Morgan who had been sent down with a Party near Quebec sent up two prisoners whom he had taken.

30th. Capt Duggin arrived with fifteen barrels of powder, and other stores from Montreal. The King's ships fell down the River.

Decemr 1st. The General [Montgomery] arrived at one afternoon with three armed schooners having troops, artillery, ammunition, provisions & clothing on board. The stores & clothing were given in charge to General Greg(?) for our Detachment. The Detachment was marched to General Montgomery's quarters; he expressed great satisfaction in receiving them & said that they were fine stout and likely fellows.

2d. The small field pieces were ordered to be carried down near to Quebec on sleds & the large cannon on Bateaux. As soon as the cannon were landed, the Bateaux were ordered to go to Point Levi to bring over scaling ladders that were made there.

3d. Our men drew their clothing; each man had a full suit allowed him as a present from the Continental Congress for the extraordinary fatigue they had underwent. The weather was rather cold.

On the 4th, they were ordered to march to St. Foy, a village near six miles distance from Quebec, to canton. They marched accordingly to St Augustine and were elegantly entertained there by the Curate of the parish, who at the same time possessed great regard for them, as well as for the glorious cause wherein they were engaged.

5th. At noon they arrived at St Foy. My company was ordered into the nunnery. It was called the General Hospital too, and was about a mile from the Palace Gate of Quebec.

6th. It was squally & cold.

7th. I had been very ill and was extremely reduced at Pere St. Joses from the 6th of November, & could not join my company until this day. A party of our men took a Sloop with a great quantity of provisions, and Three Hundred Eighty Two Dollars of specie on board.

8th. The enemies Sentinels fired from the Ramparts upon ours. It was fine weather.

9th. We began at night to bombard the Citadel- twenty seven shells were thrown into it; and we began to raise a Battery about half a mile from St Johns Gate.

10th. The enemy continued a brisk fire all day on our quarters. A party of our Train of Artillery were sent into St Rocks-- almost under the walls of the Garrison, with five mortars, and two field pieces, covered by eighty men.

11th. Forty two shells were thrown into the City in the night. The enemy returns a few, and some short that did no other damage than killing an old Canadian woman; & they burnt a number of houses in St Johns. A party of our men were employed all night on the Battery. One of our men lost his way in a snow storm, and found himself under the walls of the Citadel, where he was fired at often, and received only one wound in his thigh, with which he got off; & it was not mortal. The weather was sharp squalls with snow & sleet.

12th. We threw forty five shells again in the night. Our Battery was near finished, & the platforms were preparing for it. The enemy endeavored though unsuccessfully to annoy our People at work with shot and shells.

13th. Two of our men were apparently wounded in their legs by the enemies shot; the bones were so shattered that it was feared it would be necessary to amputate them.

14th. Five of our Canadians were wounded by another shot that penetrated through our Battery.

15th. We threw twenty four shells; and the enemy kept up a brisk cannonading that did us very little hurt. Our Battery was informed it was to mount six guns, five & twelve pounders, and a twelve inch mortar. After being briskly served for two hours, they ceased firing by the General's order. A flag of truce was sent (to) General Carleton, but he would not admit it within the Garrison. The gentleman who carried it had some conversation with the King's troops on the ramparts. Afternoon our Battery began again to play on the town. The enemy kept up a brisk fire, though they did not serve our pieces as well as ours were served, as they themselves acknowledged. My company was ordered across Charles's River to the Beau Port side, because the nunnery was now wanted to make a hospital for the sick. I was quartered at one McHenry's, a Presbetarian pastor of Quebec. Two men were killed at our Battery; one gun destroyed & a small mortar dismounted by the enemy's shot. It was now in agitation to storm the lower town.

16th. The enemy cannonaded Colonel Arnold's quarters; he therefore quitted, & took others. We had a man killed by the enemies grape shot. In the afternoon a Council of War was summoned to confer about storming the town. The majority of the Council was for storming it as soon as they could prepare properly for it, with _____ hawl's, spears, etc.

17th. There was a severe snow storm.

18th. We heard Colonel Conlon was coming from Montreal to join our army.

19th. It snowed.

20th. Was very cold. The men drew what muskets they wanted; & were employed in making spears, etc. The smallpox began to break out amongst the men.

21st. We had orders to cause our men to distinguish themselves by wearing a sprig of hemlock in their caps.

22d. The spears & ladders were ready, and everything repined a pace for the important purpose of storming the Town. "The blessings of Heaven attend the enterprise".

The 23d. The officers of our Brigade met afternoon about the subject of the storm. The General frequently visited the men, and said many encouraging things to them, relating to the storm.

24th. The Reverend Mr. Spring our Chaplain preached a sermon in the chapel of the nunnery; it was an elegant little chapel, richly adorned, and had a complete rigged small ship hanging upon it.

25th. Our Brigade was ordered to meet, and parade at Captain Morgan's quarters. The General attended there, & made a very sensible & spirited speech to them upon the subject of the approaching storm.

26th. A return was made of the men in Colonel Arnold's Detachment who were willing to storm the town; there were only three in my company consisting of sixty three, who dissented from it.

27th. Afternoon all the troops assembled at the place of rendezvous in very high spirits, and were ready to march to the attack, when an order came from the General to send them back to their quarters- because he thought the night too clear and calm for the attack-- though the day had been windy with snow.

28th. The General ordered it to be published "that he had the most sensible pleasure in seeing the laudable disposition with which the troops had moved the preceeding night for the attack. That it was with utmost reluctancy he was obliged to suppress their ardour, on account of the clearness of the night; but he must have deem'd himself as in great measure culpable for having been the cause of losing many of those brave men had he led them on to the attack-- whose lives he doubted not would be preserved by only waiting for a more favorable opportunity." He desired that all orders might be made known to the Troops at the calling of the roll; and he hoped that no soldier who was zealous for the success of that Enterprise would absent himself from his quarters at night, as he might perhaps be wanted at a minutes warning.

29th. I had the main guard at St Rocks. A Subaltern & fifteen men went in the afternoon by command of Colonel Arnold to a large distillery near Palace Gate, & brought away the overseer a prisoner, & carried him to Head Quarters. One man was shot through the leg from the Garrison walls. The enemy knocked down one of our guard house chimneys with their shot. We threw thirty shells into the Citadel in fifteen minutes; the enemy returned only a few but they kept up a very heaving cannonading on us.

30th was very windy with snow. When I was ordered off the guard I had orders to be upon the parade at four o'clock the next morning, and all the men were ordered to be there under arms at two o'clock.

31st. The Sergeant Major having neglected to call me in proper time; and Charles's River being very difficult to pass across from the highness of the tide, & badness of the weather; the attack was begun before I could leave my quarters. I was therefore obliged to fall in, in the rear with my company when I got over the River, instead of being the second company in the front, the post that was assigned me in the attack.

The ATTACK was regulated in the following manner. The General at the head of three Battalions of the New York troops was to march around by Cape Diamond, and to force his way into the Lower Town, by the Pres de Ville.

Colonel Arnold was to go round through St. Rocks; to pass Palace Gate, and to force his way with his own Brigade through the different barriers into the Lower Town, by the Sault du Matelot. In that manner, the General and the Colonel were to push on through the Lower Town with their different corps until they met.

Colonel Livingston in the meantime with a Detachment chiefly consisting of Canadians, was to make a feint about St. John's Gate; and unless they could burst it open, they were to set fire to it, and burn it with combustibles that were prepared for that purpose.

All of them were to march from their respective places of rendezvous exactly at five in the morning. Accordingly the General advanced at the head of his men to the picquets; some of them were cut by the artificers in a moment, and pulled down, the General himself assisting. He then immediately entered through the opening with his Aide de Camp, Captain Cheeseman, the Engineer and a few of his men, calling out repeatedly, but in vain, to the rest of his Troops to follow him. Whilst he was advancing with that small party, the enemy fired a volley of grape shot, & small arms that unhappily cut him off (killed him) together with his Aide de Camp, Captain Cheeseman, the Engineer and some others.

The light in the guard room was by some means knocked out at this time, and there was nothing then to have prevented the Generals Troops from entering. as we afterwards heard that the enemies guard quit their post & ran off. However Colonel Campbell instead of entering with the Troops, ordered a retreat, and carried off our wounded men to their quarters.

Colonel Arnold on the other side sent a Lieutenant & thirty men to march in front as his advance guard. He ordered the Company of Artillery, with a Brass six pounder on a sled, to march out; and the main body to follow them. The advanced party had directions to open to the right & left, as soon as they came up to a two gun Battery on a wharf where the enemy had a guard, whilst the Artillery fired a few shot at the Battery; and then to rush on with scaling ladders to mount and force the Battery. At the same time it was directed, that Captain Morgan should march round the wharf upon the ice, if it was possible, with a part of the main body, and thereby surround the enemy.

But the snow being deep; and the road, naturally, extremely bad, the Artillery could only advance very slowly. So slowly did they advance indeed, that they were obliged to leave the gun behind at last on the way. To increase the delay, the main body from the darkness of the morning; from a very heavy snow storm beating in their faces; and from the intricacy of the way were led wrong, besides they were harassed with a continual fire from the walls of the Garrison that killed, and wounded many of them.

As it proved impossible for the Artillery to get the gun along, the advanced party were ordered to attack the Battery. Some of them fired in through the port holes, while others with ladders scaled the Barricade, and took all the enemies guard prisoners consisting of thirty men. The attack was made with so much activity that the enemy had barely time to fire two guns before they were made prisoners. Not more than two or three men were lost on either side.

When the prisoners were secured our men immediately advanced to the second Barrier and attempted to force their way through it. But the main body not having got up in time for the reasons already mentioned; and the General's Troops unfortunately, having retreated, the enemy was allowed to turn their sole attention to the Sault au Matelot. So that they who attacked the second Barrier were in a moment surrounded, almost, with a fire from treble their number of the enemy posted behind the Barrier, and in the adjoining houses; and were failed in their attempts.

Unfortunately, I was far behind in the rear with my men, as I before observed; and still more unfortunately for me as I was marching past Palace Gate to join our main body we lost our way from the same cause, that they had lost theirs: and at the same time that a brisk fire was kept up upon us from the ramparts, about two hundred of the enemy sallied out of the Garrison; part of whom took post in the adjacent houses, and galled us with their fire, whilst the rest surrounded us. To add to our misery, our muskets were so wet with snow that not one of them would fire. Their distressfully circumstances we surrendered ourselves prisoners, upon being promised good quarters. We were immediately disarmed, & marched into the Garrison. When we entered Palace Gate we heard that our men had got possession of the Lower Town;

[Note: Typical of this journal the first word on the next page is shown at the bottom of the current page. On this page, the next word is "That." Unfortunately, there is no next page beginning with "That." It appears that a page is missing from the journal.]

[Now the journal continues]

me and liberty too very heartily, he began to fire very briskly upon us. "I felt vexed at his reply, and tried often very hard to give him his due, but could not get my piece to go off".

January 1st 1776. General Montgomery's body was taken up & brought into the Garrison; he was of good stature, rather slender, yet well limbed; of a graceful, though a manly port; with an easy and polite address. He was both esteemed and loved by the whole army-- who placed in him their entire confidence. His death though honourable, was greatly lamented-- for in him we lost not only an amiable and worthy friend; but a brave and experienced General. Our country suffer'd greatly by that stroke. All our officers, who were not wounded, were put into a large building called the Seminary, wherein we had good accommodations; and plenty of beds and blankets were sent us by the towns people. Those who were wounded were sent to the Hospital.

2d. The Governour gave Major Meigs liberty to go out of the Garrison to our quarters for his own and our baggage. Sixteen of us who had (not) had the small pox agreed to be inoculated. Mr. Bullen, Surgeon of Lizard, was recommended to us as a very skillful physician, and one who was very well acquainted with inoculation. We began to take preparatory medicines from him.

On the 3d we were inoculated. The Governor made us a present of a hogshead of porter.

The 4th, General Montgomery's body was very decently interr'd. We were allowed to send for four of our men to attend us.

5th. We who had been inoculated were, for the benefit of air, moved into another room. Cooking utensils and fresh meat for soup were sent into us from the Inhabitants. Major Meigs returned with our baggage.

6th. We were visited every day by a Field Officer.

7th. Nothing occurr'd.

8th. The Bishop sent us two hogsheads of port wine, six loaves of sugar, and several pounds of tea in a present, for which we sent him a letter of thanks-- at the same time begged leave to return him the tea, as the majority thought that it would have been imprudent for us to have drank it.

9th. There was a heavy snow, with the wind, from the NE.

10th. We began to prepare a petition to send to the Governor to exchange prisoners; we had no opportunity of writing or sending to our friends. The storm continued.

11th & 12th. The small pox began to appear on us; They who had them in the natural way amongst our people were extremely ill.

13th. My fever abated much. Nothing material happen'd.

14th. Mr. Levius formerly a judge of our court in New Hampshire, came to see me, and made me a very kind offer of his service. I rejoiced to find that contrary to my expectation, I had a friend in the Garrison. Captain Hubbard died of his wound.

15th & 16th. Nothing remarkable occurr'd.

17th. We sent our petition to the Governor by Major Cox the Field Officer of the Day.

18th, 19th, 20th, 21st, 22d and 23d, nothing singular happened.

24th. We were all recovered of our inoculation; I wrote to Mr. Levius for some shirts.

25th. One of our men died of the small pox-- he had them the natural way. I rec'd two shirts and some money from Mr. Levius.

26th. Our people without the Garrison, for some past nights had burnt houses, woods & vessels at St. Rocks. One of the vessels was loaded with fish belonging to the Town.

27th. A party was sent out of the Garrison to St. Rocks for wood, that was soon obliged to return by reason of our men lying in ambush and firing upon it.

28th. Colonel Hamilton sent us a fine quarter of venison in a present.

The 29th was extremely cold.

30th was more moderate. Two of our officers had very bad inflammations in their arms; and another of them was taken ill.

31st. Our people continued to burn St Rocks.

Feb 1st, 2d, 3d, 4th & 5th. Nothing remarkable occurred. The weather was variable. 6th. We were ordered by the Governor to deliver up all of our pens and ink to the Officer of the Guard.

16th. For want of pen and ink I could not keep my journal the nine preceeding days. However nothing material happened unless what follows. I already took notice that we who had been inoculated were indulged with another room for the benefit of air, and the rest of our officers were likewise permitted to visit us; but after the 6th we were not allowed to see them.

On the 14th at nine o'clock at night Colonel MacLean, Major Caldwell, and the other officers of the Guard came into our room and made us remove immediately into the room amongst the rest of our officers. Colonel MacLean said he had particular reasons for removing us so suddenly that we should be acquainted with the next day.

Accordingly on the morning of the 15th he came and told us that one of us had been conversing with one of the Sentinels. Upon an enquiry amongst ourselves we found that Lieutenant Hutchins, one day as he went to the Necessary House, overheard one of the Sentinels say that there were five hundred Yankees at Point Levi; and that he replied, very imprudently, there would be five thousand of them soon.

On the 16th being very unwell I was carried to the Hospital. All our wounded officers were in one room. I heard that our men were falling down with small pox daily in the Prison.

17th. The weather was clear and warm for the season. There was thirty Nuns in the Hospital that attended the sick very carefully; and we were visited daily by Mr. Mabane Surgeon of the Garrison, and his assistants.

18th. I had part of a tooth pulled out that was broke by a pick axe on Winter Hill.

19th. I saw one of my men. He was the first that I had seen of them-- from the time I was taken prisoner. He told me that the rest of my men had had the small pox in the prison and recovered; the poor fellow was without a shirt, which shocked me; I therefore gave him one of the few I had.

20th & 21st. We heard that our People were erecting a Battery at Point Levi. We were accused of talking to the Sentinel. A lamp was ordered to be kept therefore constantly in our room; a pane of glass was fixed in our door, and that was locked, and two Sentinels were placed on the outside of it. The weather was variable.

22d. The Garrison fired a number of guns to annex our men at Point Levi, it was said.

23d, 24th and 25th. Nothing happened. My men wrote to me to beg a little money of me. I sent them ten dollars.

26th. We had leave again to walk in the passage. We esteemed it an indulgence. The officer of the Guard inform'd us that Montreal was retaken by the Canadians;

and a Priest told us that the Congress had sent notice to the Commander of our Troops before Quebec, that they could send no more Troops to Canada; and therefore, unless he got possession of the Garrison before the 15th of March, that they had ordered him to retreat to Montreal. The Field Officer of the Day also told us that General Amherst was arrived with 10,000 Troops at New York, and that there was as many more at Halifax waiting only for the Rivers breaking up, to come to Quebec. We likewise heard that Sir John Johnson was at the head of a large body of Scots and savages, against whom General Schyler had march'd with what Troops were destined for Quebec; but that more Troops were coming to Quebec.

27th & 28th. Nothing material happened.

29th. The Field Officer of the Day inform'd us that two hundred & fifty sleds had been sent from Montreal across the lakes to bring over some of our Troops; and that there were none to bring, but one hundred that they got at Ticonderoga.

March 1st. We were no longer permitted to walk in the passage. A strong partition was made in it with a door, and a pane of glass in that; and the Sentinels were placed without this door to prevent our talking to them: Two Sentinels were likewise placed under our windows, to prevent our getting out at them, & making our escape, we imagined, though we were in the fourth story.

2d, 3d and 4th. Nothing happen'd.

5th. A Canadian came into the Garrison we heard, who said he had been taken prisoner at St Johns and set at liberty after having been carried into New York. He afterwards told us that our Troops at Cambridge had made an attempt to storm Boston, but were repulsed with the loss of 4,000 men who were partly killed & partly drowned by falling through the ice. It was said that General Lee had march'd towards New York with 3,000 men, but that before he reached it he had lost all of them by desertion for want of clothing except about 300. The Field Officer of the Day informed us that General Carleton had a copy of a letter from General Washington's to Colonel Arnold, wherein he told him that he could send him no more men to his assistance, because he could scarcely keep any of his men from deserting at Cambridge for want of clothing. We also heard that 200 men had marched near to Montreal, on their way to Quebec, but that by differing amongst themselves they had killed ten or twelve of each other, and had returned home again.

6th, 7th, 8th, & 9th. We heard of nothing material.

10th. We learned from the Field Officer of the Day that all our People were about to decamp, and to march to Montreal.

11th & 12th. Nothing remarkable came to our knowledge.

13th, 14th, 15th, 16th, 17th, 18th, 19th, 20th, 21st and 22d. We had nothing singular happen'd.

23d, 24th, 25th & 26th. The weather was very cold.

27th. A house wherein our People kept a guard on the Beau Port side was burnt by a shell thrown from the Garrison. Mr. Mabane inform'd Major Meigs, that our officers would soon be removed from the Hospital to the Seminary.

28th, 29th and 30th. Nothing occurred.

31st. We were all removed to the Seminary. There wood being scarce.

April 1. We were inform'd by Major Caldwell, the Field Officer of the Day that our men had been detected in executing a plan for escaping out of prison, and were therefore all put in irons. I was sorry to hear of their situation.

2d. Our People opened a Battery at Point Levi of four guns. Four of their shot fell into the Seminary garden; a heavy fire of shot & shells was kept up from the Garrison upon it.

On the 3d there was cannonading on both sides.

4th. Several shot were thrown from our Battery at Point Levi through the Seminary. We were granted two more small rooms to lodge in.

5th, 6th, 7th, 8th and 9th. A cannonading was kept up by both the enemy & our People.

10th. We were told by the Officer of the Day that Colonel Arnold was gone up to Montreal; and that General Lee was dying with the gout in his stomach. When he was taken ill, he was on his way to Quebec. There was a firing on both sides.

11th and 12th. The weather was mild; and the cannonading continued.

13th. The Garrison kept up a heavy fire on our People. We were informed by the

Officer of the Guard after we were in bed that in case our People without should make an attack on the Garrison, we were not upon any pretence to open our windows, for if we did, the Sentinels had orders to fire in upon us; or if we even opened our windows in the night.

14th & 15th. A smart fire was kept up on both sides; the weather was mild and the Priests began to work in the garden.

16th. The trace of earth began to appear through the snow; and the Rivers to break up. There was but little firing.

17th. The weather was moderate; we were serv'd fresh beef four days in the week.

18th. There was a constant fire either of shot or shells from the Garrison chiefly on our Peoples Battery at Point Levi.

19th. The weather was warm; but the River was yet full of loose ice.

20th. The usual cannonading was kept up.

21st. We heard that two of our men who had deserted, and came into the Garrison the preceeding night, said that 300 of our New York Troops had laid down their arms; but that after many entreaties they had been prevailed upon to take them up again.

22d. Our People opened a two gun Battery on the Beau Port side, and fired briskly from it, as well as from the one at Point Levi, for some time. The Garrison kept up a very heavy fire upon them both. There was a storm of rain sleet and snow with the wind at NE.

23d. We were inform'd by Major Cox the Field Officer of the Day that two men arrived the preceeding night from Montreal who said that Colonel Arnold had gone across the lakes with his baggage. A heavy fire particularly from the Garrison was kept up. The River began to clear of ice.

24th. We heard that our People had open'd a two gun Battery on the Heights of Abraham. The firing continued & the weather was pleasant.

25th. We expected to be sent away soon in a vessel as we began to despair of being retaken. The cannonading was continuous on both sides, but was constant from the Garrison.

26th. We were told that our New York Troops had gone home, that they fired upon our own magazine as they went off; and that what remained of Colonel Arnold's Detachment had likewise gone home. There was a very heavy fire kept on both sides; and many shells were thrown from the Garrison. We were told by Major Caldwell that the King's Troops had left Boston, & gone to the southward; that 40,000 Troops were to be sent to America in the summer; that the negroes to the southward were all to be declar'd free by His Majesty's command; and that we might depend on seeing a large number of our People that invested the Garrison drove (?) in to keep us company within three weeks.

28th. Captain Thayer, one of our officers, was detected in attempting to open a door that led up to the garret of the Seminary by the Officer of the Guard; and was immediately sent on board a vessel where he was put in irons. The weather was pleasant and there was but little firing.

29th. The Sentinels fired upon us for standing at our windows after it was dark.

30th. Colonel MacLean, Major Caldwell, Major Mackenzie, Captain McDougal, Mr. Lanwear the General's Aid de Camp, and the Officer of the Guard with a soldier came into our room, and took away Captain Lockwood, and Captain Hanchet without assigning any reason-- nay they scarcely spoke. Soon after Major Caldwell returned again, and inform'd us we were not on any account whatever to leave our apartments after the sun set. The weather was foggy with rain.

May 1st. The Officer of the Guard brought some joiners to fix a strong bolt and a lock on our door. Major MacKenzie the Field Officer of the Day informed us that Captain Lockwood and Captain Hanchet had given money, rum, bread and cheese as a bribe to the soldier, whom the other officers and he brought in with them the night before when they took those two gentlemen out, while he was a Sentinel; that he would be shot for having received the things from them; & that they were both put in irons on board of a vessel for having given them to him. The weather was cold & the snow was not yet off the ground. Nothing singular happen'd.

3d. As I went to bed about ten o'clock, I heard one of the Sentinels hail a ship repeatedly but no answer was made. Soon after some person and a ship was arrived, and immediately there was a confused noise, yet I could hear the word, fire, given. I then got up & in a few minutes I discovered a fire that appear'd to be in the Lower Town. The bells began to ring, and I thought I heard a brisk fire of small arms. We concluded then that our People had made a real attack on the Garrison. That imagination of our people being so brave fill'd us with the most joyful satisfaction. At the same time we were apprehensive that it should miscarry as our former one did. Thus between joy and fear we were so agitated that we were in universal tremours; but we soon found that we had only deceived ourselves with false hopes by observing that the fire we thought had been in Lower Town to be only a vessel on fire, and falling down the River with tide. The bells then ceased ringing and all was soon quiet. Nothing material occurred through the day.

4th. The Officer of the Guard told us that the vessel we had seen burning the night before was a Fire Ship that our People had sent up from the Island of Orleans with an intention to burn the ships that lay in the Cul-de-Sac of the Lower Town; but without succeeding. We were not permitted to speak from our windows to any person. There was cannonading on both sides. The firing continued on the [5th].

5th. About the sun's rising, to our very great mortification we saw a ship coming up the River; and soon after two more came up. They were all ships of war; the largest was a fifty, the next had sixteen, and the last fourteen guns. At noon Captains Lockwood, Hanchet, and Thayer were brought back to the Seminary. Those gentlemen inform'd us that some of the ships had gone up the River to take some of our ships that were lying at Point au Tremble. We learned that 130 men had landed from the Kings ships, and had gone out with the Troops of the Garrison to attack our People; and we could hear some firing towards the Plains.

7th. Our People decamped with great precipitation from before Quebec at the appearance of Men of War we were told; and that they left behind them most of their cannon, some powder, some baggage, and all their sick; which had filled the people in the Garrison with great spirits.

8th. Two ships came up. We were informed that 55,000 men were coming out to America; 15,000 of whom were to come to Canada. Some of the officers of the Men of War, and of the land officers who came in them were _____ us, amongst whom was Major Carleton the Governor's brother. Lieutenant McDougal a commander of one of our schooners who had been taken the previous day at Point au Tremble was brought into the Seminary; there was a considerable quantity of powder on board the schooner, he said; and he told us that our Troops had passed through Point au Tremble before he left it; and added that he expected they would make a stand little above that, where they had two Batterys to prevent ships from getting up the River. We learned too that General Thomas with 300 men had joined General Wooster the day he marched off. It was said that our Men had left fifty of their dead in a house near the town unburied; & that they had been lying in it a long time. The Canadians began to come into the town from the country.

9th. We again heard that the King's Troops had left Boston, and were gone to Halifax. There was thunder with light showers.

10th. We were told that Major Meigs was to be permitted to go home on his parole. We had leave to walk in the passage; and were told that we should have more liberty soon. Three ships arrived with Troops, the 47th Regiment from Halifax.

11th. I wrote to Mr. Livius to intercede for me to get home on parole, along with Major Meigs. He assured me for answer that he would endeavour to obtain it for me, & would supply me with what money I might want.

12th. To our great satisfaction we were permitted to walk in the garden. I received forty dollars from Mr. Levius; but he told me he was afraid that he would not be able to obtain leave for me to go home on my parole.

13th. We walked all day in the garden; and we were informed that the colonies had declared themselves independent, and that no exchange of prisoners would be made until the war ended. A ship came up.

14th. A ship sailed for Halifax.

15th. A ship came up the River. Major Meigs was told by the Governour, who sent for him, that he was to go home in a day or two on his parole. We were all busy writing letters to be sent by him.

16th. Nothing happened.

17th. A ship arriv'd. Mr. Levius came to me before noon and informed me that he had at last with much difficulty obtained leave for me to go home on my parole with Major Meigs, & that we were both to embark that same afternoon. Accordingly the Town Major came for him and me after dinner, and carried us to the Governour. We signed our parole, and were then embarked on board of a schooner; and we had been but a short time on board when an invitation came from the officers & the Commodore for us to go on board and spend the evening with them. We went & were extremely well treated by them; and we slept on board of her all night.

18th. We went ashore to breakfast: at nine o'clock in the morning we returned on board of the schooner; and immediately sailed down the River.

JOURNAL #2: INCLUDED AS APPENDIX I TO DURBEN'S JOURNAL

Transcriber's Introductory Note to Journal

I think it proper to add the two following short journals as Appendix to the proceeding one because the obstacles and hardships which the Rebels met with & underwent between Cambridge & Quebec are more fully expressed in those than in it. Had there been a possibility of so doing, I would have united them with Durben's, but by their marching in different Parties they were seldom at any place in the same day. Repetitions of those occurances which are involved in the preceeding journal are carefully avoided; and it required much pains to amend the language of those, as it did to amend Durben's.

ANONYMOUS JOURNAL

On the 19th of September three Companies of Riflemen & eleven of Musket Men embarked & sailed on board of eleven Transports to Kennebek River.

22d. We found two hundred & twenty light Batteaux ready for us; and got thirty miles up the River.

23d. As the Transports could go no further up, we put all our provision etc in the Batteaux & rowed up to Fort Western.

24th. We went up the River a mile and a half and encamped. Sixteen batteaux were allotted to every Company.

25th. We rowed seven miles up to Halfway Brook & encamped.

26th. We reached Fort Halifax, & encamped on the side of Sabasticook River; it was a rainy day.

27th. We got our Batteaux over the portage about three hundred yards-- at the Falls of Taconmick; & after rowing up four miles & a half further we encamped.

28th. At night we encamped after getting twelve miles up; in several places there was such a rippling & strong currents of the River that we were obliged to set the Batteaux up with poles.

29th. We found the River shallow & rapid in many parts; and our men by wading to track the boats, & by setting them up were much fatigued & dejected. They had everything to carry across the Portage at the Falls of Shupigan [Skowhegan], about 200 yards, and after all we advanced three miles only.

30th. The Batteaux were again track in many places, & we got up about ten miles to Norridgewalk Falls in Norrywok.

October the 1st. We got the Batteaux etc across the Portage, & encamped at night beyond all the Inhabitants. Many of our men were sick.

2d. We could only get two miles forward.

3d. By a mistake that we soon discovered, we rowed up the Seven Mile stream; & returned into the Kennebek & got seven miles up.

4th. The men were much dejected from the River's being full of rocks and shoals; but we advanced seven miles to Devils Falls; & the Portage over which we transported the Batteaux was rocky & full of precipices. At night we encamped.

5th. We let the boats eight miles up through many rapid & shallow streams, & encamped.

6th. By setting up our Boats as usual we proceeded five miles.

7th. We reached the Portage which is said to be six miles over; & we cut down the brush for a mile upon it to render the carriage of our boats etc easy. Then we encamped.

8th. Captain Morgan return'd from measuring the Portage, which he found shorter than it was computed. By the different accounts of the way that we had still to go to Quebec, our expedition began to wear a gloomy aspect.

9th. Here we left seven of our Batteaux, & began to carry the rest over a swampy country. Some of the men were unable to carry half a mile. Carrying fatigued them more than setting or tracking the Batteaux [up] the River. At night we cleared a place & encamped.

10th. Our flower [flour] was very inconvenient to carry; and for greater care in carrying, we unpack'd our pork, slung it with ropes & carried it on poles. After having carried it about two miles the men gave out with fatigue, then we encamped.

11th. We crossed about 140 roods over the end of a lake; proceeded then about half a mile, & encamped.

12th. Lieutenant Steele returned who had been sent as a scout to the Chaudiere to see if there [was] anything to oppose us; & to take prisoner an old remarkable villain of an Indian called Natanus [Natanis], whom Governor Carleton had honour'd with a Captain's commission. He had been on the Dead River all the summer; & there was found at his hut a draught of the River on birch bark, drawn with charcoal, in the cleft of a stick which was stuck in the ground. We crossed a second pond; and then after carrying everything a quarter of a mile came to a third.

The 13th & 14th. We were employ'd in getting over the Portage.

15th. We paid the Batteaux, one of which was now allowed to every mess, & every Company was divided into eight messes. Sixteen days provisions were given to each mess-- all we had. Lieutenant Steele was dispatched with twenty four men to clear the Portages; & two Indians & one man were sent off with dispatches to Quebec to get intelligence in what manner the Inhabitants would receive us; they promis'd to meet us again in ten days.

16th & 17th. We got about nine miles up the Dead River. We passed two ripplings.

On the 18th, we passed through three ripplings, & waded a little way to a Portage having the Morrishall River on our left. We had advanced about eleven miles. Then we came into a current that was very rapid a little way about half a mile from the Portage. After rowing about eight miles in very crooked still water, the River became shallow & rapid in many places, where we went up about four miles further. Our course was that day N. 26W.

19th. We had three Portages to cross, one of 18 poles; the second of 72; & the 3d of 74 poles, in getting about four miles up the River. The men complain'd of their short allowance of provisions, having only a pint lightly fill'd with flower [flour] & a less proportion of pork. And there were only remaining 12 days provisions, at that rate.

20th & 21st. Were rain.

22d. The River overflowed the place of our encampment; which obliged us to break up our camp, and embark. But the boats work'd up with so much difficulty that many preferred marching in an excessively, nay almost an incredibly bad way from its swampiness & being full of thickets. We had taken the wrong, or the left branch of the River too; & had we not met two of our men who had been sent on a hunting the day before, & who put us in the right way, we must have perished. We gained about seven miles.

23d. We cross'd the eighth Portage. The River was exceedingly rapid from the rains. One boat with five muskets & some baggage was lost; & another was overset but all the men were sav'd.

24th. A Council of War adjudged proper to send Captain Hanchet forward with fifty men to conduct Colonel Arnold to the Inhabitants with all expedition to purchase provisions; & Captain Gotridge had leave to march with them. That their boats might not detain them at the Portages, they left them all but two, & one cannon which they carried. We crossed the tenth Portage, having advanced seven miles.

25th. Our water was very bad. One of our boats sunk but nothing was lost. Another boat was drove back that detain'd me, & prevented me from getting up further. I therefore put ashore & with much difficulty could get a fire made.

26th. We cross'd three ponds. The Dead River now became very crook'd, narrow, & in many places extremely rapid. Then we cross'd another Pond & encamped near a sixth. We got sixteen miles.

On the 27th, we crossed the sixth & two other Ponds. The Portages were very difficult to get over, being quite swampy & covered with thickets. We now carried but three of our Batteaux with us.

28th. It was propos'd to make a common stock of our provisions, & to share them equally; but Gotridge refus'd to do it. We received a letter from Colonel Arnold directing us to keep N by E or N.N.E. to avoid a large swamp; & recommending the bearer of the letter for our pilot.

29th. Colonel Green having undertaken to pilot us, we came, after a march of six miles, to a large Pond & followed its winding course until dark, when we encamped; but I got over the Pond, determining to push forward to the Inhabitants.

30th. A large gutter arising from an extensive swamp & running into the lake stopped me. Colonel Green & a Major Bigelow join'd me. Being now bewildered we agreed to go to a ridge that was in sight, south of us. From there we cross'd the swamp, & kept about N.N.W. to hit Chaudiere River, or lake. We waded to our waists in crossing the gutter & swamp, & cold it was. By keeping along shore then we came at last to Antijuntuck Lake, or the Chaudiere Lake or Pond, and March'd a mile in a track & encamped.

31st. We march'd twenty six miles. We heard that two of the Batteaux had been lost with one man, some rifle muskets, ammunition & baggage, & money.

Nov'm 1st. The men were quite feeble. We came to a River which by a map, we suppos'd to be but eight miles from the Inhabitants; and marched in all twenty miles.

2d. I divided my last morsel with my friend. The men were greatly distressed; many of them not having eat for two days. I pass'd some the preceeding day who said that they had lived some time on dogs flesh; & that others had boiled their shoes, pouches, etc to eat. After having march'd about ten miles we met some Frenchmen, & a Sergeant with some oxen & oat meal, with the husks on, which we thought was sumptuous fare.

3d. We met some more provisions, & with unexpressable joy we beheld the uppermost houses on the Chaudiere. We waded a branch of the River which was very cold, & went into an Indians hut to warm ourselves. The Indian gave us some bread, butter & honey for which he made us pay extravagantly. At a house further down the River we found provisions ready dress'd for us.

4th. The landlady where I lodged being told that we came from Boston sung a French song to the tune of Yankee Doodle Dandy. Laughed very heartily.

5th. My cloaths [cloths] were so ragged that my breeches could not keep my shirt in. All the Inhabitants were kind to us.

6th. I appeared to be ably decent in Peter grubs brushes, & my boots. We march'd eleven miles to Tres Chemins Riviere without seeing a house. At night we got down, & quartered amongst the farmers.

7th. It snow'd & was very cold.

8th. We march'd hartily, under orders, to within three miles of Point Levi; where we halted to prevent our being discover'd by the enemy. We hear that armed Indians came the night before from General Schyler with an express to Colonel

Arnold; & to our great mortification we were told that a hundred soldiers arrived at Quebec last Sunday from Newfoundland; it having been without any troops before, General Carleton having withdrawn them elsewhere. We were further told that there were but 150 Canadians embodied in the Garrison, & that even many of them had been forced to take up arms. It was suppos'd that the Indians whom Colonel Arnold dispatched with the letter from the Dead River must have betray'd him as he did not return with an answer, & as the Gentleman to whom he wrote is put on board of a Frigate that sailed up the River in the evening. P.M. We march'd near to a mile on the side of St. Laurence River, in which it was said there were three hundred bushels of wheat. The enemy discover'd us.

9th. We were alarm'd by a report that the Kings Troops were coming over to attack us, upon which we run out as fast as we could; but it proved to be only a boat that attempted to rob the mill or destroy a small vessel that lay ashore. We plac'd Sentinels along shore to prevent any boats from coming over, or crossing to Town.

10th. The Frigate fir'd at the mill.

11th. It was much talked of to storm the Town. Blacksmiths were employ'd to make the Spears & hooks, & carpenters to make ladders but everything was carried on in confusion; & what better could be expected of them who were at the head of affairs having obtain'd their places only by Interest or Wealth. They could never boast of military geniuses, nor of their experience. The Commander in Chief indeed to do him justice was a clever, active, & sensible little man, and followed the sea sometime I was told. However the scheme of scaling the walls of Quebec with 800 men, with not twenty rounds of ammunition, & their arms in bad order, to attack 400 well provided in everything plainly showed that he was an able General. P.M. a topsail schooner came down the River that was suppos'd to have General Carleton on board and several vessels sail'd downwards. Some thought that the Tories were going off.

12th. Our little Army was divided into two battalions. The command of one was given to Colonel Green & the other to Major Meigs; & the Rifle Company was equally divided under their command which distressed our Corp much. Indeed we ought all to have laid down our commissions rather than to have serv'd under a man who possess'd no one quality requisite to make them good officers.

13th. It was reported that the Indians whom Colonel Arnold sent to General Schuyler were taken; that our plan would thereby be blown, & that the enemy who had hitherto supposed us to be 2000 strong would know our real force.

14th. As our Division cross'd the River Captain Morgan & others fir'd at a boat which got off from us; but as groans were heard some of the crew were probably wounded. Five hundred men were left to guard Point Levi side.

17th. A merchant found means to slip out of the Garrison to us, & took a Memorandum of the necessaries we wanted to the amount of four hundred pounds; & we were told that there were great disputes between Colonel MacLean, who commanded whom they called their regular Troops, & the Inhabitants.

18th. We learn'd that Colonel MacLean had taken all the marines & sailors out of the ships in the harbour; that he had prevail'd on the rabble of the Town to take up arms, which made them in all seven hundred strong; & that he was to sally out on us with Field Pieces on next day. Therefore as we were not more than seven hundred strong from our losses, & sickness, & as most of our ammunition was _____. The Riflemen having but two rounds each, & the Musketmen only two besides all the arms being bad condition, we march'd to Point aux Trembles, & took up our quarters. General Carleton left the Town, & went on board of a schooner which sail'd down to Quebec with two others a few hours before we arriv'd.

20th. By an express from Montreal, we heard that General Carleton had been forc'd to make his escape in a small birch canoe with two men.

21st. Major Bigelow presented two Gentlemen to Captain Morgan, who followed us from Quebec to beg protection, & that their property might be secure when the City fell into our hands. They were detained however as spies; it having an odd appearance that they should ask protection from an army that was running away. Neither of them understood a word of English; one of them was a German.

FINIS

QUEBEC JOURNAL #3

Note: This is the 3rd journal known as Appendix II in the Glasgow Library Americana manuscripts. This one is much shorter than #1 and #2.

Journal

While we were encamped at Cambridge we heard that General Washington had received letters from Gentlemen in Quebec inviting him to send Troops there; & adding that they thought it would be for the safety of the Colonies to send them. Accordingly the General ordered eleven companies of Musketeers, & three of Riflemen to march to Quebec. Colonel Benedict Arnold was appointed to command the Detachment.

September 11th, 1775. We march'd thirteen miles to Neals Tavern.

12th. We went fifteen miles to Bunkham's Meeting House.

13th. We arriv'd at Newbury Port, forty five miles NE of Boston, & encamped until the 18th

18th, when we embarked on board eleven sail of Sloops & Schooners that were ready to receive us.

19th. We sailed A.M. & next morning got into the mouth of the Kennebek River about thirty six leagues NE of Newbury Port.

21st. We stood up the River & got all up to Fort Western the 23d, about nine leagues up.

On the 26th, we got up to Fort Halifax, about six leagues further up.

On the 27th, Taconic, three miles higher.

28th. We set our Batteaux up eight miles. The River was so full of rocks & shallows that the men were obliged to get in the River to hale the boats over; & some times they fell up to their chins in holes.

29th. By setting our boats against a stream, we got to the Chasin Falls about ten miles higher.

30th. After crossing the Portage we got four miles up the stream.

October 1st. We set & haled the boats over rocks & shoals, sometimes plunging overhead from the ruggedness of the bottom, seven miles to Norywok Falls.

2d. The Portage was a wilderness of birch, pines & hemlock. ON the River side we encamped. There is good _____ (transcriber's note) & some sugar trees.

3rd. By setting, pushing, & haling our boats we got up eleven miles; we shot a mouse deer.

4th. By our usual methods we reach'd Tan Tucket Falls, called Hells Gate, eight miles higher.

5th, 6th, & 7th. We set & track'd our boats twenty miles against a shallow stream. We now left the Kennebek.

8th. There was a heavy rain.

9th, 10th & 11th. We carried our Batteaux up three quarters of a mile over a high hill; the way was incredibly bad; to the first pond on the Portage about five miles in all.

12th, 13th, 14th, & 15th. Were spent in crossing the Portage to the Dead River, which we affected with great trouble.

16th. We rowed ten miles. The River comes at one place from the NW, & runs about four perches to SE.

17th & 18th. We crossed two short Portages & got up twelve leagues.

19th. We pass'd over four Portages, _____ advancing five miles.

On the 20th, 21st, 22d. Many rains kept us in our camp.

23d. The shallowness of the River obliged us to set the Batteaux up ten miles.

24th. Before this, Colonel Innes with three company's of Musket Men turn'd homewards, being discouraged by so many difficulties. Seven boats were overset & much baggage & provisions were lost with a few guns; but we advanced nine miles.

25th. We set our boats up eight miles & crossed over two Portages.

26th. By setting the boats we got seven miles to the fourth pond & march'd over four Portages.

27th. It was agreed to leave all our boats at the Great Portage of the Chaudiere except for a few to carry the sick down that River; after having carried them over twenty miles over such mountains & rocks, & through such swamps as never were I believe pass'd by men before. Our shoulders were so bruised by carrying them that we could scarce suffer anything to touch them.

28th. We divided our flour. As for meat we had none. A letter from Colonel Arnold inform'd us that we might expect provisions in three days, which put us in high spirits, & caus'd us to eat up our bread more lavishly than we otherwise would have done; & proved hurtful to many. And Likewise told us that General Schyler had gain'd an advantage over the Ministerial Troops near St. Johns; having kill'd & taken a number of them.

29th. We march'd fourteen miles, in many places through swamps up to our knees; & over trees that for several perches together lay covering the ground.

30th. We went astray over mountains & through swamps, scarcely passable for wild beasts. After wading too a little River that was up to our waists, we march'd till night in our wt clothes.

31st. Several of [our] men had no provisions. We march'd twenty five miles. Some who had a little bread & flour divided it with Lieutenant McLellan who was very ill. One man was drown'd, & money & many other things were lost by the boats oversetting.

November 1st. Fatigue, sickness & famine made many to lag behind, but our case being desperate everyone who could, push'd on over mountains, & through such swamps as would have discouraged any traveller whatever; some not having anything for twenty four hours, & after walking twenty miles had not a morsel to put in their mouths. We pass'd some of them eating dogs that they had roasted with their skins, guts & all. Some of those men having found nothing to eat for three days. I saw a dollar offer'd for about two ounces of cake.

2d. In the morning many of us were so weak that we all stagger'd as if we had been drunk. A small stick lying across the way brought the stoutest of us to the ground. In the morning we met some cattle. The most joyful sight we had ever seen. The people that brought them told us we were then twenty miles from the nearest Inhabitants. We marched twenty miles that day.

3d. Though we had several small Rivers to wade, some of which put us up to the waist, & very cold. We got twenty miles & got to a house, the first we had seen for a month.

4th. The night was snowy. We went down the River side. There are many Inhabitants on it.

5th. We continued our march down along the River, 12 miles. Though the people were hospitable they sold us everything very dear. We paid a shilling for a three pound loaf of bread.

6th. We joined Colonel Arnold with the advance party, and halted at two o'clock. At dusk we march'd until midnight, seventeen miles.

7th. We march'd three miles further & halted till evening. A Lieutenant & twenty men were ordered forward then to see if the way was clear; they continuing their march untill two o'clock, having got within sight of Quebec. We advanced nine miles.

8th. We were quartered along the Point Levi side of the River St. Laurence, until all our men who were behind could come up to us.

13th. Most of the men who were alive, of those that were left behind, joined us & we learn'd from them that several perished through famine in the woods. We crossed the River under cover of night in long boats & canoes, some of which overset. A few of the muskets only were lost.

14th. The Frigate fired on us without doing us any damage.

21d. We march'd up the River to Point aux Tremble, our ammunition being insufficient to attack the Town of Quebec. The two men whom I left with Lieutenant McLellan up the Chaudiere join'd us & inform'd us that they buried him at the first house they came to, after he had been brought down thereto by two Indians whom Captain Smith hired for that purpose.

December 5th. We again march'd towards Quebec, & laid siege to it untill 30th December, during which some were kill'd on both sides.

FINIS.

CHAPTER THREE

WARD COMPANY JOURNALS

There were four collaborative journals written by Ward Company privates which deserve more examination for two reasons. First, these journals are almost identical in their daily entries raising the question of how such an occurrence happened and whether one was an original with the others being copies. Second, there has been an ongoing dispute since the middle of the nineteenth century as to whether the Ware or the Tolman journal is the original. Justin Smith supposedly settled this dispute in 1904 but evidence that he did not consider leads to a different conclusion.

The Ward Company collaborative journalists are:

- Ebenezer Tolman of Fitzwilliam, New Hampshire
- Joseph Ware of Needham, Massachusetts
- Ebenezer Wild of Braintree, Massachusetts
- William Dorr of Roxbury, Massachusetts

The journals of these four collaborators, Ware, Tolman, Dorr and Wild, are almost word-for-word identical in their daily entries. A few of the words are different but the similarities are too obvious to be in doubt. All of these journals start on the same day, September 13, 1775, and end on the same day, September 6, 1776. There is no doubt that they are copies of each other. That four journalists would write about their experiences on this historic expedition using almost identical entries is highly unusual.

The purpose of this chapter is to examine the Ward Company collaborative journals to make a conclusion regarding the author of the original journal. All of the available evidence regarding these journals will be examined, including some information which Justin Smith did not consider.

WILD'S JOURNAL TO BE ELIMINATED FROM CONSIDERATION

The Ebenezer Wild journal, which was published by the Massachusetts Historical Society in 1886, must be eliminated from further consideration. Contrary to the title of the journal in the MHS publication, that journal was not written by

Ebenezer Wild. Private Ebenezer Wild did write a journal of his Revolutionary War experiences, but he was not in the army in 1775 and did not go to Canada with the Arnold expedition. This journal will therefore be eliminated from further consideration as the original for the following reasons:

1. The 1913 Proceedings of the Massachusetts Historical Society reported that James M. Bugbee presented a letter to the Society in 1887 regarding the authorship of the Wild journal, stating that it had been "erroneously ascribed to Ebenezer Wild." Later in 1887, Bugbee presented what he called the "true" journal of Wild to the Society, which covered the period from 1776 to 1781. Bugbee was the editor of the true Wild journal and presumably had examined both journals to make his point regarding the error. He concluded that Winsor made a mistake when he published the Wild journal as an authentic record because it was not written by Wild.[108]

2. Ebenezer Wild's name is not in the Banks card file as a member of Arnold's corps and is not in any other list of the men in Arnold's expedition, including the list in Appendix II.

3. In 1842, Wild's wife submitted a pension application as the surviving spouse, claiming payment for Wild's service in the Revolutionary War. The pension application states that he first enlisted in the army on or about the 7th day of August, 1776. Most pension applications tended to stretch the length of service, not the opposite. It seems pretty clear that Wild's heirs did not try to claim service for the period of the Arnold expedition because he did not serve during that time.

4. There is no American or British record of an Ebenezer Wild being a prisoner at Quebec after the assault, while the entries in the MHS Wild journal make it clear that the author was a prisoner in 1776.

DORR'S JOURNAL TO BE ELIMINATED FROM CONSIDERATION

The Dorr journal was the most recent journal to be transcribed, however, its transcriber, Rebecca Goetz, makes no claim that Dorr authored the original journal. There is nothing in the journal or in Dorr's life to suggest that he was the primary or lead author. That the Dorr journal was not transcribed until 2000 makes it less likely that he was the original author. Therefore, it is this author's contention that Dorr should be eliminated from consideration as the author of the original collaborative journal.

THE WARE AND TOLMAN JOURNALS AND CLAIMS TO ORIGINAL AUTHENTICITY

Eliminating the Wild journal for the reasons explained above and discounting Dorr as the original author, we are left with the Tolman and Ware journals to be considered as the original. Their competing claims of authenticity will be examined in more detail in this chapter and a determination will be made as to who wrote the original.

Competing claims to original authenticity between the Ware and Tolman journals started in 1852 when the New England Historical and Genealogical Register (NEHGR) first published the complete text of a journal by Joseph Ware. The transcriber of the journal was William B. Trask, who was given the Ware journal by a grandson of the author, also named Joseph Ware.

When the 1852 issue of the Register containing the Ware journal came out, it was read by John Goodwin Locke, who was a resident member of the New England Historical and Genealogical Society, living in Lowell, Massachusetts. At that time, Locke was working on his comprehensive history of the Locke family, which he subsequently published in 1853. Based on his extensive research on the Locke family, of which the Tolman family was a member by marriage, Locke realized the Ware journal was identical to another journal he had been examining. Ebenezer Tolman, one of Locke's ancestors, wrote this journal. Tolman's son, William Tolman of Watertown, New York, gave the journal to Locke.

Because of his knowledge of the Tolman journal, Locke was convinced that the NEHGR had made a serious mistake. He therefore wrote a letter to William Tolman requesting a copy of the entire Tolman journal so he could compare it to Ware's journal. Locke did a comparison and found them to be identical. At that point, he was even more convinced that the Ware journal was a copy of the Tolman original.

Locke invited both William B. Trask, a long time member of the Society, and John Ward Dean, a former editor of the NEHGR and a well known historical researcher and writer, to visit his office with the Ware manuscript. There the three men examined Locke's copy of the Tolman manuscript and compared it with the Ware journal that Trask had recently transcribed.

Dean's Statement

In a note published in The American Genealogist in 1868, John Ward Dean gives the following statement regarding his meeting with Trask and Locke.

> In the year 1852, I examined, with Messrs. Locke and Trask, the two manuscripts of this journal, referred to by Mr. Locke. Mr. Trask thought, as I did, that the manuscripts were in different handwritings. As for myself, I had little doubt of it. The manuscript ascribed to Mr. Ware, showed a much more practiced pen than did that ascribed to Mr. Tolman. There were other points of dissimilarity. The capital A's in one manuscript, were always begun at the top, while in the other they were always begun at the bottom. Other letters showed similar differences. If I remember aright, the two journals were almost literally the same, to the date of imprisonment of the company, after which they differed materially. My impression at the time was that Mr. Ware, who was clerk of his company, kept the journal, but that during their mutual captivity, Mr. Tolman copied what Mr. Ware had written, and continued it as his individual journal. The occurrence of the personal pronoun I, in Mr. Tolman's manuscript, which Mr. Locke lays stress upon, occurs in this latter portion. It is evident that one manuscript was copied from the other, or that both were copied from some other manuscript. A grandson of Mr. Ware, who was familiar with his writing, asserted that the manuscript, from which the above work [meaning the Ware journal] was printed, was in his grandfather's handwriting, and that he had always heard it spoken of as his grandfather's journal. Mr. Locke asserts that a son of Ebenezer Tolman's is equally sure that his father kept the journal. The authorship must therefore remain in doubt, unless some other evidence is produced.[109]

Locke's Statement

In Appendix H of his book on the Locke family, John Goodwin Locke provides the following information on the Tolman journal.

> I have been furnished by Mr. William Tolman, of Watertown, N.Y. with a portion of a Journal, a part having been lost, which he alleges was 'kept' by his father, Ebenezer Tolman, who was a member of the same company to which Mr. Ware belonged. A comparison of this journal with what is called the original of Mr. Ware, establishes the fact that one is a copy of the other, or that both were copies of some other. They are,

with the exception of now and again a word, identically the same, save one important entry which will be noticed. A comparison also shows with considerable certainty that they were written by the same hand. The writing is very similar, and I think I am not mistaken in the opinion that he who penned the one also penned the other, and that there is a reasonable presumption that Mr. Tolman was the penman, and that the one furnished by his son is the original; and for several reasons. First, it appears to have been written at different periods, and has an older appearance than Mr. Ware's copy, which looks as though it was written all at one time, and almost with the same pen. Second, Mr. Ware does not use the personal pronoun I from beginning to end, whereas Mr. Tolman says under date of Jany. 19, 1776, 'This day I was taken...'. And lastly, two sons and two daughters of Mr. Tolman now living, all unite in saying that they have, time and again, heard their father speak of his journal as one that he 'kept' on the march and while in prison, and that they have no doubt that it is in his handwriting ... Mr. Tolman and Mr. Ware had frequent intercourse after the war, and the former may have furnished the latter with a copy of the journal.[110]

Justin Smith's Conclusions

Justin Smith evaluates both journals on the evidence that he had available and his comments are as follows:

> In the New England Historical and Genealogical Register for 1852, there appeared a journal almost identical with this attributed to Wild. It was represented as the composition of Joseph Ware, of Needham, Mass.; and it has been so attributed ever since. Just why there was so much confidence about this does not appear, for according to Mr. Winsor's notes it bore no indication of source except the words "Joseph Ware his book." If this is enough to prove authorship, what must be the number of schoolboys wickedly robbed of their copyright dues on Webster's Spelling Book.

> The simple fact is that Joseph Ware of Needham cannot have written the journal, for he did not belong to Arnold's army. The Massachusetts archives contain a roll dated Cambridge, October 5, 1775, which reports him as a corporal in Whiting's company of Heath's regiment that day. There was, however, a Joseph Ware in Ward's company of Arnold's army, for the name is down in both our lists of the prisoners of December 31st. But this is all the information that we have. Although several

Joseph Ware's appear on the Massachusetts rolls, no one by that name is reported as 'gone to Quebec,' the usual formula, and we must conclude that this was somebody who enlisted specially for the Canada campaign, and cannot be identified...

There certainly was an Ebenezer Tolman in Ward's company of Arnold's army, the company in which we find a Joseph Ware. The evidence in Tolman's favour, set over against the facts about Wild and Ware, seems decisive, so that we may boldly discard the latter two names, and attribute their journals to the former. Of course, this is not quite satisfactory, for we have not the original manuscript, and have only Mr. Locke's testimony that Tolman's copy differed very slightly from Ware's; but it is the best we can do, for the Tolman original appears to have disappeared from our ken.[111]

Based on the evidence he reviewed, Justin Smith concluded that Tolman was the original author of the collaborative journals for two reasons. First, he finds no evidence to support that Joseph Ware of Needham was actually on the expedition. Second, since Ware was not on the expedition, he finds the arguments made by Locke compelling. The most compelling of the arguments for Smith is the statement by Tolman's son, William Tolman of Watertown, NY, that the journal Locke examined in 1852 was the journal kept by his father on the expedition.

WAS JOSEPH WARE ON THE EXPEDITION?

Smith's conclusions regarding Tolman being the original author and Ware not being on the expedition do not hold up under careful scrutiny. There are additional factors supporting Ware being the author of a journal that Smith did not consider. The one argument Smith makes against the Ware journal that merits further examination is his claim that Joseph Ware from Needham, Mass. was not part of the Arnold expedition. To explore this point further, any available documentation that supports Ware being present on the expedition needs to be considered. There are four source documents that should be considered and evaluated regarding Ware's participation. The one source that is not helpful is the Ware family genealogies. The first of these was prepared by Trask and included in the NEHGR publication of Ware's journal. Two other Ware family genealogies were issued subsequently, both by Emma Forbes Ware, and both cite Trask as their source. However, Trask did not reveal his source to claim that Ware was the author of an expedition journal.

1. <u>Local Histories of Ware's Hometown.</u> These local histories typically contain information about the military experience of soldiers from the town in which they lived. Two local histories do have information about Joseph Ware of Needham and both state that he was a member of the Arnold expedition.[112] While local histories have been a valuable source, they are also often unreliable because they repeat family and community tradition and pass it off as good history. These histories by themselves do not make the case for Ware because of their dates of publication, which were subsequent to Smith's book.

2. <u>Unit Muster Roll.</u> Smith cited one muster roll from October of 1775 which does list Joseph Ware as a private in the Whiting Company, but that company was not on the Arnold expedition. Smith correctly says that there are others on this roll that have a notation next to their name stating "went to Quebec." However, his conclusion that Ware was not on the expedition because he does not have such a notation is evidence of omission but does not prove his point. It is contradicted by other information presented below that does support Ware being on the expedition. There is no persuasive evidence from the muster rolls that Joseph Ware of Needham was on the Quebec expedition. In fact, the existing muster rolls only add to the confusion about Ware's presence rather than to help resolve it.

3. <u>Pension Applications.</u> There are two relevant pension applications which confirm that Joseph Ware wrote a journal of the Quebec expedition.

First, is the pension application of Oliver Edward's heirs in 1845, which includes a deposition by Elijah Clark of Brighton, Massachusetts. It states he has "an original manuscript which has ever been known by available witnesses to be the handwriting of Joseph Ware of Needham ... and that I received the same in the form and situation which it now is, of Mrs. Shepard, a daughter of the aforesaid Joseph Ware, and the manuscript commences as follows: 'Joseph Ware his Book. A Journal of a March from Cambridge ...'" The statement goes on to state that the manuscript is "beyond doubt a genuine original true account." The list of prisoners in the Ware journal contains the name of Oliver Edwards, which is why the journal was referred to in the application.[113]

Second, and even more significant, is a pension application for Joseph Thomas, a 2nd Lieutenant in Samuel Ward's company, containing a deposition made by Ebenezer Homer of Boston in 1809, which has the following language: "I have in my possession an original written document, entitled 'A Journal of a March from Cambridge on an expedition against Quebec in Colonel Benedict Arnold's Detachment September 13th 1775, kept by Joseph Ware, a private in Captain Samuel Ward's Company in the aforesaid Detachment.' That said journal contains forty four pages, that in said Journal there are lists of Officers and Men, killed, wounded and taken prisoners at Quebec on the 31st of December, 1775 ... I further certify that I have no doubt that the Journal aforesaid is the true and genuine document which it purports to be." This application was even closer in time to the actual event than the other pension application so it must be considered as a credible source.[114]

4. Quebec Prisoner Lists. There is a relevant prisoner list which is entitled *Return of Rebel Prisoners taken at Quebec, December 31, 1775*. The handwritten cover sheet says that the list was found in Sir Guy Carleton's papers, dated 10th August 1776. This document provides a comprehensive list of the American prisoners who were captured in the attack and were being held in Quebec.[115]

There is a "Joseph Wire" on that Return who is listed as being from Captain Ward's Company. He is 22 years of age and is from Massachusetts. It is easy to see how the spelling of the name Ware could turn into Wire based on the way the name sounded to the person making out the return. Justin Smith agrees with this point. It is also true that there is no member of Captain Ward's company with a name that is similar to Ware. The entry on Quebec prisoner's role is a spelling mistake, hence proof that there was a Joseph Ware being held prisoner in Quebec.

Smith claims that the name on the list of prisoners was another Joseph Ware, but not the one from Needham. However, there is no evidence to support Smith's contention. The comprehensive list of the men that were on the Arnold expedition, contained in Appendix II, confirms that there was only one Joseph Ware and no Joseph Wire on the expedition. If Smith knew of evidence of another Joseph Ware, he did not share any sources for that information.

CONCLUSIONS ABOUT THE TOLMAN AND WARE JOURNALS

1. The Ware and Tolman journals are, in fact, two different journals written in different handwriting that are identical in their account of the Arnold expedition. There are relevant sources to support the authenticity of both journals.

2. The authenticity of each journal is supported by each author's heirs. Each states that a journal was written by his ancestor and that it is an authentic journal in that ancestor's own handwriting. This confirmation does not favor one over the other as the original. Both have the same supportive statements from the heirs and, therefore, have equal value.

3. Although documentation that Tolman was on the Quebec expedition is much more direct, there is sufficient documentation to confirm that Ware was on the expedition and wrote a journal.

4. If Ware was on the expedition, Smith's argument has no merit and his conclusion about Tolman and Ware needs to be revised to reflect new information. Justin Smith's contention that Ware did not go to Quebec is incorrect and his contention that Tolman's journal is the original is also wrong. For the reasons stated above, Ware has the better case.

5. There is ample evidence to conclude that Ware was the original author of the collaborative journals. The two pension applications cited above are sufficient proof to support this conclusion. None of the evidence favoring Tolman as the original author is as persuasive as the pension applications that support Ware.

CHAPTER FOUR

JOURNALS OF THE EXPEDITION DOCTOR

Dr. Isaac Senter wrote two different manuscript versions of his journal that are located in two different libraries and with two different provenances. Both have been claimed to be his original journal. The fact that there are two manuscripts extant that are alleged to have been written by the same person makes one question their authenticity and ask why there are two instead of just one.

The better known journal was first published by the Historical Society of Pennsylvania (HSP), which is the only journal to be transcribed to date so it is the one that has appeared in all of the previous publications described in Chapter One. The second Senter journal, located in the Rhode Island Historical Society, has never been transcribed or published until this book. Kenneth Roberts suggests that the Rhode Island journal is a copy of the other journal, which he calls the "original."[116] This conclusion is not supportable as will be shown by the following examination of the Senter journals.

Justin Smith asserts that the journal printed by the HSP is a Senter original because of the presence of a letter from Arnold referenced in the journal that was attached to the page opposite the reference. He concludes that Senter wrote the journal sometime after the expedition was finished because of the "uniformity of the penmanship." Smith makes the point that there is a very close similarity between the two journals and concludes that Senter wrote both but at different times because the handwriting is similar.[117]

H. M. Chapin, the librarian of the RIHS, wrote to William Abbatt in 1915 suggesting that the RIHS manuscript journal is "the original notes which Dr. Senter made during the expedition, or possibly a first draft from those notes, which he may have made upon his return home, and that the (Philadelphia) Ms. is probably his second draft, based either on our Ms. or upon his notes written at a later period."[118] While it is a supposition, this explanation is more compelling and makes more sense than the explanations by Smith and Roberts.

HSP OR MUNN JOURNAL

In 1846, the American Penny Magazine and Family Newspaper printed a review of the Senter journal published as No. 5 of the Bulletin of the Historical Society of Pennsylvania. The review stated that the version contained in the HSP Bulletin was "printed from a manuscript in the possession of a gentleman in this city".[119] The identity of the individual is confirmed by two sources. First is a line from an 1846 letter from Dr. Lewis Roper to Judge Thomas Ruffin. "I send you a copy of the Journal of Isaac Senter which has been published from the original manuscript in my possession."[120] Second, the Notice in the 1846 HSP publication that the existence of the manuscript journal "became known in consequence of inquiries made by Dr. Lewis Roper, of this city, who wished to add to his collections of autographs a good specimen of the handwriting of General Arnold. It was given to him, that he might extract from it an original note of that officer, which the reader will find printed on page 32. His perception of the value of the Journal induced him to communicate it to the Society by which it is published, with permission to print it."[121]

The HSP version referred to in the letter was published in 1846 and was the only version that was known at that time. Of particular interest is the introductory notice to the HSP journal explaining how Roper obtained the manuscript. The 1874 issue of The American Bibliopolist contains an advertisement by Henry Carey Baird of Philadelphia for the original manuscript of the Journal of Isaac Senter in half morocco.[122] This confirms that in 1874 the original manuscript journal was still in Philadelphia and was available for sale.

The HSP journal disappeared for a time but showed up in the middle of the twentieth century in the collection of William Allen Munn, a well known book collector. The Munn collection, consisting of 127 items, was donated to the Fordham University library by an anonymous donor on February 26, 1943. A New York Times article covering the donation states, "Among the other manuscript material in the collection is the journal of Isaac Senter, physician to Arnold's Quebec expedition in 1775."[123] The University announced that it was naming the collection in honor of "the late editor and publisher of The Scientific American and member of the patent bar, who assembled the material originally." The description of the journal in the Munn collection says that it is an, "original manuscript journal kept while on 'A secret expedition to the Province of Quebec, commanded by General Benedict Arnold.' Covers the period September 13, 1775 to January 6, 1776 ... written on one side only."[124]

The HSP journal is definitely the same journal as the one that is now in the Munn Collection at Fordham. The more pertinent question is where did the source who sold the journal to Dr. Lewis Roper obtain his copy and how do we know it was written by Senter. Senter's authorship is supported by Justin Smith:

> The authenticity of the journal is beyond question. One curious fact is sufficient proof. Senter was very proud of a certain letter that he

received from Benedict Arnold and states in his journal that it was on the opposite page. This letter has been abstracted from the manuscript, but the place where it was attached is evident. This assures us that we have before us Dr. Senter's own work."[125]

This explanation has a high degree of credibility because there is evidence that Dr. Roper removed the Arnold letter in the manuscript for the reason alluded to above. Questions still remain, however, regarding the source from which Roper obtained the journal.

In a letter dated February 23, 1900, the Historical Society of Pennsylvania stated that they had no information relative to where Dr. Roper got the manuscript. It would appear that Roper gave it to HSP and they published it, but knew nothing else about it.[126] The original letter from Arnold to Senter in the journal clearly establishes a credible connection of Senter to the HSP journal.

RHODE ISLAND HISTORICAL SOCIETY JOURNAL

The Rhode Island Historical Society journal also presents some questions that relate to its authenticity and provenance. According to written information that is included with the manuscript, it was discovered by a daughter of former Governor John Brown Francis "among some old papers of her father's." When she realized what it was, she sent the manuscript journal to Senter's granddaughter, Mrs. Crawford Allen. Mrs. Allen in turn presented the manuscript to the Rhode Island Historical Society at its meeting of April 30, 1878.[127]

The RIHS manuscript was discovered enclosed in a copy of the HSP journal and for a time it was thought that it was the missing HSP manuscript journal. However, that journal is in the Munn Collection. Even a cursory comparison of the two journals reveals that they are entirely different. So different that it is difficult to reconcile that they were written by the same person.

Two notations in the RIHS manuscript show a connection to Isaac Senter. The first is a note written to Senter by the estate of the Reverend President James Manning, President of Brown University. The note is dated July 28, 1791 and is addressed to Senter. Senter signed the note on the bottom with the words "Errors Excepted." Since Senter was alive in 1791, the note establishes a clear link to him. Senter at that time was the most prominent physician in Rhode Island so it is credible that he would have been treating Manning.

The second notation is a signature of John R. Bartlett on the back page of the journal. Although Bartlett was not yet born when Manning's estate wrote the note to Senter, he does have a connection to Governor John Brown Francis. Bartlett was Secretary of State for Rhode Island from 1855 to 1872. In addition to being active in the political life of Rhode Island, Bartlett was also a former bookseller in New York and a member of several historical and scientific societies. From 1754 until his death in 1886, he was the librarian of the John Carter Brown Library. Bartlett's credibility as a historian is beyond question so his signature on the manuscript is solid evidence that he accepted it as an authentic account by Senter.

Senter's authorship has been sufficiently established by the referenced notations to conclude that Isaac Senter wrote it prior to 1791. The number of cross outs in the manuscript and the often illegible handwriting supports the supposition that this manuscript was written by Senter during the expedition. However, it is unlikely that Senter would have written the introductory material while he was on the expedition, and those remarks lead right into the first daily entry of the journal. Therefore, it seems more likely that, as suggested by Mr. Chapin, this journal was written shortly after the expedition.

A second previously non-transcribed Senter journal presents a challenge. Because of its historical significance and because its contents have never been studied, the second Senter journal deserves to be recognized. Therefore, this author has undertaken to transcribe the second Senter journal and it is presented here for the first time. The journal is extremely difficult to read and explains why a number of words have been left out of the transcribed copy.

NEWLY TRANSCRIBED ISAAC SENTER JOURNAL

RHODE ISLAND HISTORICAL SOCIETY

To such a pitch of initiation had the contest arrived between Great Britain & the United Colonies early in the year of 1775, that it was thought necessary by the latter to take the most advantageous & effectual measures to secure our frontiers, bordering on the Lakes of Canada, from the hostile invasions of the English & their savage allies, the northern Indians. Consequently the Garrisons of Ticonderoga & Crown Point, the gates & sluces through which these incursions were to have been made, were of too much importance in the eyes of the Americans, not to attract their early attention. Already has the British Governor Carleton, commander of that colony, been authorized by a Commission as new as it was extraordinary, & arm the French Canadians & march them out of that Colony for the express purpose of subjugating the Anglo

Americans, & if he found it necessary in the completion of his work to capitally punish all those in any Colony whom he should deem rebelious opposers of his measures. Altho' the Canadians in general were not favorably disposed to comply with this despotic request, still it was too evident to the United Colonies that the arrival of the British forces in that country in the course of the lesson would enable him to, by compelling the Canadians by arms, carry out his plans into effectual operation.

At the same time, it was well known that he had already embodied a considerable number of the different tribes of savages into his service, who only waited for an opportunity to lust the blood of the intended victims of the ministerial wrath, to assemble with a rapid association & diabolical sympathy all the rest of these infernals from affiliation by their ___ & passions in ___ & laughter. When with many more aggravating circumstances as well as ___ hostilities under General Gage in New England too numerous to mention were sufficient to authorize any effective measures on our part. Indeed, to have waited to be attacked by such a barbarous combination as ever forming in Canada & threatening our frontier settlements bordering on that country would have been little short of self murder.

Thus the Americans felt & thus they reason'd, which the timid patriots & ministerial advocates unitedly represented offensive measures at this period especially in Canada as entirely unjustifiable upon the principles of reconciliation, which was the vain hope & the expectation of no small & influential part of this country. To seize the present opportunity & forestalling the designs of the enemy & to pierce him deep in the most vulnerable part was a conduct worthy of exasperated freemen.

To this end Cols Allen, Arnold & Warner, with a few more decided & patriotic characters, hastily collected a number of provincials for the occasion by a rapid march from Vermont & threw themselves successively into Ticonderoga, Crown Point & St. Johns, bring[ing] off from the latter all the cannon & prisoners which they could & garrisoned the others. This coup de main so favorable to the Americans in the infancy of their struggle, besides the prisoners & military stores achieved, paved the way for a more solid impression of American arms.

This was undertaken authoritatively by Gen'l Schuyler as chief, but for want of health carried on by the amicable, the brave intrepid Montgomery who united in character all the accomplishments of the soldier & gentleman. Had this armament followed up the first strike on the lakes early in the summer, that country in all probability would have long ere this constituted one of the United States.

While the American army were successful progressing in Upper Canada under the direction of these two generals, a plan was found for penetrating into Lower Canada through the Province of Maine directed against Quebec, its capitol. Through this unexplored wilderness, the British could form no conception of an attack from their antagonists, consequently Carleton had left it defenseless in order to meet Montgomery in the vicinity of Montreal.

Colo. Arnold who had shown no common spirit of enterprize as well as attachment to the cause of his country, was the first to solicit the conducting of this extraordinary & hazardous undertaking.

It was accordingly given him an armament selected for 1100 including officers, from the Americans camped at Cambridge, who march from thence on the 13th of Sept 1775, and arrived on the 15th at Newburyport, which on the 20th sail'd with 11 transports for the mouth of the River Kenebec where they arr'd the next day.

From this to the 23d, the transports were employ'd in ascending the stream to within a few miles of Fort Western to the head of the navigable water on the River. There were mostly finished a number of Batteaux hastily constructed with green soft pine to the number of nearly 200, which were intend'd to convey up the Kenebec all the provisions, military stores etc belonging to the army.

From this to the 25th the troops were employed in unloading the transports and in adjusting the Batteaux, & carrying all the effects belonging to the army up the falls at this Fort.

During this time, the army had been arranged into three Divisions. A part of each Division to[OK] the charge of the boats with all the stores etc, while the others were destined to march on the east bank of the Kenebec, in such progressive ___ with the batteaux as for each Division to every night encamp at the same stage.

Capt. Morgan with the three rifle companies constituted the first Division, Lieut. Col. Greene the 2d, & Lt. Col Enos the third. Two of the guides & pioneers who had been hunters in this wilderness were also engaged in the front Division to assist in discovering the least difficult passages in the woods, as well as to help clear the way in the various carrying places.

Our provisions consisted of 1st salt pork, 2d flower, 3d barrel'd beef, 4th barrel'd dry bread, 5th salt cod fish & 6th barrel'd pease, & having no artillery.

Our military effects were inconsiderable in point of hefts. We had only fuzens &

side arms with kegs of powder & ball & flints. These with a tent to each Battalion, a few boxes of candles, soap & hospital stores, constituted then nearly all the effects to be transported by water.

The batteaux were furnished with each a setting pole, oars, & pointer at the head. Thus arrang'd & equip't, we left Ft. Western, where the officers had been very entertain'd at Mrs. Howard, a polite, hospitable & excellent family, in the following order: 1. Morgan's Div. five in the a.m. of the 25th. 2d. Green's on the 26th, & 3d. Enos's on the following day.

From this to the 30th, we were employ'd in ascending the River to Fort Halifax, a distance of only 18 miles. We soon experienced how illy adapted these large & heavy boats were to force against a stream, the current of which in this stage, mostly ran much short of three knots an hour & in many places much more. In this much skill as well as strength was requir'd. In the former we generally fail'd for very few of the men had ever been acquainted with [this] kind of savage navigation. The first Division had propos'd this carrying plan before the last arriv'd. This is a large water fall & the last stands on a point of land made by the confluence of the Kenebec & Sabasticook Rivers. The Indian name of these falls is Tucconnic. Here was our fist carrying place by which we were exercised in a way little to be envied by any short of gally slaves. The rear Division did not all pass this ___ till the 2d of Oct.

From this to the 5th the two last Divisions were almost incessantly employ'd in forcing up this rugg'd stream, & before our arrival there, several of the batteaux were become so leaky that it was the work of one hand to bale one of them. Between Fort Halifax & Norrigwok, we passed two water falls, the first was call Wassarun, ___ & the second Scunkhegan.

At Norrigwalk, many of our batteaux being joined in such a shatter'd state that the Company of artificers we employ'd [had] to repair them. We now had arriv'd to the extreme settlement on this River & where there were but a few families who had but lately plac'd themselves at this frontier.

We now began to discover that courage & bodily prowess were the only requisites for conducting such an enterprize as this successfully. The water which had been taken in to the boats, as well through the leaks as over their sides, had so freshen'd the floating salt fish that we could not longer reckon on that article for support. The casks of biscuits & dry pease by the same means began to soak & burst & to finish the climax, our salt beef which was put up in hot weather was sufficiently ripon'd for the most improved modern epicures. In fine we had little else now to depend on to keep body & soul in ___, just the solid junks of salt, past[e]

153

& flower. The fact we had been able to purchase fresh meat, by the generous inhabitants through which we passed to ___ all our wants, but this could last no longer than which in this stage.

The forward Division of Riflemen who were better acquainted as well with the disadvantages of a life in the wood as well as this kind of inland navigation than the New England troops who made up the two rear ones, did not experience such a deduction in the proportion of their provisions. They however soon became pinch'd in this respect, but derived some assistance from being in the front of the whole, and excellent marksmen. Not long after we arrived at this stage before it began to rain & this added not a little to the injury of the provisions as we possessed no covering for it.

It was during our tarry here that Col. Arnold laid the foundation which finally blasted all our reward.

Measures were not only taken by the Lt. Gov'r [for] defense [of] the city against a surprise by ____ all those who were in the place, but directly destroyed all the boats, canoes etc on the south side of the Riv'r St. Lawrence for 30 miles up & down the Riv'r.

I now resume my narrative.

9th. The last Division greet Norrigwalk & in the course of the day passed a small riv'r 7 miles from hence call'd the Seven Mile Stream & encamp'd three miles above.

10th. As soon as the light would favor us we were moving & in the course of three miles we came to a fall call'd by the Hunters Caratunuc. The carrying place by this fall was about 40 rod. & we encamped a mile only in advance. The water for this day unusually rapid. The land & timber however was superior to what we had before seen on this stream.

11th. The water still continued so rapid that our oars were of little service the most of the day, & the only way we had left us to advance with the bateaux was by seizing the inclining bushes which grew on the banks of the River & by that means haul our boats forward. The distance which we advanced daily is not easily ascertained. We encamped on the June grass which grows on the sides of the Riv'r here with great frequency.

12th. This day we expected to reach to the Great Carrying Place & we accordingly arriv'd there at past 4 o'clock p.m., where we found a very considerable part of the army busily engaged in transporting boats on thin bark directly into the wilderness, leaving the Kenebec on the right & proceeding by a west course. There the Riv'r which we were now leaving appeared to come from a point east of north & as far as we could discover was one continuous impossible rapid. The rifle companies with the pioneers had pushed their way through the woods in Quest of a ____ which we were told was within 4 miles of the River. Little had been done by them to alter the face of nature in rendering the obstacles less difficult. This was a stage of extreme fatigue. Not less than 7 or 8 times were each boats crew obliged to pass before the last article was carried over. High hills, miry morasses & almost impenetrable woods were continually opposing us. Our bateaux in gen'l weighed not less than 400 lbs, which with the provisions, we made not less than 800 weight on average, to be transported by 5 or 6 hands over each carrying place. This encumbrance however was easily diminishing as scarcely a day passed without several of the boats being stove to pieces & all or part of their loading lost. It was not till the 15th before the army crossed this laborious passage. Added to our other difficulties, the number of our sick & infirm were daily increasing & so bad were several of them, that they were obliged to be transported by hand in the same way over all the carrying places. We had for several days been entirely in solid provisions, which create a constant thirst, & to allay which we got nothing but water more or less ____. The first pond which we came to was entirely surrounded by a filthy ____ & the water was as yellow as a mixture of saffron & water. This partly from its ____ quality & perhaps from the quantity we were obliged to use, brought on a vomiting & diaherrea which harassed many of the ____.

From the 15th to the 16th we were employed in crossing the first pond, & it was not till the 18th the army got across the 3d pond. Two ____ of these ponds consist of waters which were pernicious to the soldiery. The salt provisions with which they were now exclusively ____, call'd for the frequent use of drink & we were entirely dependent upon such water as nature afforded us to supply our wants. There water were not only yellow but very bitter, which brought on either vomiting or diaherrea, or both to a very considerable part of the army. The 3d pond was less injurious. At this pond we supposed ourselves only 12 miles from the Kenebec.

Note: At this point in the journal Senter writes the following two different narrations.

First. This day we met Maj'r Bigelow with detachment of the 2nd Division of the Army returning in pursuit of provisions, who informed us that they could proceed no further without. We now ascended a mountain. Our woods beyond which we expected to find a small water stream which would conduct us to what was call'd the Dead River, & after traversing this height for about 27 miles, where we began to descend in to a hideous spruce & cedar swamp, in which we labored for another mile & a half.

Second. This day we met Maj'r Bigelow & 27 men who were returning from the 2d Division in search of Provisions, & inform'd that the men forward would advance no further without. From a S.W. course which we had follow'd since leaving the Kenebec, we now varied it nearly N.W. & ascended a mountainous & ___ ___, and then descended in to a spruce & cedar swamp so deep ___ & almost impenetrable brush for a mile & a half more till we came to a stream of slow water serpentine course apparently coming from S.W. part of the high wood we had just crossed. This was mostly about 12 feet wide and frequently as many deep. There are much appearance of beaver & other amphibious animals. After following this ¾ miles we descended two miles up these waters. Here to most of us was an unofficial report. An ox had been drown from Norrigwalk by two hands who had no other duty to attend to. He was slayn by the first Division each man taking all, or part as they came up. From the 8th of the month, this poor animal [had] eaten no other food than what the ___ etc afforded him & he swam over the riv'r & drove round the ponds & at night contentedly lodged with his drivers.

The water of this riv'r, which is the W. branch of the Kenebec had a remarkable dark appearance, & scarcely when we entered it to have any motion. Here we found excellent trought (trout) in plenty as we had in most of the ponds we had pass'd.

21st. We had a south west storm through the whole of this day which blew with such violence that we had not ascended but a few miles before the water became so great that it was with greater labour we forced our way against them. Add to this embarrassment, the violence of the increasing wind threw so many trees in to the river that we were momentarily expected to be sunk. We however labored incessantly while night approached & encamped about 15 miles up the stream, but instead of resting we were obliged to watch the provisions part of the night to guard against accidents from the frequent falling of the trees around us.

We here found Col. Greene's Div which could proceed no further for the want of provisions.

By the 20th, most of the rear Division had passed this carrying place, & after passing this reverted near a mile we came in to the Dead River, a western branch of the Kenebec. This stream is about 12 feet wide & for the most part was not very deep. There were much appearance of beaver & other animals of the kind here. When we first entered on this stream, its water appeared almost motionless, till a heavy rain with a violent wind S.W. soon swelled it to that degree that by 4 in the afternoon we had a rapid cur[rent] to oppose, with the addition of a great number of trees, which were by the severity of the wind constantly thrown in & a across it.

21. The storm continued to increase. All this days ascent was accompanied with the same difficulties in a greater degree than yesterday.

Side note: All these ponds abound with [the] tastiest trought [trout], which are easily taken.

22d. Not a dry thread had any of the army all night & as the morning was serene we were in motion at its dawn. The riv'r from being dead now had become so lively that many of our boats lay submerged almost out of sight. By actual measurement it had risen 8 feet during the night & how much in the day we could not definitively ascertain. In many places the land what was dry the day before now was inundated in many places for miles, especially up such creeks & small streams as emptied themselves into it. The land party now suffered hardships equally great as with that which went by water. Since in many instances the men were obliged [to] leave the course of the stream several miles to cross those over flown places, & in several instances they had no other method left them than to fell the trees to pass upon. These difficulties retarded our advance to that degree that in two days of the most severe exertion we [were] not more than 14 miles in advance. [The] Greater part of the way the bateaux were hauled up entirely [with] the assistance we obtained from the projecting inclining branches of small trees. Boats were over sot & nothing but the lives of the crews preserved.

23d. Our water carriage was daily ___ & every hour presented fresh & unexpected difficulties. All the cooking that was done was in the night when encamped. In several places the River was so barricaded with large trees, that we were obliged to clear them away or carry our batteaux round them. Besides this we meet 2 falls so grate that we could not ascend them.

24th. We this day meet two more carrying places of 2 miles each & the stream appeared every moment to grow more wild, drawing into a smaller compass, & the high lands with a terrific appearance began to assume a threatening aspect. We had only advanced 3 miles before we began to discern the wrecks of the batteaux left by Morgan's division, occasioned by his attempting to ascend the rapids at the foot of an impossible catarac. Another was pass a short distance above this & we soon met a number of invalids returning with such accts of the almost starved condition of the advanced parties & the impassible state of the River, that we began to conclude that we had arriv'd at our <u>ne plus ultra</u> . Night was now drawn near & we made fast our boats where we could no longer force them up, & march'd a short distance where we found Col. Greene detachment halted at the foot of two imperious mountains, which were only ___ ___ ___ this wild stream. Just room to pass. Morgan's ___ division was still in advance who derived no inconsiderable assistance from a hunting party who kept in the ___ of all the other troops for the purpose of taking all the wild game they could. Our bed & covering this night was composed of the boughs of the spruce & cedar & our supper of flower & candle soup. Apprized of the ___ of the provisions in the 2nd Division, orders were left here by Col. Arnold to separate the ___ & resolute from the infirm & broken hearted with leave for the latter to return, & the former only to persevere, & we were now only waiting for the arrival of Col. Enos's party to carry them into execution.

25th. We had a fall of snow last night of about 2 inches & this morning a request was dispatched to Col. Enos & officers to attend a Council which was to consider ___ at this dismal stage. At about 11 he arriv'd with a part of his officers, while the rest of his party were still below. While in the meantime, the remainder of the invalids were going back. [Based upon] An examining into the state of the two Divisions, it was found that in Enos's there are no [can't see full word], while in Greene's they [are] nearly expended. The question being, ___ Enos Pres., whether to proceed or return. The party against going on argued that there was no provisions for the whole army to last for 5 days.

    When all the officers present voted in the following manner.   (25th)

Greene's Division	Enos's Division
For going forward.	
Lt. Col. Greene	Capt. Williams
Maj. Bigelow	Capt. McCobb
Capt. Topham	Capt. Scott
Capt. Thayer	___ Hyde
Capt. Ward	Lt. Pellis

Col. Enos who was President gave his voice for going on.

It has already been absented that in consequence of the greater difficulties the two first Divisions of the Army expected to encounter, the less they were encumbered [with] the more weighty & solid provisions. Hence it was that there were much more pork & flower, & less of the perishable articles in the last party than in either of the others. The batteaux however in general [were] full of various things. The boxes of candles, barrels of powder, flint & ball were plentifully laid in.

It ought not to escape observation that altho' Scott [I think he means Enos] voted for a part of the army to proceed, yet it is very understood both by the officers who were of his party as well by those of Col. Greene's that he had pledged himself not to go forward. As the matter was now determined by vote what parts of the army would go forward, Colonel Greene provided an order left in this place by the Commander in Chief for an equal partition of the provisions between Greene's & Enos's Divisions & solicited dividend & agreed upon their principles to go on with those only who were willing to risk it. To this, the returning party utterly refused & asserted that there was not sufficient stores to inc[lude] all that part of the army & carry through the party who were determined to go on.

Col. Enos was then call'd upon to give a propitious order for an equal division. He replied that his men were out of his power, & that they had previously determined not to part with any. However, [they] finally concluded to give up 2 1/2 barrels of flower & this was all that we could do with them. We now quit all our batteaux excepting one to each company, for the purpose of conveying the military & hospital stores. We also left the few tents which we had in the army. Each one took his pack made out of a shirt & proceeded with all the vigor & determination which the desperacy of the occasion demanded. Pursued the River & passed one fall that afternoon & encamped when we could no longer see our way thru these dismal woods.

26th. In Col. Arnold's orders which he had left behind, we were directed to rendezvous on the white island at the head of the Chaudier Lake where all the first parties except himself were to wait for us. We passed three carrying places for the batteaux this day, & that there were high precipices & craggy mountains which we were obliged to crawl up on all fours with nothing but rock, moss & trees & shrubs to support us from tumbling down. Passed one point the Rv'r ran through beyond these rugged heights, & to encamp with nothing to cover ourselves except blanket for two.

27th. We rose by day light & having no cookery we made the best of our way. In the course of the days march, the Riv'r had dwindled away to nothing but a small brook. Our course was nearly S. S.W. This day we passed 4 ponds which this crazy brook ran through. The last of which was a very beautiful one on the Appalachian heights from which this branch of the Kenebec Lake it rises. We now proceeded over this chain of mountains, till we came to s descent & then to 7 Mile Stream which heads into the Chaudier Lake. This carrying place was computed 4 __. The course of this beautiful little riv'r was about N.E. & S.E. Here we found Capt. Morgan's Division with the rest of the advanced party where we were all to be waiting for the rear of the Detachment to come up.

[The journal ends rather abruptly here.]

TWO JOURNALS OR ONE

A comparison of the language and handwriting of two journals indicates they are very different even though Isaac Senter wrote both. They are not the same journal nor is one an embellished copy of the other. They read like two different journals written by two different people documenting the same events. It is obvious that they were written at different times and the information provided above supports that the same person wrote them.

It is clear that the Munn journal is not the original. Senter did not write that journal and then subsequently produce a less detailed and extensive version represented by the RIHS journal. There is no doubt that the RIHS journal was written first. While there is no definitive evidence that it was written during the march, Mr. Chapin of the RIHS has an excellent point about the timing of its writing which cannot be easily discounted. The Munn journal was written after the RIHS journal but before Senter died.

Because of the three introductory pages, it is likely that the RIHS manuscript was written by Senter after the assault and was used by him as a guide for writing the more detailed and descriptive Munn journal, which is of a later vintage. The Munn journal contains more extensive details about the expedition and, therefore, is more informative as an historical narrative than the RIHS journal.

There is a vast difference in the language and writing style of the two journals. Neither journal has been authenticated by any credible source as being in Senter's handwriting. The entries in the Munn journal contain information consistent with being written by a physician, including the identification of three surgeon mates which does not appear in any other journal.

There is no indication why Senter felt it necessary to write two very different journals other than the fact that he wrote his earlier journal with the intention of using it as a guide to write a new and improved journal. This makes sense because his later Munn journal contains more details and is better written than the RIHS journal. Because of his reputation and prestige in Rhode Island after the war, Senter likely preferred his legacy to be represented by the more polished Munn journal.

CHAPTER FIVE

VOICES WAITING TO BE HEARD

The two expedition journals presented in this chapter have never been published. These journals are presented in order to bring them to the attention of interested readers and to promote their significance as an historical record of the Arnold expedition.

The first previously unpublished journal in this chapter was written by Private Moses Kimball. While Roberts refers to it in his book and provides specific entries, he did not reproduce it in its entirety. This journal also has unique and helpful information about the expedition including a summary of the carrying places where the men on the expedition had to portage their bateaux and supplies.

The second journal was written by Private Samuel Barney and offers expedition details from the point of view of a private from New Haven, Connecticut. It is written in simple language but has many details about the lives of the enlisted men. It offers more names of the men in his company than is provided by any of the other journals written by a private. The Barney journal has historical significance because it is a previously unpublished personal account of the Arnold expedition and, therefore, deserves recognition.

MOSES KIMBALL'S JOURNAL

Note: The words in brackets were added by Dr. George Simmons, the transcriber of the journal.

"A great deal of this is worn by time and is not legible." [This notation is written by a different hand on the journal.]

List of Carrying Places on Expedition

Carrying Places on Kennebec River

No.	Miles	Rods
1	0	80
2	0	45
3	1	0
4	0	80

Great Carrying Place

No.	Miles	Rods
1	4	0
2	3/4	0
3	1/2	0
4	1/2	0

Carrying Places on Dead River

1	0	4
2	0	8
3	0	4
4	0	15
5	3/4	0
6	0	4
7	0	3
8	0	4
9	3/4	0
10	0	8
11	3/4	0
12	0	?
13	0	2
14	0	2
15	0	15

Between Kenebec & Chaudiere

1	3/4	0
2	1/2	0
3	can't read, figures torn out	

Sept

2. An adjorum ___ of the ___ Cambridge to General Arnold

8 Winter-hill. In the morning there was some difficulty between me & my mess mates. It rose to this degree [that] Lieutenant Emerson put two of us under guard. In about a quarter of an hour he took us out. I immediately went to [Remainder of page torn out].

[Top of reverse side of torn page.]

___ I went to Plumb Island ___ boxes on board of the Eagle Scooner ___ & these lay on board.

19. 10 oclock sail'd out of the harbor & stood off on (the side) waiting for one of the vessels that got on the rocks in the harbor. The men were put on board the other vessels & we sailed in the afternoon with a fair wind & steered for Kenebec River at night ___.

[bottom half of page is destroyed]

23. Within 6 miles of Fort Western, where we arrived the 23rd & encamped.

24. On guard at the Fort at night, James McCormick, being drunken, shot Sergeant Bishop belonging to Capt Williams Company. McCormick belonging to Goodrich.

25. [McCormick] Was tried by Court Martial & found guilty of murder.

26. [McCormick] Was sentenced to be hanged & brought to the gallows but was repriv'd till General Washington's pleasure was known.

27. Got our provisions on board the battows & proceed'd up the River about 4 miles & stopp'd.

28. Proceeded up the River and found the water very Shoal in some places, which caused a rapid current and about 3 miles of ripples.

30. Arriv'd at Fort Halifax where was the first carrying place & it was 80 rods. The inhabitants of this place depend much on fishing & hunting. This day found the water very rapid. The land on this part of the River is much better than that nearer the sea. This evening we carried our Battows & provisions over.

October

1. Proceeded up the river. [There were] Bad ripples & at night [we] lodged in the woods.

2. Went about 10 miles. The weather very cold & rainy.

3. We arrived at Skowhigin Falls, which is 40 rods [a]cross.ed. Got over our Battows & provisions. The land here is thinly inhabited.

4. We arrived at Harrigen walk where was formerly an Indian town but now settled by the English. Here we took our leave of houses & settlements, entering the wide wilderness. After two days stay here, [we will face a] carrying place of one mile in length.

6. Left Harrigen Walk & went 5 miles, where we encamp'd.

7. Set out very early & went to _____ & encamped & as usual took our bottle to make a drink of grog, but found good creature(s) gone which occasion'd dull looks. The land here is very level & good but the River (is) rapid.

8. We proceeded up the River & crossed Caratunk & encamped about 3 miles above the falls. It rained all night. Clear'd up in the morning & was very cold.

9. Proceeded up River & arrived at the Great Carrying Place.

10. Went to the first pond which was 4 miles from the river.

11. Cross'd the first pond which was 3/4 of a mile wide. At this carrying place near the river, Mr. Carr [Senter] built a log house for the sick.

13. [No entry for 12th] We cross'd this carrying place to another pond. This carrying place is 3/4 of a mile wide.

14. Cross'd the pond which was 1/2 mile wide & got over the carrying place which is 1 1/2 mile in length. The woods here are chiefly cedar & hemlock.

16. [No entry for 15th] Cross'd 3d pond which is 1 1/2 mile. Same day went over 4th carrying place, being 4 1/2 in length over a boggy swamp. Found it very difficult getting over our Battows & barrels, being obliged to wade knee deep. We launched our Battows into a creek which empties itself into Dead River. Here we encamp'd, being all greatly rejoiced at (the) thought of being over (the) worst of our fatigue.

17. Set out ___. Went 18 miles up the river. Crossed one carrying place of 4 rods. We encamp'd. Fine land for game but not very good on other accounts. The woods chiefly birch & hemlock.

18. Set out up the River & overtook Col. Green & his party about 25 miles up

the Dead River. Here we reciv'd orders to get ourselves in a defensive condition. Here the land appears to be very good but the water (is) unwholesome on account of many sorts of leaves falling into the river.

19. We reciev'd orders to push on & accordingly proceeded about 5 miles. Mr Spring & Mr [Aaron] Burr, not having a pilot, missed their way & travel'd considerable time before they found their way. It rain'd hard all night.

20. This day found it tedious being both cold & rainy & our Battows very leaky. This day cross'd the 10th carrying place.

21. Nothing remarkable. The land very good.

22. March'd through tedious woods & mountains for the most part, but sometimes (were) on the bank of the River where the water was excessive(ly) rapid. The chief (trees) of the woods is hemlock & fir.

23. About this time, Col. Enos & his party turn'd about & went back.

24. Capt. Hanchet & 60 men were ordered to march on with the greatest dispatch before the main body. Same day sent back about 40 sick & weak men. In the afternoon continued our march, but slowly.

25. Continued our march. Very bad traveling.

26. Cross'd the 11th carrying place which brought us to the first pond leading to Chaudiere River.

27. Cross'd 2d carrying place which was 3 quarters of a mile. Then cross'd 2d pond. Then cross'd 3d carrying place & 3d pond. Then the 4th carrying place & 4th pond, where we left out Battows & encamp'd.

28. Went 10 miles, wading knee deep a great part of the way, & came to a place over flowing where we stop'd (for) some time, not knowing what to do, & at last were obliged to wade up to our arm pits. The ground giving way (at) every step. We got on a little Island where we were obliged to stay, [with] night coming on. We were all wet & cold. This is Saterday.

29. Cross'd a river & waded 40 rods & came to another which we cross'd, & took a wrong way & went 2 miles & came back again. Then went 2 or 3 miles & came to a bark camp & stop'd that night.

30. Came where the River Chaudiere runs out of the pond. Went 20 miles & camp'd.

31. Went 21 [miles]. Capt. Goodrich's Company kil'd our dog to eat. Camp'd.

Wensday, November 1. Travel'd 20 miles & camp'd.

2. Travel'd 4 miles & met (the group bringing) provisions. [The] same day arrived at the first French inhabitants & stop'd, which was 14 miles further.

3. Went 12 miles further. Snow'd all [day].

4. Went 16 miles.

5. Went 6 miles & stop'd at a clever old Frenchman's house where they gave us rum & bread & butter, as much as we wanted. There was two pretty girls at the same house. Stayed till the next day.

6. Marched 18 miles.

7. Marched 8 miles. Stormed all day.

8. Marched 5 miles & came in sight of Quebec.

9. Took a prisoner named McCinsy [Mackenzie] who was a midshipman. We continued at Point Leavy until the 13th.

13. In the evening we crossed the River St. Lawrwnce & went [to] Major Colwells [Caldwell's] house & there stayed & kept guard till the 19th of November.

19. We set out from the major's house about 3 oclock in the morning. At night reached [our destination] at Point aux Trembles, where we stayed until General Montgomery came down with his army.

December 3. Set out for Quebec in battows with cannon & came to Wolfe's Cove & there landed.

4. Stayed at Wolfe's Cove all day.

5. Went to a nunery which is in [the] edge of the suburbs of Quebec & there stay'd

a few days. Then went over the River St. Charles to the house of Mr. Henry, a minister, & there stay'd till the storming of Quebec.

31. An hour before day, Col. Arnold's party came into St. Rock & marched on between the water & the town [at the same time] as General Montgomery went by Cape Dimond. After daylight, the enemy sallied out at [the] public gate to that degree we were obliged to surrender. There was 375 [men] taken prisoners.

January 3, 1776. General Carleton call'd for a list of our names [and] age.

4. All the old country men were picked of & called out.

5. They were call'd again to be examined by the General.

6. They were call'd out & sent to the Barracks, about 80 in number.

10. Wednesday. Norris & Martin went to the hospital. Our living is salt pork, bisket, rice & butter & a sufficient [amount] allowed us. And if we were not cheated in our weight by one Downy who is appointed 2r Master Sergeant to deal out our provisions. For instead of being our friend, [he] proved [to be] our Enemy by defrauding us of our allowance by scanty weight & measure.

21. [We] were ordered to make a return of all tradesmen amongst us. About this time, two of our company who enlisted in Enemy service escape(d) out of town.

30. About this time, Downy made a complaint [against] 15 men which had agreed to fight their way [out] & make their escape. Two of them were found out & sent to the goal in irons.

February 12. I went to the hospital.

21. I return'd from the hospital. Nothing material happened this month.

March 1. One of our men was put in irons for abusing the sentry.

2. There was an alarm.

13. We were moved to the old goal. The same is burn proof.

24. We hear our army have left Canada & gone to the line.

26. We hear they have brought 300 prisoners to town.

28. We hear of a cessation of arms.

30. A ship from England arrived here. Brought intelligence that a French fleet from France had arriv'd at America.

April 1. I myself was put in irons with 200 more [other men].

14. Major McKinzie took Capt Morgan's Company out [of] irons.

17. We had a weeks allowance of fine beef brought in which had been kill'd 3 or 4 months. Of which they boast much.

May 4. About 9 or 10 oclock at night the town was alarm'd & we saw a fire on the water which proved to be a fire ship sent down by our army, but (it) did no damage.

6. About sunrise, 3 ships came up to town. [They] brought some troops from Boston who marched [from the ships] at 10 oclock & drove our people off.

7. Our irons was taken off.

14. A ship set sail for England with a packet.

18. Heard that Major Meigs & Capt Dearborn were gone home.

27. Ten ships arrived with troops on board.

June 1. The Hanoverians arrived & (are) said to be about 4 thousand.

5. The General came in & gave us encouragement of sending us to our own country on condition never to bear arms against the King.

6. Sent the Governor an answer.

10. [We had] A thunder storm with hail stones as large as 2 oz. balls. A young woman was kill'd by the lightening.

(?). [preceding words not legible] have had since the arrival of the first troops, and the butter we had was very ordinary, but as we are prisoners we must be glad of anything we can get. This afternoon [we] heard that we were to be exchanged and were to go from this [place] in three days & cross the Lake.

[?]. We hear the militia had voted to keep us here & not let us go home at all. Some time(s) we hear some good (news), sometimes bad [news]. This afternoon [we] heard it contradicted about the militia. We heard again we were certainly (going) to go home & very soon. About this time, one of our company was very near out of his head.

———————————

28. This day Mr. Murray informed us that we should go home in a week or ten days. Likewise that we should have each of us a shirt.

31. We heard (that) our men has[ve] taken St. John again.

July 1. We hear the Indians have kill'd numbers of the Americans.

5. One of our plans _____ which thing I fear will bring us into trouble.

6. [It] Was found out & told to Prentice [?] [that] there was 2 prisoners brought in.

13. We heard that the Commander had got down here.

14. I had a tooth pulled.

16. There was a trifle of dancing. It seemed like old times. This evening Colonel McClain arrived at town.

19. We heard that we were not to go home but [would] stay where we are.

20. This morning George Conner was taken out for talking saucy [sassy] to the Provost.

21. This morning [we] heard that the Lizard had sail'd for England. [The] Same day [we] heard we were to sail in 7 or 8 days.

[page torn & worn. Hard to decipher.]

_____ for the arrival of General Carleton.

[?] This day had a week's allowance of butter brought in which was the first we
___.

22 [?]. Last night one of our men made their escape out of goal. About this time a plan was laid for our escape.

31. Our scheme being found out. One of our men, John Hall, went out & discovered the whole of our plot. Same day they put the Sergeants in irons.

August 1. We heard we were to be delivered to Lord Howe & were not to be exchanged. But [would] lay at his disposal.

5. This afternoon Mr. Prentice & Mr. Murray came in & brought our shirts. [At the] same time they took out 35 of the men. This day is 2 months since the General came & gave us encouragement of sending us home. This afternoon we was to go on board but one of the vessels was not ready so we are to go tomorrow.

6. ___ kind (of) a parole of honour to go home this afternoon. I [have] see(n) Major Bigelow & Capt Goodrich.

7. This morning we embarked on board of the Mermaid.

8. We drawed bisket & pork, 4lbs. of each to 6 men, & 1 gill of rum to each [man].

9. Draw'd fresh beef & soft bread, 1 lb of each to a man. Rum the same as yesterday.

10. This morning a ship arrived from Bristol named Stranger.

11. This morning there was a gun fired for the sail & 2 ships sail'd about a mile down River. The sun [was] about an hour high. At night, another gun was fired & we weighed anchor ___ down the river & came to anchor.

12. Stormy weather. Hoisted sail & sailed 44 leagues & came to anchor.

13. High winds (a)head of us so we could not sail any [today].

14. Pleasant weather & a fair wind. Weighed anchor & sail'd 13 leagues & came to anchor about 12 oclock., the wind & tide (being) against us. [We were] within

a league of Choodrough, an island. This day we saw white ____. At 4 oclock weighed anchor again. The wind fair. Came to anchor about 2 oclock at night.

15. This morning about sunrise, weighed anchor & sail'd with a fair wind [until] about 3 oclock. [Went] past the Island of Pik.

16. Continued our sail in the afternoon. Bad wind at night. Stormed & ___ all night.

17. [Page worn by age.] Fair weather this morning. Saw the whales spout the water. Our course for several days past has been north & north by east. Today it is east.

18. Today our course is south, the winds easterly. We run about 5 knots an hour.

We passed Gaspa Pint, where [there] is a river [that] comes in from Biscay.

19. This morning our course was east and we were sailing along side of St. Johns Island. About 3 oclock we saw Capertune & Cape Britten. The banks of St Johns Island in some places is very red. About 4 oclock we saw a frigate on shore. Our course is south east.

20. This day our course is round about [the] islands. Not getting forward very much.

21. Contrary winds ___ poor way ahead.

22. Last night at midnight, Capt ____ anchor & lay till the sun rose about an hour high. At night for the barge was gone ashore. After weighed anchor our course was south east & by south.

23. Our course was south east for the biggest part of the day. About the middle of the afternoon, we came to the gut of Cansor & our course then was southwest & by south & we got through the gut about 10 oclock at night.

24. Our course today is south east. At 2 oclock at night, [the] wind [was] westerly. We tack'd about & went north west.

25. [Here are a mass of indistinct figures evidently referring to the degree of latitude & longitude].

26. [Top of page torn away.] The sea is very calm. No wind hardly. What there was was west a little. (In the) afternoon, we saw a very [large] number of porpoises.

27. This morning there was a dreadful sea. The wind south east. Our course southwest & by south. We ran at the rate of 7 knots an hour all day. Th[ough] some of the time we run 7 1/2 [knots] per hour.

28. This morning no wind. We lay tossing about.

29. But little wind in the morning. At noon a good N.E. wind blew our course WSW.

30. Our course the same as yesterday.

31. A very good breeze all day. Steering to the west. This day Lieut. _____ caught a dolphin of 7 or 8 lbs.

Sunday, September 1, 1776. This morning the wind shifted into the NWS. Our course is S.W. & by W. At 12 oclock the Capt. & the mate took an observation & said we were in the latitude of 30 & (a) half.

2. This day our course is S.W. & by S & by W. The wind nice.

3. In the morning for an hour the wind was S, then shifted into the N.W. From 8 to 12 oclock our course was S. (&) then tacked & went N. W. The wind W & by S. This day a t 12 oclock we were in the latitude of 37 & 19. This day I see some flying fish.

4. This morning one of our men caught a small shark. Our course is northerly. We have a head wind. Last night there was flying fish [that] came aboard of us.

5. This morning our course is N west & so continued all day.

6. Our course the same as yesterday. The wind [is] northerly.

7. A calm [sea] all day. At night [we had] a small breeze & [it] arose higher & higher.

8. This morning our course is N.W. The wind in _____. We run at the rate of 6 knots an hour. About 1 oclock we sprung our main topmast. In the afternoon we had a thunder shower.

9. Continued our course. The wind N.E.

10. Our course [is] westerly. The wind [is] southerly.

11. Our course [was] S.W. until 1 oclock, then [we] went N.W. This night we made land.

12. This morning we see land all round before us & we saw the light house. About 7 oclock there came a pilot on board of us. At 9 oclock [we] came to anchor. At 1 oclock [we] weighed anchor & sail'd again & went about 5 miles above the narrows where we came to anchor. In this harbor there is 4 or 5 hundred sail of shipping, [the] biggest part of which is transports.

13. Here we lay in the harbor in sight of New York. About 5 oclock the King's troops lay siege to the town.

14. We lay in the harbor. Nothing of [con]sequence.

15. This morning there was a land engagement between the King's troops & our people & so continued by spells all day. At 3 oclock [in the] afternoon New York was taken.

16. This night (New) York was set on fire & our men have taken everything out of town that is of any worth.

17. We have no news about having our liberty. Pleasant weather.

18. Pleasant and warm.

19. No news today.

20. Tonight at 11 oclock the Town was set on fire by our men.

21. This afternoon we hear that orders is given out that we shall be landed next Monday at 8 oclock.

22. Sunday. My disorder increases daily.

23. Those on board of Lord Sandwich came on board the Mermaid. Weighed anchor & went down between Statens Island & the main land.

24. In the morning I was landed at Elizabethtown in New Jersey & stayed there sick until the 20th of October.

19. October. My brother Joseph came to town.

20. Sunday. This morning [we] set out for home where I reach the _____.

[Here the record ends]

[The above mentioned manuscript came into my hands in the following manner: While traveling through Ohio I met DR. L.C. Walker of Jamestown, Ohio, who gave me the first information I had concerning the manuscript. He very kindly drew up a copy and forwarded it to me. It reached me shortly after December 20, 1928. This copy was made from the original long hand copy which Dr. Walker sent me. It has been checked by myself and verified by my stenographer.]

George E. Simmons
Professor of Agronomy
College of Agriculture
University of Maine
Orono, Maine
July 6, 1934

DIARY OF SAMUEL BARNEY OF NEW HAVEN, 1775-1776

September the 16th, 1775. Had this book of one Mr. Jones of Newbury Porte [Newburyport]. This book cost nine copper.

Samuel Barney

Roxbury, September 6th, 1775. Enlisted to go to Quebeck: Isaac George, Gabriel Hotchkiss, Samuel Barney, John Wise, Elijah Mix, Arch Blakeley, Roswell Ransom, Sherman Shattuck, Joseph Lewis, Daniel Jud[d], Freeman Jud[d], Allen Jud[d], Benjamin Warner, Isaac Knap, Samuel Barnes, Allen Ives

The 8th day went to Cambridge.

September the 9th was reviewed.

September the 10th. There was five [st]raglers brought to Cambridge Guard House from Roxbury.

September, Tuesday the 13th, 1775. Isaac George, Gabriel Hotchkiss, John Wise and I washed at Inn at Cambridge where Jonathan Browne lives. Marched from Cambridge to Mistick about 3 or 4 miles and next morning we marched about 3 or 4 miles to Malden and went to breakfast at William Watts; and then went on to Newt's Tavern in Lynn, which is five miles, where we got some grog and then went to Howes Tavern in Denwitch which is seven miles; and to Meeting House is 2 miles and about 1 and a half to Benjamin Dealins in Danvers and left Salem on the right hand.

September the 14th, 1775. Went on seven miles to Beverley and to Wentham Meeting House is three miles and to Ipswich to landlord John Browne is two miles and to landlord Stainers is 5 miles.

September the 16th, Saturday. Got to Newbury Porte [Newburyport] which is seven miles more.

Sunday the 17th. I went to meeting at church.

Monday, September the 18th, 1775. Slept at Abraham Simmons and went on board the sloop Britania.

Tuesday, September the 19th. Ate a breakfast of codfish and rum and got under way about six o'clock in the morning and steered about east and by south. In the afternoon sailed by the Island of Oritage and was by Piscataqua Light House and passed by the Island of Sholes about three o'clock. Boon Island about east and our course was northeast.

September, Wednesday the 20th. Past the Island of Seguin. Our course was north east by that island. This morning entered the River's mouth and the pilot boat come off. The River runs about north westerly. Came to anchor about one o'clock. This day ate a dinner of herrings and then went up to a spring and got some water and made some grog and drank it with a good stomach. From Saguin to where we anchor is 30 miles, where George and I got some beer and made some flip. About eight o'clock we got under way and rode up the River five miles and then come to and stayed all night.

September, Tuesday [Thursday] the 21st. This morning arose well and got under way about seven o'clock. This morning had a good breakfast of chocolate and went up the River three miles and came to Broxby. By Captain Christian got ashore at Gardiners Town about one o'clock. From Newburyport to Gardners Town was two hundred miles. The people say this town is fifty-five miles from Quebeck.

September, Friday the 22nd, 1775. This morning arose well but very cold; but last night we had a dance and last night there was a _____ brig launched here. This morning was whipped a man at Gardners Town, 10 stripes by verdict. Isaac George and I went up in a battow eight miles and we beat anyone that was there, but I blistered my hands very bad.

September, Saturday the 23rd. This morning arose well but lay very hard upon the barrels and it is very cold. Isaac George and I went up the River three miles to Fort Western and there we landed our barrels; and then went down again and brought up all our things about five o'clock at night, and it was very cold.

September, Sunday the 24th. This morning arose well and all the rest of our mess and George & Blakeslee too. Last night was shot a man, one Bishop, and is liked to die. This day passed off with mending clothes, and a hard shower of rain, and we was in our tent. Bishop died today about five o'clock in the afternoon.

September, Monday the 25th. This morning arose well and went to prayers and some company([es] marched off. This day was whipped one James Culverson ten stripes for taking a thirty shilling bit to change and never returned it again to one Biggs. This day had a good dinner of fish. This Culverson was drummed out of camp. This day Rueben Bishop was buried, of Captain Williams company.

September, Tuesday the 26th. This morning arose not very well. A rainy day, and in the afternoon about three o'clock, one James McCormack was to be hung and s___ upon the scaffold and was reprieved and at once.

September, Wednesday the 27th. This morning arose well and went to prayers. John Love was whipped thirty nine stripes for stealing. About noon was whipped a sailor for stealing, twenty stripes. Set out in battos and went up the River five miles and then come to and stayed all night.

September, Thursday the 28th, 1775. Arose well and ate chocolate for breakfast. Loaded our battows and went up about two miles and came to falls, Samuel Barnes, John Wise and I. From the falls to Vasselborough is forty miles, where we found a man and drinked some grog and ate a dinner of codfish; and to the next falls is one mile and a half _____. Went up the River about 8 miles and come to and stayed all night. Next morning went up to a man's house and got some milk. There is good land here.

Friday, September the 29th. This morning arose well but I lay very cold, and Isaac George, Gabriel Hotchkiss and I went in the battows and went up the River five miles to Forte Halifax and had dam's bad work to get there, and had a damned bad boat. We got up to [from] Forte Halifax to the first Carrying place and we carried our boat and then pitched our tent and made a large fire, and I lay down by it and I slept well.

Saturday, September the 30th. This morning arose well and got some chocolate and herrings, and then we loaded our battow, and Barnes, Wise and Warner went in them about a mile, and come to a bad falls that lasted about a quarter of a mile; and then went about two miles and came to Three Mile Falls, that were very bad. Then George, Hotchkiss and I went to a house and had an ox killed; and then we had to go back a mile and pitched our tents and slept.

October, Sunday the 1st. This morning arose well and went up the River 13 miles. Had some bad falls and the rest was good. This day George, Barnes and I has come to a good place.

October, Monday the 2nd. This morning arose well and it is liked to rain. George, Barnes and I goes in the boat. Went up the River one mile and a half, all bad falls, and then came to a carry where we had to carry our boats fifty rods, and set out again. Had good water three miles and then we stopped. Slept very well this night.

October, Tuesday the 3rd. 1775. This morning arose well. George, Barnes and I in the batto set out and had some very good water and then had some very bad falls, and had a leaky boat. Came up the River 8 miles, and then came to a carrying place, where we had to carry one mile and a half. The name of this place is Norridgewock.

October, Wednesday the 4th, 1775. This morning arose well but George out. The name of this place is Norrigewock. Is five miles back and wait. Name of this place is Norridgewock. Today we carried our boats over this carrying place. No more English inhabitants upon this River after this; and then come to the Indians.

October, Thursday the 5th. This morning arose well and tarried here at the carrying place all this day; and mended my jacket. Had a wheat pudding for dinner. Loaded our batto about five o'clock and went up the River about one mile, and stopped and slept. Barnes, Hotchkiss and I. George is sick.

Friday, October the 6th, 1775. This morning arose well and slept. Had some chocolate for breakfast. In the afternoon we set out and went about three miles.

Barnes, George and Wise, for I was sick. The best land I ever see. I feel better. I slept but little.

Saturday, October the 7th, 1775. Arose this morning but felt very poorly; but George, Barnes and I went in the boat and went twelve miles to the carrying place, where we carried our things seventy rod. Then we loaded our boats and went about one mile and a half; but I felt poorly all day and all night; but I stole pork and Warner stole some bread.

Sunday, October the 8th. This morning, being very rainy, I lay very late, for I was poorly and we did not move from here this day. We stayed here all day and did not feel a bit well. Made no grains all day, and now Hotchkiss is making bread.

Monday, October the 9th, 1775. This morning arose a little better than I have been. This morning clear and cold and very windy; and Wise, Warner and Hotchkiss got into the battow and there fell a storm. Then Barnes and Hotchkiss went in about seven miles and very bad going it was.

Tuesday, October the 10th. This morning arose well, and Hotchkiss, Warner and I went in the boat and went up the River five miles, and a very hard way; and then came to the carrying place which is three miles and a quarter by the chain. Allen Ives and Allen Todd and Amasa Allen went home the 6th day of October.

Wednesday, October the 11th. This morning arose well, but George is poorly yet. We ate a chocolate for breakfast without sugar, and carried over ten battows. Then we carried a barrel of flour and got almost across and left it; and then we laid by all night and then in the morning, we carried it up, then went back,

Thursday, October the 12th. This morning arose up and carried over some pork, and then came back again and carried over the Major's boat and pitched a tent.

Friday, October the 13th. This morning arose well and carried our things over this place, which is two miles. The first pond is one mile and the next is two miles, where we encamped. James Taylor, Ichabod Swaddle and [Sylvanus] Hale came into our mess. Today it snowed.

Saturday, October the 14th. This morning arose well and we carried our things over this place, which is two miles; and it rained some but we got a good fire tonight and feel well.

Monday, October the 16th, 1775. This morning arose well and carried our provisions one mile and a quarter; and drived our boats into the creek which leads to Dead River, and went up the River two miles. Wise and I pitched our tent and had some ____ for supper and felt well.

Tuesday, October the 17th, 1775. This morning arose well and got some breakfast and shaved, and hove away the shoes that Hill made us. We don't move from here today. We feel well and have cleaned our guns today.

Wednesday, October the 18th. This morning arose well. It is cold and pleasant, and there is twenty men a going to go back about two miles after fresh beef. Started late, but went up the River 10 miles and a half, and went by an Indian hut where the Ingen [Indian] spys was kept, and overtook two other companies and then stopped. Wise, Hale and I went in the boats. Good land here. We went six miles and had a carrying place about five rods, and the rest a good River.

Thursday, October the 19th. This morning arose well and it rained very hard here. We moved in the afternoon and went up the River five miles and had some bad falls.

Friday, October the 20th. This morning arose well and it rained very hard; but we moved and had our allowance shortened from three-quarters of a pound of pork to half a pound, and a final pint of flour; and we went up the River five miles and had a carrying place which was 15 rods, and then went up the River ten miles more. Rained all day. Wise, Swaddell and I in the boats. I have a bad boil and a sore shoulder. We had some bad falls. The Major's boat was overset.

Saturday, October 21st. This morning arose well but it had rained very hard and we went up the River four miles and then had a carrying place, which was 40 rods; then went up the River two miles and then had another [carrying place], which was 50 rods, and then stopped. It rained very hard.

Sunday, October the 22d. This morning arose well but lame with a boil. This morning it did let up, and we went up the River one mile and a half and had a carrying place of 80 rods; and then went up the River 100 rods and came to another carrying place and stopped. [We] were held up all the way by bushes. Taylor, Wise and I, [and] the Major and Captain got lost, but they found us in the night.

Monday, October the 23d. Arose well and stood guard. We went up the River. We carried our things over this place which is 100 rods, and then went up the River six miles, and had many bad falls, and George's boat was overset.

Tuesday, October the 24th, 1775. This morning arose well. [Isaac] George, ____,

[Theophilus] Hyde, [Simon] Winter, [Roswell] Ransom & [David] Sheldon was sent forward and to ___. Was sent back [John] Cole, [Elijah] Mix, [Josiah] Remington, _____, [Abijah] Perry, [Joseph] Curtis. Then we all set out and went up the River three miles and it snowed. Barnes, [Mark] Lun and I in the boats. We had a good place.

Wednesday, October the 25th. This morning arose well and went up the River 4 miles and had a carrying place 10 rods, and then went up the River 100 rods and has another about 8 rods, and then went up the River two miles and had a very bad way. Then another carrying place and carried over that, which is a quarter of a mile and then stopped. Barnes, Swaddell and I in a boat.

Thursday, October the 26th. This morning arose well and went up the River about half a mile and then went into a Pond and then had two more Ponds, and had a carrying place about 15 rods. We went twelve miles today, [Elijah] Marshall, Swaddel and I.

Friday, October the 27th. This morning arose well and slept on the top of a mountain and carried the boats into a Pond which is a mile, and then crossed the Pond. Then had another carrying place which is three quarters of a mile, and then went into another Pond which carried us into the great carrying place, which is four miles.

Saturday, October the 28th. This morning arose well and left out battos and took seven days provisions on our backs, and went four miles to the creek that leads to Showdare [Chaudiere].

Sunday, October the 29th. This morning arose well and it snowed but we marched ten miles and came to Showdare [Chaudiere] . This is not the Showdare Pond, for we have been lost and have traveled in the swamp.

Monday, October the 30th. This morning arose well and traveled 15 miles in the woods.

Tuesday, October the 31st. his morning arose well and it was cold and snowed. We traveled seven miles and found Showdare River. Traveled 8 miles and stopped.

Wednesday, November the 1st. This morning arose well and marched 20 miles. It snowed and our provisions was almost gone.

Thursday, November the 2d. This morning arose well and a fine day, and some of us marched off soon, and we traveled 24 miles and had news of provisions ahead; and we traveled one mile more and stopped and ate all our provisions up.

Friday, November the 3d. We rose early and marched 18 miles and found cattle and got some meat and ate hearty, and it stormed fierce. Then we went about 10 miles and I gave an Indian a Pistareen to carry us down five miles, and found houses. George gave us a loaf of bread and some butter and ate hearty, and built a house. It snowed and I had sentry guard.

Saturday, November the 4th. This morning arose well and was very lame, but went about two miles. We see two Frenchmen in a boat and they carried us 19 miles and we gave them six Pistareens for it.

Monday, November the 6th. This morning arose well and stayed here till about 4 o'clock and then marched about half a mile.

Tuesday, November the 7th. This morning arose well but very lame. We marched from Saint Maries 16 miles through the woods and it snowed very hard.

Wednesday, November the 8th. This morning arose very unwell but marched about five miles and stopped.

Thursday, November the 9th. This morning very lame and stayed all day to a white house.

Friday, November the 10th, 1775. This morning arose very sick and stayed here at the white house and it snowed very fast all day. The regulars fired cannon all day and we had news that our men took a Lieutenant and a barge. Our company marched off and left me for I was sick.

Saturday, November the 11th. This morning arose very sick and laid out a Pistareen fore butter and another for eggs. Stayed here all night.

Sunday, November the 12th. This morning arose, was better and marched 9 miles and found the Company.

Monday, November the 13th. This morning arose well and stayed here till night and then we went over the River Saint Lawrence and landed where General Wolfe did. Then a barge came along and we fired at them and killed three men.

Tuesday, November the 14th. This morning arose well and had an alarm for the regulars (British) took one of our men. We marched up to the Fort and they fired at us.

Wednesday, November the 15th. This morning arose well and went on guard down by the River.

Thursday, November the 16th. This morning came off guard. The ship fired at us and came very near. This day Sergeant Dixon was shot in the leg and died.

Friday, November the 17th. This morning arose well but it is very cold.

Saturday, November the 18th. This morning arose well and went on guard at the sentry guard.

Sunday, November the 19th. This morning came off guard and all the rest were gone, but George and I overtook them. Marched 24 miles and went in my stocking feet and was very _____ , lame and cold.

Monday, November the 20th. This morning arose well and marched one mile and a half and found the Company.

Tuesday, November the 21st. This morning arose well and got a pair of shoes and washed; and George cut my hair, and (we) made some pancakes. I laid out two pistareens and a half for rum and eggs.

Wednesday, November the 22d. This morning arose well. Isaac George, debtor, to one shilling that I paid to Salem on the way out, and to [buy] one shirt.

Thursday, November the 23d. This morning arose well but it snowed.

Friday, November the 24. This morning arose well and it snowed. But I went to the tavern and ate till I am sick.

Saturday, November the 25th. This morning arose well and am going ___ miles and met Captain Grant. And went a ___ ____ and found it near that ____ in some good ____. Then I had a fit[?].

Sunday, November the 26th. This morning arose very well and John Wise and I went about two miles; and I got three pints of rum and got some bread and milk and paid for it. This day heard that Hull was dead.

Monday, November the 26. This morning arose. The rest of the entry is cut off and unreadable.

Friday, December the 1st. This morning arose well and we all slung our packs and marched over to the Captain's, and Major Meigs came and talked to us. There were three vessels came down and we marched two miles to see General Montgomery.

Tuesday, December the 5th. This morning arose well and marched to the review and went again to (the) other side of the creek, and our mess went three or four miles and could not find no house. We loaded our guns and at last found a house where we stayed; and in the morning we drew lots to know who should eat milk.

Wednesday, November the 6th. This morning arose well and it snowed. Went over to the Captain's where we played for some wine and then found a house to go into.

Thursday, December the 7th. This morning arose well. Nothing strange happened today.

Friday, December the 8th. This morning arose well and went to the review.

Saturday, December the 9th. This morning arose well and went about three miles and called the Quarter Master to our store; and went on fatigue, and we built a battery and have 26 guns.

Sunday, December the 10th. This morning not very well and the Regulars fired all this morning.

Monday, December the 11th. This morning came off fatigue. We built a gun battery. It was very cold.

Tuesday, December the 12th. This morning was on guard and our mess house burned and the Regulars fired all the while. Came off guard.

Wednesday, December the 13th. This morning arose not very well but ate breakfast of bread and milk, but was not well. This night ate a supper of turkey.

Thursday, December the 14th, 1775. This morning arose not well for a have lumbago, and this day there was a ball come through our breastwork and killed three men and wounded two more.

Friday, December the 15th. This morning arose not well. Our men fired 16 cannon and then sent in a flag of truce for them to resign, but they won't and our men went at it again. They have killed one man and wounded another.

Saturday, December the 16th. This morning arose not well. A fine day. Last night an Indian was killed and today a Soldier was killed and three of our cannon was dismantled. They fired all the while.

Sunday, December the 17th. This morning arose no better. A stormy day. This day passed and nothing done.

Friday, December the 22d. This morning arose well and we had orders to fasten a hemlock bus to our caps.

Sunday, December the 24th. This morning arose well, and this night we had a sermon preached by Mr. Spring; and he took his text on the 2d Book of Chronicals, the twenty second chapter and twenty 9 verse. "And the fear of God was on all the Kingdoms of those countries when they heard the Lord fought against the enemies of Israel".

Monday, December the 25th. This morning arose very poorly and had orders to proceed to General Montgomery's at five o'clock in the afternoon.

Tuesday, December the 26th. This morning arose some better. We was asked who would scale the walls. There was (17)? Turned out.

Wednesday, December the 27th. This morning arose well and it snowed, and we had orders to go into Quebec and all paraded, but it cleared up and we did not go.

Saturday, December the 30th. This morning arose well and last night Sergeant Singleton deserted to the regulars. There they have been and fired cannon all day and all night.

Sunday, December the 31st. Last night we went to scale the walls. General Montgomery was killed and all our people that got into low(er) town are took prisoners. Major Meigs come out on parole of honor.

Monday, January the 1st. This morning it was very stormy and we had to retreat. The Colonel (Arnold) is wounded.

Tuesday, January the 2d. Last night was afraid that the regulars would come out and we lay on our arms all night. Major Meigs came out again on parole.

Wednesday, January the 3d. This morning arose well. Lieutenant Cooper is dead and William Goodrich too. It is very warm and Sergeant Liman [Abner Lyman] and James Moore is gone home.

Thursday, January the 4th. This morning arose well and it is very warm and rainy. We heard that the Regulars was coming out.

Friday, January the 5th. This morning arose well. Last night we heard that Joseph Goff was dead. It is very warm and rainy. Major Meigs went into Quebec.

Saturday, January the 6th. This morning arose well and it is very cold, but nothing happened today.

Sunday, January the 7th. This morning arose well. Today very pleasant and we are going to send the soldiers' things into them. There was a hundred men killed and wounded. Nathaniel Gutridge [Goodrich] is dead.

Monday, January the 8th. This morning arose well. This day it snowed and this day George Hubbard of Bedford died with the small pox. Three French prisoners died. Borbo [Barbeau] for one.

Tuesday, January the 9th. This morning arose well and it snowed very hard all night and then cleared.

Wednesday, January the 10th. This morning arose well. It is very cold today and the old Flag o' truce died.

Thursday, January the 11th. This morning arose well. It snowed very hard and the old man was buried.

[The following statement has been placed at the end of the journal: "Here the diary ends abruptly but out of necessity, as the book was filled and probably no other was to be had."]

Drawn by Sydney Adamson   Halftone plate engraved by H. Davidson

WORKING AGAINST THE FLOOD ON DEAD RIVER

CHAPTER SIX

UNKNOWN EXPEDITION COMMANDERS

Captains William Hendricks, Jonas Hubbard, Oliver Hanchett and William Goodrich are obscure figures with very little written about their lives. Hubbard and Hendricks were killed in the assault on Quebec so they lost their lives less than nine months after they first volunteered for service in the American army. The assault on Quebec, which was their only major military campaign, ended in a personal disaster with their deaths. With little in the way of a military career and not much on their personal lives, they have not been good candidates for further examination. Hanchett and Goodrich survived the assault, were taken prisoner and were held by the British until the fall of 1776. Hanchett left the army after being released, so he is similar to Hubbard and Hendricks because he had no further military career to examine. Of the four, only Goodrich had a subsequent military career.

Captain William Hendricks

There are not many details known about the life of William Hendricks. He was born on the Lowther Manor estate in East Pennsborough, Pennsylvania, Cumberland County, but no record exists of his exact date of birth. He was the grandson of Tobias Hendricks Sr., from Donegal, Ireland, the son of Albertus Hendricks. Tobias Sr. was an Indian trader and possibly the first white settler in the valley. He settled there around 1725 and became an important political leader during its early history. He subsequently served as a Judge and County Commissioner in Lancaster County. At that time, the land was included in Lancaster County and remained so until Cumberland County was formed in 1750.

Tobias Sr. wrote a letter to John Harris in 1727 where he describes himself located on "this side of ye Susquehanah."[128] His referenced land was located on the west side of the Susquehanna River. The location of that settlement was at Oyster Point, which is west of Harrisburg. His home in the Town of East Pennsborough was called Lowther Manor, which was part of the Penn family holdings. The Penn family agreed to allow the subdivision of the Lowther Manor estate in 1736. At that point, the only structures on the manor were John Harris' Ferry, Peter Chartier's trading post and the house of Tobias Hendricks Sr. An early history reported that Tobias Sr. "lived on and had charge of Lowther Manor" which he managed for the Penn family.[129] There is no record to show that Tobias Sr. ever actually took ownership of any lands in his name. Tobias Sr. died in November of 1739 leaving 6 children.

One account says that one of Tobias Sr.'s sons, Henry lived on "the old place" where William Hendricks was born, and goes on to suggest that he might be the father.[130] However, Robert Crist has a different point of view. "William's father, also Tobias, had been living in the Manor of Lowther as a representative of the Penn family for nearly forty years".[131] The consensus of opinion now is that William's father was Tobias Jr., who in the early 1740's began operating a tavern, known as the "Sign of the White Horse" or "Tobey's Stand," on a parcel of land identified as Tract No. 18 of Lowther Manor. Tobias Jr. did not actually purchase the land on which he built his tavern until the early 1770's. His tavern was an important meeting place for traders and travelers and also hosted political meetings and community events. Tobias Jr. did purchase other land in his name prior to 1750, probably for speculation, so his name was on the list of taxables in East Pennsborough in 1750 and 1762.

In terms of previous military experience, one historical sketch of the Hendricks family speculates that William "likely served" in his brother James' company during the Bouquet expedition in 1764.[132] The French and Indian War experience makes sense because Hendricks must have had some previous military experience or good political connections in order to get designated as a captain of a rifle company in 1775. There is, however, no record of William being in his brother's company.

On June 14, 1775, Continental Congress passed a resolution creating a corps of riflemen. Because of the aggressive response to the call for rifle brigades, particularly in Pennsylvania, on June 22nd Congress directed Pennsylvania to raise two more such companies. By the 11th of July, Cumberland County had raised two companies of riflemen including one organized and commanded by William Hendricks. The Cumberland County companies became part of a total of nine such companies from Pennsylvania under the command of Colonel William Thompson of Carlisle. Robert Crist states that Hendricks's rifle company roster "read like a census of Ulster" with many Scotch-Irish names.[133] Oscar Stroh states that "about two thirds of the riflemen were of Scotch-Irish descent".[134] There is no doubt that the Hendricks family had close connections to the Scotch-Irish settlers in Cumberland County.

The cost of recruiting a company of men was up to the commander and William Hendricks was able to raise his own recruiting money. On June 23, 1775, Hendricks "rec'd 50 pounds" from Robert Miller to pay recruiting expenses, presumably as a gift, and raised another 15 pounds by selling his half interest in a tract of land in Northumberland County.

According to the McCoy journal, the company departed from Carlisle on July 13th and arrived at Cambridge on August 8th. Hendricks and his company were active members of the Quebec expedition and participated in the assault on the city. Hendricks was killed in the assault and was buried in Quebec in the same burial site as General Montgomery.

John Joseph Henry described Hendricks death in his journal. "Hendricks, when aiming his rifle at some prominent person, died by a straggling ball through his heart. He staggered a few feet backwards and fell upon a bed, where he instantly expired".[135] Lieutenant Nichols, his second in command, describes his death as " ... from a volley of musketry a ball went through Capt. Hendricks' left breast and he expired in a few minutes."

In his eulogy of General Richard Montgomery, Provost William Smith said about William Hendricks, "I must not, however, omit the name of the brave Captain Hendricks, who commanded one of the Pennsylvania rifle companies, and was known to me from his infancy. He was, indeed, prodigal of his life, and courted danger out of his tour of duty."[136] Smith goes on to point out that Hendricks's commanders, Thompson and Magaw, said of him, "No fatigues of duty ever discouraged him; he paid the strictest attention to his company, and was ambitious that they should excel in discipline, sobriety, and order. His social and domestic virtues you were well acquainted with."[137] John Joseph Henry in his journal describes Hendricks as "tall, of mild and beautiful countenance ... soul animated by a genuine spark of heroism."[138]

Some have suggested that Hendricks attended the College of Philadelphia based on Smith's statement in the eulogy that he knew him from his infancy. Crist says that there is no mention of Hendricks on the student rolls of the college so they must have met elsewhere. He suggests that they met at the tavern owned and operated by William's father. Crist argues that Smith traveled in Pennsylvania before he settled there in 1754 and that he would have undoubtedly stopped at the Hendricks' tavern.[139]

According to Oscar Stroh and Henry Young, when he led the rifle company in the expedition William Hendricks was "barely 21" and was a "natural leader".[140] While he may have been a natural leader, their statement regarding Hendricks' age is not supported by the known facts about his life. Young explains this conclusion because Provost William Smith came to Pennsylvania in 1754, and, in his eulogy regarding General Montgomery, Smith said he knew Hendricks from his infancy. Thus, various writers, including Stroh and Young, concluded that Hendricks was twenty-one years old in 1775 because Smith implies he was an infant in 1754. The question is whether Smith met William prior to 1756. As indicated above, Smith is presumed to have traveled in Pennsylvania before 1754 and met William in his father's tavern.

William Hendricks' birth date is established by the date of his marriage. According to the records examined by the Cumberland County Historical Society, Hendricks was married to Mary Reynolds in 1761. If he were twenty-one in 1775, he would have been born in 1754 and married at the age of seven. This is obviously not realistic. Based on his marriage date, he must have been at least eighteen years old in 1761 making his date of birth approximately 1743. Therefore, in 1775 he would have been thirty-two years old and not twenty-one years old as some previous writers have assumed.

Although he was married at the time of his death, there is no record of any children from the marriage. It is also unclear what became of his wife Mary after his death as she does not appear in any record after 1775. The scarcity of records on William Hendricks life outside of his experience on the Quebec expedition is frustrating and surprising because of his family's substantial involvement in the history of Cumberland County.[141]

Captain Jonas Hubbard

Jonas Hubbard was born in Worcester, Massachusetts on May 21, 1739, the son of Daniel and Dorothy Hubbard. His father was an early settler of Worcester. Hubbard was described as "an active business man of ample means at the outbreak of the Revolution." One source describes his activities prior to the war as being "engaged in the cultivation of his patrimonial estate, and in the management of extensive concerns of business." He was likely farming his father's lands.

On March 7, 1759, he married Mary Stevens and they had four children. In the winter of 1774-5, Hubbard was a founding member of Timothy Bigelow's company of minutemen. Hubbard was initially appointed as an ensign but was promoted to lieutenant prior to the Lexington Alarm. Bigelow's company with Hubbard as first lieutenant marched to Cambridge on April 19 where it served for five days and then returned home. Hubbard was subsequently appointed as the captain of a company in the regiment of Colonel Jonathan Ward on May 23, 1775. Ward's company went to Cambridge after Hubbard was commissioned and documents in the Massachusetts Archives verify Hubbard's company being in

Cambridge during June, July and August of 1775. Despite his company's presence in Boston, there is no evidence that it was in the Battle of Bunker Hill.

By September, Arnold selected Hubbard as a company commander of one of the musket companies. In the Colonel Ward Regiment return, dated October 7, 1775, he is listed as "on command to Quebec." Hubbard wrote the following in a letter to his wife while his company was at Fort Western: "I know not if I shall ever see you again. The weather grows sever cold, and the woods, they say, are terrible to pass. But I do not value life or property, if I can secure liberty for my children."[142]

Hubbard is mentioned in the Pierce journal as one of three companies, the others being Hanchett and Goodrich, that would not agree to "scale the walls of Quebec" and early in December stated that they were going home. General Montgomery confirmed this situation in a December 26th letter to Schuyler, "I have discovered that three companies of Colonel Arnold's detachment are very adverse to a coup-de-main … This dangerous party threatens the ruin of our affairs."[143] Montgomery is careful to avoid identifying the names of the companies except for Hubbard's name. Montgomery was able to persuade these companies to stay and participate in the assault, but this issue had the potential to ruin the effort to conquer Canada before the assault was launched. There is no indication why Hubbard joined in this cabal against Arnold.

Hubbard was wounded in the assault on Quebec. One story mentions that he was seriously wounded and lying under the ramparts of the town and his company wanted to carry him away. At that point he told them to leave him because, "I came here to fight with you; I will stay here to die with you."[144] He was taken to the hospital but died there on January 14, 1776. Two journal accounts mention his wound. One said he was wounded in the heel and "died shortly after," and the other said he was shot in the ankle. A foot wound would not typically be considered serious, and Arnold's reference in his after action report to Congress that Hubbard was only wounded clearly indicates that Arnold believed he would recover. If the above statement about Hubbard staying with his troops is correct, he may have stayed too long to save his own life. This story of a heroic Hubbard staying with his company is at odds with the reaction of William Heth to Hubbard's death.

Simon Fobes, a member of Hubbard's company, described him as follows: "Captain Jonas Hubbard of Worcester, a stout athletic man and much esteemed and beloved by all his acquaintances." Justin Smith says "he interested himself in military matters" and describes him as a "typical patriot."[145] After Hubbard's death, "his widow and children removed to Paris, Me., where they were early settlers." On June 17, 1776, a resolution was passed by the General Assembly of Massachusetts which awarded "his wages" to Hubbard's wife, Mary. The resolution justified the payment because of her husband's sacrifice by going on "the expedition against Quebec and after his arrival there, Died."[146]

A contrary view of Hubbard was expressed by Lieutenant William Heth of Morgan's company, who offered the following blunt assessment: "Capt. Hubbard rec'd a wound through the hed of wch. he died—some weeks after, no great loss except to a wife & a few children."[147] The rifle companies seem to have had questions about Hubbard's abilities as a leader.

Simon Fobes describes a meeting with his Captain, who he says was Jonas Hubbard, in Worcester Massachusetts, in September of 1776 on his way home from Canada. As Roberts points out, this meeting could not have occurred because Hubbard had previously died of his wounds in Quebec. Fobes also describes Hubbard as a single man yet he was married in 1759 and his wife received the award from Massachusetts as described above. The Fobes recollection is a strange account that is clearly not accurate and should not cast doubt on the death of Hubbard in January of 1776. It is difficult to know to whom Fobes was referring in his account because Hubbard's lieutenants do not fit the description. One of them was still a prisoner in Quebec and the other was from Northfield, Massachusetts not Worcester. Even though Fobes mentions Hubbard by name, it is possible that Fobes was so confused about this incident after so many years had passed that he described it taking place at the wrong time and involving the wrong officer. He could have been describing an incident involving another unnamed officer under whom he served.[148]

Captain Oliver Hanchett

Oliver Hanchett was born in Suffield, Connecticut on August 7, 1741. He was the son of John Hanchett III and Mary Sheldon. His great grandfather, John Hanchett I, was the first settler in Suffield. Oliver married Rachel Gillet on May 29, 1766 and they had eight children. He was a sergeant in Phineas Lyman's Regiment in the French and Indian War.

In 1763, prior to his marriage, Hanchett fathered an illegitimate son with Sylvia Woodbridge, a daughter of Timothy Woodbridge of Stockbridge, Massachusetts, and the future sister-in-law of Captain William Goodrich.[149] Apparently such situations were not unheard of at that time. The child, named Oliver Hanchett after his father, was raised by his Woodbridge grandparents in Stockbridge. In 1778, at the age of fifteen, he enlisted in the army and served in Massachusetts and Vermont. It does not appear that Hanchett had any contact with his son because no involvement with his son and Sylvia Woodbridge in Stockbridge is mentioned in any local history. That is the primary reason why the son by Sylvia has largely gone unreported. Whether Hanchett and Goodrich knew each other in the early 1760's cannot be verified.

There is no clear indication of how and where Hanchett met Sylvia Woodbridge. One possibility is that beginning in the 1750's her father was active in the Susquehanna Company which held some of its meetings in Connecticut. Mr. Woodbridge could have taken his family with him on one of his trips to Connecticut. While the Woodbridge family was in Connecticut, Sylvia and Oliver could have met each other. The Company was an active land speculator and had many members throughout Connecticut, but there is no known connection between the Company and Hanchett or his family. There were, however, individuals from Suffield and surrounding towns in the Company, and the Woodbridge family could have stayed near Suffield while in Connecticut. A less likely possibility is that Hanchett, during the French and Indian War, passed through Stockbridge on his way north and had a short relationship with Sylvia.

After the First Continental Congress in 1774, Hanchett was selected as one of eleven men in Suffield to be on a Committee of Inspections to "promote and protect the liberties of the colonies."[150] When the Lexington Alarm occurred, Hanchett was a first lieutenant in Captain Elihu Kent's company of minutemen, consisting of one hundred fourteen men, which marched on April 20th. Kent's company returned after approximately ten days. On May 1st, Hanchett was commissioned as a captain of the 10th company in the 2nd Connecticut Regiment commanded by General Joseph Spencer. His company consisted of one hundred and three men and they marched to Cambridge on May 7th. Many of the minutemen from Kent's company subsequently enlisted in Hanchett's company. One source says his company "is thought to have participated in the battle of Bunker Hill."[151]

Hanchett was appointed as a company commander in Arnold's detachment on September 1st. He was captured by the British in the assault on Quebec. His petition to the Connecticut General Assembly described his efforts as follows. "Having arrived before Quebec, in Endeavouring to take that City by storm and by fortune of War, the Memorialist and Most of his Company who Survived the Attempt were taken, made Prisoners, and himself put in Irons, and Continued in Captivity until the Month of October, 1776."[152] During his time in prison, he claimed to have advanced the sum of one thousand dollars to the men of his company who were prisoners, which "saved them from much trouble and privation." Hanchett's claim was determined to be acceptable because he was later reimbursed by the Connecticut legislature after a prolonged process.

Hanchett also made a claim in 1782 to the Continental Congress for money that he was owed as a result of being a commander on the expedition. His claim included travel expenses, rum and wine provided to his troops, clothes and food that he bought for his company and his own wages from September 1, 1775 to December 31, 1775. Eight of Hanchett's men also submitted claims for unpaid wages during the time they were on the expedition. General Benjamin Lincoln reviewed Hanchett's claim and submitted a report to the President of Congress on June 22, 1782 concluding that "the principal part of the representations which the memorialist [Hanchett] has made are unsupported by any vouchers produced by him and rest solely on his declaration." He recommended that the claim be put on hold "until further evidence shall be given in support of the several observations." No documentary evidence of the non-wage claims was submitted by Hanchett subsequent to Lincoln's findings and presumably he was never reimbursed.[153]

Hanchett was a ringleader with two other companies in trying to undermine Arnold by strongly opposing the assault on Quebec. Thayer's journal entries on December 2nd, 7th and 8th reveal that Hanchett refused to take orders from Arnold to lead a detachment to carry arms and supplies to a forward location and later to take his company forward. In both instances, Thayer said Hanchett "abruptly refused" and in both cases he and Topham did what Arnold ordered. Pierce stated that Hanchett paraded his men in early December to begin marching home and stated that Hanchett's men would not sign up to "scale the walls of Quebec." Pierce also related that Captain Hanchett and Major Bigelow were "complained of for cowardice when doging when a ball came near them." Montgomery informed Schuyler that three companies were adverse to attack Quebec and to follow Arnold's orders and that "Captain [blank space], who has incurred Colonel Arnold's displeasure, is at the bottom of it."[154] It is generally accepted that Hanchett is the captain Montgomery was referring to in his letter. It was only the strong intervention by Montgomery that convinced Hanchett's men to stay and participate in the assault.

According to the Piece journal, Hanchett became disaffected towards Arnold on the march and asked that he and his men be released to go home early because he did not want to serve under Arnold.[155] Some have speculated that Hanchett's negative attitude arose when Arnold took his company's bateaux in order to rush ahead to the French settlements to get provisions for the men. It is also alleged that Hanchett became upset with Arnold as a result of an incident at the crossing of the St Lawrence River when the expedition first reached Quebec. The dispute between Arnold and Hanchett and the other two company commanders is an important part of the story told by Kenneth Roberts in his novel of the expedition. There is no reason to question Pierce's account. Lieutenant William Heth describes Hanchett as a colleague who was sympathetic with and supportive of Captain William Goodrich in his confrontation with Morgan, which is described in the account of Goodrich's life later in this chapter. Goodrich also supported Hanchett's dissatisfaction with Arnold.

After he was released by the British, Hanchett returned to his farm, which has been described as "a fine, beautiful spot", and was reunited with his family. He continued to live in Suffield until his death on May 26, 1816, at the age of seventy-five. There is very little information on his life after the Quebec expedition but it is clear he did not serve in the army after his release from prison.

In hindsight, Hanchett's selection by Arnold to be one of his officers was a serious mistake. His conduct during the expedition made the march and the assault much more difficult and problematic than it needed to be. Hanchett's lack of subsequent military service does not add any luster to his reputation. It is likely that Arnold was aware of the political considerations in the selection of his officers, including the fact that Connecticut needed to have at least one company commander on the expedition. Since there are no records of how many officers actually volunteered to serve under Arnold, it may well be that Hanchett was the only company grade officer from Connecticut to volunteer for the expedition.[156]

Captain William Goodrich

After beginning to write this chapter, it soon became apparent that William Goodrich was more enigmatic than most of the other officers from the expedition. Details on his early life are almost non-existent and, until now, no one had been able to identify his parents, his birthplace or date of birth. Since so little attention was paid to William Goodrich in previous histories, this author tried to identify all of the know records regarding his life. Fortunately, subsequent research began to uncover some details about Goodrich's life and a more complete picture began to emerge.

William Goodrich was born in Sheffield, Massachusetts to William and Abiah Stocking Goodrich on December 19, 1734. His father, William, is on a 1733 list of proprietors of the Third Division on the Housatonic River in the area that became known as Sheffield. All of the divisions, including the Third Division, were incorporated as the town of Sheffield in January of 1733. Some time prior to his marriage, William Jr. moved to Stockbridge. In Stockbridge, William Jr.

married Sybil Woodbridge, daughter of Timothy Woodbridge, around 1768, although there is no record in Stockbridge or any other Massachusetts town of any formal marriage. They had two children both of whom were born in Stockbridge. His son William died in 1771 at the age of one and a half and is buried in Stockbridge. There is no written record that mentions his daughter, Experience.

His civilian occupation before the war was hotel or tavern keeper. In 1773, he applied to Governor Thomas Hutchinson for a license from the Massachusetts Colony "for keeping a house of publick entertainment and that it [his property] would greatly commode travelers."[157] His petition was subsequently granted, after he obtained the approval of the selectmen of the Town of Stockbridge. He opened the first tavern in Stockbridge on the corner of Main and South Streets in a newly constructed house. This building was moved to a new location on the corner of East Main Street and Lincoln Lane in the nineteenth century and is still there today, although it has changed significantly from the original.[158] When he was appointed a company commander in April of 1775, "the tavern operated by William Goodrich fell into disuse." After his confinement in Quebec, Goodrich returned home to find his tavern had been closed and that there was a competing tavern across the street. Situated where the Red Lion Inn is today, it was owned by Anna Bingham, one of the more interesting characters in the early history of Stockbridge.[159] Reopening his tavern was not feasible so he turned to other ways of making money, including land speculation.

Presumably as a result of his connection to the Woodbridge family, Goodrich followed in the footsteps of his father-in-law, Timothy Woodbridge, and began buying up Stockbridge Indian lands. During the period between 1763 and 1786, William Goodrich was the third largest purchaser of Indian land with thirteen purchases totaling 1011 acres.[160] None of his land speculation seems to have made Goodrich any significant money. It may, however, have helped him in other areas.

After missionaries successfully converted the Stockbridge Indians to Christianity, the tribe in turn made efforts to mix well with their white neighbors, including serving in the French and Indian War. In the winter of 1774 and 1775, a number of Stockbridge Indians became minute men under the command of William Goodrich, who must have had a reasonably good relationship with the tribe at that time. There is nothing in the records to indicate how Goodrich obtained his favored status with the Indian community. However, as indicated above, since one of Goodrich's primary activities in Stockbridge during the 1770's seemed to be trading in Indian lands, he may have been able to make friends through his land acquisition activities.

In the spring of 1775, Goodrich and one of his colleagues "applied to the Committee of Safety for assistance in enlisting two companies of Indians from the western parts of the colony".[161] On April 4, 1775, the Massachusetts Provincial Congress sent a letter to the Stockbridge chief, Jehoiakim Mtohkain, through Colonel John Paterson and Captain William Goodrich, offering a blanket and a yard of ribbon to those Indian men who would enlist in the Massachusetts' militia.[162] On April 4th, the Congress also authorized Goodrich to expand the company he was enlisting to one hundred men and directed "that they may be considered as rangers." He was instructed to apply to Colonel Paterson for further instructions regarding the enlistment of the Indians. On April 11th, the Indians responded through Goodrich "asking to be allowed to fight in their own Indian way, as they were not used to train and fight English fashion."[163] There is no record of a response from the Congress but Goodrich did precede with his enlistment efforts. When the Lexington Alarm sounded, Goodrich's company, including thirty-two Stockbridge Indians, marched to Cambridge on April 22nd with Colonel John Paterson's regiment. On May 27, Goodrich's commission as captain was confirmed by the Massachusetts Provincial Congress.[164]

There is a reference to Captain William Goodrich's Company at the siege of Boston in a June 21st letter from a group of Stockbridge Indians stationed around Boston requesting that the army limit the amount of whiskey that would be made available to the Indians.[165] Some have alleged that the Goodrich Company was in the Battle of Bunker Hill but their participation has not been verified. One historian reported that the dull camp life around Boston was not compatible to the Indians and that some of them left and went home during the summer of 1775. It is unclear how many Indians were still in Cambridge with his company when Goodrich signed up with Arnold's expedition.

The selection of Goodrich as a company commander could have been motivated by Arnold's desire to have some trustworthy Indians in his expedition. Arnold was one of the few American commanders at that stage of the war who understood that the Indians were unequalled in woodcraft and could also be effective fighting troops if utilized properly and if led by a knowledgeable officer. Realizing how difficult the wilderness trek would be, Arnold wanted some men who were experienced and skilled in the art of woodcraft, which most of his men lacked. If that was Arnold's intent, it did not work out. For reasons unrelated to the expedition, there were no Stockbridge Indians among Arnold's troops, but Goodrich did command one of the companies on the expedition. Goodrich's new company included men from his original company but no Indians.

Goodrich had a difficult march to Quebec apparently suffering more than some of the other officers. Dearborn's journal entry for October 28th states that when Dearborn met up with him at the river going into Chaudière Pond, "Capt. Goodrich was almost perished with the cold, having Waded Several Miles Backwards, and forwards, Sometimes to his arm pits in Water & Ice, endeavouring to find some place to Cross this River." Dearborn described how he took Goodrich into his canoe and carried him over to the other side which presumably saved his life.[166] Goodrich is described in a footnote in Heth's journal as "a trouble maker in Arnold's army. He objected to the assault and asked to be withdrawn from Arnold's command."[167] Pierce's journal, which is a primary source of describing the discontent with Arnold, names the three officers who were unwilling to scale the walls of Quebec as Goodrich, Hanchett and Hubbard. In fact, Pierce says that on December 2nd, "Capt. Goodriches men protested they would go home."[168]

The fact that both Goodrich and Hanchett were involved with the Woodbridge sisters before the war could account for their agreement regarding Arnold. Goodrich was also from Berkshire County which was the home of John Brown and James Easton. Brown and Easton were active antagonists against Arnold, and he against them, due to their experiences in the capture of Ticonderoga in May and June of 1775. These men could have influenced the attitudes of Goodrich and his men toward Arnold. General Montgomery, referring to the discontent of the three companies, implicitly names John Brown as "being deeply concerned in this affair." Montgomery's reports about the three troublemakers in Arnold's detachment did not bode well for any plans they may have had for subsequent military careers.[169]

At the assault on Quebec, Goodrich was one of the American officers who was captured and put in prison. He was exchanged with the rest of the captured officers in the fall of 1776. While he was in prison in Quebec, the Town of Stockbridge granted Goodrich fifty acres of land in a transaction where he is described as "a white hotel keeper and a captain of minute men in the Revolution."[170] The only mention of Goodrich in captivity is found in William Heth's journal that presents a very negative portrait of Goodrich. Heth says he stole a watch from a local Canadian which Daniel Morgan found out about and demanded that he return it. Heth describes the harsh language, used by Morgan as "by G-d you shall." Goodrich still refused to give Morgan the watch. Morgan then told Goodrich "that if he did not deliver it up to Mr. Cunningham he wou'd take it from him and give him a damn'd flogging into the bargain." After more argument between the two men, Morgan grabbed Goodrich by the throat and he gave up the watch. Heth sums up Goodrich as follows, "I say that, many of us have entertained a worse opinion of him—than before—but, to increase that unfavorable opinion, a few days after, we were acquainted that, when he retreated to Point Aux Tremble, --- he led off a blooded colt, the property of Mr. Rich'd Murry—which he swap'd away for a horse, & sent one of his soldiers home with him—This we look'd upon to be such a degree of baseness that he was treated with the utmost contempt whenever he came in our room."[171]

When Goodrich returned home, he rejoined Paterson's regiment and was appointed to serve as a major without being commissioned. In response to a written request from Paterson, Goodrich was promoted to major in the Massachusetts militia by the Massachusetts War Council on June 26, 1777 and assigned to Paterson's brigade. On July 24th, Goodrich applied to Paterson for permission to resign from his regiment, which was granted. For the next two years there is no record of Goodrich's military service. He was probably still recuperating from his experiences in Quebec and trying to recover from the loss of his business. In June of 1779, Washington wrote to Goodrich authorizing him to raise a company of Stockbridge Indians to serve in the Sullivan expedition with the same pay rate as other volunteers and enlistees in that expedition. Washington wrote a subsequent letter to Goodrich on July 4th, in response to Goodrich's letter of June 30th, telling him that the conditions under which Goodrich had engaged the Indians was not acceptable, but if the Stockbridge Indians desired to serve under "the terms and conditions I mentioned I shall have no objection to the measure."[172] A company of Stockbridge Indians did serve under Sullivan on his expedition but no record exists of their activities. It is clear that Goodrich himself did not serve in that expedition as the commander of the Indians because he was appointed one of three Stockbridge town assessors in 1779, indicating that he must have been in town at that time.

By 1780, William Goodrich was in a difficult financial condition and he tried to obtain reimbursement from both the Continental Congress and the Massachusetts House of Representatives for losses that he incurred on the expedition to Quebec. His petition to the state on January 20, 1780 claims, "he was a great sufferer not only by his captivity, but also in the loss of a number of valuable items." He claims a total value of the items lost as "approx. to the amount of thirty five pounds." He attached an itemization of his losses which he titled "Account of things left at Quebeck." The list of items included a gun and side arms, shirts, blankets bedding, a beaver hat and plates, knives, forks and spoons. There is no evidence that either the federal or state legislative bodies ever acted on his requests.[173]

On October 23, 1780, Goodrich was a major in command of Captain Enoch Noble's company from Berkshire County, which marched to Bennington in response to a request by Governor Chittenden and Brigadier General Ethan Allen to "guard the frontiers in the State of Vermont." He served with the Noble Company until November 7, 1780.[174] There is no record of any other companies under Goodrich that might have accompanied Noble. Goodrich himself may have been present for that service based on the fact that he submitted a 1781 invoice to the State of Vermont, which was subsequently paid, for his service on behalf of Vermont from October 23rd to November 4th. In April of 1781, the State of Vermont authorized Goodrich to supply them with 18,000 gunflints and six tons of lead.[175] William Goodrich's service to Vermont was substantial enough to allow him to be listed as a Revolutionary officer from Vermont.

According to his pension application, James Holcomb joined a regiment from Berkshire County in May of 1781 under Colonel Fellows, Major William Goodrich and Major Skinner, which marched to White Plains and served until the surrender of Cornwallis. No other record exists showing the participation by a Goodrich detachment in that activity, although the pension application is a reliable source. On August 14, 1781, Goodrich wrote General Washington from Stockbridge stating "that there is a considerable number of old officers and other gentlemen in the County of Berkshire [who] would be happy to serve your Excellency as volunteers for a month or more if needed."[176] Washington responded on September 2nd that "the circumstances of the Campaign at present are such as will not probably require your Services." Washington goes on to tell him that the appropriate person to address his offer to is General Heath "who commands the troops in the vicinity of N. York."[177] It stands to reason that Washington's attitude toward Goodrich was influenced by the reports he received regarding Goodrich's conduct on the expedition. There is no indication that Goodrich made any request to Heath or that he served again in any military capacity. Given the petition referred to in the next paragraph it is likely that Goodrich focused his efforts on assisting Vermont, perhaps with the help of his former colleague from the Quebec expedition, Colonel Roger Enos.

In February, 1782, William Goodrich and six other former officers petitioned the Governor of Vermont and the General Court of Vermont for a vacant parcel of land south of New Haven, west of Ferrisburg and north of Monkton as a result of being wounded in defending the frontiers of Vermont "in the Battle of Johns Town in October last."[178] No record has been found of a unit commanded by William Goodrich participating in that battle and no information was found regarding a wound other than the details contained in a summary of the petition.

Sybil Goodrich died on June 21, 1782 at the age of forty. Four days after her death, William Goodrich purchased his last parcel of land in Stockbridge buying fifty acres on County Road. In 1783, Goodrich was a witness to a deed to his brother-in-law, Enoch Woodbridge, for a parcel of land in Bennington, Vermont. This is the last known land transaction involving Goodrich.[179]

The most interesting information about William Goodrich after the war involves two different activities. The first was a number of land speculation activities in the State of Vermont. On November 3, 1780, William Goodrich and sixty-four other individuals were granted a township by the Vermont legislature for a parcel of land in Franklin County near the Canadian border "six miles square as laid down in the plan herewith returned by the name of Berkshire." The town was charted by the state on August 3, 1781. Goodrich was the first land owner to transfer land in the new town which occurred on March 29, 1782 in a deed to William Maltby of Lenox, Massachusetts.[180] It does not appear that William Goodrich ever lived in the township of Berkshire so it is likely that he viewed this township as an investment and not as a potential residence. In fact, Goodrich and a number of other proprietors did not pay their required monies and as late as 1794 were listed in newspaper legal notices.

In addition to being the lead proprietor in Berkshire, Goodrich was also a proprietor in the following Vermont towns all of which were set up for land speculation prior to the end of the war. The towns of Woolcot and Starksboro in Addison County, Vershire in Orange County, Weybridge in Bennington County and the Town of Montpelier, where he followed his old expedition companion Timothy Bigelow. In each of these towns, Goodrich became one of the listed proprietors in default on his required payments beginning in 1787 and continuing through the early 1800's. Goodrich's wife Sybil was also a proprietor in Vershire and Montpelier and is on those same lists.[181] It is clear that none of his land ventures ever produced any significant money for William Goodrich.

The second post war activity was the military action, known as Shays Rebellion, which took place in Berkshire County in the first half of 1787. Berkshire County's participation in that rebellion on the side of the government involved local leaders, including General William Paterson and Colonel John Ashley. There was a detachment of approximately forty men from Sheffield that all sources seem to agree was under the command of a Captain Goodrich. There is no contemporary record that mentions the first name of Captain Goodrich and two more current histories are content to only provide the last name of Goodrich for this commanding officer. A third source identifies the leader as Captain William Goodrich and a fourth source calls the leader Captain Joseph Goodrich. There was a Joseph Goodrich in Sheffield who served in the Massachusetts militia during the Revolutionary War and attained the rank of sergeant by the end of the war. At his death in 1827, he was being referred to as Colonel Joseph Goodrich. He is a realistic possibility for the Captain Goodrich who commanded the Sheffield detachment in 1787.

The only William Goodrich who was in Sheffield during the last half of the eighteenth century, and who also had military experience, was our William Goodrich, who had been a captain during the war but was also promoted to and designated as major by both the State of Massachusetts and the State of Vermont.

It seems somewhat unlikely that he would have reverted to his old military rank of captain after the war. If anything the tendency was to inflate one's rank so it would be surprising to find our William Goodrich being referred to as captain. Moreover, as the next paragraph points out, in 1787 William Goodrich still seemed to focus his activities in the State of Vermont and not in Sheffield, Massachusetts. Based on the available evidence, in this author's opinion the leader of the Sheffield detachment in 1787 was Joseph Goodrich and not our William.

William Goodrich was in such adverse financial condition that in October of 1787 he got the Vermont General Assembly to discharge him from "all debts or demands against him" and they established a commission to supervise the use of his remaining assets to pay off all of his creditors on a pro rata basis. The three commissioners appointed to supervise his assets placed advertisements in Vermont newspapers in January of 1788 giving notice to all creditors. The process Goodrich followed seems to be a colonial version of the modern bankruptcy proceedings.[182] By 1788, Goodrich was fifty-four years old and all of his money-making ventures had collapsed.

The Stockbridge Library has a notation in their file on William Goodrich that in 1789 he led the funeral procession and made the only remarks at the funeral of Ethan Allen. There is no source cited in support of this statement and this author has not been able to find any source to support that contention. The Library file also indicates that he moved to Middlebury Vermont in the later part of the 1780's and that he died there in 1812. Since there is no record of William Goodrich being buried in the Stockbridge cemetery, initially there seemed to be some credibility to the possibility of his burial in Middlebury. The problem with the Library's information about Goodrich being buried in Middlebury is that the 1776 return of Quebec prisoners lists Goodrich's age as 37. In fact, he was born in 1734 which in 1775 would make him forty-one years old. The William Goodrich who is buried in Middlebury and died in 1812 was born in 1755 and was 57 years of age according to the inscription on his tombstone.

The birth year of 1734 is consistent with the date of the birth of his son, William, by Sybil Woodbridge, whereas the 1755 date, which is when the William Goodrich in Middlebury was born, is not. By 1812, he would have been 78 and not 57 as stated on the tombstone. The History of Middlebury identifies the William Goodrich buried in the cemetery as the son of Stephen Goodrich and says that he was born in Connecticut. The Henry Sheldon Museum in Middlebury confirms this information. This information leads to the conclusion that our William Goodrich did not spend his last years in Middlebury, Vermont. Unfortunately, no record of Goodrich's death and burial has been uncovered to date.[183]

CHAPTER SEVEN

THE LIFE AND CAREER OF COLONEL ROGER ENOS

A controversial incident that occurred during the expedition was the decision by Lieutenant Colonel Roger Enos and the three companies under his command to return to Cambridge, without authorization, before they reached Quebec. Much inaccurate information has been written about Roger Enos and his military career. One reason for this is that almost the only biographical information on his life is the favorable piece written by his descendant, Horace Hayden, and published in both the *Magazine of American History* and *March to Quebec*. The Hayden article presents Enos in a very positive manner but it has inaccuracies and leaves out some relevant history of Enos and his subsequent career. Long after the publication of the Roberts book, an article appeared in the *Connecticut Bar Journal* presenting the other side, or what might be called the prosecution's case.[184] The information that follows has been obtained from sources in the Connecticut archives, the National Archives, the Vermont archives, the history of Windsor, CT and Enos family genealogy.

Roger Enos was born in 1729 in the town of Simsbury, Connecticut to David and Mary Eno. His father David died in the Cape Breton campaign of 1745. David's father, James Eno II, was one of eleven petitioners in 1705 for a grant of land for service in the Great Swamp Fight. This grant of land later became part of Simsbury. James Eno II died in 1714 and is buried at the Old Burying Ground in Simsbury. Roger's great grandfather, James Eno I, came to America from England in 1646 and settled first in Windsor, Connecticut, and then in Simsbury. The spelling of the last name as Enos, as distinct from the original family name Eno, does not appear in any family record until Roger used it in the French and Indian War in the late 1750's. It is then used in entries in the public record of the town in 1762 and 1764 for the name of William Enos of Simsbury, and later for other members of the Eno family.

Roger Enos served in the French and Indian War in the Regiment of Major General Phineas Lyman, a well respected American provincial officer from Connecticut. He first appears on the rolls of Lyman's regiment in 1759 holding the rank of sergeant-major, but in subsequent years gained promotions. In 1760 he is listed as an ensign in the Regiment with the spelling of Enos instead of Eno. In 1761, he appears on the rolls as an adjutant as well as a captain-lieutenant of the first company, and in 1762 he appears as the commander of the fourth company that was formerly headed by Capt. John Patterson. In both years his name is listed as Enos. In 1764, he was in Israel Putnam's regiment as the company commander of the fifth company, listed as Capt. Enno. His company was in the expedition sent that year against the Pontiac Indian uprising.

His civilian trade is not known and very little is known about his life between the French and Indian War and the American Revolution, except that he was appointed, along with Israel Putnam, Rufus Putnam and Phineas Lyman, to survey lands in the Mississippi Valley that were granted by the crown to provincial troops who served in the French and Indian War. Enos also married during this time. On March 10, 1763, he married Jerusha Hayden in Windsor, Connecticut. They lived in Windsor until 1780 and had five children, one of whom, named after her mother, married Ira Allen of Vermont, brother of Ethan Allen.

In April of 1775, as a result of the Lexington Alarm, Roger Enos was appointed by the Connecticut General Assembly, as a captain, to command the 3rd Company of the Second Regiment led by Colonel Joseph Spencer. He was later commissioned as a first major in that regiment on May 1, 1775. He was promoted to lieutenant colonel in the Spencer regiment on July 1, 1775. General George Washington commissioned Enos a lieutenant colonel in the 33rd Regiment of Foot of the Continental Army on September 11, 1775, shortly before the Arnold expedition left Cambridge. Arnold selected Roger Enos to be a part of his detachment based on his French and Indian War service. Due to his rank, he was designated as one of the division commanders before the expedition left Cambridge. Arnold undoubtedly thought he was getting an experienced and qualified officer as one of his division commanders.

Since every history of the Arnold expedition to Quebec includes a discussion of the decision by the three companies in the Enos Division to turn back in late October of 1775 before the expedition reached the first French settlements, no attempt will be made here to provide a detailed description of those events. Enos' actions, however, are relevant to offer a complete story of his life and career.

After the hurricane that ravaged the expedition on October 19th through 21st, the officers and men in Enos' division determined among themselves that the situation was too grim to continue on to Quebec and that they should return to Cambridge with the sick troops. They therefore wanted to consult with all of the officers available in the rear area to make a joint decision on what to do. According to the Senter journal, on October 25th a council of war was held among eleven officers to decide whether to continue on to Quebec or to return to Cambridge. The final vote was six for going on and five for returning.

Enos voted to proceed on but all of his officers voted to go back. After the vote, the officers of the Enos division decided that they would go back anyway and Enos went back with them. When they were requested to divide the food they were carrying with those going on, they refused to do so and Enos refused to order them to either go on in accordance with the vote or to share their food. His response, according to Senter, was "that his men were out of his power, and that they were determined to keep their possessed quantity." Enos' actions at this critical point have been criticized by almost every historian, including Justin Smith and Kenneth Roberts.

When Enos returned to Cambridge with his division, he was arrested by Washington and subsequently court-martialed. The court-martial was held on December 1, 1775 and heard testimony from Enos and his officers, but no one was available to present a different perspective because all of the officers who continued on were in Canada waiting to attack the city of Quebec. The decision of the court-martial was unanimous, "that Colonel Enos was under a necessity of returning with the Division under his command, and therefore acquit him with honor."

On January 18, 1776, after his court-martial, Enos sent a letter of resignation to General Washington. The letter requests Washington's "permission to resign my command" based on his conclusion "that I do not stand in that character, at Head-Quarters, which, as a Field Officer, is necessary to my being serviceable to the great cause in which we are engaged." Washington undoubtedly made his opinion of Enos' conduct known to the officer corps in Cambridge, so Enos was aware that he had lost Washington's confidence. In his letter, Enos describes his service in the "last campaign," meaning the Quebec expedition, as "if not with good fortune, at least without censure."[185] He must mean official censure because there was a lot of unofficial censure in the American camp in Cambridge. Washington accepted Enos' resignation and he left the army. A fact not well understood is that Roger Enos never served in the Continental Army again during the war.

In November of 1776, eleven months after his court-martial, Enos was promoted by the Connecticut General Assembly to the rank of colonel and was appointed as commander of one of four state militia battalions that were being raised to join with the Continental Army near New York. His appointment called for him to serve until March 15, 1777. In May of 1777, the General Assembly appointed Roger Enos to be colonel in one of the state battalions to be raised for the "defense of this state till the first day of January next." The battalion muster roll for the Col. Enos State Regiment is dated June 1777. In the History of Greenwich, Connecticut written by Spencer Mead, Enos' regiment is said to have served in Greenwich during 1777. The history states that the troops under his command engaged in foraging so excessive that the town at a special meeting voted that the troops of Colonel Enos' regiment "have committed great outrages upon the property of some of the inhabitants of this town." The proposal then went on to request the selectmen "to apply to the field officers for redress of the aforesaid grievances." There is no record of any redress.

A year later, in June of 1778, two Connecticut state regiments, one of which was commanded by Enos, were ordered to serve in the Hudson River area for three months. Enos' battalion was raised from the 1st, 4th and 6th Brigades of Militia and it returned home in early September, although on August 8, 1778, Colonel Malcolm furloughed Enos earlier than the rest of his command. In October of 1778, Colonel Enos' regiment of state troops was ordered to the south-western part of Connecticut on the sea coast, with one company to Norwalk, one to Stamford and the rest to Greenwich to "guard and defend the Inhabitants in those parts against the invasion and incursions of the enemy by sea and land." By November 3, 1778, Enos' Regiment was again in Greenwich, so apparently the State of Connecticut officials did not learn from the 1777 experience and believed that Enos' previous experience there made him the ideal choice to go again. Enos' regiment was at Horseneck in Greenwich and stayed there until May of 1779.

Enos' troops became the subject of complaints by the citizens of Greenwich beginning in January and continuing through May of 1779. The first complaint against Enos occurred in January of 1779, where he was accused of taking lightly a complaint by Dr. Amos Mead that a soldier of his regiment "threatened a negress belonging to Mead." In April, another complaint was filed that Enos' regiment confiscated guns from a party of six men and refused to give them back. In May, the Town of Greenwich complained to the State of Connecticut that they had suffered more from Enos' Regiment than from the British. The town accused Enos of immorality and of having insulted and beaten Dr. Amos Mead. The Connecticut General Assembly reported that they found the charges against Enos' conduct as an officer without support but that he was guilty of the assault on Dr. Mead. One would think the assault would be sufficient to support the charge against Enos regarding his conduct as an officer. The Assembly avoided taking any action by arguing that since Enos was not in Hartford they could make "no decree against him." The Greenwich men protested the Assembly report but it was never modified or overturned. The state was still unwilling to find fault with Enos' leadership. In November of 1780, he made a claim for the extraordinary expenses he incurred while serving in Greenwich, and the Assembly approved a payment to him of £120.

In 1780, Enos was looking to move out of Connecticut. In March of that year, just under a year from the time he ended his service in Greenwich, he and several associates were granted land by the government of Vermont that subsequently became the town of Enosburg. It is unclear whether Enos ever lived in the town. He subsequently moved from Simsbury, Connecticut to Vermont, probably as a result of the complaints against him from Greenwich and a realization that his military career in Connecticut was damaged. There is no record that explains the reason for his move to Vermont, but he must have been encouraged by someone who had influence in Vermont, most likely his future son-in-law, Ira Allen. The move only makes sense if Enos believed that as a result of it he could revitalize his military career. According to the affidavit from his son in the pension application, Enos and his family moved to Vermont in 1781.

By June of 1781, Enos was fully entrenched in the politics of Vermont. At that time, he and three other men wrote to the Vermont Board of War offering them detailed advice on how to disperse the Vermont militia troops that were then in the field, possibly at the urging of Ira Allen.[186] The subject matter of this letter and the way it was written leaves the reader with the impression that Enos was positioning himself to obtain an appointment in the Vermont militia.

On July 10, 1781, Enos' efforts were successful, and he was appointed as a Brigadier General by the State of Vermont, which put him in charge of the entire Vermont militia. After living in Vermont for just sixteen months, Enos was able to get appointed to the highest military position in the state. The appointment of Enos is confirmed by Ira Allen in a letter to British General Haldiman on July 10th. Enos succeeded Ethan Allen, who resigned the position of militia commander to resume his study of philosophy. Enos wrote a letter to General George Washington on August 26, 1781, informing Washington that Vermont had appointed him to command the Vermont militia. Washington finally responded in a rather curt letter, dated October 6, telling Enos that he should consider himself "under the immediate command of Major Gen'l Heath, who commands the Army at the Northwest." [187]While accepting the actions of the elected government of Vermont, Washington was eager to put some restrictions on Enos' ability to act on his own or in a way that might be at odds with Washington's own strategy for the war in the north. There is no evidence that Enos ever corresponded with Heath.

On October 17th, Enos wrote to the Speaker of the Vermont House of Representatives recommending that a force of 1500 men be raised in Vermont to serve for a period of three years in order to defend that state against an expected British attack. The cost of such a step was more money than was anticipated, and the Assembly responded by appointing a committee to consider the appropriate steps to be taken "for the defence of the State in the ensuing year." Later in October and in early November, Enos corresponded with General Stark of the

New Hampshire militia regarding British troop movements in the area. On December 15, 1781, Enos resigned from active military service with the State of Vermont, having served as militia commander for five months. However, in 1787, he obtained another promotion from Vermont, this time to Major General of the 1st Vermont Division, a position that he resigned in 1791.

Between 1781 and 1792, Enos was a member of the Vermont Board of War, the Vermont General Assembly and a trustee of the University of Vermont. During those years, he played an active role in the affairs of the state. By 1792, he had resigned all public offices, and the Enos' settled down in Colchester, Vermont, with their daughter, Jerusha, who was married to Ira Allen. Ira Allen obtained a large grant of land prior to the Revolutionary War that included the Town of Colchester, Vermont and, after he married Enos' daughter in 1789, the new family settled there permanently. Roger Enos died in Colchester, Vermont on October 6, 1808, at the age of seventy-five, and is buried in Burlington, Vermont. He is buried in the same plot as Ethan Allen and his son in law, Ira Allen. In 1836, at the age of ninety-seven, Roger Enos' wife, Jerusha, submitted a claim for a pension based on her husband's military service, which was almost thirty years after his death.

Once the court-martial board acquitted Enos in 1775, he was aware that his military career in the Continental Army was finished. For the rest of his career, Enos served only in a state militia, but he made the most of those opportunities. In the state militia, he was able to continue to rise through the officer ranks to major general, first in Connecticut and then in Vermont. There is no evidence that he was ever in a battle or skirmish after the Quebec expedition and therefore no opportunity to demonstrate his abilities as a military leader in battle. Enos' ability to obtain the promotion to the top militia command in Vermont was due more to his connection to Ira Allen than to his military abilities. It is fortunate for Vermont that the British never mounted a serious attack on that state while he was in charge.

Looking at Enos' military career in the Connecticut militia, one sees the same lack of leadership in Greenwich in 1777 and 1779 that he demonstrated in the Quebec expedition, which is evidenced by his inability or unwillingness to control his men. Enos further demonstrated a significant lack of personal control in the beating of a private citizen in 1779, while his regiment was in Greenwich. Despite that record, Enos was able to parlay his previous military experience throughout his entire career into one promotion after another. His lackluster record reveals no real achievement. The ability to obtain unwarranted promotions and to retain his reputation is easier to understand in Vermont than in Connecticut.

A contemporary reaction to Enos' actions on the expedition is reflected in a letter from James Warren to John Adams in November of 1775 where Warren refers to Arnold being within a few miles of Quebec. He goes on to tell Adams "one Colonel Enos of Connecticut, with three companies he commanded as a rear guard, had come off and left him, while advanced thirty miles ahead, and perhaps at Chaudière Pond. This officer certainly deserves hanging."[188] Warren pulled no punches in his assessment of Enos. Unfortunately, no one in Connecticut accepted Warren's assessment, and Enos extended his military career much longer than was appropriate under the circumstances.

Enos was the opposite of Arnold in almost every way. Enos was indecisive and lacked the leadership ability to make hard spur of the moment decisions, to effectively lead troops in battle and to control the men in his command. There is no record of strategic planning to achieve a successful military objective or the ability to plan and implement a complicated military campaign. Enos was never a commander in a battle and never demonstrated the ability to lead his men to a victory. All of these traits were paramount in Benedict Arnold, who continually demonstrated the ability to plan campaigns and win battles, even under severe conditions. The comparison to Arnold demonstrates the limited abilities of Enos as a commander.

Although it can be said of Enos that he never changed sides as did Arnold, he was an active participant in a questionable Vermont strategy in 1781. When Roger Enos assumed command of the Vermont militia, his future son-in-law, Ira Allen, and other state leaders were engaged in secret negotiations with British General Haldiman to protect Vermont from a British invasion by joining the British side. The failed negotiations are said by many to have been a sham and were only engaged in to delay any action against the state by the British. Others, at the time, saw these actions as bordering on treason. Washington was very concerned when he was informed of Vermont's negotiations, which came at a very critical time when the American side seemed to be on the verge of losing the war. It is certainly true that no formal action was ever taken by any Vermont leader to reach a final agreement with the British. Ira Allen's subsequent account of the actions of Vermont leaders during this time frame clearly states that Enos was aware of the negotiations, although his level of involvement is unclear.

Roger Enos' military career was mediocre at best. He had no real achievement and his only claim to fame is his questionable actions on the Arnold expedition. If Enos' subsequent record had been one of valor and accomplishment, it would be credible to conclude that his action in the wilderness was an anomaly, and that it was correct of the court-martial board to give him a pass for those acts. With an impressive military record, it would be easier to find that his behavior on the expedition did not amount to desertion, and that he did actually make the appropriate decision based on the facts he had. The argument would be that his future conduct demonstrated that he deserved the promotions and that the court-martial verdict was correct. However, one cannot ignore the subsequent record of Roger Enos despite his promotions and high rank. The totality of his actions during the march belies the finding of the court-martial. Roger Enos' reputation must be judged on what he did, and not from the finding of the court or from the subsequent titles he received from Connecticut and Vermont.

Colonel Roger Enos

CHAPTER EIGHT

WHO WAS CAPTAIN SCOTT?

The answer to the question of who was the Captain Scott in the Enos division is an important historical fact that has been a mystery for over two hundred twenty-five years and it is the subject of this chapter. Captain Scott's role in the expedition is known but his identity is not, and until now the actual person who was Captain Scott has not been accountable for his role in the decision to return. This chapter intends to change that and definitively identify the Captain Scott who was in the expedition to Quebec. Before looking at Captain Scott, however, it is also appropriate to look at the lives of the other two Enos Division captains.

THE LIVES OF THE OTHER TWO ENOS DIVISION CAPTAINS

Captain Samuel McCobb

Captain Samuel McCobb was born in 1774 in Georgetown, Maine, which is located on the Kennebec River. He was the son of James McCobb, who was an important businessman and Justice of the first Court of Common Pleas in Lincoln County. Samuel was a member of the Provincial Congress which convened in Watertown, Maine, in 1775 to consider what to do about the British army in Boston. He was also a member of the local Committee of Safety and Correspondence for many years. In 1768, Samuel married Rachael Denny with whom he had three sons and six daughters.

In June of 1775, he enlisted a company of men at Georgetown using his own money and then marched to Cambridge. McCobb was in the Battle of Bunker Hill and based on his conduct in that battle was appointed as a company commander in Nickerson's Brigade. In August of 1775, he was assigned to command a company in the Arnold expedition to Quebec and was placed in the Enos Division. When he returned, his company was posted in Cambridge until January of 1776 when he was given a commission as Captain in the Continental Army.

Later in 1776, he was appointed by the state as a colonel of the militia in Lincoln County, Maine under General Lovell. His regiment served in Rhode Island and then served in the Penobscot Expedition in 1779. Subsequent to that expedition, he was appointed a Brigadier General in command of the Eastern Division of Maine where he served until the end of the war. After the war, he served for several years as a member of the General Court in the Commonwealth of Massachusetts. McCobb died in Georgetown on July 30, 1791, at the age of forty-seven.

As far as can be determined, Captain Samuel McCobb suffered no negative treatment from the political and military establishment of his state as a result of his participation in the unauthorized return from the Quebec expedition. There is no pension application from McCobb or any of his heirs to provide a more comprehensive history of his life.[189]

Captain Thomas Williams

Thomas Williams came from a distinguished family in the Berkshire area of Massachusetts. He was the eldest son of Dr. Thomas Williams of Deerfield, who was an imminent physician and brother of Ephraim Williams, the founder of Williams College. Thomas was born on May 5, 1746 in Deerfield. Rather than follow his father in the medical profession, he studied law with Colonel Hopkins of Great Barrington and prior to the war set up his own law office in Stockbridge, Mass. In 1771, he married Thankful Ashley of Stockbridge and had three children.

When the war started, he went to Cambridge on April 23rd as commander of a company of minutemen from the Stockbridge area in a regiment under Colonel John Paterson of Becket, Massachusetts. His company served for thirteen days and then he was commissioned as a Captain by the Massachusetts Provincial Congress to enlist another company under Colonel Paterson. In August of 1775, he was selected as a company commander in the Arnold expedition and assigned to Colonel Enos' Division.

Williams had a short military career. After he returned from the Arnold expedition, he resumed his military service and in 1776 he was back in Colonel Paterson's regiment where he was promoted to Lieutenant Colonel. In the spring of 1776, he was ordered to go with Paterson's regiment to Canada by a different route than the Arnold expedition followed. On his way north, his company stopped in Whitehall, New York, where he died of an unknown cause on July 10, 1776, at the age of thirty. Thomas Williams left no statement or letters regarding his participation in the Enos division's decision to return.[190]

THE IDENTITY OF CAPTAIN SCOTT

One of the most surprising facts about the Arnold expedition is that in the two hundred thirty-five years since it took place the first name of one of the Enos company commanders has never been identified. Until now, he has been referred to in all of the expedition journals and histories only as Captain Scott and no first name has been identified. The two most recent books written about the Arnold expedition refer to Scott only as Captain Scott.[191] While the names of all of the other Arnold expedition company commanders and the majority of the other officers have been known, the identity of Captain Scott has remained a mystery. This is probably the case for two reasons. First, none of the journals of the Arnold expedition mention his first name. Second, there are a number of men who served in the Revolution with the same first name as our Captain Scott. The fact that there were a number of men with the same name serving in the army inevitably causes confusion that prevents positive identification.

In the early twentieth century, Charles E. Banks tried to verify the identity of Captain Scott. In an article in the *Magazine of History*, written in 1914, Banks requested the assistance of all of its readers in his effort, saying that "His Christian name has eluded every effort I have made to fix it unmistakably." In that article, Banks goes on to focus his attention on a reference in the *History of Northampton* which describes Scott as Captain William Scott of Londonderry, New Hampshire. For some reason, Banks uses the name of Peterborough in his article but the book actually says Londonderry. In any event, the Northampton history does provide the first name as William. What Banks apparently did not realize is that the Northampton history was quoting from a pension application filed by Ebenezer Gee of Northampton, who was on the Arnold expedition and refers in his application to his company commander as Captain William Scott of Londonderry, New Hampshire.

Banks goes on to point out that there were two William Scotts from Peterborough, New Hampshire, in the Revolutionary War. Banks then explains why neither one of the two William Scotts from Peterborough is the right man leaving him with the question still unanswered. He eliminated one of the William Scotts because the family descendents denied any knowledge of their ancestor being on the Arnold expedition. The other William Scott was eliminated because he was in a British prison when the expedition left Cambridge and was on its way toward Quebec. Banks was frustrated by the results of his research because it left Scott's identity still unresolved. Since Banks' question is still unanswered, it is important to take up where he left off and definitively identify the first name of the elusive Captain Scott.[192]

WILLIAM SCOTT OF PETERBOROUGH, NEW HAMPSHIRE

There is clear and convincing evidence from three relevant sources that the Captain Scott who was in the Enos division was Captain William Scott of Peterborough,

New Hampshire. Until now, every researcher, including Charles Banks, has overlooked the first and most important source. That source is an original document written by the commander of the expedition, Benedict Arnold. In his Day Book and Ledger, which was seized by an order of the Supreme Executive Council of Pennsylvania on September 27, 1780, Arnold has entries that are dated in 1777 and 1778 where he lists cash and "sundry disbursements" that he made to the officers in the Quebec expedition. Among the officers from the expedition who are listed in his Day Book is Wm. Scott.[193] This entry from Arnold's Day Book serves as primary evidence from the commander of the expedition to establish the identity of the Captain Scott in his expedition as Captain William Scott.

The second source is a list of officers found in the National Archives and Records Administration which contains miscellaneous Revolutionary War muster rolls, payrolls, strength returns and other miscellaneous personnel, pay and supply records of American units. The record is a one-page report with a heading on the previous page that identifies the list as Commissions Granted on Recommendation of General Court. The one-page list is undated but it must be from the fall of 1775. The page shows a list of twenty-two officers that were in the Quebec expedition ranging from Lieutenant Colonel Christopher Greene to Adjutant Christian Febiger. One of the officers on the list is Captain William Scott and he is the only Scott listed.[194]

The third source is four pension applications from men serving under Captain Scott in the expedition three of who list their commander's name as William Scott. Of the four, James Moore identifies him as Captain William Scott from Peterborough, and Ebenezer Gee says he was Captain Scott of Londonderry, New Hampshire. Since there is no Captain Scott who served in the Revolutionary War from Londonderry, this is obviously a mistake. Londonderry is in the State of New Hampshire and located near Peterborough. Therefore, it appears to be a mistake as to his residence and there was only one Captain Scott from Peterborough in 1775. The other two pension applicants simply describe their commander as Captain William Scott, and do not identify his hometown.[195] There was no other Captain William Scott serving in the Revolutionary army in Boston in the summer of 1775, except for William Scott from Peterborough.

Captain William Scott of Peterborough's name appears in at least seven historical publications relating to his involvement in the Revolutionary War, but in all seven his service in the Arnold expedition is not mentioned at all. It is no wonder that Banks was thwarted in his efforts to confirm the real identity of Captain Scott. The only historical publication that did correctly identify William Scott of Peterborough as the Captain Scott in the Arnold expedition is the *Proceedings of the Worcester Society of Antiquity*, which has an article regarding the Arnold expedition written in 1912.[196] Banks did not cite this source in his 1914 article so it is not likely that he had seen it. The inaccurate and confusing information on Captain William Scott cited by Banks and the difficulty he had at that time of obtaining a list of the Scott company privates and their pension applications offers a significant contrast from the means of research and identification used today via the computer.

The name of Captain Scott need no longer remain a mystery. There is no doubt that it was Captain William Scott of Peterborough, New Hampshire who commanded one of the companies in the Enos Division.

WHICH WILLIAM SCOTT FROM PETERBOROUGH?

Because there are two William Scotts from Peterborough who became Captains in the Revolutionary Army, it makes sense to clarify which William Scott was on the Arnold expedition as a company commander. The Banks article correctly identifies two William Scotts from Peterborough but does not clarify who each one was. The distinction between the two is clarified in two publications by the same author, Jonathan Smith. First is his article in the *Proceedings of the Massachusetts Historical Society* of 1911 and second is the extensive information on the two men contained in his *The History of Peterborough in the Revolution*.

Both of these accounts point out that these two William Scotts were first cousins and were both Peterborough residents.

> In all local, regimental and other histories the records of these men both during and subsequent to the war are very much mixed; the services of the one being often accredited to the other, and vice versa. Both were in the army through the entire war and rendered honorable and even brilliant service. In the interest of historical truth the tangle should be straightened out.

This is obviously a realistic statement about the confusion in terms of correctly identifying the two William Scotts and was the reason the article appeared. Based on the information in these accounts and other genealogical information, the distinction between the two William Scotts can be made.

Captain William Scott of 1775

The Captain William Scott who was on the Arnold expedition, also apparently known as Short Bill, was born in County Derry in Ireland and was the son of

Archibald Scott. His father was a brother to Alexander, the father of the other William Scott. He was born in 1743 or 44, married Rosanna Tait (Tate), also of County Derry, in 1760 and came to America shortly thereafter and settled in Peterborough. He served in the French and Indian War in Captain Silas Brown's company soon after moving to America. By the time the Revolutionary War broke out, this William Scott is identified in the Revolutionary War history of Peterborough as the proprietor of the only store in Peterborough.

He responded to the Lexington Alarm by organizing a group of Peterborough men who marched off to join the army assembling in Cambridge. At some point prior to the Battle of Bunker Hill, he raised a new company consisting of most of the men in his original company and was appointed Captain, probably by brevet, with his first cousin, the other William Scott, as his lieutenant. His company is listed in the *History of Peterborough* and *Peterborough in the Revolution* as being in the Bunker Hill battle. In that battle, the other William Scott, his lieutenant, was wounded and left lying on the battlefield.

Surprisingly, both the genealogical book and the two local history accounts of our Captain William Scott pass over the period of his company's service, which was from Bunker Hill through December 31, 1775, without any mention of Arnold's expedition, thus giving rise to the confusion about the identity of Captain Scott. On July 7, 1776, he was commissioned as a Captain in Colonel Sargent's Regiment where he served until November of 1776. At that time, he was appointed a captain in Colonel John Stark's, afterward Colonel Cilley's regiment of the Continental Line, 1st New Hampshire Battalion. He was present in the retreat from Ticonderoga and in the Battle of Saratoga, where he was wounded in the hand. He was subsequently promoted to major and was in the Battle of Monmouth. During that battle, he was wounded by a bayonet thrust in his back when he tried to squash a mutiny in the American lines.

Our William Scott was in the Sullivan expedition in 1779 as Major of the 1st New Hampshire Regiment and became acting commander of his brigade in 1782 and 1783. In October of 1783, he was promoted to Lieutenant Colonel by brevet and then retired when the Continental Army was disbanded in late 1783. He never returned to Peterborough. After the war he moved to Greenfield, New York, where he was the first supervisor of the town, a Justice of the Peace and a promoter of the Society for the Promotion of Useful Learning. He died in Greenfield in 1815 at age seventy-one and is buried in the Bailey Cemetery.

In *The History of Peterborough in the Revolution*, he is described as earning the title of The Fighting Major, and his grandson described his hands as being "so drawn and misshapen by wounds, that they resemble bird claws rather than human hands."

Lieutenant William Scott of 1775

Lieutenant William Scott, the cousin, also known as Long Bill, was born in Townsend, Massachusetts in 1742, the son of Alexander Scott. At some time prior to the war, probably around 1750, he moved to Peterborough with his father and mother and later purchased his own farm. According to the MHS article and *The History of Peterborough in the Revolution*, he also served in the French and Indian War with his cousin. Lieutenant Scott was in another town when he learned about the fight at Lexington and went immediately to the scene of the British retreat, where he was able to get a couple of shots off as the British crossed the Charlestown Ferry.

He assisted his cousin, Captain Scott, in recruiting the original company and was appointed its first lieutenant. This is confirmed by pension applications from company members. The company of which the two William Scotts were commander and first lieutenant was in the Battle of Bunker Hill. Lieutenant Scott was wounded early in the battle with a musket ball below the knee and then when an attack occurred as he was retreating "he received in his thigh and the lower part of his body four additional balls, and bleeding at nine orifices, fainted upon the field." When the Americans finally retreated he was left on the field and was taken prisoner by the British and placed in a Boston prison. He was subsequently taken to Halifax, Nova Scotia, and put into prison there when the British evacuated Boston. In July of 1776, Lieutenant Scott and some fellow prisoners escaped and reached Boston, where he recuperated enough to join Colonel Sargent's regiment. His regiment was in the Battle for New York and in November of 1776, Lieutenant Scott was again taken prisoner, this time at Fort Washington. However, before the British could send him back to prison, he escaped by swimming the Hudson River.

Lieutenant Scott was commissioned as a Captain in January of 1777 and served until the spring of 1781. As his wounds were too severe to continue in a foot company, he resigned and entered the naval service where he served until May of 1782. After the war, this William Scott moved to Groton, Massachusetts, and then to Litchfield, New York. He was appointed as deputy storekeeper at West Point in 1784 and then went on a mission to Detroit. In 1796, he was surveying land near Lake Erie and caught a fever and died at his home in Litchfield on September 19, 1796. It is obvious that this Lieutenant Scott cannot be the Captain Scott on the Arnold expedition because he was in jail in Boston recovering from serious wounds when the Quebec expedition left Cambridge. Moreover, he was not a captain during 1775.[197]

APPENDIX I

SUMMARY OF INFORMATION ON JOURNALISTS

NO.	NAME OF JOURNAL AUTHOR	RANK	COMPANY	HOME TOWN	DATE 1" PUB	# PRINT'GS	LOCATION OF ORIGINAL MANUSCRIPT	AGE IN 1775	AGE DIED
1	ANONYMOUS	PVT	HUBBARD	UNKOWN	1900	1	UNKNOWN	UNK	UNK
2	ARNOLD, BENEDICT	COL	HQ	NEW HAVEN, CT	1903	3	HARVARD UNIV LIBRARY	35	61
3	BARNEY, SAMUEL	PVT	HANCHETT	NEW HAVEN, CT	NONE	0	NEW HAVEN HIST SOCIETY	22	52
4	DEARBORN, HENRY	CAPT	DEARBORN	NOTTINGHM, NH	1886	6	BOSTON PUBLIC LIBRARY	24	78
5	DORR, WILLIAM	PVT	WARD	DOVER, NH	2000	2	MASS HIST SOC	18	87
6	FOBES, SIMON	PVT	HUBBARD	AMHERST, MA	1878	4	UNKNOWN	19	84
7	FLANDERS, JOHN	PVT	DEARBORN	BOSCAWEN, NH	1881	1	UNKNOWN	22	75
8	GREENMAN, JEREMIAH	PVT	WARD	PROVIDENCE, RI	1978	1	UNKNOWN	18	70
9	HASKELL, CALEB	PVT	WARD	NEWBURYPORT, MA	1886	6	HARVARD UNIV LIBRARY	21	75
10	HENRY,JOHN JOSEPH	PVT	SMITH	LANCASTER, PA	1812	7	HIST SOC OF PA	19	53
11	HETH, WILLIAM	LT	MORGAN	WINCHESTER, VA	1931	2	LIBRARY OF CONGRESS	26	57
12	HUMPHREY, WILLIAM	LT	THAYER	PROVIDENCE, RI	1931	2	RHODE ISLAND HIST SOCIETY	28	79
13	KIMBALL, MOSES	PVT	DEARBORN	HAMPSTEAD, NH	NONE	0	UNKNOWN	19	33
14	MCCOY, WILLIAM	SGT	HENDRICKS	CUMBERLAND CO, PA	1776	5	UNKNOWN	28	50
15	MEIGS, RETURN J	MAJ	DIVISION	MIDDLTOWN,CT	1776	10	UNKNOWN	40	83
16	MELVIN, JAMES	PVT	DEARBORN	HUBBARDSTON, MA	1846	6	UNKNOWN	22	80?
17	MORISON, GEORGE	PVT	HENDRICKS	SHERMAN VALLEY, PA	1803	5	UNKNOWN	21	46
18	NICHOLS, FRANCIS	LT	HENDRICKS	CARLISLE, PA	1896	2	HIST SOC OF PA	38	75
19	OGDEN, MATTHIAS	CPT	VOL	ELIZABETH, NJ	1928	4	MORRISTOWN NHP LIB	21	36
20	OSWALD, ELEAZER	VOL	HQ	NEW HAVEN, CT	1846	2	NATL ARCHIVES	20	39
21	PIERCE, JOHN	SGT	HUBBARD	WORCESTER, MA	1946	2	DARTMOUTH LIBRARY	31	64
22	PORTERFIELD, CHARLES	VOL	MORGAN	WINCHESTER, VA	1901	3	UNKNOWN	21	30
23	SENTER, ISAAC	SUR	HQ	NEWPORT, RI	1846	7	FORDHAM UNIV/RIHS	22	46
24	SQUIER, EPHRAIM	PVT	SCOTT	ASHFORD, CT	1878	3	LIBRARY OF CONGRESS	27	94
25	STOCKING, ABNER	PVT	HANCHETT	HADDAM, CT	1810	4	UNKNOWN	23	80?

26	THAYER, SIMEON	CAPT	THAYER	PROVIDENCE, RI	1867	6	RHODE ISLAND HIST SOCIETY	38	63
27	TOLMAN, EBENEZER	PVT	WARD	FITZWILLIAM, NH	1917	2	UNKNOWN	27	90
28	TOPHAM, JOHN	CAPT	TOPHAM	NEWPORT, RI	1897	4	RHODE ISLAND HIST SOCIETY	33	51
29	WARE, JOSEPH	PVT	WARD	NEEDHAM, MA	1852	3	NE HIST & GEN SOCIETY	22	52
30	WILD, EBENEZER	N/A	N/A	N/A	1886	3	NOT IN EXPED	N/A	N/A

APPENDIX II

ROSTER, TABLES AND INDEX OF BENEDICT ARNOLD'S MEN WHO SERVED IN THE EXPEDITION TO QUEBEC

This roster contains a comprehensive list of Arnold expedition personnel by company. It provides name, rank and other information on each individual in the company that has been obtained from available sources. This is the first time such a roster of the participants has been published.

Tables Summarizing Information in the Roster

At the end of the roster there are three tables. **Table 1** provides a total of those men who were in the expedition when it left Cambridge. The total shown of 1066 men who left Cambridge is less than the eleven hundred number typically referred to by most historians of the expedition. However, the 1100 number was never definitive. At the end of Table 1, the total from the roster of the men who left Cambridge is compared to the total from contemporary sources. In terms of the number of men starting out on the expedition, the most detailed contemporary account is from the Orderly Book of Col. William Henshaw, who was the Adjutant General at Cambridge. His entry for September 5, 1775, which was subsequently included in Washington's General Orders, is as follows: "A detachment consisting of two lieutenant-colonels, two majors, ten captains, thirty subalterns, thirty sergeants, thirty corporals, four drummers, two fifers and 676 privates." Henshaw included the three rifle companies as a separate entity. [198]

The contemporary total is broken down as follows:

676	Privates from Henshaw
110	Captains, Subalterns, Sergeants, Corporals, Drummers & Fifers from Henshaw
	Three Rifle Co's: From Roster
86	Hendricks
86	Smith
83	Morgan
6	Volunteers Not Counted by Henshaw (Oswald, Coates, Melcher, Duncan, Burr, Ogden)

15	Staff Officers Not Counted by Henshaw (Chaplain, Adjutant, Pioneers, Quarter Masters, Commissary, Physicians and Aides)
5	Line Officers & NCO's not Counted by Henshaw
1067	**Total Number Who Left Cambridge**

Table 2 compares the company totals from the roster with the General Return of Arnold's Detachment, dated 11/29/1775. The table shows how the numbers from the roster for each company, including the headquarters company, matches the totals in the 11/29 Return.

Table 3 shows totals by company of the five columns that relate to the disposition of the men. The table can be used to determine how much each company contributed to the hardships of the expedition in each of the five categories. The company with the most men who were killed or taken prisoner was Morgan's Company and the company with the least number of men who were killed or captured in the assault was Dearborn's because he was across the river and came to the assault later than the others.

NOTE: There are five officers, Oswald, Ogden, Burr, Duncan and Melcher, all of whom were volunteers, who I arbitrarily placed in Headquarters Company. They are the only officers in the HQ Company who are not in the 11/29 Return.

ALPHABETICAL LISTING OF ARNOLD'S MEN BY COMPANY

HEADQUARTERS COMPANY

FIRST NAME	LAST NAME	RANK	CO	AGE	HOME TOWN	SOURCES	DISPOSITION
BENEDICT	ARNOLD	COL	1	35	NEW HAVEN,CT	3, 11, 28, 124	NOT CAPTURED
ROGER	ENOS	LT COL	1	46	WINDSOR, CT	1, 11, 22, 124	RETURNED
CHRISTOPHER	GREENE	LT COL	1	50	WARWICK, RI	4, 22, 26, 30	PRISONER
RETURN J	MEIGS	MAJ	1	40	MIDDLETOWN, CT	4, 11,26, 30	PRISONER
TIMOTHY	BIGELOW	MAJ	1	35	WORCESTER, MA	1, 4, 22, 30	PRISONER
CHRISTIAN	FEBIGER	ADJ	1	34	SALEM, MA	4, 21, 26, 30	PRISONER
ARCHIBALD	STEELE	LT ADJ	1	36	DONEGAL, PA	26, 28, 30, 124	PRISONER
JEDEDIAH	HYDE	Q MAST	1	37	NORWICH, CT	4, 116,124, 125	RETURNED
BENJAMIN	CATLING	Q MAST	1	37	WETHERSFIELD	11, 30, 124	PRISONER
ABIJAH	SAVAGE	Q MAST	1	34	MIDDLETOWN, CT	11,26,28,30	PRISONER
JOSEPH	FARNSWORTH	COMM'Y	1	50	MIDDLETOWN, CT	1, 29, 47, 140	RETURNED
JEREMIAH	WHEELWRIGHT	ASST	1		PORTSMOUTH, NH	25, 47, 104	RETURNED

EBENEZER	BARDWELL	ASST	1		WHATELY, MA	51	RETURNED
SAMUEL	SPRING	CHAP	1	29	UXBRIDGE, MA	28, 47, 124	NOT CAPTURED
MATTHIAS	OGDEN	VOL	1	21	ELIZABETH, NJ	28, 30, 47, 141	NOT CAPTURED
AARON	BURR	VOL	1	19	PRINCETON, NJ	28, 47, 124, 127	NOT CAPTURED
MATTHEW	DUNCAN	VOL	1	22	PHILADELPHIA,	16, 22, 26, 30, 56	PRISONER
ISAAC	MELCHER	VOL	1		PENNSYLVANIA	16, 124	NOT CAPTURED
ISAAC	SENTER	PHYS	1	22	NEWPORT, RI	28, 124, 125	NOT CAPTURED
JOHN	COATES	PHYS	1		PHILADELPHIA,	2, 16, 140, 141	NOT CAPTURED
BENJAMIN?	GREENE	AIDE	1	35	NEW LON CO. CT	2, 125	RETURNED
?	BARR	AIDE	1		UNKNOWN	2, 125	RETURNED
?	JACKSON	AIDE	1		UNKNOWN	2, 125	RETURNED
ELEAZER	AYRES	PIONERS	1	29	GRANBY, MA	1, 18, 28	RETURNED
ELEAZER	OSWALD	ADC	1	20	NEW HAVEN, CT	11, 28, 47, 140	
TOTAL OFFICERS & MEN			**25**				

THAYER'S COMPANY

FIRST NAME	LAST NAME	RANK	CO	AGE	HOME TOWN	SOURCES	DISPOSITION
SIMEON	THAYER	CAPT	2	38	PROVIDENCE,	1, 4, 26, 127	PRISONER
LEMUEL	BAILEY	LIEUT	2	29	TIVERTON, RI	28	NOT CAPTURED
WILLIAM	HUMPHREY	LIEUT	2	28	PROVIDENCE,	26, 28	PRISONER
THOMAS	PAGE	SGT	2		PROVIDENCE,	28	PRISONER
THOMAS	ELLIS	SGT	2		PROVIDENCE,	28	NOT CAPTURED
MOSES	BRYANT	SGT	2		PROVIDENCE,	28	NOT CAPTURED
SAMUEL	SINGLETON	SGT	2		PROVIDENCE,	28, 127	NOT CAPTURED
MORRIS	COCHRAN	CORP	2		PROVIDENCE,	28	NOT CAPTURED
JAMES	HAYDEN	CORP	2	28	PROVIDENCE,	28	PRISONER
SILAS	WHEELER	CORP	2	23	PROVIDENCE,	26, 28	PRISONER
THOMAS	LOW	CORP	2		REHOBETH, MA	22, 28	PRISONER
ISAAC	HAWES	FIFER	2		CHATHAM, MA	28	RETURNED
PASCO	AUSTIN	PRIV	2		PROVIDENCE,	28	NOT CAPTURED
JAMES	BARNES	PRIV	2		PELHAM, MA	28	PRISONER
JOHN	BARRETT	PRIV	2		CONCORD, MA	28	NOT CAPTURED
STEPHEN	BARTLETT	PRIV	2		AMESBURY, MA	28	NPT CAPTURED
JOHN	BLACKFORD	PRIV	2		WOODBRIDGE, NJ	28	RETURNED
SAMUEL	BLAISDELL	PRIV	2		AMESBURY, MA	28	NOT CAPTURED

JOSEPH	BOSWORTH	PRIV	2		PROVIDENCE,	28	RETURNED
JOHN	BRIDGES	PRIV	2		ANDOVER, MA	28	RETURNED
JOHN	CAMBRIDGE	PRIV	2	17	PROVIDENCE,	22, 28	NOT CAPTURED
JOHN	CARREL	PRIV	2		CONCORD, MA	28	NOT CAPTURED
WILLIAM	CLEMENTS	PRIV	2		PETERSHAM, MA	27, 28	PRISONER
RICHARD	CONDON	PRIV	2		FALMOUTH, MA	4	NOT CAPTURED
EDWARD	CONNOR	PRIV	2		WORCESTER,	27, 28	PRISONER
JOHN	COLLINS	PRIV	2	23	DURHAM, NH	28	RETURNED
BENJAMIN	DIMAN	PRIV	2		SALEM, MA	28	NOT CAPTURED
WILLIAM	DIXON	PRIV	2		DAMARISCOTTA	27, 28, 58	PRISONER
DANIEL	DEVIZER	PRIV	2		PROVIDENCE,	28	RETURNED
MOSES	EDDY	PRIV	2		DAMARISCOTTA	28, 58	RETURNED
PETER	FIELD	PRIV	2	25	SALEM, MA	27, 28	PRISONER
ISAAC	FILLEBROWN	PRIV	2		CHARLESTOWN, RI	28	RETURNED
FRANCIS	FILLEBUT	PRIV	2		CONCORD, MA	28	NOT CAPTURED
JACOB	FLANDERS	PRIV	2		SOUTHHAMPTON	28	RETURNED
ABEL	FORD	PRIV	2		WORTHINGTON, RI	28	RETURNED
BENJA,MIN	FOWLER	PRIV	2		PROVIDENCE	22	RETURNED
ELIJAH	FOWLER	PRIV	2	21	PROVIDENCE,	26, 27, 28	PRISONER
THOMAS	GEARY	PRIV	2		STONEHAM, MA	28	NOT CAPTURED
JACOB	GOOD	PRIV	2		PROVIDENCE,	28	RETURNED
CALEB	GORDON	PRIV	2		KINGSTON, NH	6, 28	NOT CAPTURED
WILLIAM	GOUGE	PRIV	2		PROVIDENCE,	28	RETURNED
SAMUEL	GRIFFITH	PRIV	2		WARWICK, RI	28	RETURNED
PATRICK	HARRINGTON	PRIV	2		NEWBURYPORT	27, 28, 130	PRISONER
CORNELIUS	HAGGARTY	PRIV	2		PROVIDENCE,	27, 28	PRISONER
MOSES	HEMINWAY	PRIV	2		PROVIDENCE,	27, 28	PRISONER
ROBERT	HILL	PRIV	2		PETERSHAM, MA	28	RETURNED
ANDREW	HINMAN	PRIV	2		LANESBORO, MA	27, 28	PRISONER
JOHN	HOLLEY	PRIV	2	27	GRISWOLD, CT	28	RETURNED
SILAS	HOOKER	PRIV	2		PROVIDENCE,	27, 28	PRISONER
SAMUEL	INGALLS	PRIV	2	22	STONEHAM, MA	27, 28	PRISONER
JONATHAN	JACOBS	PRIV	2	38	ROYALSTON, MA	26, 27, 28	PRISONER
JESSE	JEWELL	PRIV	2	22	ADAMS, MA	26, 27, 28	PRISONER
JOSEPH	JEWELL	PRIV	2		SOUTHAMPTON	7, 28	RETURNED
ELIJAH	JONES	PRIV	2		PROVIDENCE,	28	RETURNED
JOHN	LATHAM	PRIV	2		STONINGTON, CT	28	NOT CAPTURED

THOMAS	LAWRENCE	PRIV	2	22	PROVIDENCE,	26	PRISONER
DANIEL	LAWRENCE	PRIV	2	18	PROVIDENCE,	22, 26, 27, 28	PRISONER
GEORGE	LEACH	PRIV	2		MARBLEHEAD, MA	28	RETURNED
JOSEPH	LEWIS	PRIV	2		WESTERLY, RI	28	RETURNED
STEPHEN	MILLS	PRIV	2	22	SHEFFIELD, MA	26, 27, 28	PRISONER
JAMES	MONK	PRIV	2		PROVIDENCE,	28	NOT CAPTURED
JEREMIAH	MOSHER	PRIV	2		ROXBURY, MA	28	RETURNED
EDWARD	MULLIGAN	PRIV	2		MARBLEHEAD, MA	28	RETURNED
CHARLES	NUTTING	PRIV	2		WATERTOWN, MA	22, 28	NOT CAPTURED
NATHANIEL	PARKER	PRIV	2		ADAMS, MA	28, 36	NOT CAPTURED
BENONI	PATTEN	PRIV	2		PUTNEY, VT	28	NOT CAPTURED
NATHANIEL	PEASE	PRIV	2	20	ENFIELD, CT	28	RETURNED
MATTHEW	PHILLIPS	PRIV	2		DURWANDO	28	NOT CAPTURED
JOSEPH	PLASTOW	PRIV	2		UNKNOWN	28	RETURNED
JOHN	RANKIN	PRIV	2		PROVIDENCE,	27, 28	PRISONER
JOHN	ROBINSON	PRIV	2		PROVIDENCE,	27, 28	PRISONER
JOHN	RYAN	PRIV	2		MARBLEHEAD, MA	28	NOT CAPTURED
ANTHONY	SALISBURY	PRIV	2		LITTLE COMPTON	22	PRISONER
JONATHAN	SCOTT	PRIV	2		SHEFFIELD, MA	27, 28	PRISONER
ALEXANDER	SPENCER	PRIV	2		SHARON, CT	28, 105	RETURNED
JOHN	SMITH	PRIV	2		WESTFIELD, MA	28, 36	NOT CAPTURED
JAMES	STONE	PRIV	2	21	PROVIDENCE,	26, 27, 28	PRISONER
ELEAZER	THAYER	PRIV	2		MENDON, MA	28	NOT CAPTURED
JOHN	THOMPSON	PRIV	2	22	PROVIDENCE,	28	RETURNED
PATRICK	TRACY	PRIV	2	25	NEWBURYPORT	27, 28, 131	KILLED
JOHN	TURNER	PRIV	2		KINDERHOOK, NY	28, 104	RETURNED
BANISTER	WATERMAN	PRIV	2	21	STURBRIDGE, MA	26, 28, 38	PRISONER
JAMES	WELCH	PRIV	2		PROVIDENCE,	28	KILLED
BENJAMIN	WEST	PRIV	2	22	ROXBURY, MA	22, 28	PRISONER
THOMAS	WHITTEMORE	PRIV	2		LEICESTER, MA	28, 36, 119	RETURNED
DAVIS	WILLIAMS	PRIV	2		ROXBURY, MA	27, 28	PRISONER
SAMUEL	WILLIAMS	PRIV	2		DAMARISCOTTA	28, 58	NOT CAPTURED
WILLIAM	WILLIS	PRIV	2		ALBANY, NY	28	NOT CAPTURED
TOTAL OFFICERS & MEN		**87**					

DEARBORN'S COMPANY

FIRST NAME	LAST NAME	RANK	CO	AGE	HOME TOWN	SOURCES	DISPOSITION
HENRY	DEARBORN	CAPT	3	24	NOTTINGHAM, NH	1, 4, 6, 26	PRISONER
NATHANIEL	HUTCHINS	LIEUT	3	34	DUNBARTON, NH	1, 6, 26	PRISONER
AMMI	ANDREWS	LIEUT	3	27	HILLSBOROUGH	4, 6, 26, 47	PRISONER
JOSEPH	THOMAS	ENS	3	32	DEERFIELD, MA	6, 26	PRISONER
JONATHAN	PERKINS	SGT	3	28	EPPING, NH	6, 21, 22, 26	PRISONER
SAMUEL	CHERRY	SGT	3	19	LONDONDERY, NH	6	NOT CAPTURED
THOMAS	MCLUER	SGT	3	29	MERRIMACK, NH	6, 26	NOT CAPTURED
JOSEPH	LOVERING	SGT	3	25	KINGSTON, NH	6	NOT CAPTURED
MOSES	GILMAN	CORP	3	20	EPPING, NH	6	NOT CAPTURED
TIMOTHY	AHERN	CORP	3	26	GOOFSTOWN, NH	6, 65	NOT CAPTURED
JAMES	TAGGERT	CORP	3	27	HILLSBOROUGH	6, 40	NOT CAPTURED
SIMEON	SANBORN	CORP	3	22	SALISBURY, NH	6	NOT CAPTURED
CALEB	EDSON	FIFER	3	21	WAKEFIELD, NH	6, 22, 26	PRISONER
JOHN	ROBINSON	DRUM	3		CHESTER, NH	6	RETURNED
JOSIAH	ALLEN	PRIV	3	18	PEMBROKE, NH	6, 43	NOT CAPTURED
ENOCH	BAYLEY	PRIV	3	18	NEW SALEM, NH	6	NOT CAPTURED
JOHN	BEAN	PRIV	3	20	CANTERBURY, NH	6	NOT CAPTURED
JAMES	BEVERLY	PRIV	3	24	NOTTINGHAM, NH	6, 26, 30	PRISONER
JOHN	BICKFORD	PRIV	3	20	CHICHESTER, NH	6	RETURNED
EDMOND	BOYNTON	PRIV	3	22	CANTERBURY, NH	6	NOT CAPTURED
JOHN	BOWEN	PRIV	3		SALISBURY, NH	6	NOT CAPTURED
CHARLES	BURZETT	PRIV	3	23	DANBURY, CT	22, 30	PRISONER
JOHN	BURNS	PRIV	3	20	NEW BOSTON, NH	6, 22	RETURNED
JAMES	CARR	PRIV	3	20	HOPKINTON, NH	6, 83	NOT CAPTURED
JACOB	CHASE	PRIV	3	21	KINGSTON, NH	6	NOT CAPTURED
JOHN	CLARK	PRIV	3	22	BOSCAWEN, NH	6	NOT CAPTURED
ELEAZER	DANFORTH	PRIV	3		TAMWORTH, NH	6	NOT CAPTURED
ELKANAH	DANFORTH	PRIV	3	24	TAMWORTH, NH	6, 22, 26, 30	PRISONER
JOSEPH	DAVIS	PRIV	3	26	PLYMOUTH, NH	6	NOT CAPTURED
JOHN	DOBBIN	PRIV	3	23	BEDFORD, NH	6, 30, 71	PRISONER
MOSES	FELLOWS	PRIV	3	20	HALESTOWN, NH	6, 52	NOT CAPTURED
JOHN	FLANDERS	PRIV	3	22	BOSCOWEN, NH	6, 26, 30, 70	PRISONER
PATRICK	O'FLING	PRIV	3	22	BEDFORD, NH	6, 22, 71	NOT CAPTURED
JONATHAN	FOGG	PRIV	3	19	RAYMOND, NH	6, 26, 30	PRISONER

MOSES	FOLLENSBY	PRIV	3	23	WEARE, NH	6, 26, 81	PRISONER
WILLIAM	FORREST	PRIV	3	42	CANTERBURY, NH	6	NOT CAPTURED
MATTHIAS	FRENCH	PRIV	3	31	STRATHAM, NH	6	NOT CAPTURED
THOMAS	FROHOCK	PRIV	3	26	GILMARTIN, NH	6	RETURNED
DAVID	GEORGE	PRIV	3	20	DERRY, NH	6	NOT CAPTURED
JOHN	GILMAN	PRIV	3	24	WAKEFIELD, NH	6, 22	RETURNED
AMOS	HEATH	PRIV	3	27	COOS, NH	6	NOT CAPTURED
ROBERT	HEATH	PRIV	3	29	PERRYSTOWN, NH	6, 22, 30	PRISONER
JOHN PIKE	HILTON	PRIV	3	20	NOTTINGHAM, NH	6, 26	PRISONER
SAMUEL	HUGHES	PRIV	3	21	LYME, NH	6, 26, 30	PRISONER
THOMAS	HOLMES	PRIV	3	22	DERRY, NH	6, 26, 30	PRISONER
ROBERT	HOLLAND	PRIV	3	19	NEWMARKET, NH	6	NOT CAPTURED
WILLIAM	JOHNSON	PRIV	3	25	PELHAM, NH	6, 7	RETURNED
JOHN	KERR	PRIV	3	21	BEDFORD, NH	6, 71	NOT CAPTURED
ABRAHAM	KIMBALL	PRIV	3	19	HALESTOWN, NH	6, 81	NOT CAPTURED
MOSES	KIMBALL	PRIV	3	19	HAMPSTEAD, NH	6, 26, 30	PRISONER
WINTHROP	KINNISON	PRIV	3	24	EPPING, NH	6	RETURNED
DAVID	LAWLOR	PRIV	3		LITCHFIELD, NH	6	NOT CAPTURED
BRACKETT	LEAVITT	PRIV	3	23	WEARE, NH	6, 81	NOT CAPTURED
NEHEMIAH	LEAVITT	PRIV	3	23	BRINTWOOD, NH	6	RETURNED
JOHN	MANHAN	PRIV	3	24	BEDFORD, NH	6, 71	NOT CAPTURED
NATHANIEL	MARTIN	PRIV	3	19	PELHAM, NH	6, 26, 30, 73	PRISONER
MOSES	MARTIN	PRIV	3	21	RUMNEY, NH	6	NOT CAPTURED
CHARLES	MCCOY	PRIV	3	20	SUNCOOK, NH	6	RETURNED
JOHN	MCCULLOM	PRIV	3	20	PEMBROKE, NH	6, 30, 43	PRISONER
JAMES	MELVIN	PRIV	3	22	HUBBARDSTON	26, 30, 129	PRISONER
JOHN	MORGAN	PRIV	3	24	DUNBARTON, NH	6, 26	PRISONER
PATRICK	MURPHY	PRIV	3	26	BEDFORD, NH	6, 43	RETURNED
BENJAMIN	NEALY	PRIV	3	24	MEREDITH, NH	6	RETURNED
JONATHAN	NORRIS	PRIV	3	18	SUNCOOK, NH	6, 26, 30	PRISONER
JOHN	ORR	PRIV	3	23	DERRY, NH	6	NOT CAPTURED
DAVID	PAGE	PRIV	3	19	SOUTHAMPTON	6	NOT CAPTURED
WILLIAM	PRESTON	PRIV	3	21	RUMNEY, NH	6, 26, 30	PRISONER
JOHN	RAY	PRIV	3	21	BEDFORD, NH	6	RETURNED
ELIPHAZ	REED	PRIV	3	22	RUMNEY, NH	6, 26, 30	PRISONER
ENOS	REYNOLDS	PRIV	3	18	BOXFORD MA	6, 26, 96	PRISONER
JOHN	ROBINSON	PRIV	3	24	SUNCOOK, NH	6	NOT CAPTURED

SAMUEL L.	ROWELL	PRIV	3	20	DERRY, NH	6, 22	RETURNED
BRYAN	ROURKE	PRIV	3	19	NEW SALEM, NH	6	NOT CAPTURED
AARON	SERGEANT	PRIV	3	20	CANTERBURY, NH	6, 26, 30	PRISONER
VALENTINE	SERGEANT	PRIV	3	20	DERRY, NH	6	NOT CAPTURED
SAMUEL	SIAS	PRIV	3	30	NOTTINGHAM, NH	6	NOT CAPTURED
JONATHAN	SMITH	PRIV	3	24	DUNBARTON, NH	6, 26, 30	PRISONER
JOSEPH	SMITH	PRIV	3	22	PLYMOUTH, NH	6, 26, 30	PRISONER
JOSEPH	SPRINGER	PRIV	3	38	HAVERHILL, MA	6	NOT CAPTURED
PETER R.	STEVENS	PRIV	3	19	NEWBURY, MA	6	NOT CAPTURED
THOMAS	STICKNEY	PRIV	3	21	PEMBROKE, NH	6	NOT CAPTURED
JAMES	TAGGERT	PRIV	3		PETERBOROUGH	6	NOT CAPTURED
WILLIAM	TAYLOR	PRIV	3	28	HILLSBOROUGH	6, 26, 30	PRISONER
THOMAS	TOLLEY	PRIV	3	21	DOVER, NH	6	NOT CAPTURED
EBENEZER	TUTTLE	PRIV	3	18	MONTAGUE, MA	6, 18, 26	PRISONER
WILLIAM	WILLEY	PRIV	3	19	GILMARTIN, NH	6	RETURNED
JOHN	WIER	PRIV	3	17	MERRIMAC, NH	6	RETURNED
TOTAL OFFICER'S & MEN			87				

WARD'S COMPANY

FIRST NAME	LAST NAME	RANK	CO	AGE	HOME TOWN	SOURCES	DISPOSITION
SAMUEL	WARD	CAPT	4	19	WESTERLY, RI	4, 26, 27, 28	PRISONER
JOHN	CLARK	LIEUT	4	34	HADLEY, MA	4, 26, 27, 28	PRISONER
SYLVANUS	SHAW	LIEUT	4	21	NEWPORT, RI	26, 27, 28	PRISONER
JAMES	TISDALE	ENS	4	30	MEDFIELD, MA	27, 28, 124	PRISONER
AMOS	BOYNTON	SGT	4	33	FITZWILLIAM, NH	7, 26, 27, 28	PRISONER
NICHOLAS	TITCOMB	SGT	4	25	NEWBURYPORT	18	NOT CAPTURED
JOHN	SLEEPER	CORP	4	21	NEWBURYPORT	26, 28	PRISONER
NATHANIEL	BROWN	CORP	4	25	LANCASTER, MA	26, 27, 28, 57, 123	PRISONER
LUTHER	TROWBRIDGE	CORP	4	20	FITZWILLIAM, NH	8, 28	NOT CAPTURED
EDWARD	ARNOLD	PRIV	4	24	FITZWILLIAM, NH	6	NOT CAPTURED
NATHANIEL	BABSON	PRIV	4	25	NEWBURYPORT	26, 27, 130	PRISONER
JOHN	BALDARCE	PRIV	4		UNKOWN	27	NOT CAPTURED
JOHN	BARKER	PRIV	4	19	FITZWILLIAM, NH	6	NOT CAPTURED
ISRAEL	BARRETT	PRIV	4	19	CONCORD, MA	18, 26, 30	PRISONER
JABEZ	BROOKS	PRIV	4		LANCASTER, MA	27, 28, 58, 67	PRISONER

JOHN	BROWN	PRIV	4	27	NO. 5, RI	6	NOT CAPTURED
THOMAS	BUTLER	PRIV	4	18	NEWBURYPORT	27, 131	NOT CAPTURED
JOSIAH	CARR	PRIV	4	22	NEWBURYPORT	33, 130, 131	NOT CAPTURED
GILBERT	CASWELL	PRIV	4	21	CHARLESTOWN, RI	6, 26, 30	PRISONER
ENOS	CHILLIS	PRIV	4	18	NEW HAMPSHIRE	26, 30	PRISONER
JOHN	CLARKE	PRIV	4		HADLEY, MA	27, 36	NOT CAPTURED
AARON	CLEVELAND	PRIV	4		WESTMINSTER, MA	18, 27	NOT CAPTURED
MOSES	CROSS	PRIV	4	20	NEWBURYPORT	130	NOT CAPTURED
EBENEZER	DAUGHEY	PRIV	4		DORCHESTER, MA	36	NOT CAPTURED
THOMAS	DAUGHERTY	PRIV	4		CASCO BAY, ME	27, 58	NOT CAPTURED
WILLIAM	DORR	PRIV	4	18	DOVER, NH	26, 27, 30	PRISONER
JOHN	DOOLEY	PRIV	4	26	JAFREY, NH	6	NOT CAPTURED
ELIJAH	DOLE	PRIV	4	20	LANCASTER, MA	6, 26, 30, 111	PRISONER
JESSE	EMERY	PRIV	4	24	NEWBURYPORT	130	NOT CAPTURED
JOSEPH	FASSETT	PRIV	4	19	FITZWILLIAM, NH	6, 27	NOT CAPTURED
THOMAS	FISHER	PRIV	4	22	NEEDHAM, MA	26, 38	PRISONER
ENOCH	FOOT	PRIV	4	27	NEWBURYPORT	11, 26, 30	PRISONER
BATHOLOMEW	FOSTER	PRIV	4	26	WRENTHAM, MA	6, 18, 30	PRISONER
THOMAS	GAY	PRIV	4	22	WRENTHAM, MA	26, 30	PRISONER
JOSIAH	GEORGE	PRIV	4	19	NEWBURYPORT	26, 30	PRISONER
MOSES	GEORGE	PRIV	4	25	NEWBURYPORT	130	NOT CAPTURED
JOHN	GOODHUE	PRIV	4	20	NEWBURYPORT	26, 30, 131	PRISONER
MOSES	GREENLEAF	PRIV	4	22	NEWBURYPORT	131	NOT CAPTURED
JEREMIAH	GREENMAN	PRIV	4	18	PROVIDENCE,	25, 28	PRISONER
THOMAS	GOULD	PRIV	4	24	NEWBURYPORT	27, 131	NOT CAPTURED
JOHN	GRIDLEY	PRIV	4	23	MEDFIELD, MA	26, 28	PRISONER
CHARLES	HARKIN	PRIV	4		MONTAGUE, MA	27, 28	PRISONER
STEPHEN	HARRIS	PRIV	4		CHARLEMONT, MA	18, 36, 110	NOT CAPTURED
CALEB	HASKELL	PRIV	4	21	NEWBURYPORT	131	NOT CAPTURED
ELIJAH	HAYDEN	PRIV	4		WEYMOUTH, MA	27, 28	PRISONER
JOHN	HICKEY	PRIV	4		WESTERLY, RI	27	NOT CAPTURED
AZARIAH	HILLYARD	PRIV	4		NORWICH,CT	11	NOT CAPTURED
SAMUEL	HOLBROOKS	PRIV	4		BOSTON, MA	27, 28	PRISONER
BENJAMIN	KENNEY	PRIV	4		NEWBURYPORT	27	NOT CAPTURED
JOSEPH	KIRK	PRIV	4		MAINE	32	DIED/WILD
EBENEZER	LANGLEY	PRIV	4	17	DORCHESTER, MA	18, 27	NOT CAPTURED
MOSES	MERRILL	PRIV	4	19	NEWBURYPORT	26, 30, 131	PRISONER

FIRST NAME	LAST NAME	RANK	CO	AGE	HOME TOWN	SOURCES	DISPOSITION
DENNIS	MIRE	PRIV	4		NEWBURY, MA	18, 36	NOT CAPTURED
BENJAMIN	NEWMAN	PRIV	4		NEWBURYPORT	131	NOT CAPTURED
JOSEPH	OSBURN	PRIV	4		PAXTON, MA	27, 28	PRISONER
JOSEPH	PARKS	PRIV	4	25	SALISBURY, CT	6	NOT CAPTURED
WILLIAM	PAY	PRIV	4	22	NEWBURYPORT	131	NOT CAPTURED
JOSEPH	POOL	PRIV	4	19	BOSTON, MA	26, 30	PRISONER
ENOCH	RICHARDSON	PRIV	4	21	NEWBURYPORT	27, 131	NOT CAPTURED
JOHN CARR	ROBERTS	PRIV	4	20	NEWBURYPORT	27, 131	NOT CAPTURED
JAMES	RUST	PRIV	4	19	SALEM, MA	26, 30	PRISONER
JOHN	SHACKFORD	PRIV	4	19	NEWBURYPORT	26, 30, 131	PRISONER
WILLIAM	SHACKFORD	PRIV	4	22	NEWBURYPORT	27, 30	PRISONER
THOMAS	SHEPARD	PRIV	4	37	DEDHAM, MA	27, 28	KILLED
BARTHOLOMEW	SPOONER	PRIV	4	20	NEWBURYPORT	18, 131	NOT CAPTURED
BISHOP	STANLEY	PRIV	4		GLOUCESTER, MA	27, 28	KILLED
JOHN	STEVENS	PRIV	4		SALISBURY, MA	18, 27, 28	KILLED
JOHN	STICKNEY	PRIV	4	20	NEWBURYPORT	26, 30, 131	PRISONER
BENJAMIN H.	TAPPAN	PRIV	4	22	NEWBURYPORT	131	NOT CAPTURED
EBENEZER	TOLMAN	PRIV	4	27	FITZWILLIAM, NH	6, 26, 30	PRISONER
JACOB	TRUE	PRIV	4	21	NEWBURYPORT	26, 30, 131	PRISONER
JOSEPH	WARE	PRIV	4	22	NEEDHAM, MA	26, 30, 46	PRISONER
ROBERT	WORSLEY	PRIV	4	22	KEENE, NH	6, 22	NOT CAPTURED
JAMES	WILLIAMS	PRIV	4		DEERFIELD, MA	18, 27, 131	NOT CAPTURED
TOTAL OFFICERS & MEN		**74**					

HUBBARD'S COMPANY

FIRST NAME	LAST NAME	RANK	CO	AGE	HOME TOWN	SOURCES	DISPOSITION
JONAS	HUBBARD	CAPT	5	36	WORCESTER, MA	21, 28, 133	KILLED
SAMUEL	BROWN	1 LIEUT	5	25	LEXINGTON, MA	21, 26, 39, 46, 133	PRISONER
ELIHU	LYMAN	2 LIEUT	5	24	NORTHFIELD, MA	125, 133	RETURNED
JOHN	PIERCE	ENS	5	31	WORCESTER,	21, 133	NOT CAPTURED
JONATHAN	BALL	SGT	5	22	SOUTHBORO, MA	18, 26,30,124, 133	PRISONER
SAMUEL	WESSON	SGT	5		WORCESTER,	30,86,88,124,133	KILLED
MINOT	FARMER	SGT	5		HOLLIS, NH	18, 26, 88, 124	PRISONER
LUTHER	FAIRBANKS	SGT	5	21	NORTHFIELD, MA	21, 26, 30, 133	PRISONER
ABNER	BRIGHAM	CRPL	5		CRYDON, MA	18, 21, 133	RETURNED

BENJAMIN G.	BALL	PRIV	5		SPENCER, MA	18, 21, 55	RETURNED
DANIEL	BALL	PRIV	5		SPENCER, MA	14, 18, 55	RETURNED
LEMUEL	BATES	PRIV	5	20	NORTHAMPTON	18,26,30, 117	PRISONER
?	BIXBY	PRIV	5		NOT IDENTIFIED	133	RETURNED
JABEZ	BROOKE	PRIV	5		LANCASTER, MA	124	PRISONER
JOHN	BUNN	PRIV	5		LANCASTER, MA	124	NOT CAPTURED
TILLE (TILLY)	BURK	PRIV	5		CHESTERFIELD, MA	18, 88	RETURNED
JOSEPH	BURR	PRIV	5	25	NORTHFIELD, MA	26, 30	PRISONER
BENJAMIN	BUTCHER	PRIV	5		WORCESTER,	18, 133	PRISONER
DAVID	CHAMBERLAIN	PRIV	5		SPENCER, MA	55, 133	RETURNED
WILLIAM	CHAMBERLAIN	PRIV	5	22	WORCESTER,	26, 30, 124	PRISONER
PAUL	CLAP	PRIV	5	21	NORTHAMPTON	26, 30, 117	PRISONER
RUSSELL	CLARK	PRIV	5	22	NORTHAMPTON	26,30,124, 133	PRISONER
SAMUEL	COOK	PRIV	5	20	HADLEY, MA	22	NOT CAPTURED
MATTHEW	COX	PRIV	5	27	CAMBRIDGE, MA	18, 50	NOT CAPTURED
AMOS	CRITTENTON	PRIV	5		ASHFIELD, MA	22, 53	NOT CAPTURED
JAMES	CULVERSON	PRIV	5		WESTFIELD, MA	18, 82, 136	RETURNED
JOHATHAN	DALEY	PRIV	5		PLYMOUTH, MA	133	RETURNED
JOHN	DAVIS	PRIV	5		SOUTHAMPTON	133	RETURNED
PHILLIP	DONOHUE	PRIV	5		WORCESTER,	21, 133	NOT CAPTURED
THOMAS	DUNSTON	PRIV	5		AMHERST, MA	42	NOT CAPTURED
OLIVER	EDWARDS	PRIV	5	20	NORTHAMPTON	26, 30, 117	PRISONER
SIMON	FOBES	PRIV	5	19	AMHERST, MA	26, 30, 42, 124	PRISONER
SIMON	GATES	PRIV	5		WORCESTER,	18	NOT CAPTURED
JOHN	GUILFORD	PRIV	5		SPENCER, MA	55	NOT CAPTURED
JOHN	HALL	PRIV	5		WORCESTER,	21, 30, 88	PRISONER
ASA	HARRINGTON	PRIV	5		WORCESTER,	21	KILLED
MORRIS	HAYWOOD	PRIV	5		WORCESTER,	30	PRISONER
AARON	HEATH	PRIV	5	23	ALSTEAD, NH	21, 26, 30, 124	PRISONER
NATHANIEL	HEYWOOD	PRIV	5		WORCESTER,	79, 124	KILLED
BENJAMIN	HIGGINS	PRIV	5		SPENCER, MA	124	PRISONER
MORRIS	HIGGINS	PRIV	5		LEICESTER, MA	119, 124	RETURNED
ANTHONY	JONES	PRIV	5	25	ASHFIELD, MA	26, 30, 124	PRISONER
ISAAC	JONES	PRIV	5		WORCESTER,	21, 117, 133	NOT CAPTURED
ISAAC	LEWIS	PRIV	5	20	ASHFIELD, MA	18, 22	RETURNED
SETH JR	LYMAN	PRIV	5		NORTHAMPTON	117, 133	RETURNED
WILLIAM	MARTING	PRIV	5		CHELMSFORD, MA	18, 137	NOT CAPTURED

FIRST NAME	LAST NAME	RANK	CO	AGE	HOME TOWN	SOURCES	DISPOSITION
SAMUEL	MAYNARD	PRIV	5		SHREWSBURY, MA	18, 133	DIED/WILD
CHARLES	MCGUIRE	PRIV	5		WORCESTER,	30	PRISONER
JOHN	MCGUIRE	PRIV	5		WORCESTER,	21,79, 124, 133,	PRISONER
THOMAS	MCINTIRE	PRIV	5		ASHFIELD, MA	30, 141	PRISONER
GEORGE	MILLS	PRIV	5		CHESTERFIELD, MA	88	RETURNED
GEORGE JR	MILLS	PRIV	5	23	CHESTERFIELD, MA	26, 30, 88, 141	PRISONER
JOSEPH	MORSE	PRIV	5	19	FITZWILLIAM, NH	22, 93, 133	NOT CAPTURED
?	MURPHY	PRIV	5		NOT IDENTIFIED	133	RETURNED
THOMAS	NICHOLS	PRIV	5	24	WORCESTER,	21, 26, 30, 84, 141	PRISONER
LUKE	NOBLE	PRIV	5		GR BARRINGTON	30	PRISONER
FRANCIS	PAINE	PRIV	5		WORCESTER,	83, 141	PRISONER
JOSEPH JR	PARSONS	PRIV	5	20	NORTHAMPTON	26, 30, 133, 141	PRISONER
DAVID	PATCH	PRIV	5		HOLLIS, NH	30, 141	PRISONER
BENJAMIN	PHILLIPS	PRIV	5		ASHFIELD , MA	30, 141	PRISONER
DAVID	PIERCE	PRIV	5		HADLEY, MA	22, 133	DIED/WILD
WILLIOAM	PIERCE	PRIV	5			22	NOT CAPTURED
EBENEZER	POTTER	PRIV	5	23	FITZWILLIAM, NH	22, 93	NOT CAPTURED
MORGAN	PRIGHETS	PRIV	5		UNK	133	DIED/WILD
TIMOTHY	RICE	PRIV	5	30	PELHAM, MA	30, 120, 124	PRISONER
JONATHAN	ROGERS	PRIV	5	20	WESTFIELD,MA	21	RETURNED
OLIVER	SMITH	PRIV	5	23	HADLEY, MA	21, 22, 26, 30,	PRISONER
THOMAS	SMITH	PRIV	5		LANCASTER, MA	36, 124, 141	NOT CAPTURED
CYRUS	STEBBINS	PRIV	5		NORTHAMPTON	133	RETURNED
JOSIAH	STEPHENS	PRIV	5		HADLEY, MA	124, 133	RETURNED
RICHARD	STOWERS	PRIV	5		WORCESTER,	18, 94	NOT CAPTURED
ELIAS	THAYER	PRIV	5		NORTHAMPTON	117	NOT CAPTURED
SAMUEL JR	WESSON	PRIV	5		WORCESTER,	124	KILLED
TIMOTHY	WESTON	PRIV	5		WORCESTER,	86	KILLED
JOSEPH	WHITE	PRIV	5	19	MARLBORO, MA	26, 30, 124	PRISONER
THOMAS	WHITTEMORE	PRIV	5		LEICESTER, MA	119, 124	NOT CAPTURED
TOTAL OFFICERS & MEN		**76**					

HENDRICK'S COMPANY

FIRST NAME	LAST NAME	RANK	CO	AGE	HOME TOWN	SOURCES	DISPOSITION
WILLIAM	HENDRICKS	CAPT	6	21	CUMBERLAND CO	19, 28, 30	KILLED

FRANCIS	NICHOLS	LIEUT	6	38	CARLISLE, PA	19, 26, 28, 30, 115	PRISONER
GEORGE	FRANCIS	LIEUT	6	28	CUMBERLAND CO	19, 115	RETURNED
MATTHEW	IRVINE	LIEUT	6	18	CARLISLE, PA	124, 134, 135	RETURNED
JOHN	MCLELLAN	LIEUT	6	34	CUMBERLAND CO	19, 115	DIED/WILD
THOMAS	GIBSON	CRPL	6	19	CARLISLE, PA	13, 26, 30, 115	PRISONER
WILLIAM	MCCOY	SGT	6	28	CUMBERLAND CO	19, 26, 30, 115	PRISONER
JOSEPH	GREER	SGT	6		CUMBERLAND CO	13, 19, 30, 115	PRISONER
HENRY	CORNE	SGT	6	23	YORK CO, PA	13, 26, 115	PRISONER
GEORGE	ALBRIGHT	PRIV	6		CUMBERLAND CO	19, 115	NOT CAPTURED
THOMAS	ANDERSON	PRIV	6	25	CUMBERLAND CO	13, 26, 30, 115	PRISONER
PHILIP HORN	BAKER	PRIV	6	26	MANSFIELD, NJ	13, 22, 26, 30, 115	PRISONER
JOHN	BLAIR	PRIV	6	20	CUMBERLAND CO	13, 26, 30, 115	PRISONER
ALEXANDER	BURNS	PRIV	6		CUMBERLAND CO	13, 30, 115	PRISONER
PETER	BURNS	PRIV	6		CUMBERLAND CO	13, 30, 115	PRISONER
WILLIAM	BURNS	PRIV	6		CUMBERLAND CO	13, 30, 115	PRISONER
JOHN	CAMPBELL	PRIV	6		CUMBERLAND CO	19, 30, 115	KILLED
DANIEL	CARLISLE	PRIV	6		CUMBERLAND CO	13, 30, 115	PRISONER
JONATHAN	CARSWELL	PRIV	6		CUMBERLAND CO	13, 19, 115	PRISONER
ROGER	CASEY	PRIV	6		CUMBERLAND CO	123, 30, 115	PRISONER
JOSEPH	CASKEY	PRIV	6		CUMBERLAND CO	13, 30, 115	PRISONER
JOHN	CHAMBERS	PRIV	6	22	CUMBERLAND CO	13, 26, 30, 115	PRISONER
JONATHAN	CHESNEY	PRIV	6	22	CUMBERLAND CO	13, 30, 115	PRISONER
THOMAS	COOKE	PRIV	6		CUMBERLAND CO	19, 115	PRISONER
JOHN	COVE	PRIV	6		CUMBERLAND CO	19, 30, 115	PRISONER
JOHN	CRAIG	PRIV	6		CUMBERLAND CO	19, 115	NOT CAPTURED
MATTHEW	CUMMINGS	PRIV	6		CUMBERLAND CO	13, 19, 30, 115	PRISONER
ARTHUR	ECKLES	PRIV	6		CUMBERLAND CO	19, 115	NOT CAPTURED
FRANCIS	FURLOW	PRIV	6		CUMBERLAND CO	13, 30	PRISONER
PETER	FRANIER	PRIV	6		CUMBERLAND CO	13, 19, 30, 115	PRISONER
WILLIAM	GAMMELL	PRIV	6	28	CUMBERLAND CO	13, 19, 26, 30, 115	PRISONER
JOHN	GARDNER	PRIV	6		CUMBERLAND CO	13, 19, 26, 30, 115	RETURNED
DANIEL	GRAHAM	PRIV	6	20	CUMBERLAND CO	19, 26, 30, 115	PRISONER
JAMES	GREER	PRIV	6		CUMBERLAND CO	19, 26, 30, 115	PRISONER
THOMAS	GREER	PRIV	6		CUMBERLAND CO	19, 26, 30, 115	PRISONER
ELIJAH	HARDY	PRIV	6		CUMBERLAND CO	19, 115	PRISONER
JOHN	HARDY	PRIV	6		CUMBERLAND CO	13, 19, 30, 115	PRISONER
JOHN	HENDERSON	PRIV	6	20	CUMBERLAND CO	13, 19, 26, 30, 115	PRISONER

JAMES	HOGG (HOGE)	PRIV	6		CUMBERLAND CO	19, 30, 115	PRISONER
JAMES	IRELAND	PRIV	6		CUMBERLAND CO	13, 19, 30, 115	PRISONER
DENNIS	KELLY	PRIV	6		CUMBERLAND CO	19, 115	KILLED
WILLIAM	KIRKPATRICK	PRIV	6	22	CUMBERLAND CO	13, 19, 30, 115	PRISONER
DAVID	LAMB	PRIV	6		CUMBERLAND CO	19, 22, 115	NOT CAPTURED
THOMAS	LESLEY	PRIV	6		CUMBERLAND CO	13, 19, 30, 115	PRISONER
JOHN	LORAIN	PRIV	6		CUMBERLAND CO	19, 115	NOT CAPTURED
RICHARD	LYNCH	PRIV	6		CUMBERLAND CO	13, 30	PRISONER
BENJAMIN	LYON	PRIV	6	23	LANCASTER, PA	22	NOT CAPTURED
JACOB	MASON	PRIV	6	25	CUMBERLAND CO	13, 19, 30, 115	PRISONER
PHILLIP	MAXWELL	PRIV	6		CUMBERLAND CO	13, 19, 30, 115	PRISONER
JOHN	MCCHESNEY	PRIV	6		CUMBERLAND CO	19, 30, 115	PRISONER
DANIEL	MCCLELLAN	PRIV	6		CUMBERLAND CO	19, 30, 115	PRISONER
RICHARD	MCCLURE	PRIV	6	30	CUMBERLAND CO	13, 19, 26 30, 115	PRISONER
HENRY	MCCORMICK	PRIV	6		CUMBERLAND CO	19, 115	NOT CAPTURED
GEORGE	MCCULLY	PRIV	6		PITTSBURG, PA	41	RETURNED
HENRY	MCEWEN	PRIV	6	21	CARLISLE, PA	13,19,22,26,30,115	PRISONER
ARCHIBALD	MCFARLANE	PRIV	6		CUMBERLAND CO	13, 30	PRISONER
BARNABAS	MCGUIRE	PRIV	6	21	CARLISLE, PA	18, 19, 30, 115	PRISONER
JOHN	MACKLIN	PRIV	6	25	CUMBERLAND CO	13, 19, 30, 115	PRISONER
JOHN	MCMURDY	PRIV	6	20	CARLISLE, PA	19, 22, 115	NOT CAPTURED
GEORGE	MORISON	PRIV	6	21	SHERMAN VALLEY	19, 26, 30 115	PRISONER
GEORGE	MORROW	PRIV	6		CUMBERLAND CO	13, 19, 26, 30, 115	PRISONER
EDWARD	MORTON	PRIV	6		CUMBERLAND CO	13, 19, 30, 115	PRISONER
THOMAS	MURDOCK	PRIV	6		CUMBERLAND CO	13, 19, 30, 115	PRISONER
DANIEL	NORTH	PRIV	6	23	CUMBERLAND CO	13, 19, 26, 30, 115	PRISONER
DANIEL	O'HARA	PRIV	6		CUMBERLAND CO	19, 115	PRISONER
WILLIAM	O'HARA	PRIV	6		CUMBERLAND CO	13, 19, 30, 115	PRISONER
?	PRENTICE	PRIV	6		CUMBERLAND CO	19	RETURNED
JONATHAN	RAY	PRIV	6	20	CUMBERLAND CO	13, 19, 30, 115	PRISONER
JAMES	REED	PRIV	6	25	CUMBERLAND CO	13, 19, 26, 30, 115	PRISONER
GEORGE	RINEHART	PRIV	6		CUMBERLAND CO	19, 115	NOT CAPTURED
EDWARD	RODDEN	PRIV	6		CUMBERLAND CO	13, 19, 30, 115	PRISONER
WILLIAM	SHANNON	PRIV	6		CUMBERLAND CO	19, 115	PRISONER
ANDREW	SMALL	PRIV	6	19	CUMBERLAND CO	19	NOT CAPTURED
WILLIAM	SMITH	PRIV	6		CUMBERLAND CO	13, 19, 30, 115	PRISONER
WILLIAM	SNELL	PRIV	6		CUMBERLAND CO	13, 19, 30, 115	PRISONER

FIRST NAME	LAST NAME	RANK	CO	AGE	HOME TOWN	SOURCES	DISPOSITION
ROBERT	STEELE	PRIV	6	20	CUMBERLAND CO	13, 19, 26, 30, 115	PRISONER
ABRAHAM	SWAGGERTY	PRIV	6	20	CUMBERLAND CO	13, 19, 26, 30, 115	PRISONER
HUGH	SWEENEY	PRIV	6		CUMBERLAND CO	19, 115	NOT CAPTURED
EDWARD	SWEENEY	PRIV	6		CUMBERLAND CO	19, 115	NOT CAPTURED
JOHN	TAYLOR	PRIV	6		CUMBERLAND CO	134	DIED/WILD
MATTHEW	TAYLOR	PRIV	6	21	CUMBERLAND CO	13, 19, 26, 30, 115	PRISONER
ISAAC	THOMPSON	PRIV	6		CARLISLE, PA	19	RETURNED
HENRY	TURKENTINE	PRIV	6		CUMBERLAND CO	13, 19, 30, 115	PRISONER
THOMAS	WITHEROP	PRIV	6		CUMBERLAND CO	13, 19, 30, 115	PRISONER
JOSEPH	WRIGHT	PRIV	6		CUMBERLAND CO	13, 19, 30, 115	PRISONER
MICHAEL	YOUNG	PRIV	6		CUMBERLAND CO	13, 30	PRISONER
TOTAL OFFICERS & MEN		**86**					

SMITH'S COMPANY

FIRST NAME	LAST NAME	RANK	CO	AGE	HOME TOWN	SOURCES	DISPOSITION
MATTHEW	SMITH	CAPT	7	41	PAXTANG, PA	1, 19,	NOT CAPTURED
WILLIAM	CROSS	LIEUT	7	23	HANOVER, PA	19, 115	NOT CAPTURED
MICHAEL	SIMPSON	LIEUT	7	35	PAXTANG, PA	19, 115,	NOT CAPTURED
THOMAS	BOYD	SGT	7	21	DERRY, PA	19, 26, 30	PRISONER
JOSEPH	SNODGRASS	SGT	7		LANCASTER CO	19, 26, 30	PRISONER
ROBERT	DIXON	SGT	7		WEST HANOVER	19, 115, 135	DIED/WILD
ROBERT	CUNNINGHAM	SGT	7	22	LONDONDERRY	19, 26, 30, 89	PRISONER
MARTIN	WEAVER	SGT	7		UPPER PAXTANG	19, 115	NOT CAPTURED
HENRY	HERRIGAN	CORP	7		LANCASTER CO	19, 115	PRISONER
JOHN	SHAEFFER	DRUM	7	22	LANCASTER, PA	19, 26, 30	PRISONER
EDWARD	AGNEW	PRIV	7	28	LANCASTER CO	, 26, 30	PRISONER
ROBERT	ALLISON	PRIV	7	17	LITTLE YORK, PA	22	NOT CAPTURED
JOHN	ANDERSON	PRIV	7		LANCASTER CO	19, 30, 115	PRISONER
JAMES	ANGLES	PRIV	7		LANCASTER CO	19, 30, 115	KILLED
JOHN	BELL	PRIV	7		LANCASTER CO	19, 115	NOT CAPTURED
CURTIS	BINNAGLE	PRIV	7		LONDONDERRY	19, 115	RETURNED
JAMES	BLACK	PRIV	7		HANOVER, PA	19, 115	NOT CAPTURED
JOHN	BLACK	PRIV	7		UPPER PAXTANG	19, 115	NOT CAPTURED
EMMANUEL	BALLINGER	PRIV	7		PAXTANG, PA	19, 22, 115	PRISONER
HUGH	BOYD	PRIV	7		LANCASTER CO	19, 26, 30, 115	PRISONER

PATRICK	CAMPBELL	PRIV	7	24	LANCASTER CO	19, 26, 30, 115	PRISONER
PETER	CARBOUGH	PRIV	7	19	PAXTANG, PA	19, 26, 30, 115	PRISONER
SAMUEL	CARBOUGH	PRIV	7	25	PAXTANG, PA	19, 26, 30, 115	PRISONER
EDWARD	CAVANAGH	PRIV	7		LANCASTER, PA	19, 26, 30, 115	PRISONER
?	CHAMBERLAIN	PRIV	7		LANCASTER CO	62	RETURNED
WALTER	CLAYBAUGH	PRIV	7	25	LANCASTER CO	36	RETURNED
SAMUEL	COCHRAN	PRIV	7		PAXTON, PA	89	NOT CAPTURED
TIMOTHY	CONNOR	PRIV	7		BETHEL, PA	19, 30, 115	PRISONER
DANIEL	CRANE	PRIV	7		LANCASTER CO	19, 26, 30, 115	PRISONER
JAMES	CROUCH	PRIV	7		PAXTON, PA	89	RETURNED
SAMUEL	DEAN	PRIV	7		LANCASTER CO	89	RETURNED
JOHN	DIXON	PRIV	7		LANCASTER CO	19, 115	NOT CAPTURED
RICHARD	DIXON	PRIV	7		DIXONS FORD, PA	19, 115	NOT CAPTURED
JAMES	DOUGHERTY	PRIV	7	23	LONDONDERRY	19, 22, 26, 30, 115	PRISONER
ALEXANDER	ELLIOT	PRIV	7		LANCASTER CO	19, 30, 115	KILLED
TIMOTHY	FEELY	PRIV	7		DIXONS FORD, PA	19, 115	KILLED
MICHAEL	FITZPATRICK	PRIV	7		LANCASTER CO	19, 30, 115	PRISONER
THOMAS	GUNN	PRIV	7	22	LANCASTER CO	19, 26, 30, 115	PRISONER
DAVID	HARRIS	PRIV	7		HARRIS FERRY, PA	89	RETURNED
JOHN	HARRIS	PRIV	7		HARRIS FERRY, PA	19, 115	KILLED
JOHN JOSEPH	HENRY	PRIV	7	19	LANCASTER, PA	26, 28, 30, 128	PRISONER
JOSEPH	HIGGINS	PRIV	7		LANCASTER CO	19, 30, 115	PRISONER
JOHN	KENNEDY	PRIV	7		HANOVER, PA	19, 115	NOT CAPTURED
ANTHONY	LEBANT	PRIV	7	22	LANCASTER CO	19, 26, 30, 115	PRISONER
LAWRENCE	MARSHALL	PRIV	7		HANOVER, PA	19, 115	NOT CAPTURED
ALEXANDER	MCCARTER	PRIV	7		LANCASTER CO	19, 30, 115	PRISONER
HENRY	MCNALLY	PRIV	7		LONDONDERRY	19, 30, 115	PRISONER
OWEN	MCGINNIS	PRIV	7		LANCASTER CO	19, 115	RETURNED
CHARLES	MCGRANAGAN	PRIV	7		LONDONDERRY	19, 115	NOT CAPTURED
JOHN	MCKONKEY	PRIV	7		HANOVER, PA	19, 115	NOT CAPTURED
ATCHISON	MELLEN	PRIV	7		PAXTANG, PA	19, 22, 115	NOT CAPTURED
CONRAD	MYERS	PRIV	7	22	LANCASTER CO	22, 26, 30	PRISONER
HENRY	MILLER	PRIV	7		LANCASTER CO	19, 30, 115	KILLED
JOHN	MILLER	PRIV	7	24	LANCASTER CO	22, 26, 30, 115	PRISONER
INGLEHART	MORTWORTH	PRIV	7		LANCASTER CO	19, 30, 115	KILLED
ROBERT	MOORE	PRIV	7		LANCASTER CO	19, 115	NOT CAPTURED
ALEXANDER	NELSON	PRIV	7		LANCASTER CO	19, 115	KILLED

PHILLIP	NEWHOUSE	PRIV	7	21	LANCASTER CO	19, 30, 115	PRISONER
NICHOLAS	NOGLE	PRIV	7	19	LANCASTER CO	19, 26, 30, 115	PRISONER
JAMES	OLDS	PRIV	7		LANCASTER CO	19, 115	NOT CAPTURED
THOMAS	PUGH	PRIV	7		LANCASTER CO	19, 30, 116	PRISONER
WILLIAM	RANDOLPH	PRIV	7		LANCASTER CO	19, 30, 115	PRISONER
WILLIAM	REYNOLDS	PRIV	7		LANCASTER CO	19 115, 128	RETURNED
JAMES	RICHARDS	PRIV	7		PHILADELPHIA	22	NOT CAPTURED
ROBERT	RICHMOND	PRIV	7		LANCASTER CO	19, 30, 115	PRISONER
THOMAS	ROWLAND	PRIV	7		LANCASTER CO	19, 115	RETURNED
WILLIAM	RUSSELL	PRIV	7		LANCASTER CO	26	RETURNED
JOHN	RYAN	PRIV	7		LANCASTER CO	19, 115	NOT CAPTURED
CONRAD	SHAYERS	PRIV	7		LANCASTER CO	26, 30	PRISONER
MICHAEL	SHARE	PRIV	7	22	LANCASTER CO	19, 26, 30, 115	PRISONER
THOMAS	SILBOURNE	PRIV	7	24	LANCASTER CO	19, 26, 30, 115	PRISONER
SAMUEL	SMITH	PRIV	7		PAXTON, PA	19, 115	NOT CAPTURED
WILLIAM	SPARROW	PRIV	7		LANCASTER CO	19, 115	NOT CAPTURED
JAMES	STEWART	PRIV	7		LANCASTER CO	19, 115	NOT CAPTURED
HENRY	TAYLOR	PRIV	7		LANCASTER CO	19, 30, 115	PRISONER
JOHN M.	TAYLOR	PRIV	7		LANCASTER CO	19, 115	NOT CAPTURED
MICHAEL	TEEDER	PRIV	7		HANOVER, PA	19, 115	NOT CAPTURED
ROBERT	THOMPSON	PRIV	7		LANCASTER CO	19, 115	NOT CAPTURED
JOHN	TODD	PRIV	7		HANOVER, PA	19, 115	NOT CAPTURED
THOMAS	WALKER	PRIV	7		LANCASTER CO	19, 30, 115	PRISONER
MICHAEL	WANN	PRIV	7		LANCASTER CO	19, 115	DIED/WILD
JAMES	WARNER	PRIV	7		LANCASTER CO	19, 115, 128	DIED/WILD
VALENTINE	WEIRICK	PRIV	7	24	HANOVER, PA	19,22, 26,30,115	PRISONER
?	WHEELER	PRIV	7		PAXTON, PA	19, 115	NOT CAPTURED
JAMES	WILSON	PRIV	7		LANCASTER CO	19, 115	NOT CAPTURED
JOHN HENRY	YOUNG	PRIV	7		LANCASTER CO	19, 115	NOT CAPTURED
TOTAL OFFICERS & MEN		**86**					

HANCHETT'S COMPANY

FIRST NAME	LAST NAME	RANK	CO	AGE	HOME TOWN	SOURCES	DISPOSITION
OLIVER	HANCHETT	CAPT	8	33	SUFFIELD, CT	11, 24, 26, 112	PRISONER
SAMUEL	COOPER	LIEUT	8	30	PORTLAND,CT	11, 14, 24	KILLED

JAMES	KNOWLES	ENS	8	23	WETHERSFIELD, CT	11, 14, 24	NOT CAPTURED
GABRIEL	HOTCHKISS	SGT	8	19	NEW HAVEN, CT	14, 24, 26, 136	PRISONER
DAVID	SAGE	SGT	8		CHATHAM, CT	11, 14, 24, 30	PRISONER
WILLIAM	GREEN	SGT	8		WINDSOR, CT	11, 24	NOT CAPTURED
ABNER	LYMAN	SGT	8		NORTHAMPTON	24, 117	NOT CAPTURED
GERSHOM	WILCOX	CORP	8	21	MIDDLETOWN, CT	11, 14, 24, 26	PRISONER
ROSWELL	RANSOM	CORP	8	23	COLCHESTER, CT	11, 14, 24, 26	PRISONER
JEDEDIAH	DEWEY	CORP	8		SUFFIELD, CT	11, 14, 24, 30	PRISONER
THEOPHILUS	HYDE	CORP	8		SIMSBURY, CT	11, 14, 24, 30	KILLED
JONATHAN	TAYLOR	CORP	8	19	MIDDLETOWN, CT	11,14,24,26,30	PRISONER
AARON	BULL	FIFER	8		MIDDLETOWN, CT	11, 24	NOT CAPTURED
JOHN	BASSETT	DRUM	8		NEW HAVEN CO	11, 14, 24	PRISONER
AMASA	ALLEN	PRIV	8		TOLLAND, CT	11, 24, 136	RETURMED
SAMUEL	BARNES	PRIV	8	42	EAST HAVEN, CT	11, 22, 24, 136	NOT CAPTURED
SAMUEL	BARNEY	PRIV	8	22	NEW HAVEN, CT	11, 24, 136	NOT CAPTURED
SAMUEL	BIGGS	PRIV	8	25	SIMSBURY, CT	11, 14, 24, 26	PRISONER
JOHN	BISBY	PRIV	8		NORTHAMPTON	24	NOT CAPTURED
ABRAHAM	BLINN	PRIV	8		WETHERSFIELD	24	NOT CAPTURED
SAMUEL	BLISS	PRIV	8		SPRINGFIELD, MA	11, 14, 24, 30	PRISONER
ELISHIMA	BRANDEGEE	PRIV	8		CHATHAM, CT	11, 14, 24	PRISONER
RICHARD	BREWER	PRIV	8	22	CHATHAM, CT	11, 14, 24, 30	PRISONER
SAMUEL	BURRISS	PRIV	8	21	NEW HAVEN, CT	11 14, 24, 26, 30	PRISONER
WILLIAM	CALDER	PRIV	8	22	NORTHAMPTON	24	NOT CAPTURED
JOHN	COLE	PRIV	8		PLAINFIELD, CT	11, 24	RETURNED
NATHANIEL	COLEMAN	PRIV	8	20	WETHERSFIELD	11, 14, 24, 26, 30	PRISONER
JACOB	CRAW/CROW	PRIV	8		CHATHAM, CT	24	RETURNED
JOSEPH	CURTIS	PRIV	8		NORTHAMPTON	11, 24, 136	RETURNED
CHRISTOPHER	DARROW	PRIV	8	25	NEW LONDON, CT	22, 24	PRISONER
TIMOTHY	DADY	PRIV	8		NORTHAMPTON	24	NOT CAPTURED
PELLETIAH	DEWEY	PRIV	8		SUFFIELD, CT	11, 14, 24, 30	PRISONER
THOMAS	DUNPHEY	PRIV	8		NORTHAMPTON	24	RETURNED
SAMUEL	EDSON	PRIV	8		SPRINGFIELD, MA	24	NOT CAPTURED
STEPHEN	FOSBURY	PRIV	8	20	WATERBURY, CT	11, 14, 24, 30	PRISONER
ISAAC	GEORGE	PRIV	8	24	NEW HAVEN, CT	11,14,24,26,30,136	PRISONER
JOSEPH	GOFF	PRIV	8		HEBRON, CT	11, 24, 136	NOT CAPTURED
NATHANIEL	GOODRICH	PRIV	8		CHATHAM, CT	11, 14, 24, 30, 136	KILLED
WILLIAM	GOODRICH	PRIV	8		CHATHAM, CT	11, 24, 30, 136	KILLED

SYLVANUS	HALE	PRIV	8		SPRINGFIELD, MA	24	NOT CAPTURED
STEPHEN	HARRINGTON	PRIV	8	35	SIMSBURY, CT	24	NOT CAPTURED
PETER	HEADY	PRIV	8		SUFFIELD, CT	14, 24, 30, 136	KILLED
THEODORE	HOOKER	PRIV	8		CHATHAM, CT	24	NOT CAPTURED
GEORGE	HUBBARD	PRIV	8		MARLBOROUGH	11, 24, 136	NOT CAPTURED
ALLEN	IVES	PRIV	8		NEW HAVEN, CT	11, 24, 136	NOT CAPTURED
WILLIAM	JOHNSON	PRIV	8		PELHAM, NH	11, 24, 73	RETURNED
ALLEN	JUDD	PRIV	8		WATERBURY, CT	24, 136	RETURNED
DANIEL	JUDD	PRIV	8		WATERBURY, CT	11, 22, 24, 136	NOT CAPTURED
FREEMAN	JUDD	PRIV	8		WATERBURY, CT	11, 22, 24, 136	NOT CAPTURED
ISAAC	KNAPP	PRIV	8	25	NEW HAVEN, CT	11, 24, 26, 30, 136	PRISONER
EDWARD	LAWRENCE	PRIV	8	21	TOLLAND, CT	11,14,24,26,30	PRISONER
DAVID	LEAMING	PRIV	8	18	SOUTHINGTON, CT	11,, 24	NOT CAPTURED
JOSEPH	LEWIS	PRIV	8	21	BETHELAHAM, CT	11, 22, 24	NOT CAPTURED
JOEL	LOVELAND	PRIV	8		GLASTONBURY	11, 14, 24, 84	PRISONER
SETH	LYMAN	PRIV	8		NORTHAMPTON	24, 117	NOT CAPTURED
ELIJAH	MARSHALL	PRIV	8	23	WINDSOR, CT	11,24,26,30,112	PRISONER
JONATHAN	MASON	PRIV	8		WOODSTOCK, CT	11, 24, 87	NOT CAPTURED
SPENCER	MERRICK	PRIV	8		SPRINGFIELD, MA	11, 14, 24, 30	KILLED
WILLIAM	MITCHELL	PRIV	8		MIDDLETOWN, CT	11, 24	NOT CAPTURED
ELIJAH	MIX	PRIV	8		NEW HAVEN, CT	24, 136	RETURNED
JAMES	MORRIS	PRIV	8	19	SUFFIELD, CT	11, 22, 24	NOT CAPTURED
JOHN	MORRIS	PRIV	8		SUFFIELD, CT	11, 14, 24, 30	KILLED
PATRICK	NUGENT	PRIV	8		SPRINGFIELD, MA	11, 14, 24, 30, 136	PRISONER
BENJAMIN	PARSONS	PRIV	8		SPRINGFIELD, MA	24	NOT CAPTURED
ABIJAH	PERRY	PRIV	8		FAIRFIELD, CT	22, 24	RETURNED
LANCELOT	PHELPS	PRIV	8		WINDSOR, CT	24	RETURNED
JONATHAN	POMEROY	PRIV	8		SUFFIELD, CT	24	NOT CAPTURED
JOSIAH	REMINGTON	PRIV	8		SUFFIELD, CT	11, 24, 136	NOT CAPTURED
DANIEL	RICE	PRIV	8	20	WINDSOR, CT	11,14,22, 24,30	PRISONER
JOHN	RISDEN	PRIV	8	25	SUFFIELD, CT	11,14,22,24,26,30	PRISONER
ELNATHAN	SANDERSON	PRIV	8		SUFFIELD, CT	24	NOT CAPTURED
DAVID	SHELDON	PRIV	8	19	SUFFIELD, CT	12,14,24,26,30	PRISONER
ROBERT	STEPHENS	PRIV	8		SPRINGFIELD, MA	24	NOT CAPTURED
ABNER	STOCKING	PRIV	8	23	HADDAM, CT	11,14,24,26,30	PRISONER
ICHABOD	SWADDLE	PRIV	8	20	MIDDLETOWN, CT	11,14,24,26,30	PRISONER
JAMES	TAYLOR	PRIV	8		SPRINGFIELD, MA	24	NOT CAPTURED

LOTT	TOWSLEY	PRIV	8		SUFFIELD, CT	24	NOT CAPTURED
TIMOTHY	WADSWORTH	PRIV	8		WETHERSIFELD	24	RETURNED
BENJAMIN	WARNER	PRIV	8	18	NEW HAVEN, CT	11, 22,24, 136	NOT CAPTURED
SOLOMON	WAY	PRIV	8		NEW HAVEN, CT	11, 14, 24, 30	PRISONER
NOAH	WHIPPLE	PRIV	8	22	TOLLAND, CT	11, 14, 24, 24, 30	PRISONER
MOSES	WHITE	PRIV	8	19	MIDDLETOWN, CT	11, 14, 24, 26, 30	PRISONER
SIMON	WINTER	PRIV	8		SUFFIELD, CT	11, 14, 24, 30	PRISONER
JOHN	WISE	PRIV	8		NEW HAVEN, CT	11, 24, 136	NOT CAPTURED
TOTAL OFFICERS & MEN		**84**					

TOPHAM'S COMPANY

FIRST NAME	LAST NAME	RANK	CO	AGE	HOME TOWN	SOURCES	DISPOSITION
JOHN	TOPHAM	CAPT	9	33	NEWPORT, RI	27, 30	PRISONER
JOSEPH	WEBB	LIEUT	9	22	NEWPORT, RI	27, 30	PRISONER
EDWARD	SLOCUM	LIEUT	9	26	TIVERTON, RI	22, 23, 27, 30, 36	PRISONER
NATHANIEL	CHURCH	LIEUT	3	43	LITTLE COMPTON	28, 34, 133	PRISONER
STEPHEN	TIFT	ENS	3	22	NEWPORT, RI	26, 30, 49	PRISONER
MATTHEW	COGGSHALL	SGT	9	19	NEWPORT, RI	26, 30	PRISONER
JOHN	FINCH	SGT	9	21	NEWPORT, RI	26, 28, 30	PRISONER
RUEBEN	JOHNSON	SGT	9	23	NEWPORT, RI	26, 28, 30	PRISONER
DANIEL	BOOTH	CRPL	9		NEWPORT, RI	26, 30	PRISONER
CHARLES	KING	DRUM	9		SHEFFIELD, MA	30	RETURNED
EBENEZER	ADAMS	PRIV	9		KINGSTON, RI	27	NOT CAPTURED
MARMADUKE	ALLYN	PRIV	9		WOODSTOCK, CT	11	RETURNED
BENJAMIN	ATWELL	PRIV	9		MONTVILLE, CT	11	NOT CAPTURED
CHARLES	BARTLETT	PRIV	9		LEBANON, CT	11	DIED/WILD
ISAAC	BEATTY	PRIV	9	22	VIRGINIA	26, 30	PRISONER
JOHN	BENTLEY	PRIV	9	22	NEW SHOREHAM	26, 30	PRISONER
JOHN	BAILEY	PRIV	9	17	LITTLE COMPTON	11	RETURNED
JONATHAN	BILL	PRIV	9	19	LEBANON, CT	11	NOT CAPTURED
HUGH	BLACKBURN	PRIV	9		WESTMORELAND	30	KILLED
ARCHIBALD	BLAKELY	PRIV	9		NEW HAVEN, CT	11, 136	NOT CAPTURED
ELIJAH	BOARDMAN	PRIV	9		WETHERSFIELD, CT	11	NOT CAPTURED
TIMOTHY	BURDEEN	PRIV	9	17	KITTERY, ME	23, 58	RETURNED
TOBIAS	BURKE	PRIV	9		CT VALLEY, CT	30	PRISONER

JEREMIAH	CHILD	PRIV	9	32	NEWPORT, RI	30	PRISONER
PHINEAS	CHILD	PRIV	9		WOODSTOCK, CT	11	RETURNED
MICHAEL	CLANCY	PRIV	9		MASSACHUSETTS	18, 30	PRISONER
WILLIAM	CLARK	PRIV	9	20	NEWPORT, RI	26, 30	PRISONER
NOAH	COLEMAN	PRIV	9		COLCHESTER, CT	11	RETURNED
JOHN	CONLY	PRIV	9		SUFFIELD, CT	11	NOT CAPTURED
THOMAS	CROSSMAN	PRIV	9		NEW LONDON, CT	22	RETURNED
TIMOTHY	CULVER	PRIV	9		NEW HAVEN, CT	136	NOT CAPTURED
JOHN	DARLING	PRIV	9	21	WINCHENDON, MA	26, 30	PRISONER
OLIVER	DUNNELL	PRIV	9	23	LYNN, MA	26, 30	PRISONER
BENJAMIN	DURFEE	PRIV	9	31	NEWPORT, RI	26, 30	PRISONER
CHARLES	FERGUSON	PRIV	9		CONNECTICUT	11	RETURNED
EBENEZER	FLAGG	PRIV	9		NEWPORT, RI	99	NOT CAPTURED
JOSEPH	FORWARD	PRIV	9	42	SIMSBURY, CT	11	NOT CAPTURED
BAKER	DARLING	PRIV	9		NEWPORT, RI	30, 133	PRISONER
BENJAMIN	FOWLER	PRIV	9		KINGSTON, RI		RETURNED
SAMUEL	GEER	PRIV	9	21	MILFORD, CT	26, 30	PRISONER
JAMES	GREEN	PRIV	9		WALDOBORO, ME	30	PRISONER
CALEB	HACKER	PRIV	9	18	NEWPORT, RI	30	KILLED
OLNEY	HART	PRIV	9		NEWPORT, RI	23, 27	DIED/WILD
JOSEPH	HURLEBURT	PRIV	9	23	WETHERSFIELD, CT	11	RETURNED
BENJAMIN	IRVIN	PRIV	9	21	NEWPORT, RI	30	PRISONER
PATRICK	KELLEY (KELLY)	PRIV	9		LENOX, MA	18, 30	PRISONER
JOSEPH	KENYON	PRIV	9	20	CHARLESTOWN, RI	26, 27, 30	PRISONER
ELIHU	JOHNSON	PRIV	9		TOLLAND, CT	11	RETURNED
MARTIN	LEWIS	PRIV	9		FARMINGTON, CT	11	RETURNED
LOT	LOVELAND	PRIV	9	20?	GLASTONBURY, CT	11, 84	DIED/WILD
JOHN	LINDON	PRIV	9		WALPOLE, MA	18, 30	PRISONER
MARK	LUN	PRIV	9		CONNECTICUT	11	RETURNED
THEOPOLIS	LUTHER	PRIV	9		WOODSTOCK, CT	11	RETURNED
BENJAMIN	LYON	PRIV	9		WOODSTOCK, CT	11	NOT CAPTURED
JAMES	MOORE	PRIV	9		SIMSBURY, CT	11	NOT CAPTURED
?	MORGAN	PRIV	9		NOT IDENTIFIED	133	KILLED
SAMUEL	NICHOLS	PRIV	9	29	TRURO, MA	26, 27	RETURNED
NATHANIEL	NORTON	PRIV	9	20	SUFFIELD, CT	11	RETURNED
DANIEL	OWEN	PRIV	9		WINDSOR, CT	11	NOT CAPTURED
WILLIAM	PITMAN	PRIV	9	24	NEWPORT, RI	26, 30	PRISONER

FIRST NAME	LAST NAME	RANK	CO	AGE	HOME TOWN	SOURCES	DISPOSITION
GIDEON	PORTER	PRIV	9	23	WINDSOR, CT	11	RETURNED
THOMAS	PRICE	PRIV	9	27	NEWPORT, RI	26, 30	PRISONER
THOMAS	RICHARDSON	PRIV	9	36	NEWPORT, RI	23	PRISONER
PHILLIP	ROLLINS	PRIV	9	30	WINCHENDON, MA	26, 30, 36	PRISONER
ANTHONY	SALISBURY	PRIV	9	22	LITTLE COMPTON	26, 30	PRISONER
BENJAMIN	SCOTT	PRIV	9		WOODSTOCK, CT	11	RETURNED
SHERMAN	SHATTUCK	PRIV	9		NEW HAVEN, CT	136	NOT CAPTURED
ELIJAH	SHELDON	PRIV	9		SUFFIELD, CT	11	NOT CAPTURED
?	SHEPPARD	PRIV	9		NOT IDENTIFIED	133	DIED/WILD
CHARLES	SHERMAN	PRIV	9	19	NEWPORT, RI	26, 30	PRISONER
ZACHARIAH	SMITH	PRIV	9		WOODSTOCK, CT	11	RETURNED
ALEXANDER	SPENCER	PRIV	9	20	SHARON, CT	11	DIED/WILD
WILLIAM	THOMAS	PRIV	9	19	NEWPORT, RI	26, 30	PRISONER
WILLIAM	TEW	PRIV	9		NEWPORT, RI	99	NOT CAPTURED
BENJAMIN	TRIM	PRIV	9	21	NEWPORT, RI	26, 30	PRISONER
WILLIAM	UNDERWOOD	PRIV	9	23	TOWNS END, RI	26, 30	PRISONER
LYON	WENTWORTH	PRIV	9		WETHERSFIELD, CT	11	RETURNED
AMARIAH	WINCHESTER	PRIV	9		NEWPORT, RI	22, 23	NOT CAPTURED
TOTAL OFFICERS & MEN		**77**					

GOODRICH'S COMPANY

FIRST NAME	LAST NAME	RANK	CO	AGE	HOME TOWN	SOURCES	DISPOSITION
WILLIAM	GOODRICH	CAPT	10	37	STOCKBRIDGE, MA	4,17,18,29, 30, 76	PRISONER
JOHN	CUMSTON	LIEUT	10	24	SACO, ME	17,29,30,36,58	PRISONER
ZEBEDIAH	SABIN	LIEUT	10	24	WILLIAMSTOWN	17, 97	RETURNED
DAVID	PIXLEY	LIEUT	10	29	STOCKBRIDGE	5, 22, 113	NOT CAPTURED
ASHLEY	GOODRICH	SGT	10	27	LENOX, MA	17, 26, 29, 30	PRISONER
AUGUSTUS	DRAKE	SGT	10	34	STOCKBRIDGE	26, 29, 30	PRISONER
EZRA	PARKER	SGT	10	30	NO. ADAMS, MA	69, 109	NOT CAPTURED
RUEBEN	CAREY	CRPL	10		STOCKBRIDGE	17, 18	NOT CAPTURED
JOSHUA	FINCH	CRPL	10	31	STOCKBRIDGE	17, 18, 22, 113	NOT CAPTURED
MOSES	BARNUM	CRPL	10		STOCKBRIDGE	17, 22	NOT CAPTURED
ELIJAH	ALDEN	PRIV	10	19	ASHFIELD, MA	26, 30	PRISONER
OLIVER JR	AVERY	PRIV	10	22	CHARLEMONT, MA	26, 30	PRISONER
ROSWELL	BALLARD	PRIV	10		LENOX, MA	17, 30	PRISONER
THOMAS	BENEDICT	PRIV	10		LENOX, MA	17, 22	NOT CAPTURED

AMOS	BRIDGE	PRIV	10		SHUTESBURY, MA	30	KILLED
BENJAMIN	BUCKMAN	PRIV	10	19	AMHERST, MA	26, 30	PRISONER
SAMUEL	BUCKMAN	PRIV	10	19	AMHERST, MA	22, 26, 30	PRISONER
JOSEPH	CAMFIELD	PRIV	10		NEW MARLBOROUGH	17, 18	NOT CAPTURED
JOHN	CAMPBELL	PRIV	10		HAMPSTEAD, NH	22	NOT CAPTURED
DAVID	CARR	PRIV	10	20	ASHFIELD, MA	23, 133	NOT CAPTURED
JABEZ	CHALKER	PRIV	10	26	PITTSFIELD, MA	26, 30	PRISONER
JESSE	CLARK	PRIV	10		LEE, MA	17, 22, 95	PRISONER
NOAH	CLUFF	PRIV	10		BERKSHIRE CO	22, 30	PRISONER
ELDAD	CORBETT	PRIV	10		MYRFIELD, MA	17, 18	NOT CAPTURED
THOMAS	DART	PRIV	10		PITTSFIELD, MA	17, 18	NOT CAPTURED
NATHAN	DAVIS	PRIV	10		LEE, MA	17, 22, 75, 95	RETURNED
ABNER	DAY	PRIV	10	26	STOCKBRIDGE	26, 30, 113	PRISONER
SAMSON	DOE	PRIV	10		DOVER, NH	17, 22	RETURNED
PAUL	DORAN	PRIV	10	25	CAMBRIDGE, MA	26, 30	PRISONER
WILLIAM	DOUGLAS	PRIV	10		KENNEBEC CO	17, 18, 142	NOT CAPTURED
DANIEL	DOYLE	PRIV	10	32	CAPE ANN, MA	26, 30	PRISONER
FESTUS	DRAKE	PRIV	10	37	STOCKBRIDGE	26, 30	PRISONER
ASA	DURHAM	PRIV	10		LANESBOROUGH	22	NOT CAPTURED
JARED	FITCH	PRIV	10		STOCKBRIDGE	17, 18	RETURNED
ROSWELL	FOOT	PRIV	10	17	BRADFORD, MA	26, 30	PRISONER
FENNER	FOOTE	PRIV	10		LEE, MA	22, 75, 95	NOT CAPTURED
JOSIAH	FREEMAN	PRIV	10		NORTHAMPTON	17, 18	NOT CAPTURED
BENJAMIN	FULLER	PRIV	10		LEE, MA	75, 95	NOT CAPTURED
SAMUEL	GILSON	PRIV	10		NEW MARLBOROUGH	75, 95	NOT CAPTURED
JOHN	GOVE	PRIV	10		STOCKBRIDGE	17, 18, 113	NOT CAPTURED
ROBERT	JONES	PRIV	10		STOCKBRIDGE	17, 18, 113	NOT CAPTURED
JOHN	LEE	PRIV	10	29	"DERWANDA"	26, 30	PRISONER
NATHANIEL	LORD	PRIV	10		ARUNDEL, ME	30, 58, 142	PRISONER
NATHAN	LYON	PRIV	10		ASHFIELD, MA	17, 18	NOT CAPTURED
STEPHEN	LYON	PRIV	10		ASHFIELD, MA	17, 18	NOT CAPTURED
JAMES	MCCORMICK	PRIV	10		NO. YARMOUTH	137	RETURNED
EDWARD	NASON	PRIV	10	20	ARUNDEL, ME	58, 95, 142, 143	NOT CAPTURED
CALEB	NORTHRUP	PRIV	10	26	LENOX, MA	26, 30	PRISONER
JOHN	PARROTT	PRIV	10	48	CAPE ANN, MA	26, 30	PRISONER
AMASA	PARKER	PRIV	10		SWANZY, NH	22, 102	NOT CAPTURED
BENJAMIN	PEARCE	PRIV	10		GROTON, MA	30	PRISONER

JOHN	PERCIVAL	PRIV	10	21	LEE, MA	22, 75	NOT CAPTURED
DAVID	PETTIS	PRIV	10	20	AMHERST, MA	26, 30	PRISONER
JOSIAH	ROOT	PRIV	10	21	LEE, MA	18, 26, 30, 113	PRISONER
DAVID	ROSS	PRIV	10		WESTFIELD, MA	17, 18	NOT CAPTURED
CHARLES	SABIN	PRIV	10		WILLIAMSTOWN	97	DIED/WILD
JOHN	SABIN	PRIV	10		WILLIMASTOWN	97	NOT CAPTURED
NEHEMIAH	SEALEY	PRIV	10		NEW LEBENON, NY	17, 18	NOT CAPTURED
JONATHAN	SHARP	PRIV	10		FALMOUTH, MA	17, 95, 101	NOT CAPTURED
RICHARD	SHOCKLEY	PRIV	10	22	WELLS, ME	26, 30	PRISONER
JOHN	TAYLOR	PRIV	10	24	MYRFIELD, MA	18, 26, 30	PRISONER
ROBERT	THOMPSON	PRIV	10		GAGEBOROUGH	17, 18	NOT CAPTURED
JAMES	THORTON	PRIV	10		KENNEBEC CO	17, 18, 58	NOT CAPTURED
MIAL	THORNTON	PRIV	10		KENNEBEC CO	17, 18, 58	NOT CAPTURED
RICHARD	VINING	PRIV	10	21	OTIS, MA	18, 22, 113	RETURNED
JOHN	WATROUS	PRIV	10		COLCHESTER, CT	17, 95	NOT CAPTURED
WALTER	WELCH	PRIV	10		PITTSFIELD, MA	17, 18	NOT CAPTURED
ELIJAH	WEST	PRIV	10		GROTON, MA	22	NOT CAPTURED
SAMUEL	WEST	PRIV	10		HADLEY, MA	17, 18	NOT CAPTURED
MOSES	WHITNEY	PRIV	10		HATFIELD, MA	17, 18	NOT CAPTURED
TOTAL OFFICERS & MEN		**70**					

MORGAN'S COMPANY

FIRST NAME	LAST NAME	RANK	CO	AGE	HOME TOWN	SOURCES	DISPOSITION
DANIEL	MORGAN	CAPT	11	40	WINCHESTER, VA	1,26,30,35, 39	PRISONER
JOHN	HUMPHREY	LIEUT	11	28	WINCHESTER,	26,30,35,39,138	KILLED
WILLAIM	HETH	LIEUT	11	26	WINCHESTER,	26,30,35,39,138	PRISONER
PETER BRYAN	BRUIN	LIEUT	11	23	FREDRICK CO,	22, 26, 30, 35	PRISONER
WILLIAM	FICKHIS	SGT	11		FREDRICK CO,	30, 35	PRISONER
CHARLES	PORTERFIELD	SGT	11	21	WINCHESTER,	30, 35	PRISONER
JOHN	DONALDSON		11		FREDRICK CO,	30, 35, 138	PRISONER
JOHN	ROGERS	CORP	11	25	WINCHESTER,	26, 30, 35, 138	PRISONER
BENJAMIN	GRUBB	CORP	11	22	FREDRICK CO,	26, 30, 35	PRISONER
JOHN	ALFORD	PRIV	11	17	FREDRICK CO,	35	RETURNED
DANIEL	ANDERSON	PRIV	11	22	WINCHESTER,	26, 30, 35	PRISONER
ROBERT	ANDERSON	PRIV	11		WINCHESTER,	26, 30, 39	RETURNED

WILLIAM	BALL	PRIV	11			WINCHESTER,	26, 30, 39	RETURNED
ISAAC	BEETLEY	PRIV	11			PENNSYLVANIA	35	RETURNED
CURTIS	BRAMINGHAM	PRIV	11			FREDRICK CO.	30	PRISONER
ABSALOM	BROWN	PRIV	11	25		FREDRICK CO.	26, 30, 35	PRISONER
JEHU/JOHN	BROWN	PRIV	11	23		FREDRICK CO.	26, 30, 35	PRISONER
WILLIAM	BROWN	PRIV	11			FREDRICK CO.	138	NOT CAPTURED
JOHN	BURNS	PRIV	11			FREDRICK CO.	30, 35	PRISONER
BENJAMIN	CACKLEY	PRIV	11			FREDRICK CO.	30, 35	PRISONER
THOMAS	CHAPMAN	PRIV	11	23		FREDRICK CO.	26, 30, 35, 138	PRISONER
ROBERT	CHURCHILL	PRIV	11			FREDRICK CO.	30, 35, 138	PRISONER
JAMES	CLIFTON	PRIV	11			PENNSYLVANIA	138	1 RETURNED
JOHN	COCHRAN	PRIV	11			FREDRICK CO.	26, 30, 138	PRISONER
RICHARD	COLBERT	PRIV	11			FREDRICK CO.	30, 35	KILLED
JOHN	CONNOR	PRIV	11	25		MARYLAND	30, 35	PRISONER
CHRISTOPHER	DALTON	PRIV	11			FREDRICK CO.	30, 35, 138	PRISONER
DANIEL	DAVIS	PRIV	11	22		FREDRICK CO.	26, 30, 35	PRISONER
GILBERT	DEHART	PRIV	11	24		NEW JERSEY	30, 35	PRISONER
PATRICK	DOOLAND	PRIV	11			FREDRICK CO.	30, 35	PRISONER
DANIEL	DURST	PRIV	11	20		FREDRICK CO.	30, 35	PRISONER
CONRAD	ENDERS	PRIV	11			FREDRICK CO.	35	RETURNED
TIMOTHY	FEELY	PRIV	11			FREDRICK CO.	30, 35, 138	PRISONER
SOLOMON	FITZPATRICK	PRIV	11	25		FREDRICK CO.	26, 30, 35	PRISONER
WILLIAM	FLOOD	PRIV	11	21		FREDRICK CO.	22,,26,50, 35,138	PRISONER
SPENCER	GEORGE	PRIV	11			FREDRICK CO.	30, 35	PRISONER
JEREMIAH	GORDON	PRIV	11			FREDRICK CO.	30, 35	PRISONER
GEORGE	GREENWAY	PRIV	11			WINCHESTER,	35, 39	RETURNED
WILLIAM	GREENWAY	PRIV	11	21		WINCHESTER,	23, 26, 30, 35, 39	PRISONER
DAVID	GRIFFITH	PRIV	11	26		FREDRICK CO.	26, 30, 35	PRISONER
CHARLES	GRIM	PRIV	11	20		WINCHESTER,	22,26,30,35,39,138	PRISONER
JOHN	HARBISON	PRIV	11	29		FREDRICK CO.	22, 26, 30, 35	PRISONER
MATTHEW	HARBINSON	PRIV	11			FREDRICK CO.	30, 35	KILLED
MARK	HAYES	PRIV	11			WINCHESTER,	35, 39	RETURNED
ADAM	HEISKELL	PRIV	11	21		WINCHESTER,	26, 30, 35, 39	PRISONER
GEORGE	HEISKELL	PRIV	11			WINCHESTER,	35, 39	RETURNED
GEORGE	INNIS	PRIV	11			WASHINGTON, PA	30, 128	DIED/WILD
?	JACKSON	PRIV	11			NOT IDENTIFIED	125	RETURNED
ROWLAND	JACOBS	PRIV	11	21		FREDRICK CO.	26, 30, 35, 138	PRISONER

ADAM	KURTZ	PRIV	11	22	WINCHESTER,	26, 30,35,39, 138	PRISONER
FREDERICK	KURTZ	PRIV	11		WINCHESTER,	35, 39	RETURNED
EDWARD	LEEDES	PRIV	11		NEW JERSEY	30, 35	PRISONER
PETER	LAUCK	PRIV	11	21	WINCHESTER,	26,30,35,39,138	PRISONER
SOLMON	LAUCK	PRIV	11		WINCHESTER,	35, 39	RETURNED
ARTHUR	MCCORD	PRIV	11	23	FREDRICK CO	147	RETURNED
HENRY	MCGOWAN	PRIV	11		FREDRICK CO,	35	RETURNED
JOHN	MEAD	PRIV	11	22	FREDRICK CO,	26, 30, 35, 138	PRISONER
JOHN	MCGUIRE	PRIV	11	24	FREDRICK CO,	28, 35, 138	PRISONER
BENJAMIN	MCINTIRE	PRIV	11	23	FREDRICK CO,	26, 30, 35, 138	PRISONER
GEORGE	MERCHANT	PRIV	11		FREDRICK CO,	26, 28, 35	PRISONER
ROBERT	MITCHELL	PRIV	11		FREDRICK CO,	22, 30, 35	PRISONER
JOHN	MOORE	PRIV	11		FREDRICK CO,	35, 39	KILLED
CORNELIUS	NORRIS	PRIV	11		FREDRICK CO,	30, 35, 138	KILLED
JOHN	ORAM	PRIV	11	22	BALTIMORE, MD	26, 30, 35	PRISONER
JOHN	PIERCE	PRIV	11	22	WESTMORELAND PA	22, 26, 30, 35	PRISONER
HEZEKIAH	PHILLIPS	PRIV	11		SOUTHWEST, VA	30,35,36, 108	PRISONER
JEDEDIAH	PHILLIPS	PRIV	11	21	SOUTHWEST, VA	26, 30, 35	PRISONER
JEREMIAH	RIDDLE	PRIV	11		FREDRICK CO,	28, 30, 35	PRISONER
BENJAMIN	RODERICK	PRIV	11	22	FREDRICK CO,	28, 30, 35	PRISONER
WILLIAM	RUTLEDGE	PRIV	11		FREDRICK CO,	30, 35, 138	KILLED
JOHN	SCHULTZ	PRIV	11	22	WINCHESTER,	22, 26,30, 39, 138	PRISONER
CHARLES	SECREST	PRIV	11	23	FREDRICK CO,	26, 30, 35	PRISONER
EDWARD	SEEDES	PRIV	11		FREDRICK CO,	30, 35	PRISONER
JOHN	SMOOT	PRIV	11		FREDRICK CO,	22	RETURNED
JACOB	SPERRY	PRIV	11	25	WINCHESTER,	22,26,30, 39, 138	PRISONER
JOHN	STEPHENS	PRIV	11	22	FREDRICK CO,	26, 30, 35, 138	PRISONER
SETH	STRATTON	PRIV	11		WINCHESTER,	35, 39	RETURNED
SOLOMON	VEAL	PRIV	11	23	BENNINGTON CO, NJ	26, 30, 35	PRISONER
JACOB	WARE	PRIV	11		FREDRICK CO,	30, 35, 138	PRISONER
JESSE	WHEELER	PRIV	11		FREDRICK CO,	30, 35	PRISONER
THOMAS	WILLIAMS	PRIV	11	30	FREDRICK CO,	26, 30, 35	PRISONER
DAVID	WILSON	PRIV	11		FREDRICK CO,	30, 35	KILLED
PETER	WOLF/WOLFE	PRIV	11		FREDRICK CO,	30, 35	KILLED
TOTAL OFFICERS & MEN		**83**					

MCCOBB'S COMPANY					ALL RETURNED	
FIRST NAME	**LAST NAME**	**RANK**	**CO**	**AGE**	**HOME TOWN**	**SOURCES**
SAMUEL	MCCOBB	CAPT	12	31	GEORGETOWN, ME	1, 3, 15
BENJAMIN	PATTEE	LIEUT	12	39	GEORGETOWN	3, 15
JOHN	RIGGS	LIEUT	12		FALMOUTH, ME	3, 15
MASON	WATTLES	SGT	12		WISCASSET, ME	3, 15
JOHN	TAGGART	SGT	12		PITTSON, ME	3, 15
ELIPHALET	FOSTER	SGT	12		WINTHROP, ME	3, 15, 18
ABNER	WADE	SGT	12		WOOLWICH, ME	3, 15
BILLY	FOSTER	CORP	12		WINTHROP, ME	3, 15
JAMES	FLEMING	CORP	12		GEORGETOWN	3, 15
WILLIAM	BUTLER	CORP	12		WINTHROP, ME	3, 15
JAMES	WORKS	CORP	12		WINTHROP, ME	3, 15, 22
JEREMIAH	BUTLER	DRUM	12		PAWNALBORO	3, 15
WILLIAM	BAKER	FIFER	12		HAVERILL, MA	3, 15
WILDER	KIDDER	FIFER	12	21	WINTHROP, ME	3, 15, 22
JACOBUS	BAILEY	PRIV	12		WOOLWICH, ME	3, 15
JOSIAH	BAILEY	PRIV	12		WOOLWICH, ME	3, 15
JOHN	BALL	PRIV	12		WOOLWICH, ME	3, 15
WILLIAM	BISHOP	PRIV	12		WINTHROP, ME	3, 15
GEORGE	BOULTOR	PRIV	12		HALLOWELL, ME	3, 15
SAMUEL	BOYD	PRIV	12		WINTHROP, ME	3, 15
SAMUEL 3R	BRIGGS	PRIV	12		STOUGHTON, MA	3, 15, 22
JAMES	BUCK	PRIV	12		GEORGETOWN	3, 137
JOSEPH	CHANDLER	PRIV	12		WINTHROP, ME	3, 15
ROGER	CHASE	PRIV	12		WINTHROP, ME	3, 15
SETH	DELANO	PRIV	12		WINTHROP, ME	3, 15
JEREMIAH	DUDLEY	PRIV	12		WINTHROP, ME	3, 15, 22
JAMES P	EVANS	PRIV	12		HALLOWELL, ME	3, 15, 22
NATHANIEL	FAIRBANKS	PRIV	12		WINTHROP, ME	3, 15, 22
JOSEPH	FARLEY	PRIV	12		HALLOWELL, ME	3, 15
TIMOTHY	FARRINGTON	PRIV	12		WINTHROP, ME	3, 15
THOMAS	FOOT	PRIV	12		GEORGETOWN	3, 15
DAVID	FOSTER	PRIV	12		WINTHROP, ME	3, 15
WILLIAM	GILCREASE	PRIV	12		GARDNERSTWN	3, 15
ANDREW	GLEADEN	PRIV	12		WISCASSET, ME	3, 15

JAMES	GORDON	PRIV	12		HALLOWELL, ME	3, 15
ENOCH	GREENLEAF	PRIV	12		GEORGETOWN	3, 15
MARTIN	HALL	PRIV	12		GEORGETOWN	3, 15
SAMUEL	HARPER	PRIV	12		ACWORTH, NH	8, 15
PETER	HEALL	PRIV	12		GEORGETOWN	3, 15
EBENEZER	HILTON	PRIV	12		WOOLWICH, ME	3, 15
JOSEPH	HILTON	PRIV	12		WOOLWICH, ME	3, 15
JAMES	JOHNSON	PRIV	12		WINTHROP, ME	3, 15
JOSEPH	JORDAN	PRIV	12		GARDNERSTOWN	3, 15
WILLIAM	LANCEY	PRIV	12		HALLOWELL, ME	3, 15
JOHN	MCKNIGHT	PRIV	12		GARDNERSTWN	3, 15
ENOCH	MOFFAT	PRIV	12		GARDNERSTWN	3, 15, 22
RUEBEN	PAGE	PRIV	12		HALLOWELL, ME	3, 15
EBENEZER	PLACE	PRIV	12		WINTHROP, ME	3, 15
SAMUEL	PLUMMER	PRIV	12		WINTHROP, ME	3, 15
TIMOTHY	PLUMMER	PRIV	12		WOOLWICH, ME	3, 15
JEDEDIAH	PREBLE	PRIV	12		PAWNALBORO	3, 15
WILLIAM	PULLIN	PRIV	12		WINTHROP, ME	3, 15
JOHN	PUMROY	PRIV	12		GARDNERSTWN	3, 15
EBENEZER	RICHARDSON	PRIV	12		CANAAN, MA	3, 15, 33
BENJAMIN	ROLLINS	PRIV	12		ST. GEORGES, ME	3, 15
JOSEPH	SELF	PRIV	12		SCARBORO, ME	15, 22
ELIAB	SHAW	PRIV	12		WOOLWICH, ME	3, 15, 22
GEORGE	SMITH	PRIV	12		WINSLOW, ME	3, 15
STEPHEN	STUART	PRIV	12		WOOLWICH, ME	3, 15
EPHRIAM	STEPHENS	PRIV	12		PETERBOROUG	9
JOHN	TAYLOR	PRIV	12		WINTHROP, ME	3, 15
DANIEL	TIBBETTS	PRIV	12		GOULDSBOROUGH	3, 67
JAMES	TIBBETTS	PRIV	12		BOOTHBAY, ME	3, 67
THOMAS	TOLMAN	PRIV	12		HALLOWELL, ME	3, 15
WILLIAM	USHER	PRIV	12		HALLOWELL, ME	3, 15
SAMUEL	WALKER	PRIV	12		WINTHROP, ME	3, 15
NATHANIEL	WEBB	PRIV	12		WOOLWICH, ME	3, 15
ABEL	WHITTIER	PRIV	12		WINTHROP, ME	3, 15
SOLOMON	WHITTER	PRIV	12		PAWNALBORO	3, 15
LEMUEL	WILLIAMS	PRIV	12		WOOLWICH, ME	3, 15
CHRISTOPHER	WOODBRIDGE	PRIV	12		WISCASSET, ME	3, 15

FIRST NAME	LST NAME	RANK	CO	AGE	HOME TOWN	SOURCES
DANIEL	WYMAN	PRIV	12		PAWNALBORO	3, 15
SAMUEL	YOUNG	PRIV	12		WINTHROP, ME	3, 15
TOTAL OFFICERS & MEN		**73**				

COLBURN'S COMPANY

ALL RETURNED

FIRST NAME	LST NAME	RANK	CO	AGE	HOME TOWN	SOURCES
OLIVER	COLBURN	CAPT	13	35	GARDINERSTOWN	18, 25
BENJAMIN	COLBURN	LIEUT	13		GARDINERSTOWN	18, 25
JOSEPH	BURNS	ENS	13		GARDINERSTOWN	18, 25
PHILLIP	NORCROSS	SGT	13		GARDINERSTOWN	18, 25
ROGERS	LAPHAM	SGT	13		GARDINERSTOWN	18, 25
FRANCIS	FULLER	SGT	13		GARDINERSTOWN	18, 25
DENNIS	JENKINS	SGT	13		GARDINERSTOWN	18, 25
ANDREW	GOODWON	CORP	13		GARDINERSTOWN	18, 25
THOMAS	AGREY	CORP	13		GARDINERSTOWN	18, 25
EZRA	CUSHING	CORP	13		GARDINERSTOWN	18, 25
SAMUEL	NORCROSS	FIFER	13		GARDINERSTOWN	18, 25
DAVID	AGREY	PRIV	13		GARDINERSTOWN	18, 25
OLIVER	ALLEN	PRIV	13		GARDINERSTOWN	18, 25
DAVID	BERRY	PRIV	13		GARDINERSTOWN	18, 25
THOMAS	COLBURN	PRIV	13		GARDINERSTOWN	18, 25
EZRA	DAVIS	PRIV	13		GARDINERSTOWN	18, 25
SAMUEL	DEMON	PRIV	13		GARDINERSTOWN	18, 25
EDWARD	DOROTHY	PRIV	13		GARDINERSTOWN	18, 25
TIMOTHY	DWYER	PRIV	13		GARDINERSTOWN	18, 25
TIMOTHY	FITCH	PRIV	13		GARDINERSTOWN	18, 25
THOMAS	FOSTER	PRIV	13		GARDINERSTOWN	18, 25
EDWARD	FULLER	PRIV	13		GARDINERSTOWN	18, 25
STEWART	FULLER	PRIV	13		GARDINERSTOWN	18, 25
JEREMIAH	GOODWIN	PRIV	13		GARDINERSTOWN	18, 25
THOMAS	HALEY (KALEY)	PRIV	13		GARDINERSTOWN	18, 25
WILLIAM	HALEY	PRIV	13		GARDINERSTOWN	18, 25
JOSIAH	HALL	PRIV	13		GARDINERSTOWN	18, 25
NATHAN	HALL	PRIV	13		GARDINERSTOWN	18, 25
JAMES	LAPHAM	PRIV	13		GARDINERSTOWN	18, 25

FIRST NAME	LAST NAME	RANK	CO	AGE	HOME TOWN	SOURCES
OLIVER	LAPHAM	PRIV	13		GARDINERSTOWN	18, 25
DAVID	LAWRENCE	PRIV	13		GARDINERSTOWN1	18, 25
CALEB	LOUD	PRIV	13		GARDINERSTOWN	18, 25
ANDREW	MCCAUSLAND	PRIV	13		GARDINERSTOWN	18, 25
JAMES	MCCAUSLAND	PRIV	13		GARDINERSTOWN	18, 25
JOSEPH	PARKER	PRIV	13		GARDINERSTOWN	18, 25
WILLIAM	PHILBROOK	PRIV	13		GARDINERSTOWN	18, 25
JOHN	SMITH	PRIV	13		GARDINERSTOWN	18, 25
JOSEPH	STACKPOLE	PRIV	13		GARDINERSTOWN	18, 25
ABNA	STEVENS	PRIV	13		GARDINERSTOWN	18, 25
BENJAMIN	WELCH	PRIV	13		GARDINERSTOWN	18, 25
JOHN	WHITING	PRIV	13		GARDINERSTOWN	18, 25
TOTAL OFFICERS & MEN		**41**				

SCOTT'S COMPANY

ALL RETURNED

FIRST NAME	LAST NAME	RANK	CO	AGE	HOME TOWN	SOURCES
WILLIAM	SCOTT	CAPT	14	31	PETERBOROUG	1, 137
JAMES	SPRAGUE	LIEUT	14	39	UNION, CT	66, 137
ANDREW	PETERS	LIEUT	14		MENDON, MA	98
RICHARD	BUCKMASTER	LIEUT	14	45	SALEM, MA	18
JOHN	TAGGART	ENS	14	25	PETERBOROUG	110
JOSIAH	MONROE	SGT	14	30	PETERBOROUG	9, 110
JOHN	SWAN	SGT	14		PETERBOROUG	9, 22
ER	CUSHING	SGT	14	24	WEYMOUTH,MA	18, 22, 145, 146
JAMES	SCOTT	CORP	14		PETERBOROUG	9, 22, 110
CHARLES	WHITE	CORP	14	26	PETERBOROUG	9, 22, 110
ANDREW	BAILEY	CORP	14		PETERBOROUG	9
DANIEL	READ	DRUM	14		MEDFORD, MA	110
JONATHAN	BARNETT	PRIV	14		PETERBOROUG	110
JOHN	BLAIR	PRIV	14		PETERBOROUG	9, 110
ZACCHEUS	BLOOD	PRIV	14		STODDARD, NH	110
NATHANIEL	BURROUGHS	PRIV	14		PETERBOROUG	110
JOHN	CALDWELL	PRIV	14	18	DUBLIN, NH	22
SAMUEL	CALDWELL	PRIV	14	24	PETERBOROUG	110
WILLIAM	COCHRAN	PRIV	14	35	PETERBOROUG	110

ASA	DAVISON	PRIV	14	39	PRESTON, CT	48, 118, 137
THOMAS	DOUGLAS	PRIV	14		KEENE, NH	9, 64
JABEZ	DOW	PRIV	14		KENSINGTON, NH	9
DAVID	EMERY	PRIV	14	22	FAIRFIELD, ME	22
RICHARD	EMERY	PRIV	14	13	PETERBOROUG	9, 110
JEREMIAH	FAIRFIELD	PRIV	14		PETERBOROUG	9, 110
JOHN	FERGUSON	PRIV	14	17	CHESHIRE CO. NH	22
SEABRID	FITCH	PRIV	14		CONNECTICUT	137
EBENEZER	GEE	PRIV	14	21	WESTHAMPTON	117
JONATHAN	GEORGE	PRIV	14		LONDONDERRY	9, 36
RICHARD	GILCHRIST	PRIV	14	22	DUBLIN, NH	22, 110
JOSEPH	GREEN	PRIV	14		PETERBOROUG	110
JACOB	GREGG	PRIV	14	18	PETERBOROUG	9, 110
JOHN	GRAHAM	PRIV	14		PETERBOROUG	9, 110
WILLIAM	GRAHAM	PRIV	14		PETERBOROUG	9, 110
JOHN	HALFPENNY	PRIV	14		PETERBOROUG	9, 110
JAMES	HOCKLEY	PRIV	14	19	PETERBOROUG	9, 110
JOHN	HILLSGROVE	PRIV	14		TEMPLE, NH	110
JONATHAN	HOIT	PRIV	14		POPLIN, NH	9
SAMUEL	HUNTOON	PRIV	14		KINGSTON, NH	9
BENJAMIN	JACKMAN	PRIV	14		ROWLEY, NH	22
WILLIAM	KEMP	PRIV	14		PETERBOROUG	110
JAMES	KENNEDY	PRIV	14	25	COLRAIN, MA	22
SOLOMON	LEONARD	PRIV	14		PETERBOROUG	9
JOHN	LOVE	PRIV	14		STOWE, MA	136, 136
JAMES	MARSHALL	PRIV	14		PETERBOROUG	110
JOHN	MATTHEWS	PRIV	14		PETERBOROUG	9, 110
JONATHAN	MASON	PRIV	14		LYME, NH	22
GEORGE	MCCLURG	PRIV	14	47	PETERBOROUG	9, 110
ROBERT	MCCLURG	PRIV	14	20	PETERBOROUG	9, 110
RANDALL	MCALLISTER	PRIV	14	31	PETERBOROUG	110
JAMES	MCKEEN	PRIV	14	35	PETERBOROUG	9, 110
ARCHIBALD	MCMILLAN	PRIV	14		NEW BOSTON, NH	110
JAMES	MITCHELL	PRIV	14		PETERBOROUG	9, 110
WILLIAM	MITCHELL	PRIV	14		PETERBOROUG	9, 110
TIMOTHY	MIXTER	PRIV	14	47	PETERBOROUG	9, 110
JAMES	MOORE	PRIV	14	21	PETERBOROUG	9, 22, 110

JOSIAH	MUNROE	PRIV	14		LEXINGTON, MA	110
ISAAC	PAGE	PRIV	14		LONDONDERRY	110
JEREMIAH	PROCTOR	PRIV	14		PETERBOROUG	110
JOHN	RAINO	PRIV	14		PETERBOROUG	110
RICHARD	RICHARDSON	PRIV	14	21	PETERBOROUG	110
JOHN	RITCHIE	PRIV	14	25	PETERBOROUG	9, 110
DAVID	ROBBE	PRIV	14	23	PETERBOROUG	110
AMAZIAH	ROBERTS	PRIV	14		WINCHESTER, NH	9
JOHN JR	ROBINSON	PRIV	14		PETERBOROUG	110
JOHN	ROW	PRIV	14		PORTSMOUTH, NH	9
DAVID	SCOTT	PRIV	14	26	PETERBOROUG	110
THOMAS	SCOTT	PRIV	14	23	PETERBOROUG	110
WILLIAM JR	SCOTT	PRIV	14	19	PETERBOROUG	110
SAMUEL	SMITH	PRIV	14		BEDFORD, NH	110
EPHRIAM	SQUIER	PRIV	14	27	ASHFORD, CT	118, 137
ROBERT	STEWART	PRIV	14	26	SALEM, NH	18, 22, 36
JAMES	STINSON	PRIV	14		PETERBOROUG	9, 110
JOHN 3RD	SWAN	PRIV	14	31	PETERBOROUG	110
JAMES	TAGGERT	PRIV	14	37	PETERBOROUG	9, 110
JOHN	TAGGERT	PRIV	14		PETERBOROUG	110
SAMUEL	TREADWELL	PRIV	14	34	PETERBOROUG	9, 110
JOHN	TUCKER	PRIV	14		PETERBOROUG	110
SIMEON	TYLER	PRIV	14	21	BOXFORD, MA	118, 137
DAVID	WHITE	PRIV	14	17	PETERBOROUG	9, 110
GEORGE	WILSON	PRIV	14		PETERBOROUG	110
MICHAEL	WOODCOCK	PRIV	14		PETERBOROUG	9, 110
JOSEPH	WORKER	PRIV	14		PORTSMOUTH, NH	9
TOTAL OFFICERS & MEN		**83**				

WILLIAM'S COMPANY

ALL RETURNED

FIRST NAME	LAST NAME	RANK	CO	AGE	HOME TOWN	SOURCES
THOMAS	WILLIAMS	CAPT	15	29	STOCKBRIDGE, MA	1, 77
ORRINGH	STODDARD	LIEUT	15	33	STOCKBRIDGE	22, 113, 114
ISAAC	DAVIS	LIEUT	15	39	LEE, MA	4, 95
LUKE	DAY	LIEUT	15		W. SPRINGFIELD	17, 18

251

ISAAC	MARSH	SGT	15		STOCKBRIDGE, MA	104, 113
DAVID	JOHNSON	SGT	15		WILLIAMSTOWN	96
RUEBEN	BISHOP	SGT	15		STOCKBRIDGE	136
HEMAN	WATSON	CRPL	15		W. STOCKBRIDGE	17, 18
NATHANIEL	RAWSON	CRPL	15		W. STOCKBRIDGE	17, 18
SILAS	LINCOLN	CRPL	15		HARTWOOD, MA	17, 18
SAMUEL	DAVIS	DRUM	15		HARTWOOD, MA	17, 18
ELIJAH	ALFORD	PRIV	15		BECKET, MA	22
JAMES	ALLEN	PRIV	15		HARTWOOD, MA	17, 18
JONATHAN	ALLEN	PRIV	15		SALEM, MA	17, 18
DAVID	AMES	PRIV	15		HOLLIS, NH	17, 18
ASA	BAIRD	PRIV	15		BECKET, MA	22
AARON	BEARD	PRIV	15		BECKET, MA	17
ELNATHAN	BREDEN	PRIV	15		STONEHAM, MA	17, 18
ELKANAH	BISHOP	PRIV	15		STOCKBRIDGE	77, 113
JARED	BISHOP	PRIV	15		STOCKBRIDGE	77, 113
CALEB	BOYNTON	PRIV	15		W. STOCKBRIDGE	22
SAMUEL	BOYNTON	PRIV	15		STOCKBRIDGE	17, 18, 113
ABNER	BRUCE	PRIV	15		HARTWOOD, MA	17, 18
ROBERT	CALLAGHAN	PRIV	15	30	GLOUCESTER, MA	17, 18
JOHN	CHAPLIN	PRIV	15	17	HARTWOOD, MA	17, 18
RICHARD	COLE	PRIV	15		MEDFORD, MA	17, 18
TIMOTHY	COLE	PRIV	15		HARTWOOD, MA	17, 18
WILLIAM	COLE	PRIV	15		HARTWOOD, MA	17, 18
SAMUEL	COOK	PRIV	15		HADLEY, MA	17, 18
NICHOLAS	COTTERELL	PRIV	15		WORTHINGTON, MA	17, 18
ABEL	CRANE	PRIV	15		HARTWOOD, MA	17, 18
THOMAS	CROSMAN	PRIV	15		NEW LONDON, CT	22
ELNATHAN	CURTIS	PRIV	15		STOCKBRIDGE	17, 18, 113
WILLIAM	DANIELS	PRIV	15		UPTON, MA	17, 18
JAMES	DEAN	PRIV	15		MARBLEHEAD, MA	17, 18
JOHN	DEANE	PRIV	15		SALISBURY, CT	17, 18, 113
SAMUEL	DILL	PRIV	15		NANTUCKETT, MA	17, 18
DAVID	DUNNELS	PRIV	15		LANESBOROUG	96
SIMEON	ELWELL	PRIV	15		HADLEY, MA	17, 18
THOMAS	EVERDON	PRIV	15		HOLLISTON, MA	102
ARTHUR	FENNER	PRIV	15	34	CRANSTON, RI	17, 18

JOHN	GARDINER	PRIV	15		PITTSFIELD, MA	17, 18
GERSHOM	GRAHAM	PRIV	15		STOCKBRIDGE	17, 18
BARTHOLEMEW	HARRIS	PRIV	15		BRATTLEBORO, VT	57
ELNATHAN	HIGBEE	PRIV	15	21	CHATHAM HTS, MA	17, 18
JESSE	HOOKER	PRIV	15		STOCKBRIDGE	17, 18, 113
NEHEMIAH	IDE	PRIV	15	15	STOCKBRIDGE	17, 18, 113
JOHN	INGRAHAM	PRIV	15		BECKET, MA	17, 18
SAMUEL	INGRAHAM	PRIV	15		BECKET, MA	17, 18
JOSEPH	JONES	PRIV	15		STOCKBRIDGE	17, 18, 113
DANIEL	KNAPP	PRIV	15	22	STOCKBRIDGE	22, 113
JOHN	MACK	PRIV	15		W. STOCKBRIDGE	17, 18
WILLIAM	MANSELL	PRIV	15		DEDHAM, MA	17, 18, 22
ANDREW	MESSENGER	PRIV	15		W. STOCKBRIDGE	17, 18
BILLE	MESSENGER	PRIV	15	18	BECKET, MA	22
ABEL	MATTOON	PRIV	15		BECKET, MA	17, 18
PERSE	MOORE	PRIV	15		BECKET, MA	17, 18
JOHN	MUDGE	PRIV	15		W. STOCKBRIDGE	17, 18
BANI	NETTLETON	PRIV	15		W. STOCKBRIDGE	17, 18
WILLIAM	OSBORN	PRIV	15		STOCKBRIDGE	17, 18, 113
FRANCIS	PAINE	PRIV	15		STOCKBRIDGE	22, 113
DAVID	PALMER	PRIV	15		W. STOCKBRIDGE	18, 22
SAMUEL	PRINDLE	PRIV	15		SPOFFORD, N H	22
DANIEL	REED	PRIV	15		LANESBOROUG	96
JONATHAN	RAWSON	PRIV	15		STOCKBRIDGE	22, 113
JAMES	RUSSELL	PRIV	15		W. SPRINGFIELD	101
JONATHAN	SIKES	PRIV	15		WILBRAHAN, MA	17, 18
JOSEPH	SINN	PRIV	15		WESTFIELD, MA	17, 18
CHRISTOPHER	SLOMAN	PRIV	15		BOSTON, MA	17, 18
DANIEL	SWEETLAND	PRIV	15		SOMMERS	17, 18
ELDAD	TAYLOR	PRIV	15		BECKET, MA	17, 18
NICHOLAS	WARD	PRIV	15		STOCKBRIDGE	17, 18, 113
PHANUEL	WARNER	PRIV	15		WILBRAHAN, MA	17, 18
MELATIAH	WEEKS	PRIV	15		BECKET, MA	17, 18
THOMAS	WHITNEY	PRIV	15		LANESBOROUG	17, 18
ELISHA	WILLIAMS	PRIV	15		STOCKBRIDGE	17, 18, 113
GEORGE	WILLIAMS	PRIV	15		SALEM, MA	96
TOTAL OFFICERS & MEN		77				

GUIDES, SCOUTS & INDIANS

FIRST NAME	LAST NAME	RANK	CO	AGE	HOME TOWN	SOURCES	DISPOSITION
SAMUEL	BERRY	SCOU	16	38	VASSALBORO	22, 58	RETURNED
DENNIS	GETCHELL	SCOU	16	51	VASSALBORO	58, 61	RETURNED
JOHN	GETCHELL	GUID	16	56	VASSALBORO	58, 61, 165, 123	RETURNED
NEHEMIAH	GETCHELL	GUID	16	31	VASSALBORO	58, 61, 92	RETURNED
JEREMIAH/ JOHN	HORN	GUID	16		VASSALBORO	58, 92, 128	RETURNED
ISAAC	HULL	GUID	16		WATERVILLE, ME	74, 142	RETURNED
NATHAN	PARLIN	GUID	16	25	NORIDGEWOCK	22, 32, 58	NOT CAPTURED
JOHN	MCCURDY	GUID	16		BRISTOL, ME	58, 78	RETURNED
LUKE	SAWYER	GUID	16	15	NORIDGEWOCK	22, 32, 36, 58	NOT CAPTURED
CHRISTOPHER	JACQUIN	GUID	16		TOCONOC FALLS	31, 58, 76, 125, 139	RETURNED
J.M.	GWINN	VOL	16		VIRGINIA	28	NOT CAPTURED
JOHN JR	MARSH	GUID	16	24	RIPLEY, ME	58, 76, 85, 122	PRISONER
JOSEPH	WESTON	VOL	16	43	KENNEBEC, ME	57, 144	RETURNED
	OUANOCHT	INDIAN	16		MAINE	91	RETURNED
JOSEPH	ENEAS	INDIAN	16		MAINE	76, 91	RETURNED
	SABATIS	INDIAN	16		SKOWHEGAN	91, 76, 123	PRISONER
	NATANIS	INDIAN	16		VASSALBORO	91, 123	PRISONER
TOTAL OFFICERS & MEN		**15**					

1125	ABOVE TOTAL OF OFFICERS & MEN ON EXPEDITION

TABLE 1		ARNOLD'S MEN WHO LEFT CAMBRIDGE
TOTAL MEN IN EXPEDITION FROM ABOVE		1125
LESS:	MEN WHO CAME LATER:	
	COLBURN'S COMPANY	41
	GUIDES/SCOUTS	15
	HQ CO. CAME LATER	3
TOTAL MEN LEAVING CAMBRIDGE FROM ROSTER		**1066**
TOTAL MEN WHO LEFT CAMBRIDGE PER CONTEMPORARY SOURCES		**1067**

TABLE 2			COMPARISON OF ROSTER WITH ARNOLD'S 11/29 RETURN		
COMPANIES	COMPANY TOTAL TO BEGIN MARCH	RETURN OR DIED IN WILD		TOTALS AT 11/29/75	ARNOLD 11/29 GENERAL RETURN
THAYER	87	28		59	59
DEARBORN	87	15		72	72
WARD	74	1		73	73
HUBBARD	76	21		55	55
HENDRICKS	86	8		78	78
SMITH	86	13		73	73
HANCHETT	84	12		72	72
TOPHAM	78	25		53	53
GOODRICH	70	7		63	63
MORGAN	83	17		66	64
MCCOBB	73	73		0	0
SCOTT	83	83		0	0
WILLIAMS	77	77		0	0
TOTALS	1041	380		664	662
HEADQUARTERS	23	9		11	13
TOTAL	1066	389		675	675

TABLE 3	DISPOSITION OF MEN BY COMPANY					
	EXPEDITION IN WILDERNESS			ATTACK ON QUEBEC		
	RETURNED	DIED IN WILD	TOTAL OF MEN WHO LEFT	KILLED	PRISONERS	NOT CAPTURED
HEADQUARTERS	9	0	9	0	9	7
THAYER	28	0	28	2	31	27
DEARBORN	15	0	15	0	31	41
WARD	0	1	1	3	35	35
HUBBARD	18	3	21	6	31	18
HENDRICKS	6	2	8	3	63	12
SMITH	10	3	13	7	36	30
HANCHETT	12	0	12	7	31	33
TOPHAM	20	5	25	3	33	17
GOODRICH	6	1	7	1	26	37
MORGAN	16	1	17	8	57	1
TOTAL	140	16	156	40	383	258

EXPLANATION REGARDING EIGHT OFFICERS AND ONE GUIDE FROM THE ROSTER

An explanation is needed for the names from the roster listed below. The first name of six of these men, Hyde, Buckmaster, Coates, Ayres, Farnsworth and Church, has never been clearly identified. Due to journals, letters and other sources, most histories identify their last names, except for Dr. Coates, who is identified in a letter but is not widely recognized as a participant. However, except for Farnsworth, no one has previously provided first names, even though they are all officers. This is the first time their full names are identified. A previous identification regarding Isaac Hull was a mistake that needs to be corrected. Two of the officers, Steele and Savage, were initially line officers in one of the companies, but were appointed by Arnold to new staff positions after the expedition started. Their names have been previously known, but the 11/29 general return only makes sense if their new staff positions are acknowledged.

- Joseph Farnsworth, Commissary. The name of Joseph Farnsworth is confirmed by an entry in the Journals of the Continental Congress from May 24, 1776 where he was awarded payment of wages and rations for being employed in the commissary general's department. The authorized pay was in the amount of "£10 lawful money per month and 3 rations [per day]" when he was "employed as commissary to Colonel Arnold's detachment." All of his Revolutionary War experience involved serving as a captain with the commissary general's department. Joseph Farnsworth served in the 1777 Battle of Bennington in his capacity as commissary. He had previously served as commissary in Charlestown, New Hampshire in 1766 during the Pontiac Uprising where he provided supplies to the British Army in that area. He was born in Middletown, Connecticut on August 12, 1744, but moved to Bennington, Vermont after his Revolutionary War service. From October of 1781 to February of 1784, he was commissary general of the State of Vermont. He married Elizabeth Carruthers at Middletown on November 6, 1776 and he died on May 27, 1794 in Bennington.[199]

- Archibald Steele, Lieutenant Adjutant. Archibald Steele was born in Lancaster County, Pennsylvania in 1742. He joined Matthew Smith's rifle company with the rank of lieutenant and started out on the expedition in that company. Arnold selected Steele to lead a group of eight men from various companies to seek out the route and blaze the way to Canada. He was appointed as an assistant adjutant to Christian Febiger at some point during the expedition but also continued to serve as first lieutenant in Smith's Company.

256

Captain Smith did not show up for the battle, so Steele took command of the rifle company during the assault as its highest ranking officer on the field. Steele was captured but escaped and "returned after a long and trying march through the wilderness to Washington's Army, which was then in New Jersey." As a result of the march, his confinement and journey back, Steele "had broken his health to such an extent that Washington assigned him to the commissary department." He ended up serving in the commissary department in various capacities until he was finally discharged from the army in 1821, having served for an amazing forty-six years. He died in Philadelphia on October 29, 1832 at the age of ninety.[200]

- Lieutenant Jedediah Hyde, Quarter Master Enos Division. Until now, all references to Hyde have simply described him as Lieutenant Hyde. However, there is a partial list of officers on Arnold's expedition found in the NARA files. One of the names on that list is Lieutenant Jedediah Hyde. Since there were no other officers on the expedition named Hyde, this has to be the Lieutenant Hyde in Enos' division. The only Jedediah Hyde who was a lieutenant in the continental service in 1775 was Jedediah Hyde of Norwich, Connecticut. The list of officers and his subsequent quarter master career is definitive evidence that the Quarter Master Hyde on the expedition was Jedediah Hyde from Norwich.

Jedediah Hyde was born on August 24, 1738 and married Elizabeth Brown, also of Norwich, in 1780. He served with Captain Coit's Company in the Battle of Bunker Hill, where he was slightly wounded. According to Johnston's Record of CT Men, he was Quarter Master Sergeant of the 4th Regiment of the Connecticut Line from Jan. 1, 1777 to Jan. 1, 1780, and was then appointed "Conductor of Military Stores" on the general staff. After his war service, he moved to Hyde Park, Vermont, where he died on May 29, 1822. The village of Hyde Park was named after him because he obtained a large grant of land in Vermont which included that town. He applied for a pension in 1820 but did not list his service in the Quebec expedition in that application.[201]

- Abijah Savage, Quarter Master. Savage started out the expedition as a lieutenant in Captain Oliver Hanchett's Company. When Lieutenant Hyde returned with the Enos Division, Savage was appointed by Arnold as the second quarter master of the expedition to replace Hyde. Abijah Savage was born in Middletown, Connecticut in 1744 and was in the French and Indian War as a unit commander in 1761. Savage married Martha Torrey on August 22, 1765 and they had fourteen children. He entered the service on May 1, 1775 as a second lieutenant in Return J. Meigs' Company of Colonel Wylly's Connecticut regiment. He was on the Quebec expedition and was taken prisoner in the attack on Quebec.[202]

- Dr. John Coates, volunteer surgeon. The September 13, 1775, letter from Jesse Lukens is sufficient proof that Dr. Coates was a volunteer on the expedition. He is the second physician referred to in the November 29th General Return. Lukens' letter specifically identifies him as, "Dr. Coates, who goes as a surgeon." After returning from Quebec, Coates was assigned to command a company in the 11th Pennsylvania Regiment. Coates served as its commander until he was wounded in his right hand in a skirmish at Piscataway, New Jersey, and then resigned from the Army on September 7, 1777. There was a report that said his wound "renders his middle finger useless, and in good measure deprives him of the use of his hand." There is no record of his subsequent career or any other personal information on his life. [203]

- Captain Eleazer Ayres, Head of Pioneers. Captain Ayres is mentioned in the journals of Melvin, Dearborn and Henry as being head of the pioneers on the expedition. None of those journal entries mention a first name of Captain Ayres. Arnold's Day Book contains a list of officers on the expedition to whom he provided funds. One of the names on Arnold's list is a Captain E. Ayres. This is obviously the Captain Ayres referred to in the journals. No first name of the Ayres on the Quebec expedition appears in any contemporary record.

  The best assumption that can be made is that the head of the pioneers came from one of the New England states as did all of the other officers in the expedition. One reason is that in the summer of 1775, there were very few men in Cambridge from outside the New England states. The only Ayres with a first name beginning with "E", who was in the Revolutionary War from a New England town in 1775, was Eleazer Ayres from Granby, Massachusetts. He is not listed as an officer but Arnold could easily have given him a brevet position. Therefore, the best assumption that can be made until someone locates additional documentation is that the Ayres on the expedition was Eleazer Ayres from Granby, Massachusetts.[204]

- Lieutenant Nathaniel Church. Lieutenant Church was the leader of one of the detachments selected by Arnold to blaze the trail to Quebec. The available evidence supports the conclusion that this

Lieutenant Church was Nathaniel Church from Captain Topham's Company. Lieutenant Church is mentioned by Arnold, Oswald and Pierce in their journals as well as in a letter from Arnold, dated October 31st, but no first name is given. He was not in the Enos Division because Pierce named him in an entry on November 18th, which was long after Enos had returned.

In his 1874 publication of an extract from Arnold's Day Book, John B. Linn asserts that the Lieutenant Church on the Quebec expedition was Thomas Church of Pennsylvania. Mr. Linn cites no source for this conclusion and no documentation has been discovered that supports Linn's conclusion. Unfortunately, the Day Book does not contain the first name of Lieutenant Church. Lieutenant Thomas Church did go to Quebec, but not until 1776, when he was a captain, and not a lieutenant, in Anthony Wayne's regiment that marched to the relief of Quebec. The fact that he was not mentioned in the Lukens' letter supports the contention that he was not one of the Pennsylvania volunteers in the expedition.

All of the genealogical information that is available regarding the Church family, as well as relevant state or local records, has been reviewed to attempt to give a first name to Lieutenant Church. Only one soldier named Church has been found who was a lieutenant in 1775 and was in Cambridge as well. That person is Nathaniel Church from Little Compton, Rhode Island, who was a first lieutenant in Colonel Thomas Church's Rhode Island Regiment. His regiment marched to Cambridge in 1775, right after the Lexington Alarm. He was in Captain John Topham's Company, which would make sense because all of the officers and NCO's in Topham's Company were from Rhode Island.

Nathaniel Church was born in 1732 to Caleb and Margaret Church. He married Sarah Wood in 1757 at Little Compton. He joined the army in May of 1775 and served as a first lieutenant with the company under Captain William Ladd in Newport and Bristol in the Rhode Island regiment of Colonel Thomas Church. In June, the Church regiment went to Cambridge. At the end of 1775, he was promoted to captain of the 10th Company, 1st Regiment. He was a recruiting officer at Little Compton in 1777, major in the Newport County Militia in 1778, lieutenant colonel in the militia in 1779 and lieutenant colonel commandant in 1780. In 1780, his regiment was called out for service within the State of Rhode Island. In 1787, he was on the committee to conduct a lottery to obtain funds to build a parsonage for his church.

Nathaniel died at Little Compton on February 5, 1825, at the age of ninety-three.[205]

- Lieutenant Richard Buckmaster. Lieutenant Buckmaster was one of the officers that testified at the Enos court-martial in support of Enos' actions. Contemporary records show that the only Buckmaster who was a lieutenant in the army in 1775 was named Richard. Therefore, it stands to reason that he must be the Lieutenant Buckmaster who was in Enos' Division. Richard Buckmaster was born in Boston, Massachusetts in 1729. He later moved to Salem and entered into the service in 1775. He was subsequently a Lieutenant in the 4th Continental Infantry in 1776 and an adjutant in the 6th Massachusetts Regiment from January 1777 to June 1779. Buckmaster was promoted to captain in Nixon's Massachusetts Regiment in June of 1779 and died in November of 1779. [206]

- Isaac Hull, Guide and Messenger for Arnold. Although there were multiple men by the name of Isaac Hull who served in the Revolutionary War, the Isaac Hull on the Quebec expedition was from Waterville, Maine. Phyllis J. Hughes, the genealogist for the Hull Family Association provided documentation regarding the Isaac in Waterville and agreed that he was the Hull on Arnold's expedition. There are no details about this Isaac Hull other than his presence in Waterville beginning in 1773 and ending in 1779. He is presumed to be a descendant of Richard Hull. Confusion regarding the identity of Isaac Hull was initiated in the republication of the Humphrey journal by the Rhode Island Publication Society where the editors refer to Arnold's messenger in a footnote as Lieutenant Isaac Hull. This reference is incorrect, but, unfortunately, it has been picked up and used in a subsequent history of the expedition.[207]

SOURCES FOR NAMES ON THE EXPEDITION ROSTER

This section contains 147 bibliographical sources, by number, that were used to confirm the names of the men in each company who are included in the above expedition roster. The number shown in the roster under the column labeled "Source" corresponds to the number in the bibliographical sources below. The expedition journals are listed by number near the end of the sources with no bibliographical details. However, complete bibliographical information on the expedition journals is provided in Chapter One.

PRIMARY

1. Arnold, Benedict. Day Book and Ledger: Oct. 6, 1777 to 1779. *American Historical Record,* Vol. 3, May 1874: 220-222.

2. Arnold, Benedict. *General Report on the Detachment, November 29, 1775.* Library of Congress.Washington Papers 1741-1799. Series 4. General Correspondence. [Detachment strength by company].

3. (Banks, Charles E.). *A Roster of Officers and Men Composing the Two Battalions Commanded by Col. Benedict Arnold Detached for an Expedition against Quebec through the Wilderness, September 1775.* New Haven Museum and Historical Society, n.d.

4. *Commissions Granted on Recommendation of General Court.[List of Arnold's Officers],* Misc. Revolutionary War Rolls, M346. National Archives and Records Administration, Misc. Rev War Rolls, General Staff: Field & Staff & Line Officers 1775-1783.
   a. www.footnote.com/ image/ #991045.

5. Goodrich, John E., comp. & ed. *Rolls of the Soldiers in the Revolutionary War, 1775 to 1783.* Rutland, VT: State of Vermont, 1904.

6. Hammond, Isaac W., comp. & ed. *Rolls of the Soldiers in the Revolutionary War, 1775 to May 1777;* Concord, N.H.: State of New Hampshire, 1885.

7. --- *New Hampshire Troops in the Quebec Expedition:* 209-212; 214-222. [Dearborn's Company]. Also Arnold Expedition Historical Society. www.arnoldsmarch.com/research/rosters/Dearborns_Company.pdf.

8. --- *A List of the Men in Capt Ward's Company in Col. Benedict Arnold's Detachment:* 213. Also in Arnold Expedition Historical Society.
   a. www.arnoldsmarch.com/research/rosters/Wards_Company. pdf.

9. --- *New Hampshire Men in the Service of Massachusetts Regiments:* 739-741. Appendix. [Peterborough Men in Captain William Scott's Company, October 6, 1775].

10. Henshaw, William. "Orderly Books of Col. William Henshaw, October 1, 1775 through October 3, 1776."[Summary of men on expedition who left Cambridge]. *Proceedings of the American Antiquarian Society for April 1947,* 1948: 19-234.

11. Johnston, Henry P., ed. *Record of Service of Connecticut Men in the War of the Revolution*. Hartford: Adjutant General's Office, 1889.

12. --- *The Quebec Expedition, 1775*: 91-93. [List of CT men in Hanchett's Company and other men from CT in expedition].

13. Letter From William McCoy [McCay] to Mr. Francis Nichols; [List of American Prisoners of War in Hendricks Company at Quebec in Canada, 1776]. *Pennsylvania Magazine of History and Biography*. Vol. 32, 1908: 118-119.

14. *A List of the Officers and Soldiers Taken at the Defeat of Quebec the 31st of December 1775 Belonging to Capt. Oliver Hanchett.* Connecticut State Archives, Revolutionary War, Vol. III: 649.

15. *A List of Capt. Samuel McCobb's Company in 5th Regiment of Foot, October 6, 1775.* History of Bath and Environs: 56.

16. Lossing, Benson J. Incidents of the Siege of Boston, in 1775. [Letter from John Lukens]. *American Historical Record*, Vol. I, 1872: 546-570.

17. *Massachusetts Archives, Military Records, Revoluitionary War Period, 1775-1787.* Commonwealth of Massachusetts. [Muster rolls of companies of Captains Thomas Williams and William Goodrich].

18. *Massachusetts Soldiers and Sailors of the Revolutionary War*, 17 vols. Boston: Secretary of the Commonwealth, 1896.

19. Muster rolls of Col. William Thompson's Battalion of Riflemen. Hendricks' Company: 23-27; Smith's Company: 39-42. *Pennsylvania Archives*. 2nd ser., vol. X, 1896.

20. Muster Roll of Company Under Command of Capt. David Bradish in Col. Phinney;s Reg (Condon). *Collections and Proceddings of Maine Historical Society*. Vol. VII, Jan. 1878: 166-167.

21. *A Muster Roll of Capt. Jonas Hubbard's Company in the 32d Regiment of Foot in the Continental Army Station'd in Dorchester, Sept. 1, 1775.* N.A.R.A. M 246, Revolutionary War Rolls, Mass. 32d Regiment of Militia, 1775. www.footnote.com/ image/#10115883.

22. National Archives and Records Administration. *Revolutionary War Pension Files. M804, Record Group 15, Records of the Veterans*

Administration. Includes an estimated 80,000 pension and bounty-land warrant application files. Also at www.footnote.com.

23. *Partial List of Men in the Rhode Island Companies of Arnold's Expedition.* [Addendum to Topham's Journal] Newport: Society of Sons of the Revolution in the State of Rhode Island, 1902: 53-56. Also Arnold Expedition Historical Society. www.arnoldsmarch.com/research/rosters/Rhode_Islanders.pdf.

24. Pierce, John, Paymaster General. *A Pay Roll of Capt. Oliver Hanchet's Company in Benedict Arnold's Detach. on Continental Service.* Papers of the Continental Congress, M247, Letters From Maj Gen Benjamin Lincoln, Vol. 1, page 440, Item # 149, 3 Jan'y 1776. Also at www.footnote.com/ image/#424193.

25. Putnam, Eben. "Muster Roll of a Company of Minute Men under the Command of Oliver Colburn, Colonel Arnold's regiment." *Putnam's Monthly Historical Magazine.* Vol. I, May, 1892-April, 1893: 32. Also at Arnold Expedition Historical Society.
    a. www.arnoldsmarch.com/research/rosters/Oliver%20 Colburn%20Company.pdf.

26. *Return of Rebel Prisoners Taken at Quebec, Dec'r 31ˢᵗ 1775.* [Return is dated July 27, 1776]. Colonial Office 42/35: 139-143. British National Archives. Also in Misc. Rev. Rolls in N.A.R.A. at www.footnote.com/ images #9972178; #9972177;9972178; 9972179; 9972180; 9972181; 9972182; 9989000; 9989003.

27. Roll of Captain Topham's Company, 1775. [June 10, 1775]. New England Historical and Genealogical Register, Jan. 1901, 82-83.

28. Stone, Edwin M., ed. [Appendix with Thayer Co. muster roll]. *The Invasion of Canada in 1776: including the journal of Captain Simeon Thayer, describing the perils and sufferings of the army under Colonel Benedict Arnold, in its march through the wilderness to Quebec.* Providence, R.I., 1867: 103-104. Also Arnold Expedition Historical Society.

29. Walton, E.P., ed. *Records of the Governor and Council of the State of Vermont.* Vol. II, Montpelier, VT: J. & J.M. Poland, 1874.

30. Ware, Joseph. *New England Historical and Genealogical Register,* April 1852. Addendum to Ware's Journal showing list of American troops at Quebec that were killed, wounded or taken prisoner: 129-145.

SECONDARY

31. Allen, James, comp. Account of Arnold's Expedition. *Collections of the Maine Historical Society.* Vol. I. Portland: Maine Historical Society, 1831, 387-416.

32. Allen, William. *The History of Norridgewock.* Norridgewock, ME: Edward J. Peet, 1849

33. *American Monthly Magazine.* Daughters of the American Revolution. Vol. 36, Jan.-June 1910: 183; 409-410.

34. Arnold, James N., ed. *The History of the Church Family.* Providence: The Narragansett Historical Publishing Company, 1887.

35. Barton, Lewis N., comp. *List of Members of Daniel Morgan's Rifle Company.* In Men and Events of the Revolution in Winchester and Frederick County, VA. Winchester, VA: Winchester-Frederick County Historical Society, 1975: 55-58. Also at web site of Arnold Expedition Historical Society. www.arnoldsmarch.com/research/rosters/Morgans%20Company.pdf.

36. Banks, Charles E. *Card File.* In the Papers of Charles E. Banks. Boston: Massachusetts Historical Society, n.d.

37. Banks, Charles E. Arnold's Expedition to Quebec in 1775: a preliminary note on the personnel of the detachment. *Magazine of History with Notes and Queries,* Extra # 50, 1916.

38. *A History of the County of Berkshire, Massachusetts in Two Parts.* Pittsfield, MA: Samuel W. Bush, 1829.

39. Boogher, William Fletcher, comp. *Gleanings of Virginia History. An Historical and Genealogical Collection Largely from Original Sources.* [A Partial List of Capt. Daniel Morgan's Company of Winchester, Frederick Co., VA., July, 1775]. Washington, D.C.: William Fletcher Boogher, 1903: 171

40. Browne, George Waldo. *The History of Hillsborough, New Hampshire 1735-1921.* 2 vols. Hillsborough, NH: Town of Hillsborough, 1922.

41. Burton, Clarence M. "George McCully in Quebec." *The Magazine of History with Notes and Queries.* Extra # 10, 1910: 67-68.

42. Carpenter & Morehouse, comp. *The History of the Town of Amherst, Massachusetts.* Amerst, MA: Carptenter & Morehouse, 1896.

43. Carter, Rev. N.F. *History of Pembroke, N.H. 1730-1898,* 2 vols. Concord, N.H.: Republican Press Association, 1895.

44. Cartmell, T.K. *Shenandoah Valley Pioneers and Their Descendants: A History of Frederick County Virginia from its Formation in 1738 to 1908.* Winchester, VA: T.K. Cartmell, 1909. [Morgan and His Men: 102-104].

45. Chatto, Clarence and Clair E. Turner, comp. *War History.* East Somerset County Register, 1911-1912.

46. Clarke, George Kuhn. *History of Needham Massachusetts, 1711-1911.* George Kuhn Clarke, 1912.

47. Codman, John. *Arnold's Expedition to Quebec.* 1901.

48. Coles, H.R. Remsen. *Genealogical Record of the Davison, Davidson, Davisson Family of New England.* New York: H.R. Remsen Coles, 1899.

49. Cowell, Benjamin. *The Spirit of 76 in Rhode Island.* Boston, 1850.

50. Cox, Rev. Henry Miller. *The Cox Family in America.* New York: Henry M. Cox, 1912.

51. Crafts, James M. *History of the Town of Whately, Mass. 1661-1899.* Whately, MA: Town of Whately, 1899.

52. Dearborn, John J., coll. *The History of Salisbury, New Hampshire From the Date of Settlement to the Present Time.* Manchester, N.H.: William E. Moore, 1890

53. *Descendants of Abraham Crittenden.* Rootsweb, June 2001. www.archiver. rootsweb.ancestry.com/th/read/MAFRANKL/2001-06/0993914741.

54. Dodge, Mary Cochran, comp. *A List of the Soldiers in the War of the Revolution From Worcester, Mass.* Worcester, MA: Col. Timothy Bigelow Chapter, Daughters of the American Revolution, 1902.

55. Draper, James. *History of Spencer, Massachusetts from Its Earliest Settlement to the Year 1860.* Worcester, MA: H.J. Howland, 1860.

56. Duncan, Mary Ann (Dobson). *Duncan's in the Revolution- Pennsylvania.* The Genealogy Bug, 2003. homepage.rootsweb.ancestry.com/-dobson/pa/parev.htm.

57. Fenner Family Genealogy. www.fennerfamily.com.

58. Fisher, Carleton E. and Sue G. Fisher, comp. *Soldiers, Sailors and Patriots of the Revolutionary War Maine.* Louisville, KY: National Society of the Sons of the American Revolution, 1982.

59. Flickinger, B. Floyd. "Captain Morgan and His Riflemen." *Winchester-Frederick County Historical Society Journal,* 2002: 43-62.

60. Frazier, Patrick. *The Mohicans of Stockbridge.* Lincoln, NE: University of Nebraska Press, 1992.

61. Getchell, Everett Lamont. "The Family of Samuel Getchell of Salisbury, Mass." *The New England Historical and Genealogical Register.* Vol. LXIII, 1909: 265-270.

62. Graham, James. *The Life of General Daniel Morgan.* New York: Derby & Jackson, 1856.

63. Green, Mason A. *Springfield 1636-1886, History of Town and City.* Springfiled, MA: City of Springfield, 1886.

64. Griffin, S.G. *A History of the Town of Keene.* Keene, N.H.: S.G. Griffin, 1904.

65. Hadley, George Plummer. *History of the Town of Goffstown 1733-1920.* Concord, NH: The Rumford Press, 1922.

66. Hammond, Rev. Charles. *The History of Union, Conn.* New Haven, CT: Price, Lee and Atkins, 1893.

67. Hanson, J.W. *History of Gardiner, Pittston and West Gardiner 1602 to 1852.* Gardiner, ME: William Palmer, 1852.

68. Harris, Alex. *A Biographical History of Lancaster County, Being a History of Early Settlers and Eminent Men of the County.* Lancaster, PA: Alex Harris, 1872.

69. *History of Berkshire County, Massachusetts with Biographical Sketches of Its Prominent Men,* 2 vols. New York: J.B. Beers & Co., 1885.

70. *Historic Boscawen*. Boscawen, N.H.: Boscawen Women's Club for Old Days, 1971.

71. *History of Bedford, New Hampshire from 1737*. Concord, N.H.: Town of Bedford, 1903.

72. *History of Cumberland and Adams Counties*. Chicago: Warner, Beers, 1886.

73. Hobbs, L. Frances. *Pelham: Old Days & Old Ways*. Pelham, N.H.: Pelham Historical Society, 1975.

74. Hull Family Association. Family information on Isaac Hull from Watertown, ME.

75. Hyde, Rev. C.M. and Alexander Hyde. *The Centennial Celebration and Centennial History of the Town of Lee, Mass*. Springfield, MA: Town of Lee, 1878.

76. "Indians in the Revolution [Maine]". *Spragues Journal of Maine History*. Vol. VI. Nov. 1918, Jan. 1919: 105-112.

77. Jones, Electra. *Stockbridge Past and Present, or Records of an Old Mission Station*. Springfield, MA: Samuel Bowles & Co, 1854.

78. *Lincoln County News*. "John McCurda of Bristol, Maine who was guide for Arnold Expedition. The story is based on research done by the Bremen County Historical Society." In issue of June 29, 2005.

79. Lincoln, William. *History of Worcester, Massachusetts, From Its Earliest Settlement to September 1836*. Worcester, MA: Charles Hersey, 1863.

80. Little, George Thomas, comp. *Genealogical and Family History of the State of Maine*. Vol. III. New York: Lewis Historical Publishing Company, 1909.

81. Little, William. *The History of Weare, New Hampshire 1735-1888*. Lowell, MA: S.W. Huse & Co., 1888.

82. Lockwood, Rev. John H. *Westfield and Its Historic Influences, 1669-1919*. Westfield, MA: John H. Lockwood, 1920.

83. Lord, C.C. *Life and Times in Hopkinton, N.H. in Three Parts*. Concord, N.H.: C.C. Lord, 1890.

84. Loveland, J.B. and George Loveland. *Genealogy of the Loveland Family in the United States of America.* Fremont, Ohio: Loveland and Loveland, authors, 1895.

85. John Marsh, Jr., "Owner of the Orono Island That Bears His Name." *Spragues Journal of Maine History.* Vol. 2, Oct. 1914: 202-205.

86. Marvin, Abijah Perkins. *History of Worcester County Massachusetts From Its First Settlement to the Present Time,* 2 vols. Boston: Abijah Perkins Marvin, 1879.

87. Mason, Edna Warren, comp. *Descendants of Captain Hugh Mason in America.* New Haven, CT: Tuttle, Morehouse & Taylor Company, 1937.

88. Mills, Borden H. *George Mills: A Soldier of the Revolution with a Genealogy of His Descendants.* Albany, N.Y.: Borden H. Mills, 1911.

89. Morgan, George H. *Centennial. The Settlement, Formation and Progress of Dauphin County, Pennsylvania, From 1785 to 1876.* Harrisburg, PA: Commissioners of Dauphin County, 1877.

90. Morison, George Abbot. *History of Peterborough, New Hampshire.* Rindge, New Hampshire: Richard R. Smith, 1954.

91. *NEBODA, Abenaki People of Maine.* Lewiston, ME, www.neboda. org.

92. North, James W. *The History of Augusta From the Earliest Settlement to the Present Times.* Augusta, ME: Clapp and North, 1870.

93. Norton, Rev. John A. and Joel Whittemore. *The History of Fitzwilliam, New Hampshire, From 1752 to 1887.* New York: Burr Printing House, 1888.

94. Nutt, Charles. *History of Worcester and Its People.* New York: Lewis Historical Publishing Co., 1919.

95. Paine, Silas H., Collector. "Soldiers of the Champlain Valley." *Proceedings of the New York State Historical Association.* Vol. XVII, 1919: 301-428.

96. Perley, Sidney. *The History of Boxford, Essex County, Massachusetts From Earliest Settlement Down to the Present Time.* Boxford, MA: Sidney Perley, 1886.

97. Perry, Arthur Latham. *Williamstown and Williams College.* Williamstown, MA: Arthur L. Perry, 1904.

98. Peters, Edward Frank and Eleanor Bradly Peters, comp. *Peters of New England, A Genealogy and Family History.* New York: Knickerbocker Press, 1903.

99. Peterson, Rev. Edward. *History of Rhode Island.* New York: John S. Taylor, 1853.

100. Powers, William H. *Powers-Banks Ancestry.* Ames, Iowa: John Leslie Powers, 1921.

101. Raynor, Ellen M. and Emma L. Petitclerc. *History of the Town of Cheshire, Berkshire County, Mass.* Holyoke, MA and New York: Clark W. Bryan & Company, 1885.

102. Read, Benjamin. *The History of Swanzey, New Hampshire From 1734 to 1870.* Salem, MA: The Salem Press, 189

103. Reed, Parker McCobb. *History of Bath and Environs, Sagadahoc County, Maine, 1607-1894.* Portland, ME: Parker McCobb Reed, 1894.

104. Roll of Ancestors. *Register of the Empire State Society of the Sons of the American Revolution.* 1899: 361-583.

105. Sedgewick, Charles A. *General History of the Town of Sharon, Litchfield County Conn.: From Its First Settlement.* Amenia, New York: Charles Walsh, 1877.

106. Sheldon, George. *A History of Deerfield, Massachusetts.* Deerfield, MA: George Sheldon, 1896.

107. Sherrow, Doris. *A Portland Revolutionary War Veteran, Parts I and II.* www.portlandct.org/Portland/history/history20.htm, November 2000.

108. Shively, Scott. *Hezekiah Phillips, An American Patriot,* 2006. www.stonesandbones.us/phillips.html.

109. Silliman, Sue Imogene, State Historian. *Michigan Military Records, Bulletin No. 12.* Lansing, Mich.: Michigan Historical Commission, 1920.

110. Smith, Jonathan. *Peterborough New Hampshire in the American*

Revolution. Peterborough, NH: Peterborough Historical Society, 1913.

111. Somers, Rev. A. N. *History of Lancaster, New Hampshire.* Lancaster, N.H.: Town of Lancaster, 1898.

112. Stiles, Henry R. *The History and Genealogies of Ancient Windsor Connecticut.* Hartford: Case, Lockwood & Brainard Company, 1891.

113. The Stockbridge Massachusetts Recruiting Center-Continental Army. *Berkshire Genealogist.* Vol. 18, Fall 1997: 126-127.

114. *Stoddard Family Genealogy.* www.freepages.genealogy.rootsweb. amcestry.com/~marci/stoddard.html.

115. Stroh, Oscar H. *Thompson's Battalion and/or The First Continental Regiment.* Harrisburg, PA: Graphic Services, 1976.

116. Sullivan, Sandi. *Captain Jedediah Hyde.* www.sandisullivan.com/ Hyde%203.htm:60.

117. Trumbull, James Russell. *History of Northampton, Massachusetts From Its Settlement in 1654.* Northampton, MA, 1902.

118. Waldo, Loren P. *The Early History of Tolland.* Hartford: Loren P. Waldo, 1861.

119. Washburn, Emory. *Historical Sketches of the Town of Leicester, Massachusetts.* Boston: Emory Washburn, 1860.

120. Waters, Rev. Wilson. *History of Chelmsford, Massachusetts.* Chelmsford, MA: Town of Chelmsford, 1917.

121. White, Emma Siggins, comp. *The Kinnears and Their Kin: A Memorial Volume of History, Biography and Genealogy.* Kansas City, MO: Thomas-Dart Printing Co., 1916.

122. White, Percia H. John Marsh, Interpreter. In *Maine in History and Romance.* Lewiston, ME: Lewiston Journal Company, 1915: 123-126.

123. Williamson, William D. *The History of the State of Maine.* 2 vols. Hallowell, ME: Glazier, Masters & Co., 1832.

124. Ellery Bicknell Channing, "A Chapter in the War of the American

Revolution." *Proceedings of the Worcester Society of Antiquities*. Vol. XXV. 1912, 99-101, 108-109.

125. Isaac Senter Journal.

126. Simon Fobes Journal.

127. Simeon Thayer Journal.

128. John Joseph Henry Journal.

129. James Melvin Journal.

130. Henry Dearborn Journal (HSP).

131. Caleb Haskell Journal.

132. Jeremiah Greenman Journal.

133. John Pierce Journal.

134. William McCoy Journal.

135. George Morison Journal.

136. Samuel Barney Journal.

137. Ephraim Squier Journal.

138. William Heth Journal.

139. Benedict Arnold Journal.

140. Eleazer Oswald Journal.

141. Matthias Ogden Journal.

142. Roberts, Kenneth. "Arnold's Letters." *March to Quebec, Journals of the Members of Arnold's Expedition*. Garden City, New York: Doubleday & Company, Inc., 1946.

143. Roberts, Kenneth. *Arundel*. "Notes on a few Nason's gathered from various sources during the writing of Arundel and the Lively Lady". 15 copies. Copy in Kenneth Roberts Papers in the Dartmouth College Library, 19

144. Balderama, Abby and Joseph Weston. The Canaan, Somerset Co. ME Gen Web Project. www.rootsweb.ancestry.com/~mecanaan/data/westjos.htm.

145. Nash, Gilbert. *Historical Sketch of Town of Weymouth, Mass.* Weymouth: Weymouth Historical Society, 1885, 71.

146. Cushing, James Stevenson. *Genealogy of the Cushing Family.* Privately Printed, 2009, 145.

147. *Return of Sick and Wounded in General Hospital, Nov. 25 to Decemr 2, 1775.* N.A.R.A. Revolutionary War Service Records.

APPENDIX III

GRAPHIC ILLUSTRATION OF ARNOLD'S MARCH

The idea of Appendix III is to present a two page graphic illustration of the expedition to Quebec. My friend, Marvin Michalson, introduced me to this concept when he showed me a graphic visualization of Napoleon's campaign in Russia in 1812-1813. That famous graphic showing the decreasing size of Napoleon's Grand Armée as it marched to Moscow and back was developed by Charles Joseph Minard. My friend Marv found it in a book entitled *The Visual Display of Quantitative Information* by Edward R. Tufet. The graph shows the consistent loss of men by Napoleon on his campaign so that by the time he returns to his starting point his manpower has been reduced to almost nothing. It was a stunning representation of what happened to Napoleon's army and the visual impact was much more impressive than I anticipated. The Minard graphic also plotted the temperature under the graph of the declining manpower, which enables the viewer to see the connection between the two.

Marv suggested that this type of graphic might be equally useful to depict the expedition to Quebec, even though the loss of manpower was not as dramatic as Napoleon's. With a skeptical agreement to see what I could do with this concept, I came to realize that a graphic illustration of the Arnold expedition is indeed interesting and helps to visualize some of the factors that affected the march and how those factors seemed to influence troop strength.

While a visual depiction will not help everyone to better understand a complicated military campaign that involved marching through a virgin wilderness, many will find it a helpful aid. It can surely supplement the written words of the journals and various histories of the expedition in a different way.

The two page graphic in Appendix III features the following six items presented visually so that a more in-depth understanding of the expedition can be attained.

- Weather: shows the three significant weather events that were experienced by the men. The hurricane in October was arguably the single most significant external factor encountered on the march. Weather information was found in the expedition journals and *Early American Winters, 1604-1820* by David Ludlum.
- Troop Strength: shows the number of men in the expedition at

twelve landmark points on the route and how the troop strength both increased and decreased as the march progressed. The troop strength figures are derived from the roster and tables in Appendix II

- Days in the field from the time the expedition left Cambridge until the assault on Quebec on December 31, 1775. The days are tied into the landmarks and show the days traveled between each landmark and the cumulative days as the march proceeded. This information was derived from the journals.

- Twelve key landmarks on the route starting at Cambridge and ending with the assault on Quebec are highlighted by vertical lines. The dates that these landmarks were attained are shown beginning at Cambridge on September 11, 1775. The landmarks are located on the graphic based on miles traveled between them and not on days.

- Elevation of the twelve landmarks in order to visualize the elevation changes that the men encountered on the march. Declining elevations can be as difficult as rising elevations and some of the most difficult conditions were encountered on the Chaudière River between the return of the Enos Division and reaching the first French settlements. The elevation figures are derived from Stephen Clark's book, *Following Their Footsteps,* and the abstract on *Geological Influences on Benedict Arnold's March to Quebec* by geologist Bruce F. Rueger.

- Number of miles traveled between the landmarks as well as cumulative miles traveled. It is interesting to note that, contrary to expectation, there is no relationship between the miles traveled and the number of days that it took to travel those miles. Stephen Clark's book was helpful as was Bruce Rueger's abstract and MapQuest.

One connection that is readily apparent is the return of the Enos Division on October 26th and two events that preceded it. Those events were the significant elevation change that occurred at the Great Carrying Place on September 7th and the three day hurricane beginning on the 19th of October. Both of these were unforeseeable to the men and both made the expedition more difficult, thus contributing to the decision of the Enos Division and the resulting loss of troop strength.

Food supply is one important factor that is not depicted in this graphic. There is no doubt, based on the journal entries of the men, that the food supply was diminishing as the days passed. The primary reason for not including food supply is there is no good contemporary source that recorded anything other than general comments about the declining food supply. We don't really know precisely how much food was lost between September 11ᵗʰ and October 26ᵗʰ or how much food the Enos Division took back to Cambridge when it returned. Misinformation, unsubstantiated assertions or a best guess about food does not serve any purpose and would only detract from the known quantitative details that are contained in the graphic display. The same problem is also present in trying to plot temperature details in the same way as is shown in the Minard graph. There is not enough factual information from contemporary sources to include temperature.

WEATHER			HURRICANE AT SEA			

TROOP STRENGTH # OF MEN		1060 MEN			1116 MEN	

DAYS	5 DAYS	4 DAYS		4 DAYS	13 DAYS	4 DAYS
CUMMULATIVE DAYS	5		9		13	26
DATE (1775)	9/11	9/16		9/20	9/23	10/7
LAND MARKS ON ROUTE	CAMBRIDGE	NEWBURYPORT	MOUTH OF KENNEBEC RIVER	FORT WESTERN	GREAT CARRYING PLACE	

ELEVATION OF ROUTE (IN FEET)	40'	10' 90 MI 44 MI	0'	50' 46 MI	85 MI 450'	13 MI
CUMMULATIVE MILES		44 MI	134 MI	180 MI		265 MI

276

3 DAY HURRICANE | SNOW AND COLD WEATHER | SNOW STORM

1091 MEN

1063 MEN

THREE COMPANIES RETURN WITH 230 MEN PLUS COLBURN & GUIDES 56 MEN

683 MEN | 680 MEN | 680 MEN | 677 MEN

423 MEN KILL OR CAPTURE

254 MEN

5 DAYS	10 DAYS	8 DAYS	10 DAYS	16 DAYS	32 DAYS	
30	35	45	53	63	79	111
10/11	10/17	10/26	11/3	11/13	11/29	12/31
CARRY PONDS	DEAD RIVER	ENOS DIVISION RETURNS	FRENCH SETTLEMENTS	REACH QUEBEC	POINT AUX TRMBLES	QUEBEC ASSAULT

1650'

18 MI   1150'

1150'

51 MI

575'   20 MI   575'

20 MI

54 MI

509"

278 MI	298 MI	316 MILES	367 MILES	431 MI	451 MI	471 MI

WORKS CONSULTED

Bibliographical details on the sources for all of the printings of the expedition journals are provided in Chapter One and will not be listed again in this bibliography. The primary objective in this bibliography is to provide a comprehensive listing of sources relating to the Arnold expedition and the sources that were used to explore the lives of its officers and journal writers.

PRIMARY SOURCES

Arnold, Benedict. Arnold's Letters on his expedition to Canada in 1775. *Maine Historical Society Collections.* Vol. 1, 341-416. Portland, Maine: Maine Historical Society, 1831.

Arnold, Benedict. *American Historical Record.* Vol. 3, May 1874: 220-222. Day Book and Ledger, 1777-1779

Chase, Philander D., ed. *The Papers of George Washington, Rev War Series,* Vols. 2 & 3. Charlottesville: University Press of Virginia, 1987-1988.

Clark, William Bell, ed. *Naval Documents of the American Revolution.* Vols. 1-3. Washington, DC: Government Printing Office, 1964-1973.

"Committee of Safety Records." *Collections of the New Hampshire Historical Society.* Vol. III, 1868: 18-20; 64; 71; 78-79. [Roger Enos].

Connecticut Archives. Revolutionary War, Series I, Vols I,III,XIV . Hartford, 1763-1820 [Roger Enos].

Dearborn, General Henry. *Arnold's Expedition to Quebec.* 23 pages. New York Public Library, Harkness Manuscript Collection, 1816.

Force, Peter, ed. *American Archives. 9 vols.* Washington, D.C., 1837-1853. Also at American Archives Documents of the American Revolution 1774-1776. Northern Illinois University. www.dig.lib.niu.edu/amarch

Ford, Worthington C. et al, ed. *Journals of the Continental Congress.* Washington, D.C., 1904-1937. www.memory.loc.gov/ammem/amlaw/lwjc.html.

Ford, Worthington C., coll. & ed. *The Writings of George Washington*. Vol. III, *1775-1776*. New York and London: G.P. Putnam's Sons, 1889.

Henry, John Joseph. "Letters of Hon. John Joseph Henry." *Pennsylvania Magazine of History and Biography*. Vol. 20, 1896: 568-570.

Hoadly, Charles J. *The Public Records of the State of Connecticut, From October, 1776 to February, 1778*. Hartford: Case, Lockwood & Brainard Company, 1894.

Letters and Certificates From the Revolutionary Papers of Col. Francis Nichols. *The Pennsylvania Magazine of History and Biography*. Vol. 32, 1908: 108-112.

Military Affairs and Haldiman Papers. *Collections of the Vermont Historical Society*. Vol.II, 1871: 189-196.[Roger Enos].

Revolutionary War Pension Files. National Records and Archives Administration, M804, Record Group 15, Records of the Veterans Administration. Includes over 80,000 application files. Also on www.footnote.com.

Roberts, Kenneth, Comp. and Ann. *March to Quebec: Journals of the Members of Arnold's Expedition*. Garden City, New York: Doubleday & Company, Inc, 1946.

Walton, E.P., ed. *Records of the Governor and Council of the State of Vermont*. Montpelier: J. & J.M. Poland, 1874.

Washington Papers. *Library of Congress, Manuscript Division, 1741-1799*. Series 4. GeneralCorrespondence.1697-1799.

Willis, William. *Journals of the Rev. Thomas Smith and the Rev. Samuel Deane, Pastors of the First Church in Portland*. Portland: Joseph S. Bailey, 1949.

SECONDARY SOURCES

Abbatt, William. "A Neglected Name: Dr. Isaac Senter." *Annals of Medical History*, Vol. II, 1920: 381-383.

Abbatt, William. "Arnold and Montgomery at Quebec." *The Magazine of History with Notes and Queries*. Vol. 1, 1905: 13-17.

Allen, Barbara. *Report to Stephen Darley on Captain William Goodrich From Records in the Library.* Stockbridge Library, Museum and Local Archives, January 2010.

Allen, William. Account of Arnold's Expedition. *Collections of the Maine Historical Society.* Vol. 1, 1831: 386-416.

Americana Exchange. A rare book bibliographical database of entries from bookseller catalogs and rare book auctions. www.americanaexchange.com

Arnold Expedition Historical Society Newsletter, 1975-1979. Arnold Expedition Historical Society. Gardiner, Maine.

Arnold, James N., ed. *The History of the Church Family.* Providence: The Narragansett Historical Publishing Company, 1887.

Banks, Charles E. "Captain Scott of Enos' Detachment." *The Magazine of History with Notes and Queries.* Vol. XVIII, January-June 1914: 271-273.

—. *Papers and research material regarding Benedict Arnold's Expedition against Quebec, 1775-1776. Includes handwritten copies of letters and jouornals, including Hendricks, Ware and Heth; newspaper clippings and portions of published articles; copies of maps; and correspondence regarding research with other scholars and institutions.* Ms. N-1782. 1 narrow box and 9 vols in cases. Boston: Massachusetts Historical Society, 1922.

---..Arnold's Expedition to Quebec in 1775; a preliminary note on the personnel of the detachment. *Magazine of History with Notes and Queries,* Extra # 50, 1916: 10 pages.

Bell, Richard G. "The Court-Martial of Roger Enos, I and II." *Connecticut Bar Journal.* Vols. 73 & 74, 1999 and 2000: 428-461; 299-312.

Alex. Harris. *Biographical History of Lancaster County, Pennsylvania.* Lancaster, PA: Elias Barr & Co., 1872.

Bird, Harrison. *Attack on Quebec: the American Invasion of Canada, 1775.* New York: Oxford University Press, 1968.

Boatner, Mark H. *Encyclopedia of the American Revolution.* New York: David McKay Company, Inc, 1975.

Campbell, Frederic L. Benedict Arnold In Maine. *Sun Up, Maines Own Magazine*, May 1931: 16, 29.

Case, Lafayette Wallace, ed. *The Goodrich Family in America*. Chicago: Goodrich Family Memorial Association, 1889.

Celebration of the Bi-centennial Aniversary of the Town of Suffield, Conn. Hartford: Wiley, Waterman & Eaton, 1871.

Chandler, Lorraine. *Lt. Jeremiah Greenman.* www.familytreemaker.genealogy. com/user/c/h/a/Lorraine-Chandler/WEBSITE-0001/u.

Clark, Stephen. *Following Their Footsteps: A Travel Guide & History of the 1775 Secret Expedition to Capture Quebec.* Shapleigh, ME: Stephen Clark, 2003.

Clarke, George Kuhn. *History of Needham Massachusetts, 1711-1911.* Needham, MA: George Kuhn Clarke, 1912.

Coburn, Louise Helen. *The Passage of Arnold Through Skowhegan.* Skowhegan, ME: Louise H. Coburn, 1922.

Codman, John. *Arnold's Expedition to Quebec.* New York: The Macmillan Company, 1902.

Coffin, Charles Carleton, comp. *The History of Boscawen and Webster, From 1733 to 1878.* Concord, N.H.: Republican Press Association, 1878.

Coffin, Charles, comp. *The Lives and Services of Major General John Thomas; Colonel Thomas Knowlton; Colonel Alexander Scammell; Major General Henry Dearborn.* New York: Robert, Hovey & King, 1845.

Collins, W.E. "Arnold's Expedition to Quebec." *Collections of the Berkshire Historical & Scientific Society*, vol. I, 1894: 57-67.

Commemorative Biographical Encyclopedia of the Juniata Valley. Chambersburg, PA: J.M. Runk & Co., 1897.

Cornwall, Edward H, "Family of George Stocking." *The New England Historical and Genealogical Register.* Vol. L, 1896: 171-176.

Crist, Robert G. *Captain William Hendricks and the March to Quebec, 1775.*

Carlisle, PA: Hamilton Library and Historical Association of Cumberland County, 1960.

Cutter, William Richard, comp. *New England Families, Genealogical and Memorial*. New York: Lewis Historical Publishing Company, 1915.

Davenport, John Scott. *The Frontier Hendricks*. Dorothy N. Lloyd Memorial Hendricks Research. April 10, 1993 letter to Col. Meredith E. Hendricks.

Davis, Curtis Carroll. "Mrs. Warner's Winter Warfare, A Momemto of Arnold's Campaign." *Lancaster County Historical Society Journal*, 1980: 125-131.

Desjardin, Thomas A. *Through a Howling Wilderness, Benedict Arnold's March to Quebec in 1775*. New York: St. Martin's Press, 2006.

Dodge, Mary Cochran, comp. A *List of Soldiers in the War of the Revolution from Worcester, Mass*. Worcester: Worcester D.A.R., 1902.

Dorr, Charley. *Descendants of Edward Dorr*. www.gencircles.com/users/cdorr/1/data/959.

Duis, E. Dr. *The Good Old Times in McLean County, Illinois*. Bloomington, Indiana: Leader Publishing and Printing House, 1874.

Egle, William Henry, ed. "The Pattang Company Before Quebec, 1775." *Notes and Queries: Historical, Biographical and Genealogical*. 3rd ser., vol. I, 1887: 249-250.

Egleston, Thomas.*The Life of John Paterson, Major-General in the Revolutionary Army*. New York and London: G.P. Putnam's Sons, 1898.

Evans, Charles. *American Bibliography: A Chronological Dictionary of all Books Pamphlets and Periodical Publications in the United States of America Down to and Including the Year 1820*. 12 vols. Chicago: Charles Evans, 1903-1934.

French, Allen. *The First Year of the American Revolution*. New York: Octagon Books, 1968.

Gabriel, Michael P. *Major General Richard Montgomery, The Making of an American Hero*. Teaneck, NJ: Fairleigh Dickenson University Press, 2002.

Gansser, Capt. Augustus H., ed. & comp. *History of Bay County, Michigan and Representative Citizens.* Chicago: Richmond & Arnold, 1905.

Gardner, Frank A. "The Organization and Personnel of the Expedition." *Danvers Historical Society, Historical Collections.* Vol.13, 1925: 38-50.

Gephart, Ronald M, comp. *Revolutionary America 1763-1789, A Bibliography.* 2 vols. Washington, D.C.: Library of Congress, 1964

Goelet, Ogden. *The Library of the Late Ogden Goelet of New York.* New York: American Art Association Anderson Galleries, Inc., 1935
--- Part One. Benedict Arnold Manuscript Journal, 10-15.
--- Part Two. John Pierce Manuscript Journal, 149-154.

Greenwood, Isaac. "The Stockbridge Indians During the American Revolution." *New England Historical and Genealogical Register.* Vol. LIV, January 1900: 162-164.

Hadley, E.D. "General Henry Dearborn." *The Granite Monthly, Vol. XLVII,* 1915: 409-412.

Handley, Christopher Simpson, comp. *Annotated Bibliography of Diaries Printed in English, Diaries 1780 to 1817.* 3rd Edition. Vol. IV. Tyne and Wear, England: Hanover Press, 2002.

Hatch, Robert M. *Thrust for Canada: The American Attempt on Quebec in 1775-1776.* Boston: Houghton Mifflin, 1979.

Hayden, Horace Edwin. "General Roger Enos, A Lost Chapter of Arnold's Expedition to Canada, 1775". *Magazine of American History.* Vol. XIII, 1885: 463-476. Also in Kenneth Roberts' *March to Quebec.*

Henderson, Denis L. *General Oliver Hanchett.* www.worldconnect.rootsweb. ancestry.com/cgibin/igen.cgi?op=GET8db=limmeadenis51.

Henry, William Louis, comp. *Lineage of John Joseph Henry.* Detroit: W.L. Henry, 1909.

"Note on the Heth Journal". *Proceedings of the Virginia Historical Society at the Annual Meeting held Dec. 21-22, 1891,* 1892: 320n.

Hildreth, S.P. *Biographical and Historical Memoirs of the Early Pioneer Settlers of Ohio*. Cincinnati: H.W. Derby & Co., 1852.

Hines, Ezra Dodge. *Arnold's March From Cambridge to Quebec*. Salem, MA: The Salem Press, 1898.

History of Ashtabula County, Ohio. Philadelphia: William Brothers, 1878.

History of Cumberland and Adams Counties Pennsylvania. Chicago: Warner, Beers & Co., 1886.

Howes, Wright, comp. *U.S.iana (1650-1950)*. New York: The Newberry Library, 1963.

Hubbard, Harlan Page. *One Thousand Years of Hubbard History*. New York: Harlan Page Hubbard, 1895.

Hughes, Phyllis J., Genealogist. *Information on Isaac Hull of Kennebec County, Maine*. Hull Family History Database, Hull Family Association, 2010.

Huston, James A. "The Logistics of Arnold's March to Quebec." *Military Affairs*, Dec., 1968: 110-124.

Jones, Charles H. *History of the Campaign for the Conquest of Canada*. Philadelphia: Porter & Coates, 1882.

Jones, Electra. *Stockbridge Past and Present, or Records of an Old Mission Station*. Springfield, MA: Samuel Bowles & Co., 1854.

Jordan, Francis, Jr. *The Life of William Henry of Lancaster, Pennsylvania, 1729-1786*. Lancaster, PA, 1910.

Kapp, James Edward. *Early Perry County People (Prior to 1830)*. The Perry Historians, n.d.

Kilbourne, James Dwight. *Virtutis Praemium: The Men Who Founded the State Society of the Cincinnati of Pennsylvania*. Rockport, ME: Picton Press, 1998.

Kingsley, Orson. *Report to Stephen Darley*. Topic: Major William Goodrich in Middlebury. Research Center, Henry Sheldon Museum, Middlebury, VT, February 2010.

Laughlin, Jean. *Report to Stephen Darley* Topic:The McCoy Name in various records. Mifflin County Historical Society, 2010.

Le Moine, Sir James M. "Arnold's Assault on the Sault-au-Matelot Barriers, 31st December, 1775." *Literary and Historical Society of Quebec, Transactions # 12*, 1876-1877: 40-70.

Le Moine, Sir James M. "The Assault of Brigadier-General Richard Montgomery and Colonel Benedict Arnold in Quebec in 1775. A Red Letter Day in the Annals of Canada." *Royal Society of Canada, Proceedings and Transactions*, 1899: 457-466.

Leake, Isaac Q. *Memoir of the Life and Time of General John Lamb*. Glendale, New York: Benchmark Publishing Company, 1970.[Eleazer Oswald, 130, 149, 168, 202-3, 209, 330, 344, 359].

Leavitt, Miss Emily Wilder. *John Melvin of Charlestown and Concord, Mass., and His Descendants*. Boston: David Clapp & Son, 1901-1905.

Lincoln, William. *History of Worcester. Massachusetts, From Its Earliest Settlement to September 1836*. Worcester: Charles Hersey, 1862.

Line of Descent for Joseph Farnsworth of Dorchester, Mass. www.newsarch.rootsweb.com/th/read/VTGEN/2001-04/6986761022.

Locke, John Goodwin. *Book of the Lockes: A Genealogical and Historical Record of William Locke of Woburn*. Appendix H. Boston and Cambridge: John Goodwin Locke, 1853.

MacDougall, Walter M. "Arnold's Expedition to Quebec, 1775." *Down East Magazine*. Vol. 22, Sept 1975: 36-40.

MacLean, Allen. "Arnold's Strength at Quebec." *Military Collector and Historian*, Autumn 1977: 137-139.

Martin, James Kirby. *Benedict Arnold Revolutionary Hero, An American Warrior Reconsidered*. New York and London: New York University Press, 1997.

Matthews, William, comp. *American Diaries: An Annotated Bibliography of American Diaries Written Prior to the Year 1861*. Boston: J.S. Canner & Company, 1959.

"The McCobb Family of Maine." *Genealogy: A Journal of American Ancestry.* Vols. I & II, 1912: 244-245

McCoy, Chauncey E. and Raymond M. Bell. *John McCoy, His Children and Grandchildren.* McCoy and Bell, 1990.

McSpadden, Joseph Walker. *The South in the Building of the Nation,* vol XI. Richmond, VA: The Southern Historical Publication Society, 1909.

Mead, Daniel. *A History of Greenwich, Fairfield County, Conn.* New York: Baker & Godwin, Printers, 1857.

Mead, Spencer P. *Ye Historie of Ye Old Town of Greenwich, County of Fairfield and State of Connecticut.* New York: The Knickerbocker Press, 1911.

Meigs, Rick. *Return Jonathan Meigs 1st.* Meigs Family History and Genealogy, www.meigs.org/rjm90.htm.

Miles, Lion G. "Anna Bingham: From the Red Lion Inn to the Supreme Court." *The New England Quarterly.* Vol. 69, June 1996: 287-299. [Footnote on William Goodrich, 289-290].

Mills, Borden. *George Mills: A Soldier of the Revolution.* Albany: Borden Mills, 1911.

Mills, William H. "Benedict Arnold's March to Canada." *Magazine of American History, with Notes and Queries,* Feb. 1885: 143-154.

Morrison, Leonard Allison and Stephen Paschall Sharples. *History of the Kimball Family in America From 1634 to 1897.* Boston: Damrell & Upham, 1897.

Morrissey, Brendan. *Quebec 1775: The American Invasion of Canada.* Oxford, UK: Osprey Publishing, 2003.

Munn, Charles A. *Rare Americana Including Selections from the Collection of the Late Charles A. Munn.* New York: American Art Association, Inc., January 21 and 22, 1926.

Nichols, Charles J. "The March of Benedict Arnold Through the District of Maine." *Sprague's Journal of Maine History.* Vol. XI, 1923: 145-150; 195-208.

Nichols, Francis. *Proceedings of the Delaware County Historical Society*. Vol. 1, Sept 29, 1895-Dec. 5, 1901: 26-29.

North, James W. *The History of Augusta from the Earliest Settlement to the Present Times*. Augusta, ME: Clapp and North, 1870.

Online, Family Treemaker. *Lt. Jeremiah Greenman*. familytreemaker.genealogy. com/users/c/h/a/Lorraine-Chandler/WEBSITE-0001/UHP-0327.html.

Oswald, Ginny. *Eleazer Oswald's Descendants*. June 29, 2001. www.genforum. genealogy.com/oswald/messages/263.html.

Park, Edward. Could Canada Have Ever Been Our Fourteenth Colony? *Smithsonian*, December 1987: 40-49.

Pierce, Frederick Clifton. *Pierce Genealogy*. Worcester, MA: Press of Charles Hamilton, 1880.

Report to Stephen Darley From Dewey Research Center. Topic: Major William Goodrich in Sheffield." Sheffield Historical Society, 2010.

Rikes, David M. *Report to Stephen Darley*. Topic: Information in the Cumberland Historical Society and Hamilton Library on the William Hendricks Family, including the Hendricks genealogy file. Cumberland County Historical Society and the Hamilton Library, January 2010.

Roger Enos- Revolutionary War General. Eno Family Association. www.enofamily. org.

Rowland, Bob. "Tobias Hendricks: A Family Tradition of Service." *Cumberland County History*. Vol. 20, Summer/Winter 2003: 49-55.

Sabin, Joseph. *Bibliotheca Americana: Dictionary of Books Relating to America from Its Discovery to the Present Time*. 29 vols. New York: J. Sabin's Son, 1879.

Seymour, Keith M. *The Descendants of Thomas Hanchett*. San Francisco: Keith M. Seymour, 1985.

Smith, Albert. *History of the Town of Peterborough, Hillsborough County, New Hampshire*, Boston: George H. Ellis, 1876.

Smith, Jonathan. *Peterborough New Hampshire in the American Revolution.* Peterborough: Peterborough Historical Society, 1913.

Smith, Jonathan. "Two William Scotts of Peterborough, N.H." *Proceedings of the Massachusetts Historical Society, vol. XLIV,* 1911: 495-502.

Smith, Justin H. *Arnold's March from Cambridge to Quebec: A Critical Study, together with a reprint of Arnold's Journal.* New York: G.P. Putnam's Sons, 1903.

—. *Our Struggle for the Fourteenth Colony: Canada in the American Revolution.* New York: G.P. Putnam's Sons, 1907.

Smith, Justin H. "The Prologue of the American Revolution." *The Century Illustrated Monthly Magazine.* Vol. LXV, Nov. 1902-April 1903: 72-94;351-369; 529-544; 713-731.

Stanley, George Francis Gilman. *Canada Invaded, 1775-1776.* Toronto: Samuel Stevens Hakkert and Co., 1977.

Stiles, Henry R. *The History and Genealogies of Ancient Windsor Connecticut.* Hartford: Cass, Lockwood & Brainard Company, 1891.

Sullivan, Sandi. Captain Jedediah Hyde. www.sandisullivan.com/Hyde%203. htm:60.

Thayer, Bezaleel. *Memorial of the Thayer Name, From the Massachusetts Colony of Weymouth and Braintree, Embracing Genealogical and Biographical Sketches of Richard and Thomas Thayer and Their Descendants from 1636 to 1874.* Oswego, N.Y.: R.J. Oliphant, 1874.

Tobias, Sr. v Tobias, Jr. December 23, 2004. www.sio.midco.net/ltsco/hendricks/toby%20v%20toby.html.

Trask, William B. Genealogy of the Ware Family. *New England Historical and Genealogical Register.* April 1852: 129-145.

Walker, J. Samuel. *The Perils of Patriotism: John Joseph Henry and the American Attack on Quebec, 1775.* Lancaster, PA: Lancaster County Historical Society, 1975.

Walworth, Rueben. *Genealogy of William Hyde of Norwich*. vol. 1, Albany: Joel Munsell, 1864.

Ward, Christopher. *The War of the Revolution*. 2 vols. New York: The Macmillan Company, 1952.

Wells, Gabriel. *Rare Books from the Estate of the Late Gabriel Wells*. Catalogue No. 1. New York: Charles S. Boesen, n.d.

Whaples, Meigs H. *An Historical Sketch of Return Jonathan Meigs, A Revolutionary Hero of Connecticut*. Colonel Jeremiah Wadsworth Branch, Connecticut Society, Sons of the American Revolution, 1918.

Wheeler, William Ogden, comp. *The Ogden Family in America, Elizabethtown Branch, and Their English Ancestry*. Philadelphia: J.B. Lippincott Company, 1907.

Whitemore, William H. *The American Genealogist Being a Catalogue of Family Histories and Publications*. Albany, N.Y.: Joel Munsell, 1868.

Williams, Stephen W. *The Genealogy and History of the Family of Williams in America*. Greenfield, MA: Merriam & Mirick, 1847.

Winter, Florence Small. *The Kennebec-Chaudiere "Arnold" Trail*. Augusta, ME: RJ Printing, 1978.

Wright, James Osborne, comp. *Catalogue of the American Library of the Late Samuel Latham Mitchell Barlow*. New York: 1889.

Young, Henry J. The Spirit of 1775, A Letter of Robert Magaw, Major of the Continental Riflemen. *John & Mary's Journal*, 1975: 6-50.

Zinn, Donna Heller. *Search of Records Report to Stephen Darley*. Topic: George Morison from Records in Cumberland and Perry County. The Perry Historians, 2010.

END NOTES

The Arnold expedition journals that are cited in these End Notes will refer to pages in *March to Quebec* for those journals that are included by Kenneth Roberts in his book. All other journal citations will identify the publication in which the journal appears and its page number. The bibliographical details from the expedition journal bibliography in Chapter One will not be repeated in these End Notes. Any of the books in that bibliography that are cited in the End Notes will only use the author's name from the Chapter One bibliography along with the page number in the relevant book. The references to Justin Smith are for his book *Arnold's March from Cambridge to Quebec* unless otherwise stated.

INTRODUCTION

1. Charles E. Banks. Papers and research material regarding Benedict Arnold's Expedition against Quebec. Massachusetts Historical Society. Ms. N-1782, 1922.
2. The seven officers are William Hendricks, Oliver Hanchett, Jonas Hubbard, William Goodrich, Samuel McCobb, Thomas Williams and Captain Scott.
3. When he researched and wrote his two books on Arnold's expedition and the campaign to conquer Canada, Justin H. Smith was Professor of Modern History at Dartmouth College. He was born in New Hampshire and received his advanced degrees from Dartmouth and the Union Theological Seminary. Early in his career, he worked for publishing companies. First at Scribner's Sons and then at Ginn & Co., where he became a partner in 1890. He was a professor at Dartmouth from 1899 until he resigned in 1908 to work on two books relating to Mexico and Texas. He published *The Annexation of Texas* in 1911 and later published *The War with Mexico*, for which he won a Pulitzer Prize in 1920. He died in Brooklyn, New York in 1930.
4. Banks Papers.

CHAPTER ONE

5. Banks Papers.
6. Christopher Ward. *The War of the Revolution*. New York: The MacMillan Company, 1962: 448. Introduction to notes on Chapter 13.
7. The only other military campaign during the Revolutionary War that approaches the number of journals produced by the Arnold expedition

is the Sullivan Expedition in 1779. There are at least twenty-six extant journals written by officers and NCO's from that expedition but none from privates.

8. Codman wrote this comment in his book regarding the expedition entitled *Arnold's Expedition to Quebec*. New York: Mcmillan Company, 1901, 1. It was quoted in the Abbatt reprinting of the Topham journal in *Magazine of History*, Extra # 50: 1.

9. Charles H. Jones, *History of the Campaign for the Conquest of Canada*. Philadelphia: Porter & Coates, 1882.

10. Greenman started out his service in the army as a private but later in the war he was promoted to officer status. Greenman's account is not as well known as the account by Joseph Plumb Martin which has been reprinted a number of times by different publishers.

11. Samuel Knapp, *Life of Aaron Burr*. New York: Wiley & Long, 1835. Introduction to Appendix which published Arnold's Journal, 205.

12. "Rare Books From the Estate of the Late Gabriel Wells." *Catalogue No. 1*. New York: Charles S. Boesen, n.d., 8-13.

13. Donation of the Arnold manuscript journal to the Harvard Library. Harvard Library online catalog.

14. Jared Sparks Collection of Documents, Harvard Library. Calendar, 39.

15. Justin Smith, 26-27.

16. The Library of the Late Ogden Goelet of New York. Part I. New York: American Art Association Anderson Galleries, Inc., 1935: 10-15.

17. James Kirby Martin. *Benedict Arnold Revolutionary Hero, An American Warrior Reconsidered*. New York: New York University Press, 1997.

18. Justin Smith, footnote # 3, 264.

19. *Historical and Biographical Annals of Columbia and Montour Counties Pennsylvania*. Chicago: J.H. Beers & Co., 1915: 626; *Proceedings of the American Antiquarian Society*. New Ser., vol. 31, Apr. 13, 1921-Oct. 19, 1921: 208; Historical Magazine with Notes & Queries, vol. III, 1859: 284-5; *American National Biography Online*, Feb. 200. www.anb.org/articles/16/16-02855.html; *Pennsylvania Magazine of History & Biography*, vol. 4, 1880: 252-253; Joseph Towne Wheller. *The Maryland Press, 1777-1790*. Chapter 3. Archives of Maryland Online; Isaac Leake. *Memoir of the Life and Times of General John Lamb*. Glendale, NY: Benchmark Publishing Company, 1970: 130, 149, 168, 202-2, 209, 330, 344, 359; Ginny Oswald. *Eleazer Oswald's Descendants*. www.genforum.genealogy.com/oswald/messages/263.html.

20. John Wingate Thornton was a well-known lawyer who practiced in Boston after graduating from Harvard in 1840. He was a founding member of the New England Historic and Genealogical Society and wrote a number of articles for their magazine. In addition to writing for *NEHGR*, he also authored a number of books. One of his interests was in collecting rare books on Americana and he was a well- respected

book collector in the nineteenth century. When he died in 1878, among other items in his collection were the manuscript journals of Henry Dearborn, which were ultimately purchased by the Boston Public Library. It was the manuscript journal in Thornton's collection that was transcribed and published by the Massachusetts Historical Society.

21. Banks Papers.

22. E.D. Hadley. "General Henry Dearborn". *Granite Monthly*, new Ser., vol. 5, 1915: 409-412; *Dictionary of American Biography*, vol. 5. Charles Scribner's Sons, New York, 1930: 174-176; Dearborn manuscript regarding Arnold's Expedition to Quebec. New York Public Library, Harkness Manuscript Collection, 1816; Charles Coffin. *The Lives and Services of Major General Henry Dearborn*. New York: Robert, Hovey & King, 1845; Daniel Goodwin, Jr. *The Dearborns*. Chicago Historical Society's Proceedings, 1844: 20-40

23. Meigs Family History & Genealogy. www.meigs.org/rjm90.htm; S.P. Hildreth, *Biographical and Historical Memoirs of the Early Pioneer Settlers of Ohio*, 258-278 ; Meigs H. Whipples. *An Historical Sketch of Return Jonathan Meigs, A Revolutionary Hero of Connecticut*. Col. Jeremiah Wadsworth Branch, Connecticut Society, Sons of the American Revolution, 1918.

24. William Matthews, *American Diaries: An Annotated Bibliography of American Diaries Written Prior to the Year 1861*. Boston: J.S. Cannor & Company, 1959: 118.

25. E. Littell. *Litell's Living Age*, Vol. 10. Boston: Waite, Peirce & Company, 1846: 48.

26. *Decker Book Catalogue*, 042-020, 1959

27. Jared Sparks Letter is quoted in *The Collection of Geo. M. Williamson* catalogue. The Anderson Auction Co., Jan. 30-31, 1908: 9.

28. William Abbatt. A Neglected Name: Dr. Isaac Senter. *Annals of Medical History*, vol. 2, 1920: 381-383; Dr. Senter and His Descendants. *Magazine of History with Notes & Queries*, Extra # 41-44, 1916: i-ix; Rev. Timothy Alden. A *Collection of American Epitaphs and Inscriptions with Occasional Notes*. Vol. 3, New York, 1814; Dr. Isaac Senter Papers, *RIHS*, MSS 165.

29. Review of Stone's book of the Thayer journal is found in *North American Review*, vol. CVII. Boston: Ticknor and Fields, 1868: 375.

30. Justin Smith, 32-33.

31. Kenneth Roberts. *March to Quebec, Journals of the Members of Arnold's Expedition*. Garden City, NY: Doubleday & Co., 1946, xiii.

32. Justin Smith, 33.

33. *North American Review*, 375-376.

34. Bezaleel Thayer. *Memorial of the Thayer Name*. Oswego: Bezaleel Thayer, 1874; *Spirit of 76 in Rhode Island*, 283-295; Edwin M. Stone, 70-80.

35. *Magazine of History*, Extra # 50, Topham's journal, 1.
36. Topham Journal, Society of the Sons of the Revolution in the State of Rhode Island, 1902: 57-60.
37. Introduction to Topham Journal. *Magazine of History*, 1; *Spirit of 76 in Rhode Island*, 348-349.
38. Justin Smith, 35-38.
39. Humphrey Journal 1984: 9.
40. William Richard Cutter. *New England Families, Genealogical and Memorial*. New York: Lewis Hist. Publishing Co., 1915: 615; William Humphrey pension application; Humphrey Journal, 1984.
41. Justin Smith, 45-48.
42. Celebration of the One Hundred and Fiftieth Anniversary of the First Settlement of Nelson, New Hampshire 1767-1917. Nelson: Nelson Picnic Association, 1917, 137-147; John Goodwin Locke. *The Book of Lockes: A Genealogical and Historical Record of William Locke of Woburn*. Boston: John G. Locke, 1853. Appendix H. 323.
43. Ware journal, *NEHGR*, 142.
44. William B. Trask. Genealogy of the Ware Family. *NEHGR*, Apr. 1852: 129-145; George Kuhn Clarke. *History of Needham, Massachusetts, 1711-1911*. Needham: George K. Clarke, 1912: 484-485.
45. Greenman journal, Bray and Bushnell, xlviii-xliv.
46. Jeremiah Greenman pension application; *The Search for Lt. Jeremiah Greenman*. www.randisgeneabzyadventurer.blogspot.com/2007/search-for-it-jeremiah-greenman; Bray and Bushnell, journal, xiii-xxviii; Lt. Jeremiah Greenman. www.familytreemaker.genealogy.com/user/c/h/a/Lorraine-Chandler/WEBSite-0001/u; E. Duis. *The Good Old Times in McLean County, Illinois*. Bloomington: Leader Publishing, 1874: 746-747.
47. MHS online catalog containing a description of William Dorr's journal.
48. Charley Dorr. *Descendants of Edward Dorr*. www.gencircles.com/users/cdorr/1/data/959; Goetz, Senior Thesis; James W. North. *The History of Augusta From the Earliest Settlement to the Present Times*. Augusta: Clapp and North, 1870: 848; William Dorr pension application.
49. Tarbox, *Life of Israel Putnam*, 214-215.
50. Introduction to Haskell journal, Withington, 4.
51. *The William Randolph Hearst Collection*, Part I. New York: Parke-Bernet Galleries, Inc., 1938: 35-37.
52. Obituary. Newburyport Herald. Vol. 4, Issue 61, May 19, 1801.
53. Caleb Haskell pension application; *Massachusetts Soldiers and Sailors of the Revolutionary War*. Boston: Secretary of the Commonwealth, 1896, 433.
54. Sleeper's statement is found in Caleb Haskell's pension application, NARA pension records.

55. *Massachusetts Soldiers and Sailors*, 295; *The Knickerbocker or New York Monthly Magazine*, vol. 6, 1834: 169.

56. Francis Jordan, Jr. *The Life of William Henry of Lancaster, Pennsylvania, 1729-1786*. Lancaster: Francis Jordan, Jr., 1910

57. Henry Letter to Francis Nichols. Letters of John Joseph Henry. *Pennsylvania Magazine of History & Biography*, vol. 20, 1896: 568-570.

58. William Louis Henry. *Lineage of John Joseph Henry*. Detroit: W.L. Henry, 1909; Francis Jordan, Jr. *The Life of William Henry of Lancaster, Pennsylvani*a; Samuel J. Walker, 60-70; *The Perils of Patriotism John Joseph Henry and the American Attack on Quebec, 1775*. Lancaster: Lancaster County Historical Society, 1975.

59. Roberts, 651.

60. Goelet catalogue, Part II, 149-155.

61. Frederick Clifton Pierce. *Pierce Genealogy*. Worcester: Press of Charles Hamilton, 1880, 84; Roberts, *March to Quebec*, 3rd ed., 651-652; Worcester Vital Records, Births and Deaths for John Pierce.

62. Justin Smith, 42-43.

63. Emily Wilder Leavitt. *John Melvin of Charleston and Concord, Mass. and His Descendants*. Boston: David Clapp & Son, 1901-1905: 291-299; James Melvin pension application; *Massachusetts Soldiers and Sailors*, 626.

64. Typescript of Kimball Journal is found in the Rauner Manuscripts, Dartmouth College Library. It is "Kenneth Roberts' copy with ms. notations".

65. Leonard A. Morrison and Stephen P. Sharples. *History of the Kimball Family in America From 1634 to 1897*. Boston: Damrell & Upham, 1897: 331; G.F. Kimball. *Kimball Family News*. Feb. 1903: 69-71 and Apr. 1902: 57-58.

66. Charles C. Coffin. *History of Boscawen and Webster, From 1733 to 1878*. Concord: Republican Press Assoc., 1878: 250-251.

67. Edith F. Dunbar & Charles M. Flanders. *The Flanders Family: From Europe to America*, 2nd Ed. www.tc.umn.edu/~vanes002/flanders/book.html, 120 ; Corser vs. Flanders, Ancient Faces, 1783. www.ancientfaces.com/research/story/386793.

68. Matthews, 120.

69. Wright Howes, 560.

70. Roberts, 543.

71. *The Maine Reader*, Introduction to Stocking journal, 37-38.

72. Justin Smith, 40-42.

73. *Midland Rare Books Catalogue* 41-196, 1948.

74. Edward H. Cornwall. "Family of George Stocking." *NEHGR*, vol. 50, 1896, 171-176; Augustus H. Ganser. *History of Bay County Michigan and Representative Citizens*. Chicago: Richmond & Arnold, 1905: 171-176; The Maine Reader, 37-38.

75. Joseph Sabin. *Bibliotheca Americana: Dictionary of Books Relating to America From Its Discovery to the Present Time.* New York: J. Sabin's Son, 1879: 36.
76. Henry journal, 395.
77. Henry J. Young. The Spirit of 1775, A Letter of Robert Magaw. *John and Mary's Journal,* 1975: 26.
78. Henry Journal, 395.
79. Letters of John Joseph Henry, 568-570.
80. Raymond Bell and Chauncey E. McCoy. *McCoy Journal,* 11-12.
81. Chambersburg: J.M. Runk & Co., 1897: 489; Jean Laughlin. Report to Stephen Darley regarding the McCoy Name. Mifflin County Hist. Soc., 2010; Chauncey E. McCoy and Raymond M. Bell. *John McCoy, His Children and Grandchildren.* Privately Printed, 1990; Bell and McCoy, McCoy Journal.
82. Roberts, 573.
83. Matthews, 113.
84. *Simon Fobes Goes to War.*
85. Simon Fobes pension application; *History of Ashtabula County, Ohio.* Philadelphia: Williams Brothers, 1878, The Simon Fobes Family. www.freepages.history.rootsweb.ancestry.com/~arkbios/Ashtabula/ fobess.txt.; Fobes Journal, autobiographical information.
86. Justin Smith, 54.
87. There is a notation in the Squier pension file at NARA: "Journal of Ephraim Squier forwarded to Library of Congress Feb. 9, 1909."
88. Ephraim Squier pension application; *Magazine of American History,* Preliminary note to Squier Journal, 685-686
89. Justin Smith, 54-55.
90. Roberts, 503.
91. William Henry Egle. Provincial Papers. State & Supply Transcripts of County of Cumberland. Toboyne Township Taxables, PA Archives, 1898; James E. Kapp. *Early Perry County People.* The Perry Historians, n.d.; Donna Heller Zinn. Search of Records on George Morison for Stephen Darley. The Perry Historians, 2010.
92. James Graham. *Life of General Daniel Morgan.* New York: Derby & Jackson, 1856. Appendix B, 464.
93. John Marshall. *The Life of George Washington Commander in Chief of the American Forces.* New York: Walton Book Company, 1930, footnote, 62.
94. Note on the Heth Journal. *Proceedings of Virginia Historical Society* at the Annual Meeting held Dec. 21-22, 1891, 1892: 320n.
95. Banks Papers. Notation regarding his handwritten copy of Heth's journal.
96. Introduction to Heth Journal. Winchester Virginia Historical Society, footnote, 37.
97. B. Floyd Flickinger, Introduction to Heth Journal, Winchester

Virginia Historical Society, 27-35; Orderly Book of Major William Heth of Third Virginia Regiment, May 15-July 1, 1777. *Virginia Hist Soc Collections*, vol. 11, 1892: 319-329.

98. Joseph Walker McSpadden. *The South in the Building of the Nation.* Richmond: Southern Historical Publication Society, 1909: 308-309; Marcus J. Wright. Letter From a Revolutionary Officer. *Publications of Southern History Association*, vol. 6, 1900: 245-257.

99. Proceedings of New Jersey Historical Society, introduction to Ogden Journal, 17-18.

100. Marie Blades, *The March to Quebec: A Mystery Solved.* Morris County Historical Society, 1980; *Some Charges of a Very High Nature: The Court-Martial of Col. Matthias Ogden*, Parts I-IV, www.greensleeves. com/berkshire, 2010; William Ogden Wheeler. *The Ogden Family in America, Elizabethtown Branch and Their English Ancestry.* Philadelphia: J/B. Lippincott Company, 1907, 132-134.

101. Sarah Barney pension application; Introduction to Barney's Journal by great grandson. New Haven Museum and Historical Society; House of Representatives, 25th Congress, 2d Session, Rep. No. 420, Report on Sarah Barney petition regarding pension application.

102. Letters and Certificates from the Revolutionary Papers of Col. Francis Nichols. *PMHB*, vol. 32, 1908: 108-112; James D. Kilbourne. *Virtutis Praemium: The Men Who Founded the State Society of Cincinnati of Pennsylvania.* Rockport: Picton Press, 1998: 728-733; *Proceedings of the Delaware County Historical Society*, vol. 1, Sept. 29, 1895-Dec. 5, 1901: 26-29; Heitman, 413.

103. Introductory comments on the Anonymous journal. *American Antiquarian and Oriental Journal*, 224.

104. Wickersham State Historic Site. Division of Parks and Outdoor Recreation, Alaska Department of Natural Resources, website.

105. Joy Werlink, Washington State Historical Society, email to author, January 13, 2009.

CHAPTER TWO

106. Melvin Journal, 449.
107. Thayer Journal, 286.

CHAPTER THREE

108. James M. Bugbee, Report of Letter Regarding Wild Journal. *Proceedings of Massachusetts Historical Society*, vol.46, October 1912-June 1913: 305-306.

109. William H. Whitmore. *American Genealogist*. Albany: Joel Munsell, 1868, footnote, 84.
110. John Goodwin Locke. *Book of Lockes*, 323.
111. Justin Smith, 45-48
112. George Kuhn Clarke. *History of Needham Massachusetts, 1711-1911*. Needham: George K. Clarke, 1912: 484-485; Joseph E. Fiske. *History of Wellesley, Mass.* Boston: Pilgrim Press, 1917: 43.
113. Oliver Edwards Pension Application.
114. Joseph Thomas Pension Application.
115. Return of Rebel Prisoners Taken at Quebec, Dec'r 31, 1775. British Archives, Colonial Office, 42/35: 139-143.

CHAPTER FOUR

116. Roberts, 193.
117. Justin Smith, 30-32.
118. *Magazine of History with Notes & Queries*, Extra # 41-44, 1916: i-viii.
119. *American Penny Magazine and Family Newspaper*, vol. 11, No. 3, May 1846.
120. Letter Lewis Roper to Thomas Ruffin, April 27, 1846. J.G. DeRoulhac Hamilton. *Papers of Thomas Ruffin*. Raleigh: Edwards & Broughton Printing Co., 1918.
121. Introduction to Senter Journal. Bulletin of HSP, 4.
122. *The American Bibliopolist*, vol. 6, No. 61-2, Jan.-Feb. 1876, Ad in back of book on page 4 of ads.
123. New York Times, Feb. 26, 1943 and March 7, 1943
124. Fordham University Library Online Catalog. Munn Collection. Contains a description of the Senter manuscript Journal.
125. Justin Smith, 30.
126. Letter to Charles E. Banks, Rhode Island Historical Society, Senter Papers, MSS 165, Box 2, Folder 6.
127. *Proceedings of Rhode Island Historical Society* 1877-1878, Special Meeting, April 30, 1878, 24-25, regarding "original journal kept by Dr. Isaac Senter".

CHAPTER FIVE

128. Letter of Tobias Hendricks. Cited in *History of Cumberland and Adams Counties, Pennsylvania*. Chicago: Warner, Beers & Co., 1886: 276.
129. *History of Cumberland and Adams Counties*, 276
130. *History of Cumberland and Adams Counties*, 276.
131. Robert G. Crist. *Captain William Hendricks and the March to Quebec,*

1775. Carlisle: Hamilton Library and Historical Association of Cumberland County, 1960: 12.

132. John Scoot Davenport, *The Frontier Hendricks*, vol. I, 1991-1993, The Frontier Hendricks Association, April 10, 1993 Letter to Col. Meredith Hendricks, 7.

133. Crist, 12.

134. Stroh, 16.

135. Henry Journal, 378.

136. William Smith. *An Oration in Memory of General Montgomery and of the Officers and Soldiers, who fell with him, December 31, 1775.* New York: John Anderson, 1776: 39-40.

137. William Smith, 40 footnote.

138. Henry Journal, 302.

139. Crist, 13.

140. Stroh, 36; Young, 17.

141. Crist. *Captain William Hendricks and the March to Quebec, 1775*; Davenport, *The Frontier Hendricks*; Bob Rowland. Tobias Hendricks: A Family Tradition of Service. *Cumberland County History*, vol. 20, Summer/Winter 2003: 49-55; Report to Stephen Darley regarding Information in the Cumberland Historical Society on the William Hendricks Family, including the genealogy file, January 2010; Tobias, Sr. v Tobias, Jr. www.sio.midco.net/Itsco/hendricks/toby%20v%20 toby.html; Henry J. Young, 6-50.

142. Mary Cochran Dodge, *List of Soldiers in the War of the Revolution from Worcester, Mass.* Worcester: DAR, 1902: 17; William Lincoln. *History of Worcester,* 1862: 232.

143. Montgomery to Schuyler, December 26, 1775. www.familytales.org/ dbDisplay.php?id=ltr_rim3016&person=rim.

144. Dodge, 18; Lincoln, 232.

145. Smith, 54.

146. Resolution and award to Hubbard's wife is in Roberts, *March to Quebec,* 573.

147. Heth Journal, Winchester Virginia Hist. Soc., 51.

148. Mary Cochran Dodge. *A List of Soldiers in the War of the Revolution from Worcester, Mass.* Worcester: Worcester DAR, 1902: 17-18; Harlan P. Hubbard. *One Thousand Years of Hubbard History.* New York: Harlan P. Hubbard, 1895: 422-426; George Mills, 11; *Massachusetts Soldiers & Sailors,* 433; Heitman, 305.

149. Keith M. Seymour. *The Descendants of Thomas Hanchett.* San Francisco: Keith M. Seymour, 1985,

150. Letter of William Loomis, Town of Suffield Historian, to Charles E. Banks, May 23, 1896. Banks Papers.

151. *Celebration of the Bi-centennial Anniversary of the Town of Suffield, October 12, 1870.* Hartford: Wiley, Waterman & Eaton, 1871: 44.

152. Hanchett petition to Connecticut General Assembly, June 8, 1778. Connecticut State Archives, Series I,

153. Hanchett claim to Continental Congress, June 5, 1782 and Benjamin Lincoln's response, June 28, 1782. NARA, Papers of Continental Congress, Letters of Maj. Gen. Benjamin Lincoln, Roll 162: 446-451.

154. Thayer, 269; Pierce, 701.

155. Pierce, 703-704.

156. Heitman, 271; Letter to Charles E. Banks, Banks Papers; Ct State Archives, Rev. War, Series I ; Bi-Centennial of Suffield, 43-45; Stone, Thayer, 82; Oliver Hanchett. www.worldconnect.rootsweb.ancestry.com/cgibin.cgi?op=GET8db=limmeadenis51; Keith M. Seymour. *The Descendants of Thomas Hanchett*. San Francisco: Keith M. Seymour, 1985: 52-53; Thayer Journal; Pierce Journal.

157. Petition of Goodrich to Lt. Governor Thomas Hutchinson, Feb. 19, 1773. Mass Archives, III, 570-571.

158. Information and old town map in the Stockbridge Library confirms the moving of the house.

159. Lion G. Miles, Anna Bingham: From the Red Lion Inn to the Supreme Court. *New England Quarterly*, vol. 69, June 1996: 289-290.

160. Lion G. Miles. The Red Man Dispossessed: The Williams Family and the Alienation of Indian Land in Stockbridge, Mass. 1736-1818. *New England Quarterly,* vol. 67, March 1995.

161. Isaac Greenwood. The Stockbridge Indians During the American Revolution. *NEHGR*, vol. 54, Jan. 1900: 162-164.

162. Stockbridge Indians During the American Revolution, 162-163.

163. Stockbridge Indians During the American Revolution, 163.

164. Goodrich commission as Capt in *Massachusetts Soldiers and Sailors in Revolutionary War*, 595.

165. Thomas Egleston. *The Life of Major-General John Paterson*. New York: G.P. Putnam's Sons, 1878: 44-45.

166. Dearborn journal, 138.

167. Heth journal, Winchester VA Hist. Soc., 117-118.

168. Pierce journal, 689.

169. Montgomery to Schuyler, December 26, 1775.

170. Stockbridge, Massachusetts. *Proprietor's Record Book, Meeting of May, 1776*. "Granted to William Goodrich (a white hotel keeper and a captain of minute-men in the Revolution) in consideration of his having an ox killed, fifty acres of land".

171. Heth journal, Winchester VA Hist. Soc., 117-118.

172. Washington to Goodrich, June 19, 1779. Washington Papers LOC, #150290; Washington to Goodrich, July 4, 1779. Washington Papers LOC, #150379.

173. Goodrich reimbursement claims. State: November 20, 1780. Mass. Archives, 186:72; Federal: Goodrich Letter to Philip Schuyler, July

24, 1777. Philip Schuyler Papers, New York Public Library, Box 33. No. 790.

174. State of Vermont. Rev. War Rolls. Major William Goodrich and Staff. 808.

175. State of Vermont. Rev. War Rolls, 789.

176. Goodrich to Washington, Aug 24, 1781. Washington Papers LOC, image 46.

177. Washington to Goodrich, Sept. 2, 1781. Washington Papers LOC, image 230094.

178. Goodrich petition to VT in Feb 1782 in NARA Revolutionary War Service records. William Goodrich Petition, image 18105121.

179. Barbara Allen. Report to Stephen Darley on Records in Stockbridge Library Relative to William Goodrich. Their records show that "in 1783 he signed a deed in Bennington, Vermont".

180. Appendix to Deming's Vermont Officers, 126. "Chartered June 22, 1781 to William Goodrich and 59 others".

181. There are various newspaper legal notices in the late 1780's, 1790's and early 1800's regarding defaults on Vermont land. An example is *The Rutland Herald*, Vol. 12, Issue 12, 3/22/1806, regarding the proprietors of Vershire, Vermont who are delinquent on the money owed. William Goodrich is one of the listed proprietors. Also *Vermont Journal*, vol. 4, issue 196, 4/30/ 1787 for Montpelier, Vermont, of which both William and Sybil Goodrich are listed as delinquent. There are a number of ads listing Goodrich as delinquent on various land deals in Vermont in the 1780s and 90's, which shows a pattern of defaulting on his obligations.

182. A legal notice was published in Vermont newspapers in 1788 stating that on October 23, 1787, the General Assembly of Vermont passed an act "discharging Maj. William Goodrich, of Pawlet, State of Vermont, from all debts or demands against him". *Vermont Journal*, vol. 5, issue 238, 2/18/1788.

183. Schuyler Papers, 1777, May-Dec., Box 33, No. 41, New York Public Library; Barbara Allen, Report to Stephen Darley on Capt. William Goodrich from Records in Stockbridge Library, Jan. 2010;Lafayette W. Chase. *The Goodrich Family in America*. Chicago: Goodrich Family Memorial Association, 1889; Thomas Egleston, *The Life of John Paterson* ; *The Stockbridge Indians During the American Revolution*, 162-164; Orson Kingsley, Report to Stephen Darley on Major William Goodrich in Middlebury, VT., Henry Sheldon Museum, Feb. 2010; Stockbridge Past and Present, ; Lion Miles, Anna Bingham, 287-299; Lillian Preiss. *Sheffield, Frontier Town*. Sheffield: Sheffield Bicentennial Committee, 1976; Report to Stephen Darley from Sheffield Historical Society on Major William Goodrich in Sheffield, March, 2010.

CHAPTER NINE

184. Richard G. Bell. The Court-Martial of Roger Enos, I and II. *Connecticut Bar Journal*, vols. 73 & 74, 1999 and 2000: 428-461, 299-312.
185. Enos resignation letter to Washington, *American Archives*, 4th, 4: 768.
186. Letter from Roger Enos, Samuel Fletcher, Samuel Herrick and Gideon Armsbury to Board of War, June 23, 1781. *Records of the Governor and Council of the State of Vermont*. Vol. 2. Montpelier: J. & J.M. Poland, 1874: 109.
187. Washington to Enos, Oct 6, 178. George Washington Papers at Library of Congress, image 230213.
188. James Warren to John Adams, November 14, 1775. *Warren Letters*, vol. I. Boston: Massachusetts Historical Society, 1917: 181-182.

CHAPTER TEN

189. The McCobb Family of Maine. *Genealogy: A Journal of American Ancestry*, vol. 1: 244-245; Samuel McCobb pension application.
190. Stephen W. Williams. *The Genealogy and History of the Family of Williams in America*. Greenfield: Merriam & Mirick, 1847: 264-265; Stockbridge Past and Present, 172-173, 255-256 ; Heitman, 483
191. Thomas Desjardin, *Through a Howling Wilderness, Benedict Arnold's March to Quebec in 1775*, New York: St. Martin's Press, 2006; Arthur S. Lefkowitz, *Benedict Arnold's Army: The 1775 American Invasion of Canada During the Revolutionary War*. New York: Savas Beattie, 2008.
192. Charles E. Banks, *Magazine of History with Notes & Queries*, vol. 18, January-June 1914, 271-273.
193. Benedict Arnold Day Book and Ledger, 1777-1779. *American Historical Record*, vol. 3, May 1874: 220-222.
194. List of Arnold Officers. Misc. Revolutionary War Rolls. M346. NARA. Image #991045.
195. The four pension applications that mention Captain Scott being their company commander on the Quebec expedition are: Ebenezer Gee of South Hampton, MA, W4679, who does not give Scott's first name; James Moore of Sharon, New Hampshire, W17158, who gives Scott's first name as William; David Emery of New Hampshire, W24123, who gives his first name as William; Robert Stewart, S43185, also mentions William Scott's first name.
196. *Proceedings of Worcester Soc of Antiquity*, vol. 25, 1912: 87.
197. Charles E. Banks. *Magazine of History*, 271-273; Mary E. Harrell. *The Scot Family: An Account of Lieutenant Colonel William Scott of Peterborough, N.H. and His Descendants*. Cincinnati: M.E. Harrell, 1967; Albert Smith. *History of the Town of Peterborough, Hillsborough*

County, New Hampshire. Boston: George H. Ellis, 1876: 155-158, 244-250; Jonathan Smith. *Peterborough New Hampshire in the American Revolution,* 316-324; Jonathan Smith. Two William Scotts of Peterborough. N.H. *Proceedings of MHS,* vol. 45, 1911: 495-502.

APPENDIX II

198. Orderly Books of Col. William Henshaw, Oct. 1, 1775 through Oct. 3, 1776. *Proceedings of the American Antiquarian Society for April 1947,* 1948.
199. Joseph Farnsworth pension application; Records of the Governor and Council of the State of Vermont. Montpelier: J. & J.M. Poland, 1874, 126; Line of Descent for Joseph Farnsworth of Dorchester, Mass. www.newsarch.rootsweb.com/th/read/VTGEN/2001-04/6986761022.
200. Alex Harris. *Biographical History of Lancaster County, Pennsylvania.* Lancaster: Elias Barr & Co., 1872: 561-562; William H. Egle. The Pattang Company Before Quebec, 1775. *Notes & Queries: Historical, Biographical and Genealogical.* 3rd Ser., vol. 1, 1887: 249-250; D.F. Magee. Col. Archibald Steele. *Papers Read to Lancaster County Historical Society,* Fri. Feb., 1921, vol. 25, No. 2, 1921: 11-13.
201. *Captain Jedediah Hyde.* www.sanisullivan.com/Hyde%203.htm:60; Rueben Walworth. *Genealogy of William Hyde of Norwich,* vol. 1. Albany: Joel Munsell, 1864; Jedediah Hyde pension application.
202. Abijah Savage pension application; CT Archives, Rev. War, Series I; Ct Men in Revolution, 91.
203. Heitman, 161; www.11thpa.org/History.html.
204. Arnold Day Book and Ledger; *Mass. Soldiers and Sailors,* 380; *Massachusetts Revolutionary War Soldiers for Belchertown and Granby,* www.viganet.org/usa/one/state/revwar/putnam/part2.html.
205. Arnold Journal; Pierce Journal; Topham Company Roll, 1778, NARA Muster Rolls; James N. Arnold. *The History of the Church Family.* Providence: Narragansett Historical Publishing Co., 1887: 50.
206. *Massachusetts Soldiers & Sailors,* 762; Heitman, 130; Benedict Arnold, List of Officers.
207. Phyllis J. Hughes. *Hull Family History Database,* Hull Family Association, 2010.

INDEX